UNCONSCIONABILITY IN EUROPEAN PRIVATE FINANCIAL TRANSACTIONS

Protecting the Vulnerable

Given the unprecedented recent turmoil on financial markets, we now face radically challenged, 'post-Lehman' assumptions on protecting the vulnerable in financial transactions. This collection of essays explores conceptions of, and responses to, unconscionability and similar notions across Europe with specific reference to financial transactions. It presents a detailed analysis of concepts of unconscionability in Europe against a backdrop of Commission initiatives aimed, variously, at securing a single market in financial services, producing greater coherence in EC consumer protection law and consolidating European private law. This analysis illustrates, for example, that concepts of unconscionability depend on context and can be shaped by a variety of factors. It also illustrates that jurisdictions may choose to respond to questions of unconscionability through a variety of legal instruments located in different branches of the law rather than through a single doctrine. Thus this collection illuminates many of the obstacles facing harmonisation in this area.

MEL KENNY is Reader in Commercial Law at the University of Leicester.

JAMES DEVENNEY is Deputy Head of Durham Law School and Director of the Durham University Institute of Commercial and Corporate Law.

LORNA FOX O'MAHONY is Professor of Law at the University of Durham.

CONTENTS

CONTRIBUTORS

CRISTINA AMATO
Professor of Law, Faculty of Law, University of Brescia

IMMACULADA BARRAL-VIÑALS
Professor of Law, Faculty of Law, University of Barcelona

DAVID CAPPER
Reader in Law, Queen's University, Belfast

PETER CARTWRIGHT
Professor of Consumer Protection Law, School of Law, University of Nottingham

OLHA O. CHEREDNYCHENKO
Senior Lecturer in Private Law, Centre for Law and Governance, Faculty of Law, VU University of Amsterdam

AURELIA COLOMBI CIACCHI
Reader in Law, Centre for European Law and Politics, University of Bremen

JAMES DEVENNEY
Deputy Head Durham Law School and Director of the Durham University Institute of Commercial and Corporate Law

KAREN FAIRWEATHER
Graduate Teaching Assistant, Durham Law School

MAGDALENA HABDAS
Lecturer in Law, Faculty of Law and Administration, Department of Civil and Private International Law, University of Silesia, Katowice

AXEL HALFMEIER
Professor of German and International Private and Economic Law, Frankfurt School of Finance and Management

STANISLAW KALUS
Professor of Law, Faculty of Law and Administration, Department of Civil and Private International Law, University of Silesia, Katowice

MEL KENNY
Reader in Commercial Law, University of Leicester

SARAH NIELD
Reader, School of Law, University of Southampton

LORNA FOX O'MAHONY
Professor of Law, Durham Law School

PETER ROTT
Associate Professor in European Private Law, University of Copenhagen

SÉVERINE SAINTIER
Senior Lecturer, School of Law, University of Sheffield

ANDRIUS SMALIUKAS
Associate Professor, Faculty of Law, Vilnius University; Attorney at Law: Varul, Vilgerts, Smaliukas (Vilnius)

WARREN SWAIN
Lecturer in Law, Durham Law School

EMMANUEL VOYIAKIS
Lecturer in Law, Brunel Law School; Barrister (Greece)

STEPHEN WADDAMS
Goodman Schipper Chair, Faculty of Law, University of Toronto

JOHN WIGHTMAN
Senior Lecturer, Kent Law School

CHRIS WILLETT
Professor of Consumer Law, Leicester de Montfort Law School

TONI WILLIAMS
Professor of Law, Kent Law School

QI ZHOU
Lecturer in Law, University of Sheffield

Introduction: conceptualising unconscionability in Europe

MEL KENNY, JAMES DEVENNEY AND LORNA FOX O'MAHONY

Unconscionability is not a simple, easily defined concept. While unconscionability even within the common law is essentially contested, in Europe unconscionability or its equivalents is an even broader concept which is to be found in a plurality of sources; it is therefore perhaps best described as a multi-dimensional concept taking its place in a polycontextual environment of national contract laws and instruments aimed at protecting the vulnerable in a variety of contexts: arising variously in consumer, family or non-professional transactions. Traditionally, in some private law systems, unconscionability may only be resorted to sparingly, as an exception to the fundamental principle of freedom of contract; in others it may be resorted to more widely as an instrument of ensuring ideas of fairness or solidarity between contracting parties. Similarly, the concept may involve stringent procedural or more invasive substantive approaches; and the effective level of protection produced by either of these approaches may vary considerably. In yet other legal orders and within those orders in specific fields of law unconscionability may be delivered indirectly through the intervention of substantive constitutional law (fundamental rights) or, alternatively, and less spectacularly, through property law principles. Some form of unconscionability or its equivalent may thus be found in all European legal orders.

This book represents the results drawn and developed from the conference 'Conceptualising Unconscionability in Europe', an event held at Durham Castle on 8–9 September 2008. The conference was held as the first of a series of events organised within the work programme 'Credit and Debt: protecting the vulnerable in Europe'; a project placing special emphasis on vulnerability in financial transactions and based at the Centre for Law and Legal Studies at Leeds Law School. The project

owes its genesis to work originally organised under the umbrella of the Commission's Sixth Framework Programme (FP6) on the protection of vulnerable family sureties, an ambitious Transfer of Knowledge project coordinated by Dr Aurelia Colombi Ciacchi at the Centre for Law and Politics at Bremen University and Professor Stephen Weatherill at the Institute of European and Comparative Law at Oxford and based at the Centre for Law and Politics at Bremen University. It was only logical to develop in this project some of the ideas which can be traced to that original research in Bremen – with the valuable collaboration of Professor Gert Brüggemeier (Bremen), Professor Gerry McCormack (Leeds) and Professor Sjef van Erp (Maastricht).

The project would not have been possible without the generous support it has received from Marie Curie research funds through the European Commission (European Reintegration Grant 223605) within the Seventh Framework Programme (FP7). In Brussels we are grateful for the assistance of Pascale Dupont, Chantal Huts and Laurent Correia, our FP7 project officers. The first stage of the work programme and the Durham conference was organised by the editors of this volume.

This work is divided into two parts: in Part I of this work we focus on fleshing out the broad contours of the concept of unconscionability. Colombi Ciacchi begins with a comparative exploration of the relationship between the concepts of freedom of contract and unconscionability in Europe. She notes that there has always been a degree of antagonism between these two concepts but examines whether freedom of contract and unconscionability could converge (Chapter 1). Waddams then engages in an examination of the theoretical basis of unconscionability in English law (Chapter 2). Barral Viñals and Saintier go on to explore concepts of unconscionability in Spanish and French Law (respectively in Chapters 3 and 4). Voyiakis then examines various theoretical justifications of doctrines of unconscionability, with particular emphasis on the value of choice (Chapter 5). Wightman, in his contribution, sets unconscionability discourse in the context of relational contract theory (Chapter 6). The section concludes with Zhou's paper, which explores the concept of unconscionability from an economic perspective (Chapter 7).

Part II goes on to elaborate the concept of unconscionability in the specialised context of financial transactions. Swain and Fairweather, Capper and Nield in their opening contributions examine the changing responses to unconscionability in England and Wales. Swain and Fairweather begin by looking to the early development of usury and

judicial regulation in the seventeenth and eighteenth centuries (Chapter 8); Capper analyses the development of the doctrine of misrepresentation (Chapter 9); and Nield the evolution of notions of unconscionability for borrowers in England and Wales (Chapter 10). Cartwright and then Williams reflect on regulatory responses to unconscionability: Cartwright on the lessons which can be drawn for the financial services industry (Chapter 11) while Williams supplies a critical analysis of the fairness regimes governing UK financial contracts (Chapter 12). Cherednychenko then develops the analysis by examining unconscionability in financial transactions in Europe and asks how public and private law approaches could be converged (Chapter 13). This theme is further elaborated by Smaliukas, Kalus and Habdas and Amato in their contributions on the development of the notion of unconscionability in the contexts of: post-soviet era legal transplants (Smaliukas, Chapter 14); loan agreements in Poland (Kalus and Habdas, Chapter 15); and financial contracts and junk titles (Amato, Chapter 16). The section concludes by looking at unconscionability in financial transactions in the context of particular EU harmonisation initiatives: Rott and Halfmeier on the Markets in Financial Instruments Directive (Chapter 17) and Willett on unfairness under the Consumer Protection from Unfair Trading Regulations 2008 (Chapter 18).

The book concludes with a final chapter by Kenny, Devenney and Fox O'Mahony on the elaboration of unconscionability in Europe in the light of a fundamentally contested private law paradigm, threatened by the treble challenges presented by constitutionalisation, European regulation and codification. Moreover, as the authors argue, since the collapse of Lehman Brothers and the advent of the Credit Crunch, our discourse is placed in the context of radically changed understandings of vulnerability, risk and responsibility (Chapter 19).

The organisers and editors are particularly indebted to all those who submitted proposals, held papers, chaired sessions and made contributions to the conference. We are particularly grateful to all those who went on to contribute to this volume and to Professor Allan Beever (Southampton) and Howard Johnson (Bangor) for their academic support. Our thanks also to Professor Teresa Rodriguez de la Heras (Carlos III, Madrid), Dr Magdalena Zielińska and Dr Jakub Szczerbowski (Olzstyn), Blanka Tomančáková (Olmuc), Steve Greenfield and Guy Osborn (Westminster) and Professor Roger Halson (Leeds). Crucial support has also been given by the highly dedicated staff at Cambridge University Press; in particular we would like to thank Richard Woodham, Daniel Dunlavey, Brenda Burke and Finola O'Sullivan for

their efficient management of the production process. Editorial assistance to the project was enthusiastically delivered by Claire Devenney. Research assistance to the project was provided by Gabe Cantu (Durham). In Leeds we remain grateful for ongoing support for the project to Professor Gerry McCormack, Professor Roger Halson and Professor Dagmar Schiek.

Any conference and any project relies on the cooperation and dedication of many otherwise unsung members of the support staff, we would like to take the opportunity to thank Rupert and Joanne Prudom, Claire Graham (Prudhoe), Helen Hewitson, Patricia Bell, Julie Platten, Rachel Tucker, Hayley Wharton and Sarah Menday-Hall at Durham Law School for their inexhaustible patience and practical help. We would also like to thank the staff at Durham Castle and Event Durham for the professional organisation of the conference. We are also indebted at an institutional and material level to the Institute of Corporate and Commercial law at Durham and to the Centre of European Law and Legal Studies at Leeds. We are also grateful to University College, Durham and Hatfield College, Durham for their generous hosting of the conference. Information on the ongoing work and forthcoming events under the project can be obtained from the programme coordinators.

CAMBRIDGE
UNIVERSITY PRESS

University Printing House, Cambridge CB2 8BS, United Kingdom

One Liberty Plaza, 20th Floor, New York, NY 10006, USA

477 Williamstown Road, Port Melbourne, VIC 3207, Australia

314-321, 3rd Floor, Plot 3, Splendor Forum, Jasola District Centre, New Delhi - 110025, India

79 Anson Road, #06-04/06, Singapore 079906

Cambridge University Press is part of the University of Cambridge.

It furthers the Universitay's mission by disseminating knowledge in the pursuit of education, learning and research at the highest international levels of excellence.

www.cambridge.org
Information on this title: www.cambridge.org/9780521190534

First published 2010

A catalogue record for this publication is available from the British Library

Library of Congress Cataloging in Publication data
Unconscionability in European private financial transactions : protecting the vulnerable / [edited by] Mel Kenny, James Devenney, Lorna Fox O'Mahony.
p. cm.
ISBN 978-0-521-19053-4 (Hardback)
1. Unconscionable contracts – Europe. 2. Law – Europe – English influences.
3. Financial services industry – Law and legislation – Europe. 4. Consumer protection – Law and legislation – Europe. I. Kenny, Mel. II. Devenney, James.
III. Fox O'Mahony, Lorna. IV. Title.
KJC1062.U53 2010
346.402–dc22
2010000696

ISBN 978-0-521-19053-4 Hardback

UNCONSCIONABILITY IN EUROPEAN PRIVATE FINANCIAL TRANSACTIONS

Protecting the Vulnerable

Edited by

MEL KENNY

JAMES DEVENNEY

LORNA FOX O'MAHONY

CAMBRIDGE
UNIVERSITY PRESS

1

Freedom of contract as freedom from unconscionable contracts

AURELIA COLOMBI CIACCHI

Freedom of contract: from the form to the substance

'Conceptualising unconscionability in Europe' means also conceptualising the relationship between freedom of contract and protection from unconscionable contracts. Freedom of contract and protection of vulnerable parties in contract law have traditionally been understood as antagonistic, conflicting principles. Legislative rules or doctrines providing remedies against unconscionable contracts are mostly seen as exceptions to the principle of freedom of contract. The high rank of this principle, which relies on the liberty and autonomy of private individuals vis-à-vis public powers, leads to the assumption that exceptions to freedom of contract should possibly be avoided, or, at least, restricted to a minimum.

Scholars who see freedom of contract and weaker party's protection as conflicting principles tend to challenge the predominance of freedom of contract, if they share a concern for social justice in contract law.[1] For example, the Social Justice Manifesto[2] criticised the European Commission's approach according to which in the Common Frame of Reference for a European contract law (CFR) exceptions to freedom of contract could only be admitted if justified by good reasons.[3] The Manifesto raised the

[1] See M. W. Hesselink, 'The Principles of European Contract Law: Some Choices Made by the Lando Commission', in *Principles of European Contract Law* (preliminary reports Verenigung voor Burgerlijk Recht) (Deventer: Kluwer, 2001) 7, 49; B. Lurger, 'The "Social" Side of Contract Law and the New Principle of Regard and Fairness', in A. S. Hartkamp, M. Veldman et al. (eds.), *Towards a European Civil Code*, 3rd edn (Nijmegen, The Hague: Ars Aequi Libri, Kluwer Law International, 2004) 273ff; T. Wilhelmsson, 'Varieties of Welfarism in European Contract Law' (2004) 10 *European Law Journal* 712ff.

[2] Study Group on Social Justice in European Private Law, 'Social Justice in European Contract Law: A Manifesto' (2004) 10 *European Law Journal* 653.

[3] So the Commission's Communication 'A More Coherent European Contract Law: An Action Plan', Brussels, 2.2.2003, COM (2003) 68 final, 62.

provoking question: 'Why should the principle of freedom of contract have such a privileged position . . .? Why not reverse the burden of proof so that those who wish to deregulate market transactions should have the burden of explaining the potential advantages to be gained by the parties to these transactions from the absence of mandatory rules?'[4]

This chapter, being written by a co-author of the Social Justice Manifesto, endorses the proposition that fairness and solidarity should be the guiding principles in contract law. However, it does not view fairness and solidarity as conflicting with freedom of contract. It starts from the assumption that this antagonism derives from an old, formal understanding of freedom of contract, which was barely compatible with modern twentieth-century private law, and is certainly no longer fit for purpose in the twenty-first century.

It is submitted that the modern understanding of freedom of contract is a substantive one.[5] Achieving substantive freedom of contract involves preventing and eliminating the harm caused by an unconscionable contract to a party who was only formally, but not substantively free to conclude it. The same applies if one party is only formally, but not substantively free to terminate a contract whose conditions have been unilaterally changed by the other party. Precisely because self-determination is crucial to private law, private law has to provide remedies for contracts that are the product of a factual subjugation of the weaker party.[6]

There is an evident parallelism between freedom and equality. Today, nobody doubts that attaining equality in the sense of non-discrimination requires more than simple, formal equal treatment. Taking the equality principle seriously means embracing a substantive understanding of equality, which includes the need for positive action to counterbalance existing factual and social imbalances that make people dramatically unequal. Similarly, taking freedom of contract seriously means embracing a substantive understanding of this freedom, which includes the need for positive action to counterbalance existing factual and social constraints that make one contractual party dramatically less free than the other.

[4] Study Group on Social Justice in European Private Law (n. 2 above) 663–4.

[5] See Canaris, 'Wandlungen des Schuldvertragsrechts – Tendenzen zu seiner "Materialisierung"' (2000) 200 *Archiv für die civilistische Praxis* 273; S. Grundmann, 'European Contract Law(s) of What Colour'? (2005) 1 *European Review of Contract Law* 184; O. Cherednychenko, *Fundamental Rights, Contract Law and the Protection of the Weaker Party* (Munich: Sellier, 2007) 10–11 and passim.

[6] Cf. BVerfG 7 February 1990, BVerfGE 81, 242; BVerfG 19 October 1993, BVerfGE 89, 214. Also nn. 12, 15 below.

Some scholars conceptualise the difference, which this chapter expresses in terms of 'form' and 'substance', in terms of 'negative' and 'positive' freedom of contract. These scholars consider the freedom from (state) intervention in the contractual relationship as the negative side of freedom of contract, whereas they view the positive side of this freedom in the self-determination and free development of personality of both contracting parties.[7]

The substantive understanding of freedom of contract is no longer a pure scholarly construct. It has already been acknowledged by the highest courts of some continental legal systems such as Germany and Slovenia, and by lower courts in other legal systems such as Greece.[8]

Substantive freedom of contract as a human right or constitutional principle: Germany, Slovenia, Greece and the Netherlands

A common thread which connects the developments concerning the principle of substantive equality and the principle of substantive freedom of contract is their constitutional dimension. All continental European doctrines on substantive freedom of contract, of which this author is aware, have so far embedded this principle in national constitutions or in the European Convention on Human Rights.

Germany

Article 2(1) of the Federal Constitution (*Grundgesetz*, GG) of 1949 reads: 'Every person shall have the right to free development of his personality insofar as he does not violate the rights of others or offend against the constitutional order or the moral law.' This provision was defined in 1957 by the German Federal Constitutional Court (Bundesverfassungsgericht, BVerfG) as a catch-all fundamental right[9] to general freedom of action, embracing all manifestations of freedom which are not covered by other, more specific, fundamental rights.[10] Among the manifestations of freedom which

[7] J. H. Niewenhuis, 'Contractvrijheid, een weerbarstig beginsel', in T. Hartlief and C. J. J. M. Stolker (eds.), *Contractvrijheid* (Deventer: Kluwer, 1999) 25–6; C. Mak, *Fundamental Rights in European Contract Law. A Comparison of the Impact of Fundamental Rights on Contractual Relationships in Germany, the Netherlands, Italy and England* (Alphen aan den Rijn: Kluwer Law International, 2008) 26, 28.

[8] See below. [9] *Auffanggrundrecht*.

[10] BVerfG 16 January 1957, BVerfGE 6, 32 (known as '*Elfes*' case). An English translation of this judgment is available at www.iuscomp.org/gla/.

are not covered by other specific fundamental rights there is freedom of contract. Indeed, in German case law and literature this principle has been generally considered protected by the Constitution in the framework of Article 2 (1) GG.[11]

However, more than thirty years passed after the establishment of the constitutional dimension of freedom of contract in 1957, before a *substantive* understanding of this freedom was acknowledged. The first BVerfG decision which relied on a substantive understanding of freedom of contract was the 'Commercial Agent' judgment of 1990.[12] The case dealt with an agency contract which excessively restricted the agent's professional freedom after termination of the contractual relationship. The BVerfG stated (my translation):

> [P]rivate autonomy is based on the principle of self-determination, and thus requires that the conditions of free self-determination be in fact actually present. If the bargaining power of one of the contracting parties is so heavily disproportionate that the contractual regulation becomes factually one-sided, this makes the contract heteronomous. Where there is an absence of approximate equality of bargaining power between the parties, then a fair balancing of their interests cannot be reached by the means of contract law alone. Even when the legislator refrains from creating mandatory contract law for certain aspects of life, that in no way means abandoning the field of contract practice to the free play of power. Rather, the general clauses of private law, which have the effect of prohibiting excessive power, first and foremost those in §§ 138, 242, 315 BGB,[13] are to be applied as integrative instruments. It is precisely in the elaboration and application of these general clauses that fundamental rights are to be observed. The corresponding protective mandate of the

[11] See W. Höfling, *Vertragsfreiheit. Eine grundrechtsdogmatische Studie* (Heidelberg: Müller, 1991); M. Bäuerle, *Vertragsfreiheit und Grundgesetz: Normativität und Faktizität individueller Vertragsfreiheit in verfassungsrechtlicher Perspektive* (Baden-Baden: Nomos, 2001) with further references.

[12] BVerfG 7 February 1990, BVerfGE 81, 242 ('*Handelsvertreter*') (1990) *Juristenzeitung* 691, comment Wiedemann; AP No. 65 to Article 12 GG, comment Canaris. For further discussion see (in chronological order) P. Derleder, 'Unterlegenenschutz im Vertragsrecht. Ein Modell für das Arbeitsrecht?' (1995) *Kritische Justiz* 320–39; C.-W. Canaris, *Grundrechte und Privatrecht* (Berlin, New York: de Gruyter, 1999) 49; G. Brüggemeier, 'Constitutionalisation of Private Law – The German Perspective', in T. Barkhuysen and S. D. Lindenbergh (eds.), *Constitutionalisation of Private Law* (Leiden: Nijhoff, 2006) 59; Cherednychenko (n. 5 above) 245–6; Mak (n. 7 above) 70–5, 281–2.

[13] § 138 *Bürgerliches Gesetzbuch* (BGB, German Civil Code) provides the nullity of immoral contracts or other acts of private autonomy, § 242 BGB requires the debtor to behave according to good faith, § 315 BGB states that if the contractual performance is to be unilaterally determined by one party, this determination shall be fair and equitable.

> Constitution is directed here to the judge, who has to enforce the objective basic decisions of fundamental rights in cases of imbalanced contractual parity, using the means of private law.

In the 'Commercial Agent' case, the civil judgment impugned by the agent's constitutional complaint was declared unconstitutional by the BVerfG on ground of violation of the agent's fundamental right to professional freedom under Article 12 GG.[14] In this decision, the BVerfG established the doctrine of substantive freedom of contract, but it did not expressly devise this substantive freedom as a constitutional right. A definition of substantive freedom of contract as a constitutional right was provided by the BVerfG only three years later, with the famous 'Suretyship' judgment of 1993:[15]

> [A]t least for the sake of legal certainty, a contract may not be challenged or adjusted in every instance in which the equality of bargaining power is disturbed. However, if there is a typical case scenario, which reveals a structural inferiority of one contracting party and in which the consequences of the contract for the inferior party are unusually onerous, then the civil law must react and enable corrective measures. That follows from the fundamental guarantee of private autonomy (Article 2 (1) GG)[16] and the principle of the social state (Articles 20 (1), 28 (1) GG) . . . For the civil courts, it follows that they are under a duty to interpret and apply the general clauses so as to ensure that contracts shall not serve as a means to hetero-determination [*Fremdbestimmung*].

In this decision, the BVerfG treated the substantive dimension of freedom of contract as an integral aspect of the fundamental right to the free development of personality and the general freedom of action under Article 2 (1) GG. Precisely because of the violation of the surety's fundamental right to private autonomy and freedom of contract under Article 2 (1) GG, the BVerfG allowed the surety's constitutional complaint and

[14] *Grundgesetz für die Bundesrepublik Deutschland*, in force since 1949.

[15] BVerfG 19 October 1993, BVerfGE 89, 214 ('*Bürgschaft*'). See M. Habersack and R. Zimmermann, 'Legal Change in a Codified System: Recent Developments in German Suretyships Law' (1999) 3 *Edinburgh Law Review* 272; Brüggemeier (n. 12 above); P. Rott, 'German Law on Family Suretyships: An Overrated System', in A. Colombi Ciacchi (ed.), *Protection of Non-Professional Sureties in Europe: Formal and Substantive Disparity* (Baden-Baden: Nomos, 2007) 51–69; C. U. Schmid, 'Private Suretyships as a Socio-Legal Crucible of Modern Private Law', ibid., 31–40; Cherednychenko (n. 5 above) 232–48, 256–7, 281–9, 306–31; Mak (n. 7 above) 75–82, 169, 180, 242–6, 276.

[16] Article 2 (1) GG reads: 'Everyone has the right to the free development of his personality insofar as he does not violate the rights of others or offend against the constitutional order or the moral code.'

declared the unconstitutionality of the civil judgment which did not challenge the validity of the suretyship.

The suretyship in question was a classic example of an unconscionable contract. A young woman with low education and very low income stood surety for her father's huge business debt, without being aware of the risk she was running. Against the backdrop of this case, the BVerfG constructed a general unconscionability doctrine, whose requirements are the 'structural inferiority' of one contractual party and the 'unusually onerous' consequences of the contract for the inferior party.[17] Thus one may say that, since the 'Suretyship' judgment, for the BVerfG freedom of contract also means freedom from unconscionable contracts.[18]

In 2001, the BVerfG confirmed the principles of the 'Suretyship' judgment in a case concerning a prenuptial agreement.[19] A pregnant woman wanted to marry the child's father. The man only agreed to the marriage on condition that the woman contractually renounced her right of maintenance granted by matrimonial property law in case of divorce. The woman agreed and a prenuptial agreement was concluded. The BVerfG acknowledged that the woman's self-determination and freedom of contract at the time of the conclusion of the agreement was so heavily limited that the agreement itself was not an act of autonomy but was the exact opposite of self-determination, which the court in both the 'Suretyship' judgment and this judgment expressed with the word *Fremdbestimmung* (hetero-determination) of the weaker party. Thus the Constitutional Court quashed the civil court judgment which violated the woman's fundamental right to private autonomy and freedom of contract (Article 2 (1) GG) insofar that the civil judges did not challenge the validity of the prenuptial agreement.

Four years later, in two decisions of 2005 on life insurance contracts,[20] the BVerfG seems to have broadened even more its understanding of the constitutional principle of private autonomy as substantive freedom of contract. In the first case,[21] an insurer had transferred a contract

[17] See A. Colombi Ciacchi, 'Non-Legislative Harmonisation of Private Law under the European Constitution: The Case of Unfair Suretyships' (2005) 13 *European Review of Private Law* 285.

[18] Paradoxically, freedom of contract can also mean to protect someone against him/herself: R. Singer, 'Vertragsfreiheit, Grundrechte und der Schutz des Menschen vor sich selbst' (1995) *Juristenzeitung* 23.

[19] BVerfG 6 February 2001, BVerfGE 103, 89 (2001) *Neue Juristische Wochenschrift* 957.

[20] BVerfG 26 July 2005, 1 BvR 782/94 and 1 BvR 957/96 (2005) *Neue Juristische Wochenschrift* 2363; BVerfG 26 July 2005, 1 BvR 80/95 (2005) *Neue Juristische Wochenschrift* 2376.

[21] 1 BvR 782/94 and 1 BvR 957/96.

to another insurance company, without being obliged by law to obtain the insured person's consent. This change worsened the position of the insured person and left him without a remedy. In the second case,[22] the law of insurance contracts did not guarantee that premium payments of the insured person were adequately taken into account in the calculation of surplus insurance benefits. In both cases, the BVerfG acknowledged a lack of substantive private autonomy of the insured person and found that the legislator was under a duty to modify the law of life insurance contracts so as to provide the insured person with effective remedies. The BVerfG inferred this duty from the constitutional protection of private autonomy (Article 2 (1) GG) and property (Article 14 (1) GG).

In these 'Life Insurance' decisions, the insured persons were not vulnerable on grounds of age, education, inexperience or poverty. The contracts were not unusually disadvantageous for them. The lack of substantive freedom of contract consisted in the general inequality of bargaining power between insurance companies and consumers, as well as in the general lack of freedom of choice of every insured person after the conclusion of a life insurance policy. Hence one may argue that the BVerfG in these judgments extended the scope of its substantive understanding of freedom of contract. Accordingly, every situation where one contracting party (before or after the conclusion of the contract) can no longer exercise its substantive self-determination and is therefore dominated by the other party now gives rise to a state's duty to intervene and provide for a legal remedy.

Slovenia

The jurisprudence of the Slovenian Constitutional Court offers another subtle example of substantive understanding of freedom of contract. A milestone in this regard is a judgment of 1994 concerning a credit agreement with an excessive interest rate.[23] Such cases are normally dealt with under the provision of usurious contract (*oderuška pogodba*), which is now codified in Article 119 of the Slovenian Code of Obligations (CO).[24] According to this Article, a contract is usurious if there is a

[22] 1 BvR 80/95.

[23] U-I-202/93 (6.10.1994), *Official Journal* No. 74/94. See Š. Mežnar, 'Family Suretyships in Slovenia – an Underestimated Problem', in A. Colombi Ciacchi (ed.), *Protection of Non-Professional Sureties in Europe: Formal and Substantive Disparity* (Baden Baden: Nomos, 2007) 247, 256–7.

[24] Obligacijski zakonik, *Official Journal* No. 83/2001.

manifest disproportion between the obligation of the two contractual parties, which is a consequence of the exploitation by one party of the other party's distress, severe financial problems, inexperience, recklessness or dependence on another person. The exploiting party must have acted in order to achieve benefits for him/herself or for another person. If all these requirements are met, the contract is null and void. Alternatively, the injured party can claim for an adjustment of the contract within five years from its conclusion. However, the injured party bears the burden of proof of the requirements of Article 119 being met. Needless to say, it is very difficult for him/her to provide such evidence.[25]

In the case decided by the Slovenian Constitutional Court in 1994, the usury requirements were not met. Theoretically, the contract could have been deemed immoral and declared null and void under Article 86 CO.[26] However, Slovenian civil courts were reluctant to avoid a contract solely on the basis of the immorality clause. They required the applicability of other, more specific causes of action, such as impermissible subject matter of the contract, impermissible motive, or, indeed, usury.[27]

This self-restraint of the civil courts was challenged by the Constitutional Court in 1994. The Constitutional Court found that the autonomy of both contractual parties was protected by the Slovenian Constitution of 1991,[28] namely in Article 35 (protection of personality rights)[29] and Article 74 (freedom of business).[30] On this basis, the Constitutional Court held that the validity of contracts that evidently violated basic principles of contract law such as good faith and fair dealing, equal performance, or prohibition of abuse of rights, had to be

[25] Š. Mežnar (n. 23 above) 253–4.

[26] Article 86 (1) CO reads: 'A contract that contravenes the Constitution, compulsory regulations or moral principles shall be null and void if the purpose of the contravened rule does not assign any other sanction or if the law does not prescribe otherwise for the case in question.' See Mežnar (n. 23 above) 255.

[27] Ibid., 256. [28] *Ustava Republike Slovenije.*

[29] Article 35 Slovenian Constitution reads: 'The inviolability of the physical and mental integrity of every person, his privacy and personality rights shall be guaranteed.'

[30] Article 74 Slovenian Constitution reads:

(1) Free economic initiative shall be guaranteed.
(2) The conditions for establishing commercial organisations shall be established by law. Commercial activities may not be pursued in a manner contrary to the public interest.
(3) Unfair competition practices and practices which restrict competition in a manner contrary to the law are prohibited.

examined by civil courts regardless of whether they could be qualified as usurious.[31]

Slovenian scholars welcomed this judgment, which 'introduced a substantive rather than formal examination of unfair contracts'.[32] In 1998, the Slovenian Constitutional Court confirmed the principles of its 1994 decision.[33] Finally, in 2005 the Slovenian Supreme Court abandoned its restrictive jurisprudence on the immorality clause. By explicitly referring to the Constitutional Court judgment of 1994, the Supreme Court held that Article 86 CO represented a direct legal basis for the nullity of a contract that evidently violated basic moral principles, such as the principle of good faith and the principle that freedom of contract is subject to limitations. It found that civil courts were obliged to declare a contract null and void when it evidently contravened such basic moral principles, regardless of whether the contract met the requirement of other, more specific provisions, such as the prohibition of usury. In particular, the Supreme Court suggested that a gross violation of the principle of equal performance could be sanctioned by Article 86 CO independently of the usury in the contract.[34]

The double meaning of freedom of contract (formal and substantive) is well reflected in the difference between the reasoning of the Slovenian Constitutional Court and the Slovenian Supreme Court. Like the German Federal Constitutional Court in the 'Suretyship' case, the Slovenian Constitutional Court in the credit agreement case of 1994 similarly established a substantive understanding of personal autonomy and freedom of contract, which also implies freedom from unconscionable contracts. By contrast, the Slovenian Supreme Court in 2005, by mentioning the 'principle that freedom of contract is subject to limitations', revealed a view of the principles of good faith, fairness and equal performance as conflicting with the principle of freedom of contract. This corresponds to the traditional formal understanding of the principle.

Greece

In Greece there is no Constitutional Court. Nevertheless, Greek civil courts have begun to view the substantive freedom of contract as a constitutional right, exactly like the German and Slovenian Constitutional Courts. In 1999,

[31] U-I-202/93 (6.10.1994) (see n. 23 above). [32] Mežnar (n. 23 above) 256.

[33] U-I-123/95. Mežnar (n. 23 above).

[34] Case II Ips 409/2004 (7.4.2005). Mežnar (n. 23 above).

the Athens Court of First Instance adjudicated a family suretyship case along the same pattern as the 'Suretyship' decision of the BVerfG,[35] explicitly referring to the German judgment. The facts of both cases were very similar: young people with low education and very low incomes had entered into suretyships without being aware of the risk.

The Athens Court of First Instance found that freedom of contract was a fundamental principle that governed both the conclusion and the content of contracts and derived from the principle of self-determination enshrined in Article 5 (1) of the Greek Constitution.[36] Since each person that takes part in private law transactions falls within the scope of protection accorded by Article 5 (1) and each person can equally invoke the constitutionally recognised principle of self-determination, the right of the stronger party cannot prevail. The freedom of contract can fulfil its mission only where the contractual parties act on an equal basis and in the context of a balancing of their opposing interests. If one of the contracting parties is in a superior position and in practice unilaterally dictates to the other party the contents of the contract, this superiority results in a situation whereby the other party is unable to exercise its private autonomy. Of course the legal order cannot take care of all cases in which the balance in the bargaining power between the two parties is disturbed. However, if there is a typical case scenario, which reveals a structural inferiority of one of the contracting parties, then the legal order has to react and enable the necessary adjustments. If the contractual obligations are manifestly disproportionate and unusually onerous for one party, and the contractual provisions are the result of a structural inequality of bargaining power, the civil courts have the duty to provide remedies by applying the general principles of private law such as good morals (Article 179 of the Greek Civil Code (AK)) or good faith (Articles 178 and 288 AK). In particular, when young people with low education

[35] Three Member Court of First Instance of Athens 7241/1999, (2000) NoV, 1146ff. See Y. Erifillidis, 'Greece', in A. Colombi Ciacchi and S. Weatherill (eds.), *Regulating Unfair Banking Practices in Europe: The Case of Personal Suretyships* (Oxford University Press, 2010). See further Γ. Δέλλιο, Ατομικά Δικαιώματα, Ιδιωτικό Δίκαιο, προστασία καταναλω τών και εγγυήσεις τραπεζικών δανείων (G. Dellios, Private Rights, Private Law, Consumer Protection and Guarantees for Bank Loans) (2003) *Digesta* 382, 383 and Γ. Μεντή, Όρια της ευθύνης του εγγυητή στις τραπεζικές καταναλωτικές συμβάσεις (G. Mentis, Limits to the Guarantor's Liability in Bank Consumer Contracts) (2004) ChrID, 185,187.

[36] *Σύνταγμα* (Syntagma), in force since 1975, Article 5(1) reads: 'All persons shall have the right to develop freely their personality and participate in the social, economic and political life of the country, insofar as they do not infringe the rights of others or violate the Constitution and the good usages.' See Erifillidis (n. 35 above).

and no experience in business enter into a suretyship for a business loan, without having been informed by the bank about the suretyship's risk and without having a personal financial interest in the suretyship, and the guaranteed amount is disproportionate to their financial capacity, the contract contravenes well-established principles of morality.

Therefore, one may say that for the Athens Court of First Instance, freedom of contract also means freedom from unconscionable contracts.

The Netherlands

As in Greece, in the Netherlands there is no Constitutional Court. Yet similarly the German 'Suretyship' judgment has been a source of inspiration, in particular for scholars. Snijders recently embraced a substantive understanding of freedom of contract which is quite similar to the BVerfG's concept. He demonstrated that Article 8 of the European Convention of Human Rights (ECHR) not only protects privacy as the right to be left alone, but also the right to personal autonomy and self-determination, which in turn encompasses freedom of contract. Accordingly, a civil court adjudicating a contract entered into under pressure, could consider it to violate Article 8 ECHR. This would apply, for example, to family suretyships where a family member and a bank employee exercised pressure on a private surety.[37]

Already in the late 1960s, Dutch scholars considered freedom of contract as an unwritten fundamental right.[38] Snijders' reliance on the ECHR instead of the Dutch Constitution (*Grondwet*, GW) as a source of the fundamental right to substantive freedom of contract is not casual. In the Netherlands, the ECHR may even be said to rank higher than the domestic constitution. Under Article 120 GW, Dutch courts are not allowed to test acts of parliament against the national constitution. However, they are not prevented from testing the compliance of domestic statutes with international treaties. In fact, quite often the ECHR is applied in the adjudication of private law cases. Moreover, certain ECHR provisions can be directly invoked before Dutch courts on the basis of Article 93 and 94 GW.[39]

[37] H. J. Snijders, 'Privacy of Contract', in K. Ziegler (ed.), *Human Rights and Private Law: Privacy as Autonomy* (Oxford: Hart, 2007) 105.

[38] A. G. Maris, 'Dient de wet bijzondere regelen te bevatten ten aanzien van de civielrechtelijke werking van grondrechten, en, zo ja, welke?' in *Handelingen Nederlandse Juristen-Vereniging 1969, first part* (Zwolle: W. E. J. Tjeenk Willink, 1969) 12ff; Mak (n. 7 above) 42.

[39] Ibid. 17.

Substantive freedom of contract and the horizontal effect of fundamental rights

The case law and scholarly doctrines outlined under the previous section can be explained in terms of either the 'vertical' or the 'horizontal' constitutionalisation of contract law. The 'Life Insurance' cases decided by the BVerfG in 2005 are examples of vertical constitutionalisation. This means that legislative provisions are invalidated on ground of their unconstitutionality and/or the legislator is obliged to reform a certain subject matter. By contrast, the 'Commercial Agent' and 'Suretyship' judgments of the BVerfG, as well as the Slovenian and Greek judgments, are examples of horizontal constitutionalisation. This means that no legislative provisions are declared unconstitutional, but the constitution helps in other ways to determine the rights and duties of the parties in a horizontal, private law relationship.[40]

The 'Commercial Agent' and 'Suretyship' judgments of the BVerfG and the Slovenian and Greek judgments on substantive freedom of contract are examples of *indirect* horizontal effect. The indirect horizontal effect doctrine assumes that it is not private parties, but only the state and its civil courts that are bound by fundamental rights. In the subject matter at stake, the state must ensure that the enforcement of a contract does not violate the self-determination and free development of personality of one contracting party. This state duty involves both the legislator and the courts. Accordingly, civil courts must avoid or adjust unconscionable contracts by applying the open norms of the Civil Codes, such as the prohibition of immoral contracts or the good faith principle, which shall be interpreted in the light of fundamental rights.

Snijders' construction instead is an example of *direct* horizontal effect. His proposal implies that civil courts take the Human Rights Convention as the direct parameter of validity of contractual claims. Accordingly, an unconscionable contract which disregards the substantive self-determination of one contracting party is considered to violate Article 8 ECHR. However, from the viewpoint of outcomes, there is no substantial difference between the indirect and direct horizontal effect approach.[41]

[40] Cf. A. Colombi Ciacchi, 'The Constitutionalisation of European Contract Law: Judicial Convergence and Social Justice' (2006) 2 *European Review of Contract Law* 167.

[41] Cf. A. Colombi Ciacchi, 'Horizontal Effect of Fundamental Rights, Privacy and Social Justice', in Ziegler (n. 37 above) 53; C. Mak (n. 7 above) 158ff.

Both approaches lead to the protection of substantive freedom of contract through a declaration of the invalidity of the unconscionable agreement or a judicial adjustment of its content.

The constitutional dimension of freedom of contract: actual acknowledgments in Italy, France and Poland

Italy

The Italian Constitution (*Costituzione italiana*, Cost.) is as old as the German Constitution[42] and the Italian Constitutional Court (Corte costituzionale) plays an equally important role in private law as the BVerfG in Germany. Not surprisingly, the acknowledgment of the constitutional dimension of private autonomy is in Italy almost as old as in Germany. As early as the 1960s, the Corte costituzionale[43] held that freedom of contract, although not a constitutional value itself, was indirectly protected by the constitution as it was functionally related to the freedom of economic initiative enshrined in Article 41 Cost.[44] The Constitutional Court acknowledged that the freedom of economic initiative and private autonomy were not unlimited and could be counterbalanced by other, higher-ranked socio-economic values which are constitutionally relevant.[45]

In fact, the Italian Constitution does not regulate the freedom of economic initiative in the chapter devoted to the citizens' rights and duties, but in the chapter regulating economic relationships. Therefore the freedom of economic initiative is less well protected than personal

[42] It entered into force on 1 January 1948, one year before the *Grundgesetz*.

[43] Corte cost. 20 February 1962, no. 7; Corte cost. 8 April 1965, no. 30; Corte cost. 13 March 1969, no. 37; available at www.cortecostituzionale.it/giurisprudenza. For more recent confirmations of the same principles see Corte cost. 3–15 May 1990, no. 241; Corte cost. 22–30 June 1994, no. 268; Corte cost. 6–17 March 2000, no. 70, ibid.

[44] An English translation of the Italian Constitution is available at www.servat.unibe.ch/icl/it00000_.html. Article 41 Cost. reads:

(1) Private economic enterprise is free.
(2) It may not be carried out against the common good or in a way that may harm public security, liberty, or human dignity.
(3) The law determines appropriate planning and controls so that public and private economic activities may be directed and coordinated towards social ends.

[45] Corte cost. 13 March 1969, no. 37; Corte cost. 7 May 1976; at: www.cortecostituzionale.it/giurisprudenza.

liberties.[46] The wording of Article 41 (2) Cost. mentions the social utility, the liberty, dignity and safety of human beings as limitations of private economic initiative. According to the Constitutional Court, the need to achieve social utility justifies both the setting of restrictive conditions for the operativity of freedom of contract, and the modification or elimination of contract terms which conflict with social utility.[47]

The prevalent opinion in academic literature follows the Constitutional Court's approach and considers Article 41 Cost. as an indirect constitutional legal basis of freedom of contract.[48] Some Italian scholars focus instead, like the German scholars and courts, on the self-determination aspect of private autonomy, as a manifestation of the freedom to decide on one's own personal and patrimonial legal sphere.[49] These scholars prefer to rely on the human rights clause in Article 2 (1) Cost.,[50] which has also served as legal basis for the development of personality rights in Italian law. However, this approach to freedom of contract is criticised both by those who deny the open-norm character of Article 2 Cost.,[51] and by those who do not view freedom of contract as an individual liberty.[52] Moreover, the Constitutional Court explicitly denied the possibility of considering contractual autonomy as a human right protected by Article 2 (1) Cost.[53]

In Italy, a substantive understanding of freedom of contract has not yet been explicitly acknowledged. However, it is submitted that both this understanding and its constitutional dimension is fully compatible with the Italian legal culture. Two examples will be given here:

[46] See G. Alpa, 'Libertà contrattuale e tutela costituzionale' (1995) 35 *Rivista critica di diritto privato* 49–50.

[47] Corte cost. 20 February 1962, no. 7 (n. 43 above).

[48] See P. Rescigno, 'L'autonomia dei privati' (1967) *Iustitia* 3; A. Pace, 'Libertà "del" mercato e "nel" mercato' (1993) *Politica del diritto* 327, 329; G. Alpa (n. 46 above).

[49] See G. Guarino, *L'organizzazione pubblica*, vol. I (Milan: Giuffré, 1977) 134; id., 'Pubblico e privato nella economia. La sovranità tra Costituzione ed istituzioni comunitarie' (1992) *Quaderni costituzionali 39*.

[50] Article 2 (1) Cost. reads: 'The Republic recognizes and guarantees the inviolable rights of man, both as an individual and as a member of the social groups in which one's personality finds expression, and it requires the performance of imperative political, economic, and social duties.'

[51] A. Pace (n. 48 above) 327.

[52] G. Alpa (n. 46 above) 45, 48. He seems to limit the contract law relevance of Article 2 Cost. to agreements which create some sort of community.

[53] Corte cost. 21 March 1968, no. 16, available at www.cortecostituzionale.it/giurisprudenza.

First, contractual restrictions of the economic freedom of the weaker party, as in the German *Handelsvertreter* case, could be dealt with by giving horizontal effect to the freedom of economic initiative under Article 41 Cost. The preparatory works to the Italian Constitution demonstrate that Article 41 was meant to protect this freedom not only vis-à-vis the public power, but also vis-à-vis private economic powers.[54] It follows therefrom that Article 41 Cost. can be given direct horizontal effect in contractual relationships.[55]

Second, a substantive understanding of all constitutionally protected freedoms is implicit in Article 3 (2) Cost., according to which '[i]t is the duty of the Republic to remove all economic and social obstacles that, by limiting the freedom and equality of citizens, prevent full individual development and the participation of all workers in the political, economic, and social organization of the country'. Since the heading of Article 3 Cost. reads 'Equality', it has been generally acknowledged that Article 3 (2) enshrines the principle of substantive equality. However, this provision not only mentions the economic and social obstacles that limit the citizens' equality: it also mentions the economic and social obstacles that limit the citizens' *freedom*. In fact, substantive freedom of contract and substantive equality are closely intertwined. If a contract is concluded between one party who is substantively free to determine its content, and another party who lacks this substantive freedom, there is a substantive inequality between the contracting parties.

France

In France, the traditional enlightenment conception of freedom of contract as a natural human liberty[56] lost its appeal; in the twentieth century, as state intervention and protection of weaker parties grew, notions of (formal) freedom of contract were undermined. Unsurprisingly therefore, before 1997 the Constitutional Council (Conseil constitutionnel) denied the constitutional nature of the principle of freedom of contract.[57]

[54] See Lucifero's intervention during the meeting of the first subcommission on 10 September 1946: see Pace (n. 48 above) 330.

[55] Ibid.

[56] See G. Rouhette, 'Liberté contractuelle et droit constitutionnel en France', in *Freedom of Contract and Constitutional Law*, Proceedings of the Colloquium of the International Association of Legal Science (Jerusalem: Hamaccabi Press, 1994) 23.

[57] Cons. const. 3 August 1994, no. 94–348, *La semaine juridique (Juris-Classeur périodique)* 1995.II.22404, comment Y. Broussolle.

However, as from 1997, the Constitutional Council gradually moved towards an acknowledgment of the constitutional dimension of this principle. In 1997, the Council held that freedom of contract was not a constitutional value, but its infringement could endanger constitutionally guaranteed rights and liberties.[58] In 1998,[59] it affirmed that severe intrusions into legally concluded contracts, i.e. violations of the principle of economy of contracts (*économie des conventions et contrats*), could be considered as an infringement of the liberty rights enshrined in Article 4 of the 1789 Declaration of the Rights of Man and of the Citizen (*Déclaration des Droits de l'homme et du citoyen*).[60] This finding was then confirmed in two decisions of 1999 and 2000.[61]

Finally, in December 2000, the Constitutional Council explicitly acknowledged the constitutional value of freedom of contract.[62] In the two years thereafter, the Council seemed to have withdrawn this acknowledgment and resumed its previous, more restrictive jurisprudence.[63] In 2003 however,[64] it reaffirmed with a more comprehensive reasoning the constitutional rank of freedom of contract, relying on both Article 4 and Article 16 of the 1789 Declaration.[65] This judgment was

[58] Cons. const. 20 March 1997, no. 97–388 DC, (1998) *Revue trimestrielle de droit civil* 99, comment N. Molfessis, JCP 1997.I.4039, comment M. Fabre-Magnan.

[59] Cons. const. 10 June 1998, no. 98–401 DC, (1998) *Revue trimestrielle de droit civil* 796, comment N. Molfessis.

[60] Article 4 of this Declaration reads: 'Liberty consists in being able to do anything that does not harm others: thus, the exercise of the natural rights of every man has no bounds other than those that ensure to the other members of society the enjoyment of these same rights. These bounds may be determined only by Law.'

[61] Cons. const. 23 July 1999, no. 99–416 DC (1999) *Actualité juridique, droit administratif* 700, comment J.-E. Schoettl; Cons. const. 7 December 2000, no. 2000–436 DC (2001) *Actualité juridique, droit administratif* 18, comment J.-E. Schoettl.

[62] Cons. const. 19 December 2000, no. 2000–437 DC, (2001) *Revue trimestrielle de droit civil* 229, comment N. Molfessis; (2001) *Revue du droit public et de la science politique* 267, comment J.-E. Spitz.

[63] Cons. const. 27 November 2001, no. 2001–451 DC; Cons. const. 12 January 2002, no. 2001–455 DC; Cons. const. 27 December 2002, no. 2002–464 DC. See F. Moderne, 'La liberté contractuelle est-elle vraiment et pleinement constitutionnelle?' (2006) *Revue française de droit administratif* 2, 9.

[64] Cons. const. 13 January 2003, no. 2002–465 DC.

[65] Article 16 *Déclaration des Droits de l'homme et du citoyen* reads: 'Any society in which no provision is made for guaranteeing rights or for the separation of powers, has no Constitution.'

welcomed by French scholars as a 're-evaluation of freedom of contract in the legal order'.[66]

The new approach of the French Constitutional Council seems to converge with the approaches of the German Constitutional Court insofar as freedom of contract is seen as a manifestation of the constitutional principle of general freedom of action. Time will tell whether the *Conseil constitutionnel* will also develop its jurisprudence towards a substantive understanding of freedom of contract. Arguably, this understanding could be based on Article 4 of the *Déclaration des Droits de l'homme et du citoyen*, according to which the exercise of the freedom rights of every person 'has no bounds other than those that ensure to the other members of society the enjoyment of these same rights'.[67] In other words: the freedom of one contracting party to determine the content of the contract must be limited if the other contracting party is not in a position to enjoy the same freedom.

Poland

The Polish Constitutional Court, in a decision of 2003 concerning a tenancy agreement,[68] held that freedom of contract, although not explicitly mentioned in the constitution, had a constitutional dimension since it was connected with the constitutional principle of protection of personal freedom and the obligation to respect the freedoms of others. The court went on to state that freedom of contract might also be regarded as inherent to the principles of social market economy, protection of ownership, labour law and protection of private and family life, as well as the right to decide about one's personal life. It considered freedom of contract as a corollary of the protection of the general freedom of the person in Article 31 of the Polish Constitution.[69] It follows from this Article, in the Constitutional Court's opinion, that nobody can be forced to or

[66] B. Mathieu, 'La promotion constitutionnelle de la liberté contractuelle en matière de droit du travail' (2003) *Dalloz* 641; C. Herrmann and C. Perfumi, 'France', in G. Brüggemeier, A. Colombi Ciacchi and G. Comandé (eds.), *Fundamental Rights and Private Law in the European Union*, vol. I, *A Comparative Overview* (Cambridge University Press, 2010).

[67] See n. 60 above.

[68] *Trybunał konstytucyjny*, 29 April 2003, SK 24/02, (2003) 4A OTK ZU [33].

[69] Article 31 Polish Constitution (*Konstytucja*), in force since 1997, reads:

(1) Freedom of the person shall receive legal protection.
(2) Everyone shall respect the freedoms and rights of others. No one shall be compelled to do that which is not required by law.
(3) ...

forbidden from concluding an agreement and that nobody can be forced to choose a particular contracting party or agree on specific contract terms unless the law provides otherwise.[70]

Unlike the Italian Constitutional Court, the Polish Constitutional Court did not derive freedom of contract from the freedom of economic activity.[71] It relied instead, like the German Constitutional Court and the French Constitutional Council, on the principle of general freedom of the person. It is submitted that from this starting point, the step towards an acknowledgment of the substantive dimension of freedom of contract can be easily made.

Substantive freedom of contract as a common European fundamental right?

It may be argued that the German, Slovenian and Greek case law and Snijders' opinion[72] witness the beginning of a Europe-wide development of the understanding of freedom of contract as freedom from unconscionable contracts. One single step separates the Italian, French and Polish acknowledgments of the constitutional dimension of freedom of contract from the German, Slovenian, Greek and Dutch doctrines on substantive freedom of contract as a constitutional or human right.

Actually, the constitutional dimension of freedom of contract could be acknowledged in all countries where the principles of self-determination, free development of personality and/or general freedom of the person are enshrined in the constitution. This is for example the case in Ireland[73] and Spain.[74]

However, neither a written constitution nor a legal culture of application of constitutional norms in private law is a necessary prerequisite for

[70] *Trybunał konstytucyjny*, 29 April 2003 (n. 68 above). Cf. A. Jańczuk and J. Krzemińska, 'Poland', in Brüggemeier, Colombi Ciacchi and Comandé (n. 66 above).

[71] The Court explicitly denied this derivation and stressed the different scope of application of freedom of contract and freedom of economic activity. See *Trybunał konstytucyjny*, 29 April 2003 (n. 68 above).

[72] See n. 37 above.

[73] Article 40 (3) no. 1 of the Irish Constitution (*Bunreacht na hÉireann*) of 1937 reads: 'The State guarantees in its laws to respect, and, as far as practicable, by its laws to defend and vindicate the personal rights of the citizen.'

[74] Article 10 (1) of the Spanish Constitution (*Constitución Española*) of 1978 states: 'The dignity of the person, the inviolable rights which are inherent, the free development of the personality, respect for the law and the rights of others, are the foundation of political order and social peace.'

the development of the understanding of substantive freedom of contract as a fundamental right. Snijders demonstrated that this understanding could also be based on Article 8 ECHR. This would provide a potential legal basis for the principle of substantive freedom of contract both in legal systems without a written constitution like the UK and in legal systems such as in the Netherlands and Sweden, where a written constitution exists but where civil courts, when adjudicating cases involving fundamental rights, prefer to rely on the ECHR.

At least an indirect horizontal effect of constitutional norms or human rights has been acknowledged by the judiciary in a large number of EU Member States, including the UK.[75] Freedom of contract as substantive self-determination can be invoked in contract cases either on the basis of constitutional norms or Article 8 ECHR. The rights enshrined in the Convention and in the common constitutional tradition of the Member States are, according to Article 6 of the EU Treaty and the established jurisprudence of the ECJ, common fundamental rights and principles of the European Union. Therefore, the principle of substantive freedom of contract as freedom from unconscionable contracts has the potential to become a truly common European fundamental principle.

The process towards the acknowledgment of such a common European principle may take a long time. In Germany, the constitutional dimension of freedom of contract was established in the late 1950s, but it took more than thirty years to achieve a substantive understanding of freedom of contract as freedom from unconscionable contracts. In other countries such as Poland and France, freedom of contract has been acknowledged as a constitutional principle only in the 2000s. In these and other EU Member States, a substantive understanding of this freedom could possibly be established in the next thirty to forty years. Time will tell whether and when the prophecy in this chapter will become reality.

[75] See G Brüggemeier, A. Colombi Ciacchi and G. Comandé (eds.), *Fundamental Rights and Private Law in the European Union*, vol. 1, *A Comparative Overview* (Cambridge University Press, 2010).

2

Protection of weaker parties in English law

STEPHEN WADDAMS

Since the nineteenth century, writers on English contract law have emphasised the enforceability of contracts and have tended to marginalise the instances in which contracts have been set aside for unfairness. In dealing with consideration it has been common to point out that inadequacy of consideration is not, in itself, a defence to contractual obligation, and from this it has been inferred that, if there is sufficient consideration to meet the test of contract formation, the contract must be enforceable. Sir Frederick Pollock in his first edition (1876) wrote that it was:

> a distinguishing mark of English jurisprudence that the amount of the consideration is not material. 'The value of all things contracted for is measured by the appetite of the contractors, and therefore the just value is that which they be contented to give'. It is accordingly treated as an elementary principle that the law will not enter into an inquiry as to the adequacy of the consideration.[1]

Sir William Anson (1879) followed the same line, and made the point more forcefully:

> So long as a man gets what he bargained for Courts of law will not ask what the value may be to him, or whether its value is in any way proportionate to his act or promise given in return. This would be 'the law making the bargain, instead of leaving the parties to make it'.[2]

As both writers were aware, however, this was not the whole story, because courts of equity had often set aside contracts on a variety of grounds related (in general terms) to unfairness. Pollock mentioned this

I am very grateful to Brendan Donovan for his assistance in preparing this chapter.

[1] F. Pollock, *Principles of Contract at Law and in Equity* (London: Stevens & Sons, 1876) at 154, quoting Hobbes, *Leviathan* (1660) Part I, ch. 15.

[2] W. R. Anson, *Principles of the English Law of Contract* (Oxford: Clarendon Press, 1879) at 63, quoting Alderson B in *Pilkington* v. *Scott* 14 M & W 657, 660.

aspect of English law with a somewhat awkward sidenote in his chapter on consideration (chapter IV):

> Inadequacy *plus other things* in Equity: see chap. XI.
>
> Inadequacy of consideration coupled with other things may however be of great importance as evidence of fraud, &c., when the validity of a contract is in dispute: and it has been considered (though, it is believed, the better opinion is otherwise) to be of itself sufficient ground for refusing specific performance. This subject, which is by no means free from difficulty, will be examined under the head of Undue Influence, Ch. XI, *post.*[3]

Anson, closely following both the form and the substance of Pollock's work, dealt with the matter as follows:

> Equity so far takes adequacy of consideration into account in dealing with contracts, that if a contract is sought to be avoided on the ground of Fraud or Undue Influence, inadequacy of consideration will be regarded as strong corroborative evidence in support of the suit. [Reference followed to what Anson, like Pollock, considered the doubtful power of the court to deny specific performance on this ground.][4]

English courts, after 1875, administered law and equity together, and one of the principal stated purposes of Pollock's book was to consider English law and equity as a whole. However his approach to this question, followed in starker form by Anson, tended to marginalise the power of the court to set aside disadvantageous contracts. The statement of the general principle of law, followed by mention two pages later of a power to set aside contracts in 'equity' suggests that the power is exceptional. The categories of 'fraud, &c.' and 'fraud or undue influence' suggest rare and closely defined instances, scarcely affecting the general principles of contract law. The reference to inadequacy of consideration as a matter only of *evidence* tends to suggest that it has little effect on substantive law, and the emphasis of both writers on the power of the court of equity to refuse specific performance (leaving the promisee with a right to full damages) tend to distract the reader from the far more significant power of the court to *rescind* the contract (leaving the promisee with no remedy at all). The postponement of the subject to a later chapter also tends to suggest that it is not directly relevant to the most basic principles of contract law, and that relief on ground of unfairness is conceptually exceptional. The tendency to marginalise the issue reached a peak in Halsbury's *Laws of England* (1907–15) where unconscionable contracts

[3] See n. 1 above, at 156. [4] See n. 2 above, at 65.

were excluded altogether from the article on Contract, and dealt with, anomalously, in a different volume in the article on Fraudulent and Voidable Conveyances.

The power of English courts to set aside contracts on grounds broadly relating to unfairness and inequality of exchange was, however, considerably wider than the extracts from Pollock's and Anson's books suggest. The first published treatise on English contract law (by John Joseph Powell, 1790) included a long chapter entitled 'Of the Equitable jurisdiction in relieving against unreasonable Contracts or Agreements'.[5] Powell stated that the mere fact of a bargain being *unreasonable* was not a ground to set it aside in equity:

> for contracts are not to be set aside, because not such as the wisest people would make; but there must be fraud to make void acts of this solemn and deliberate nature, if entered into for a consideration.[6]

But Powell went on to point out that 'fraud' in equity had an unusual and very wide meaning:

> And agreements that are not properly fraudulent, in that sense of the term which imports deceit, will, nevertheless, be relieved against on the ground of inequality, and imposed burden or hardship on one of the parties to a contract; which is considered as a distinct head of equity, being looked upon as an offence against morality, and as unconscientious. Upon this principle, such courts will, in cases where contracts are unequal, as bearing hard upon one party . . . set them aside.[7]

Powell gave as an example the very common provision in a mortgage that unpaid interest should be treated as principal and should itself bear interest until paid. Powell wrote that 'this covenant will be relieved against as fraudulent, because unjust and oppressive in an extreme degree'.[8]

The very wide meaning thus given to the concepts of 'fraud' and 'fraudulent' indicates that the power to set aside contracts was much wider than at first appears. Pollock, in his chapter on duress and undue influence, also explained to his readers that 'fraud' could not be taken at face value:

> The term fraud is indeed of common occurrence both in the earlier and in the later authorities: but 'fraud does not here mean deceit or

[5] J. J. Powell, *Essay upon the Law of Contracts and Agreements*, 2 vols. (London, 1790) vol. II, at 143.

[6] Ibid., at 144. [7] Ibid., at 145–6. [8] Ibid., at 146.

> circumvention; it means an unconscientious use of the power arising out of these circumstances and conditions' and this does not come within the proper meaning of fraud, which is a misrepresentation . . . made with the intent of creating a particular wrong belief in the mind of the party defrauded. Perhaps the best word to use would be imposition, as a sort of middle term between fraud, to which it comes near in popular language, and compulsion, which it suggests by its etymology.[9]

It is significant that Pollock, in elucidating the meaning of the word fraud, should consciously look for an equally ambiguous word (imposition), suggesting, on the one hand, the taking of unfair advantage, and, on the other hand, actual compulsion.

Relief against forfeiture

The court of equity commonly gave relief against forfeitures of all kinds. The most clearly established case was that of a mortgage. Mortgage documents usually provided that, on default in repayment, the land should be forfeited to the mortgagee. The courts consistently refused to enforce this simple provision, despite the fact that it was well known and perfectly clear. Whatever form of words was used – even if the document evidenced an outright conveyance of the land – the court, if convinced that the substance of the transaction was a mortgage, refused to enforce the document and permitted the borrower to redeem the land:

> So that in every mortgage the agreement of the parties upon the face of the deed, seems to be, that a mortgage shall not be redeemable after forfeiture . . . and a mortgage can no more be irredeemable than a distress for rent-charge can be irrepleviable. The law itself will control that express agreement of the party; and by the same reason equity will let a man loose from his agreement, and will against his agreement admit him to redeem a mortgage.[10]

No restriction, even by express agreement, was permitted on the right to redeem. In *Spurgeon* v. *Collier* (1758) Lord Northington said that 'a man will not be suffered in conscience to fetter himself with a limitation or restriction of his time of redemption. It would ruin the distressed and unwary, and give unconscionable advantage to greedy and designing

[9] See n. 1 above, at 527.

[10] *Howard* v. *Harris* (1683) 1 Vern 190, 192. This passage from the argument of successful counsel was cited, with page reference and near quotation, as having assisted in establishing the law on the point, by R. H. Coote, *A Treatise on the Law of Mortgage* (London: Butterworth, 1821) at 22.

persons.'[11] This last sentence compendiously illustrates the impact of the separate but interlocking concepts that have run through the unconscionability cases: lack of consent, avoidance of unjust enrichment, and deterrence of wrongdoing. A few years later the same judge again linked the concepts of reason, justice, freedom of consent, and deterrence of trickery:

> The court, as a court of conscience, is very jealous of persons taking securities for a loan, and converting such securities into purchases. And therefore I take it to be an established rule, that a mortgagee can never provide at the time of making the loan for any event or condition on which the equity of redemption shall be discharged, and the conveyance absolute. And there is great reason and justice in this rule, for necessitous men are not, truly speaking, free men, but, to answer a present exigency, will submit to any terms that the crafty may impose upon them.[12]

The rule was that the mortgagee could stipulate for no collateral advantage, and so strict was this rule that it came to be applied so as to cause the setting aside of agreements that were perfectly fair and reasonable. It was easier for the nineteenth-century English legal mind to accept a rigid rule that in no circumstances may a mortgagee stipulate for a collateral advantage (a rule that, for better or worse, happened to be the law) than a general power to relieve against unfair transactions. So, ironically, in the name of upholding the sanctity of contracts, transactions were set aside that were *not* unfair. In a decision of the House of Lords in 1904 Lord Halsbury remarked, with evident irritation, that 'a perfectly fair bargain made between two parties to it, each of whom was quite sensible as to what they were doing, is not to be performed because at the same time a mortgage arrangement was made between them'.[13] Ten years later the House of Lords restored flexibility by appealing to the underlying original reason for the intervention of the courts:

> It was, in ordinary cases, only where there was conduct which the Court of Chancery regarded as unconscientious that it interfered with freedom of contract. The lending of money, on mortgage or otherwise, was looked on with suspicion and the courts were on the alert to discover want of conscience in the terms imposed by lenders . . . [I]t is inconsistent with the objects for which [the rules of equity] were established that these rules should crystallise into technical language so rigid the letter can defeat the underlying spirit and purpose.[14]

[11] (1758) 1 Eden 55, at 59 (Sir R. Henley). [12] *Vernon* v. *Bethell* (1762) 2 Eden 110, 113.

[13] *Samuel* v. *Jarrah Timber and Wood Paving Co.* [1904] AC 323, 325.

[14] *Kreglinger* v. *New Patagonia Meat and Cold Storage Co. Ltd* [1914] AC 25, 36–8 per Lord Haldane.

Penalties

Forfeiture in its various forms has obvious advantages to the secured party, and it is not surprising that attempts were made by lenders to secure equivalent advantages without the immediate transfer of the property to be forfeited. The growth of the penal bond represented such an attempt. A common form of the bond was a covenant to pay a fixed sum of money unless some other act was performed by a certain date. The effect was to secure the performance of the other act, which might itself be the payment of a sum of money that had been lent by the obligee to the obligor.

The court of equity gave relief from such bonds on much the same principle as in cases of mortgages. The bond was, in substance, a device to secure repayment of a loan, and the legitimate interest of the lender was in repayment of the principal (together with interest and costs) and no more. In 1880 the law on the point, out of keeping though it was with the spirit of the nineteenth century, was explained by Bramwell LJ (who, though not himself sympathetic, accepted that this was the law) as follows:

> [T]he Court of Chancery said that a penalty to secure the payment of a sum of money or the performance of an act should not be enforced; the parties were not held to their agreement; equity in truth refused to allow to be enforced what was considered to be an unconscientious bargain.[15]

Another judge said, in 1900:

> The Court of Chancery gave relief against the strictness of the common law in cases of penalty or forfeiture for nonpayment of a fixed sum on a day certain, on the principle that failure to pay principal on a certain day could be compensated sufficiently by payment of principal and interest with costs at a subsequent day.[16]

Important also was the obvious factor that a borrower in urgent need was apt to sign too readily an extravagant penal bond: the need for the funds was always immediate, and the possibility of enforcement of the bond remote.

[15] *Protector Loan Co.* v. *Grice* (1880) 5 QBD 592, 596.

[16] *Re Dixon* [1900] 2 Ch 561, 576, per Rigby LJ.

Persons borrowing on the expectation of future ownership of property

The English courts of equity relieved against transactions entered into by persons expecting to own property in the future. The typical case was of the 'expectant heir', and this phrase, together with the otherwise obsolete phrase 'catching bargain', is generally used to denote this branch of English law, but the jurisdiction was not restricted to heirs: it extended to every kind of case in which the borrower expected to become the owner of property in the future. Commonly the substance of the transaction was a loan, but the transaction took the form of a sale of the expectancy, or of the reversion. The court would set aside the transaction unless the purchaser proved that he had given full value. As in the case of mortgages and penalties, the situation is one in which experience shows that a person, pressed with the immediate need for money, is apt to sell a future interest at an undervalue – sometimes at a gross undervalue: again, the need for money is immediate, and the interest given up seems remote. So ready was the court to set aside such transactions that the rule came to seem too rigid: a statute of 1867 provided that such transactions should not 'be opened or set aside merely upon the ground of undervalue'.[17] The statute, however, did not affect the general jurisdiction of the court to set aside unconscionable transactions,[18] and this line of cases supplies an important illustration of that wider jurisdiction, before and after 1867.[19] Pollock said, in his first edition, that 'practically the question is whether in the opinion of the court the transaction was a hard bargain'.[20]

Undue influence

Disadvantageous contractual transactions have frequently been set aside for 'undue influence'. This phrase covers a number of different circumstances. It may apply to an openly hostile relationship where one party threatens the other with adverse consequences if the agreement is not made. Such a case was *Williams* v. *Bayley*[21] where a son had forged his father's signature to promissory notes, and the creditor threatened to prosecute the son unless the father agreed to pay the debt. More commonly the phrase has been applied to situations related to fiduciary

[17] 31 & 32 Vic. c. 4. [18] *Earl of Aylesford* v. *Morris* (1873) 8 Ch 484, 490.
[19] See the passage quoted at n. 25, below. [20] See n. 1, above, at 534–5.
[21] (1866) LR 1 HL 200.

duties where one party reposes trust in the other. Certain categories of case have been said to give rise to a presumption of undue influence, but it is not necessary for the weaker party to bring his case into a recognised category: any case in which there is a relationship of trust or confidence may qualify for relief. A recent instance of a case that does not readily fall into any pre-existing category is one where an employee guaranteed her employer's debts. The guarantee was set aside by the English Court of Appeal. Millett LJ used strong language, very reminiscent of the older equity cases:

> This transaction cannot possibly stand ... It is an extreme case. The transaction was not merely to the manifest disadvantage of Miss Burch; it was one which, in the traditional phrase, 'shocks the conscience of the court'. Miss Burch committed herself to a personal liability far beyond her slender means, risking the loss of her home and personal bankruptcy, and obtained nothing in return beyond a relatively small and possibly temporary increase in the overdraft facility available to her employer, a company in which she had no financial interest. The transaction gives rise to grave suspicion. It cries aloud for an explanation.[22]

Closely related, and perhaps conceptually indistinguishable,[23] are cases where the relationship between the parties is categorised as fiduciary.

Unconscionable transactions

The courts of equity exercised a general jurisdiction to set aside transactions that they regarded as very unfair. In 1818 it was said that:

> a court of equity will inquire whether the parties really did meet on equal terms; and if it be found that the vendor was in distressed circumstances, and that advantage was taken of that distress, it will avoid the contract.[24]

In 1888, summarising the cases, Kay J said:

> The result of the decisions is that where a purchase is made from a poor and ignorant man at a considerable undervalue, the vendor having no independent advice, a court of equity will set aside the transaction. This will be done even in the case of property in possession, and *a fortiori* if the interest be reversionary. The circumstances of poverty and ignorance of the vendor and absence of independent advice throw upon the purchaser,

[22] *Credit Lyonnais Bank Nederland NV* v. *Burch* [1997] 1 All ER 144, 152.
[23] See *Lloyds Bank* v. *Bundy* [1975] QB 326 (CA).
[24] *Wood* v. *Abrey* (1818) 3 Madd 417, 423, per Leach VC.

> where the transaction is impeached, the onus of proving, in Lord Selborne's words, that the purchase was 'fair, just and reasonable'.[25]

Was undervalue alone a sufficient ground for relief? This question is not easy to answer because of the elusive meaning of 'fraud'. There are, indeed, many statements by courts and commentators to the effect that undervalue alone was insufficient, but these cannot be taken at face value because of frequent indications that a gross undervalue created a 'presumption of fraud': where there was a large inequality of exchange the court could presume, without any separate proof, that the disadvantaged party must have been labouring under some sort of mistake or disability, or else must have been influenced by necessity, or by some sort of pressure, or by a relationship with the stronger party.[26] Some cases suggest that the presumption was practically irrebuttable: Joseph Story (1836) spoke in this context of 'the most vehement presumption of fraud'.[27] Inequality of exchange was not, in itself, conclusive, but it does not follow that it was irrelevant: a large inequality of exchange often seems to have called for some sort of explanation (which might be that a part-gift was intended, or that the inequality was caused by risks fairly allocated by the transaction).[28] An attempt in the twentieth century by Lord Denning[29] to restate a general principle in terms of unfairness and inequality of bargaining power was rejected by the House of Lords,[30] but the older cases were not overruled.

Consumer credit

Since the beginning of the twentieth century, legislation has empowered the court to set aside loan and credit transactions that are found to be (broadly speaking) very unfair.[31]

[25] *Fry* v. *Lane* (1888) 40 Ch D 312, 322. Lord Selborne's words were from *Aylesford* v. *Morris*, n. 18 above, 491.

[26] *Earl of Chesterfield* v. *Janssen* (1751) 2 Ves Sen 125, *Heathcote* v. *Paignon* (1787) 2 Bro CC 167.

[27] J. Story, *Commentaries on Equity Jurisprudence as administered in England and America* (Boston: Hillard Gray & Co., 1836) at 250.

[28] *Rotheram* v. *Browne* (1747) 8 Bro PC 297 (part gift), *Mortimer* v. *Capper* (1782) 1 Bro CC 156 (inherent risk).

[29] *Lloyd's Bank* v. Bundy, n. 23 above.

[30] *National Westminster Bank Plc* v. *Morgan* [1985] AC 686 (HL).

[31] Moneylenders Act 1900 (excessive harsh and unconscionable), Consumer Credit Act 1974, ss. 137–40 (extortionate, grossly exorbitant, grossly contravenes ordinary principles of fair dealing), Consumer Credit Act 2006, s. 140A (unfair).

Lenders and third parties

A common situation arising in cases of loan guarantees is that the guarantor is induced to enter the transaction because of some kind of influence exercised by the principal debtor. The problem is whether, and in what circumstances, the lender, not having precise knowledge of the relationship between the guarantor and the principal debtor, should be precluded from enforcing the contract of guarantee. The typical case has been a guarantee given by a wife to secure her husband's debts, or those of his business. But many kinds of relationship raise the same problem. In *Credit Lyonnais* v. *Burch*, mentioned earlier, where an employee gave a guarantee to secure the debts of her employer, the English Court of Appeal held that the bank was precluded from enforcing the guarantee, and that it was not sufficient for the bank to recommend independent advice:

> The bank had actual notice of the facts from which the existence of a relationship of trust and confidence between Mr Pelosi and Miss Burch could be inferred. It knew that they were respectively employer and junior employee working in a small business and should have 'appreciated that the possibility of influence exist[ed]'.[32]

In a later case the House of Lords laid down detailed rules for the guidance of lenders in such circumstances. Dealing with the case of husband and wife, Lord Nicholls said:

> For the future a bank satisfies these requirements if it insists that the wife attend a private meeting with a representative of the bank at which she is told the extent of her liability as surety, warned of the risks she is running and urged to take independent advice. In exceptional cases the bank, to be safe, has to insist that the wife is separately advised.[33]

The House of Lords was conscious of conflicting policies, desiring, on the one hand, to protect the vulnerable guarantor and, on the other hand, not to make it practically impossible for spouses to raise money on jointly owned property. Despite the genuine endeavours of the court to satisfy these conflicting objectives, it is difficult to avoid doubts as to the feasibility of the court's enterprise, because a guarantor who is truly under the influence of a stronger spouse will not be effectively

[32] See n. 22 above, at 155.

[33] *Royal Bank of Scotland Plc* v. *Etridge (No. 2)* [2002] 2 AC 773.

protected by the measures proposed. A short private meeting in an office at a bank cannot realistically be expected to displace the continuing influence of a stronger spouse in whose company the weaker spouse will be immediately before and after the meeting. Then there is the consideration that the transaction can easily be restructured in the form of a direct advance of cash to the weaker spouse; if he or she is truly under the influence of the other spouse documents can readily be prepared and executed whereby money is paid into the account of the weaker spouse and paid over, after a shorter or longer interval of time, to the other; the precautions imposed by the House of Lords would not apply in those circumstances. Moreover, there is the awkward consideration that, in the case of a guarantee secured by a mortgage on the matrimonial home, it will, if the spouses are still living together, be the stronger spouse – the very party who allegedly has been responsible for the impugned transaction – who will benefit from having it set aside, thus creating an incentive for self-serving evidence and self-serving admissions. From the public policy point of view difficult questions arise: is it an essential aspect of freedom that persons should have unrestricted power to borrow money on the security of their assets, or are some restraints acceptable or desirable, and if so what restraints, and on whom, and in respect of what assets? These are questions on which opinions differ widely; they are not questions that the court is well-placed to determine.

Conceptualising unconscionability

Very often it has been asserted that the underlying reason for refusal to enforce unfair contracts is absence of consent on the part of the promisor, and this is implied by such concepts as cognitive incapacity, undue influence and coercion. Consensual capacity is, no doubt, a relevant, necessary and useful perspective on the problem, but it does not supply a complete explanation, and in certain respects it is misleading.

The principal attraction of the 'consent' approach is that it apparently enables relief for unfairness to be reconciled with a theory that requires enforcement of all voluntary agreements. Thus sanctity of contracts can be maintained in theory, those contracts that are not enforced being not, truly speaking, contracts at all. The objections to this, as a complete explanation, are that it is fictitious, artificial, and circular, and that it distorts the concept of consent in cases where that concept is really needed, such as mistake.

In many cases where relief is given, consent, in every ordinary sense of the word, is present. The vendor of land who sells for a tenth of its value, or the accident victim who settles a claim for a small sum in cash, usually knows what the terms of the agreement are, and intends to agree to those terms. Relief has been regularly given against forfeitures and penalties, even to sophisticated and knowledgeable parties. It is not plausible to say here that the party seeking to set aside the contract has not assented to its terms. The ordinary tests of assent, subjective and objective, are fully met in most such cases. If it were argued that, where the contract is unfair, there is no 'true' assent,[34] the answer would be that a test would then be needed of what amounts to 'true' assent, and this necessarily reintroduces some test of fairness.

A second general approach to unconscionability has been to focus on the wrongful conduct of the party seeking enforcement. This is suggested by concepts such as equitable fraud and duress. There is confusion in the usage of the word 'unconscionable'. The older usage was to refer to the *transaction* as unconscionable; the attitude of the party seeking enforcement might be described as 'unconscientious' or 'unconscionable' or 'fraudulent', but these usages referred to the impropriety of seeking enforcement (now that the transaction has been adjudged unfair) not to any wrongful conduct at the time of the transaction itself.[35] On the other hand a number of modern courts have suggested that it is the *conduct* of the party seeking enforcement that must be shown to be unconscionable, thereby implying the need to establish some kind of wrongdoing.[36]

Many older cases cannot be explained as depending on the defendant's wrongful conduct. In 1873, in granting relief to a plaintiff from an improvident bargain, Lord Selborne said that the defendant:

> is not alleged or proved to have been guilty of deceit or circumvention, and the plaintiff has no merits of his own to plead. He comes into court to be relieved from the consequences of a course of very wilful and culpable folly and extravagance. I think him entitled to the relief which he asks; but I think it is not unjust that he should obtain it at his own expense.[37]

[34] J. Murray, 'Unconscionability, Unconscionability' (1969) 31 *University of Pittsburgh Law Review* 1.

[35] See L. A. Sheridan, *Fraud in Equity: A Study in English and Irish Law* (London: Pitman & Sons, 1957).

[36] E.g., *Hart* v. *O'Connor* [1985] AC 1000 (PC), *National Westminster Bank v. Morgan*, n. 30 above.

[37] *Earl of Aylesford* v. *Morris*, n. 18 above, 499.

Costs were refused, and in some analogous cases a successful plaintiff has actually been ordered to pay the defendant's costs.[38] These cases show plainly that proof of wrongdoing on the part of the stronger party was not required. Even though the party seeking enforcement has acted perfectly properly and entirely in good faith, there are cases where the transaction has been set aside. If, as in the 1873 case mentioned, the plaintiff has 'no merits of his own' and has caused the difficulties entirely by his own 'wilful and culpable folly and extravagance' he may still be entitled to relief. He should pay the expenses attributable to his folly, but this does not mean that he should suffer the consequences of full enforcement of what might be a disastrous contract; justice is sufficiently done if he pays the costs (to both parties) of the legal proceedings that his folly has made necessary.

There are many other cases in which relief has been given despite the absence of wrongful conduct on the part of the party seeking enforcement. Maritime salvage cases supply two kinds of examples. Salvage agreements were not infrequently set aside both on the ground that too small a sum had been agreed (undue advantage being taken of the salvors) and on the opposite ground that too large a sum had been agreed (undue advantage thereby being taken of the ship in distress). Wrongdoing, in any ordinary sense, was not required in either kind of case. In one of the cases setting aside a receipt 'in full payment' of salvage services on the ground that the payment was too small, the judge (Dr Lushington) said, 'I do not mean to say that this receipt was not honestly obtained, but the inclination of the court is to look at the circumstances of the case, and not to allow a paper to operate as a bar.'[39] In the opposite case, where a salvor took advantage of a ship's difficulties in order to obtain what the court considered to be an extravagant payment, the agreement was again set aside.[40] The agreement was described by the court as 'inequitable', 'unjust', 'unreasonable' and 'extortionate',[41] but it does not appear that the salvor had committed or threatened any legal

[38] L. Field and others, *Daniell's Chancery Practice,* 6th edn (London: Stevens, 1884) at 1180, 'Where securities are ordered to be delivered up because the bargain has been unconscientious judgment is generally given for the plaintiff upon the terms that he shall repay the defendant the amount actually advanced or paid by him, with interest; and the defendant being looked upon as a mortgagee for that amount, he was treated as such, and the plaintiff ordered to pay him his costs'.

[39] *The Silver Bullion* (1854) 2 Sp 70, 75. Also *Akerblom* v. *Price Potter Walker & Co.* (1881) 7 QBD 129 (CA).

[40] *The Port Caledonia and The Anna* [1903] P 184.

[41] Ibid., 189–90 (Bucknill J).

wrong. Again, undue influence may be established without proof of wrongdoing.[42]

The concept of unjust enrichment, though not before the twentieth century under that name, has been very influential. In a treatise published anonymously in 1737 the author, generally taken to be Henry Ballow, asserted the power of the court of equity to set aside very burdensome contracts, giving as the reason that 'no man should be a Gainer by another's Loss'.[43] This phrase, like phrases in many of the cases, old and modern, such as 'advantage taken of weakness',[44] and 'deriving immoderate gain',[45] strongly suggests that the principal underlying value to be weighed against the value of enforcing the contract is the avoidance of unjust enrichment. Unjust enrichment has been, since the middle of the twentieth century, recognised as a source of obligations independent of contract, but there is, in this context, a close interrelation between the two concepts: if the contract is enforceable the enrichment is not unjust, but if the enrichment is unjust the contract is unenforceable. It is not satisfactory to say that, before unjust enrichment can be considered, the contract must *first* be set aside, because the concept of unjust enrichment has itself been highly relevant in determining the enforceability of the contract. Nevertheless, unjust enrichment, standing alone, does not explain every case. A person who agrees to sell or to purchase property or services, even at fair market value, may be entitled to set aside the contract if it was induced by undue influence,[46] or by wrongful threats.[47] Thus the concepts of consent and of wrongdoing cannot be entirely dispensed with.

There is much debate, and little consensus, about the theoretical basis of contract law.[48] To every theory that seeks to explain why contracts are enforced, unconscionability appears as an exception, anomaly, or limitation: the criteria of enforceability are apparently satisfied, yet the contract

[42] *Allcard* v. *Skinner* (1887) 36 Ch D 135, *Williams* v. *Bayley* (1866) LR 1 HL 200. See P. Birks, 'The Burden on the Bank', in F. Rose (ed.), *Restitution and Banking Law* (Oxford: Mansfield Press, 1988) 199–200.

[43] [Henry Ballow], *A Treatise of Equity* (London, 1737) 11.

[44] *Earl of Chesterfield* v. *Janssen*, n. 26 above, 157.

[45] See B. Crawford, 'Comment' (1966) 44 *Canadian Bar Review* 142.

[46] See *Griesshammer* v. *Ungerer* (1958) 14 DLR (2d) 599 (agreement to purchase dancing lessons).

[47] See M. Trebilcock, *The Limits of Freedom of Contract* (Cambridge MA: Harvard University Press, 1993) 81.

[48] The principal theories are discussed by S. Smith, *Contract Theory* (Oxford University Press, 2004).

is not enforced. This is true whether the fundamental purpose of contract law is taken to be giving effect to the will of the promisor, or protecting the reliance or expectation of the promisee, whether dealing with promises or bargains, whether resting on principles of morality or of social utility, and whether primarily concerned with justice between individuals or with social welfare.

Theories seeking to explain the positive reasons for enforcement of contracts do not, naturally enough, usually emphasise the excuses for non-performance, but some attempts have been made to discern in the doctrine of unconscionability the positive implementation of valuable social policy. It has been suggested that the willingness of courts to set aside contracts reflects the egalitarian values of the welfare state.[49] There is undoubtedly some substance in this suggestion: a society that acknowledges a duty to give positive assistance to its poorest members can hardly fail to sympathise with a poor and weak person who seeks relief from a very disadvantageous contract.

Nevertheless, there are several reasons why contract law cannot be satisfactorily viewed as a primary tool for the redistribution of wealth. With some exceptions (mainly in monopoly situations) the law does not compel the making of contracts. Even where power is given to reopen or to rewrite a contract, there is usually no power to compel parties who have not dealt with each other at all to enter into a contract. Because of this, the ability of contract law to redistribute wealth in society will always be very strictly limited. Its scope of operation is restricted, on the whole, to granting relief to those who happen to have entered into disadvantageous contracts.

The extent of relief for mistake or unconscionability is usually the restoration of the status quo before the contract was made. If there was an inequality of wealth between the parties before the contract was made, the most that the court will do, if it grants relief, is to restore that situation. It may prevent the weaker party from throwing away the little wealth that she has, but it will not make her wealthier.

Contract law gives attention to individual transactions, not, generally, to the overall wealth of the parties. Thus, wealthy parties benefit at the

[49] See R. Brownsword, G. Howells, and T. Wilhelmsson (eds.), *Welfarism in Contract Law* (Aldershot: Dartmouth, 1994), Eric Posner, 'Contract Law in the Welfare State: A Defense of the Unconscionability Doctrine, Usury Laws, and Related Limitations on the Freedom to Contract' (1994) 24 *Journal of Legal Studies* 283, S. Waddams, 'Unconscionable Contracts: Competing Perspectives' (1999) 62 *Saskatchewan Law Review* 1.

expense of the poor by doctrines of mistake, as where a bank erroneously credits a customer's account, or where a wealthy party signs a contract that contains a clerical error. Even in the case of relief for unconscionability, a wealthy party may benefit at the expense of a poorer party, as in the case of a wealthy farmer who sells his farm to an impecunious speculator for one-tenth of its value. The court, if inclined to give relief, will not be deterred by the consideration that the farmer is wealthier than the buyer, and that he would remain wealthier even if the transaction were enforced. It should be noted too that the court, in a contract case, lacks the mechanism to assess the wealth of the parties. If redistribution of wealth were to become a central feature, the court would have to contemplate a full examination of both parties' wealth, with assessment of income and valuation of capital assets, with opportunity for the other party to dispute the evidence. Such a process would, to say the least, be inconvenient in the course of a civil action.

Relief from contractual obligation is specific to the parties. Even if the court had the means to judge the wealth of the parties, it could not compare the plaintiff with other potential recipients of welfare, who might be more deserving, nor could it compare the defendant with other potential contributors, who might have a greater ability to pay. Apart from the fact that the court lacks the machinery to operate a means test and a system of taxation, there are grave political and institutional objections to ad hoc taxation and distribution of the proceeds by individual judges.

The beneficiaries of the relief that contract law can give are rarely the very poor. They are people with something to lose, and with the means and energy to seek to regain it. As we have seen, the courts gave relief to expectant heirs who squandered their inheritance, and to landowners who sold their land at an undervalue. These were deserving cases, but they were by no means representative of the poorest members of their society. The greater the wealth lost, the more useful is the law to the party seeking relief. Thus, the benefit of a judicial power to set aside contracts increases with the wealth of the weaker party. Litigation is often inaccessible to the poor.

The law of insolvency must also be considered. If a debtor has many creditors, but only one is before the court, as is usual in a contract case, it cannot be right for the court to give relief against one creditor only. The effect will probably be to benefit, not the debtor, but the other creditors. There may well be a case for consumer bankruptcy, or a stay of proceedings against a needy debtor, but such a stay should bind all the creditors, and the court, in contract litigation, lacks the mechanism to achieve that result.

The considerations mentioned in the preceding paragraphs tend to suggest reasons why policy, standing alone, has not been adopted by courts as the primary criterion for setting aside unfair contracts. But it does not follow that policy has been irrelevant. The word 'policy' has often been used in the sense of general residual considerations of justice between the parties, and in this sense it weighs in favour of giving relief from very harsh transactions. 'Policy' has also been used in the sense of giving due attention to the effect that a proposed rule or principle is likely to have on future cases. In this latter sense policy considerations have most frequently been adduced not as a primary reason for granting relief, but as a reason for restraint lest, in the words of an eighteenth-century judge, the court should 'throw every thing into confusion and set afloat all the contracts of mankind'.[50]

As part of recent attempts to harmonise European law, several documents have been published with a view to laying the groundwork for what may eventually become a contract code that incorporates both common law and civil law traditions. The *Draft Common Frame of Reference* (2008) includes the following:

> II – 7:207 Unfair exploitation
>
> (1) A party may avoid a contract if, at the time of the conclusion of the contract:
>   (a) the party was dependent on or had a relationship of trust with the other party, was in economic distress or had urgent needs, was improvident, ignorant, inexperienced or lacking in bargaining skill; and
>   (b) the other party knew or could reasonably have been expected to have known this and, given the circumstances and purpose of the contract, exploited the first party's situation by taking an excessive benefit or grossly unfair advantage.
>
> (2) Upon the request of the party entitled to avoidance, a court may if it is appropriate adapt the contract in order to bring it into accordance with what might have been agreed had the requirements of good faith and fair dealing been observed. . . .
>
> II – 7:208 Third persons
>
> (1) Where a person for whose acts a party is responsible or who with a party's assent is involved in the making of a contract:

[50] *Griffith* v. *Spratley* (1787) 1 Cox Ch 383, 388 (Eyre LCB).

(a) causes a mistake, or knows of or could reasonably be expected to know of a mistake; or
(b) is guilty of fraud, coercion, threats or unfair exploitation, remedies under this Section are available as if the behaviour or knowledge had been that of the party.

(2) Where a third person for whose acts a party is not responsible and who does not have the party's assent to be involved in the making of a contract is guilty of fraud, coercion, threats or unfair exploitation, remedies under this Section are available if the party knew or could reasonably be expected to have known of the relevant facts, or at the time of avoidance has not acted in reliance on the contract.[51]

Here are several concepts very familiar to English lawyers. The factors mentioned in 7:207 (a) (dependence, trust, economic distress, urgent needs, improvidence, ignorance, inexperience, lack of bargaining skill) largely echo expressions used in English courts and tend to suggest lack of consent. The concept in paragraph (b) of 'knew or could reasonably be expected to have known' echoes the equitable concept of constructive notice. The requirement of the means of knowledge on the part of the stronger party tends to suggest an element of wrongdoing, but the open-ended indication of what it is that might reasonably have been known ('this' referring to the list in 7:207 (1) (a), and 'the relevant facts' in 2:708 (2)) leaves much flexibility. The phrases 'excessive benefit' and 'grossly unfair advantage' echo phrases like 'immoderate gain' and 'undue advantage', and suggest unjust enrichment. But lack of consent, wrongdoing, and unjust enrichment are not expressly required to be proved. The provision in 7:208 on third persons echoes the concerns of the English courts discussed above in attempting to deal with the responsibility of lenders to guarantors influenced by family members and others. The inclusion of these various elements in a carefully considered international document suggests that it may not be possible to reduce the issue to a single governing concept: several concepts, not wholly commensurable, appear to be simultaneously in play.

One interesting phrase in 7:208 (1)(b) is 'given the circumstances and purpose of the contract'. This invites the court to look at the real substance of the transaction and ask whether the enrichment can be justified

[51] C. von Bar, Eric Clive, H. Schulte-Nolke, and others (eds.), *Principles, Definitions and Model Rules of European Private Law. Draft Common Frame of Reference. Interim Outline Edition*, prepared by the Study Group on a European Civil Code and the Research Group on EC Private Law (Acquis Group) (Munich: Sellier, 2008). These provisions were adapted from O. Lando and H. Beale (eds.), *Principles of European Contract Law* (The Hague, 1999).

by the allocation of risks properly inherent in the particular kind of transaction. The sale of a reversionary interest in land is, on the face of it, a sale of an interest in land. If that were the real substance of the transaction, that is, if the seller were dealing in a fair market for the purchase and sale of future property interests, a very large enrichment to *either* party would be wholly defensible if it arose from risks inherent in the purchase and sale of property, for example an unexpected rise in land values after the date of the contract. The allocation of that risk is the very nature of the contract, and the buyer takes a corresponding risk of a fall in values: general contractual principles give strong support for enforcement *even if there is a substantial enrichment to the buyer*. The buyer, in that case, would simply have made a profitable, legitimate bargain. But, if the real substance of the transaction is a loan, the court will compare the net effect of the transaction with the terms on which money could be borrowed in a fair market for the lending of money, and will not allow the lender to extract what is, in effect, an extravagant rate of interest. The point was made in an eighteenth-century case:

> An annuity may be purchased at as low a rate as you can, provided it was the original negotiation to purchase and sell an annuity: but if the treaty began about borrowing and lending, and ends in the purchase of an annuity, it is evident, that it was only a method or contrivance to split the payment of the principal and usurious interest into several instalments, and consequently that it was a shift . . .. So, in the case of goods or merchandise it is lawful to sell as dear as you can, on a clear bargain by the way of sale: but if it is first proposed to borrow, and afterwards to sell goods beyond the market price, this is usurious.[52]

Another interesting phrase is in the closing words of 7:208, allowing avoidance of a contract induced by a third party 'if the [other contracting] party . . . at the time of avoidance has not acted in reliance on the contract'. This phrase recognises a distinction between what Anglo-American lawyers might call the 'expectation interest' and the 'reliance interest'. Where the weaker party has, by his or her own foolishness, caused *actual out of pocket loss*, there is a strong argument for requiring the weaker party, *as a condition of relief*, to reimburse the other party's actual loss. But this concept does not support full enforcement of the stronger party's expectation interest. The distinction corresponds to that made in some of the English equity cases, discussed above, where the weaker party was successful in setting aside the impugned transaction,

[52] *Earl of Chesterfield* v. *Janssen*, n. 26 above (Lord Hardwicke).

but was required to pay the other party's costs, and suggests that a choice of 'all or nothing' is not always necessary or desirable.

The fact that these provisions have been included in a draft to which European civil and common lawyers have both contributed strongly suggests that it is no less important now than it was 250 years ago to avoid transactions that would 'ruin the distressed and unwary, and give unconscionable advantage to greedy and designing persons'.[53] The intertwining, then and now, of elements of consent, wrongdoing, unjust enrichment, and policy suggests that the problem has had multiple dimensions, and that it has not been confined to a single conceptual category.

[53] See n. 11, above.

3

Freedom of contract, unequal bargaining power and consumer law on unconscionability

IMMACULADA BARRAL-VIÑALS

Introduction

This chapter examines the compatibility of the common law concept of *unconscionability* with various categories in civil law, with particular reference to Spanish legislation, which has no general principle that corresponds directly to that of unconscionability, at least to the extent that this term exists in common law systems.[1] Yet, Spanish law, in Article 1255 of the nineteenth-century Spanish Civil Code (hereafter CC), also provides a number of disparate tools that limit the basic principles of freedom of contract and free will, thereby offering similar remedies to those available in common law. The chapter focuses on the interpretation of the general good faith clauses contained in Articles 1258 CC and 116–7 of the Catalan Civil Code (hereafter CCCat) as a general remedy in a nineteenth-century liberal Civil Code, as well as additional prohibitions such as *pactum commissorium*. It then analyses an unusual text in the Spanish system that seeks to counter the imbalance between parties: the 1908 Act for the Repression of Usury. Finally, I conclude by turning my attention to the present-day situation which defends the rights of the weaker parties in consumer law and, in particular, to unfair contract terms (UCT).

Freedom of contract and the interpretation of the good faith clause in the Spanish Civil Code of 1889

The nineteenth-century Spanish Civil Code was founded on the basis of liberal doctrine and, as such, freedom of contract was placed at the heart of its contractual regulations. This was in clear contrast to the limits

1 See S. M. Waddams, *The Law of Contracts*, 5th edn (Toronto: Canada Law Books, 2005) 313 ff.

previously placed on commercial transactions and the control wielded by the guilds and professional corporations.[2] Articles 1254 to 1260 CC lay down the general theory of contracts in a context in which the parties are deemed equals in their respective bargaining power[3] and at liberty to discuss any terms of the contract.[4] The CC thus established the main principles of traditional transactions – equality between the two contracting parties and the free will or autonomy of the parties as general principles of freedom of contract under Spanish law.

The principle of freedom of contract, laid down in Article 1255 CC, refers not only to the free will of the parties to determine the content and terms of the contract, but also to the freedom to decide whether a party wishes to enter into a contract or not. But, in keeping with the liberal tradition, the Civil Code includes good faith in contractual transactions as a nuance of the principle of freedom of contract.[5] And, as such, the basic principle of *pacta sunt servanda* – i.e. the parties must comply with the agreement – is not unlimited. An indirect limit is placed on the freedom of contract in the interpretation of the general good faith clause.[6] This general clause has been seen as a way of introducing a social and extra-legal ethic in the positivism of the Civil Codes through the court's application of the law.[7] It is through the application of this tool that a term deemed unconscionable can be declared void, despite having been agreed to under the terms of the contract.

Formally, Article 1258 CC might be understood as a clause for interpreting a contract when its terms fail to demonstrate the precise wishes of the contracting parties. But, as De Castro[8] says, the principle of good faith is not the kind of tool of interpretation that sanctions precise knowledge of the exact meaning of the terms; other rules are provided for that purpose in Articles 1281ff CC. Good faith is concerned with

[2] The foundation of the Civil Code meant the introduction of a secure, transparent law system for the new bourgeoisie, see F. Wieacker, *Historia del derecho privado europeo*, trans. F. Fernández (Madrid: Aguilar, 1957) 240.

[3] Arts. 1254 and 1256 CC. [4] Art. 1255 CC. [5] Art. 1258 CC.

[6] Art. 1258 CC. In addition, in the construction of fair trade in the regulation of contracts, a party has to rely on Art. 1255 mentioning 'public order' as a limit to the freedom of contract, considering this term to include the main features of fair trade: human dignity, respect for private property, freedom of enterprise, etc. See L. Diez-Picazo, *Fundamentos de Derecho Civil Patrimonial: I. Introducción y teoría del contrato* (Madrid: Civitas, 1993) 129 ff.

[7] For a discussion of the contradictions of this general clause in the civil law's codified systems, see F. Wieacker, *El principio general de la buena fe*, trans. J. L. Carro (Civitas: Madrid, 1982) 32 ff.

[8] F. De Castro, *El negocio jurídico* (Civitas: Madrid, 1985) 89 ff.

assuming the objective responsibility for each party's conduct in the contractual relationship and has three representations: loyalty between the parties when interpreting the contract; respect for the confidence of the other party as regards the terms of the contract; and responsibility for the meaning of the contract to be construed against the party that imposed its inclusion (*contra proferentem*).[9]

The main consequences of this proposition are easily identified as: (1) that good faith is not the subjective representation of justice in a contract; and (2) that the party that draws up a clause is liable for the exact meaning of that clause in accordance with the principle of good faith. This point lies at the heart of the regulation of standard terms and is discussed further below. Moreover, the good faith interpretation clause is a standard of normal contractual conduct that the parties have recourse to, relying on the confidence and security of transactions: that is to say, in fair trade. This is the expression used by the Catalan Civil Code in Articles 111–7 appealing to good faith in all private transactions and fair trade. In this sense, the good faith clause can be applied to the entire legal system.

This 'general interpretation clause of good faith' approach is to be found primarily in continental civil systems,[10] whereas in common law systems, at least in the English system, greater attention is given to suppressing bad faith than to promoting good faith in contractual transactions.[11] This would seem to explain why the Green Paper on the review of the consumer *acquis* calls for a general European principle of good faith, at least in consumer law.[12] In fact, opinions on this matter are also divided because of the existing good faith clauses in the main legal systems that are applicable also to consumer transactions.[13] The resulting Proposal for a Directive of the European Parliament and of the Council on consumer rights[14] in Articles 2–14 defines 'professional diligence' as a quality commensurate with honest market practice and/or the

[9] See J. L. Lacruz, *Elementos de Derecho Civil* (Barcelona: Libreria Bosch, 1994), vol. II–2, 533; For more on this idea of granting the courts the possibility of innovating in their interpretation of the law, even in contradiction of the law, see Wieacker, n. 2 above, 51.

[10] Similar articles are to be found in 1258 CC in 242 BGB, Art. 1175 Codice Civile. The French Civil Code refers to 'equity', which can likewise be defined as 'natural justice' (Art. 1135).

[11] See E. McKendrick, *Contract Law* (London: Macmillan, 2003) chaps. 12 and 17.

[12] The Green Paper on the Review of the *Consumer Acquis* can be consulted at: ec.europa.eu/consumers/rights/cons_acquis_en.htm#outcome (last accessed January 2009).

[13] See Commission Staff Working Paper: *Report on the outcome of the public consultation on the green paper on the review of the consumer acquis*, 2008, 6.

[14] Proposal for a Directive of the European Parliament and of the Council on Consumer Rights, COM(2008) 614 final text presented, 8 October 2008.

general principle of good faith in the trader's field of activity. This solution, should it be enforced, would strengthen both the principle of good faith and also controls on unfair contract terms. This concept is discussed further below.

Thus, unconscionability as a remedy to enforce certain contracts in common law is paralleled in the Spanish legal system in the shape of the good faith clause,[15] which allows the terms of a contract to be interpreted in accordance with normal and fair trade.

Imbalance between parties and limits to the freedom of contract

The good faith clause can be usefully invoked in cases of doubt concerning contractual terms, but it will only result in a contract being deemed unenforceable when good faith is unable to provide a correct remedy. As such, it is more limited in its extent than unconscionability and it is for this reason that we find special cases of agreement that are forbidden on the grounds of unfairness even when seen in the liberalist point of view contained within the Spanish Civil Code of 1889. In these cases, and in line with the Roman tradition, even though the parties operating under these conditions of freedom of contract might be in agreement over certain forbidden clauses, they would be without effect. Two types of forbidden pact serve to highlight this concept of unfair practice: firstly, the prohibition of *pactum commissorium*[16] – i.e. the pact in a credit contract that allows the creditor to retain the property of the pledged item or mortgaged land in case of no payment; and secondly, the non-admission of clauses excluding liability in case of fraudulent misrepresentation (*dolus*).[17] However, these are isolated examples, and should be viewed from the outset as normal limits to the freedom of contract.

The case of *pactum commissorium* is similar to the forfeiture of mortgaged land on the debtor's default, which the common law courts have not enforced for being unconscionable.[18] However, for Spanish law, the problem is not the mortgage or the pledge itself, but rather the possibility that the mortgagee – the creditor – has of retaining the property of the mortgaged land or pledged item. This possibility is clearly forbidden according to Articles 1859 and 1884 CC. The *pactum commissorium* is concerned with the credit system, and even the Civil Code was

[15] Art. 1258 CC, 111–7 CCCat. [16] Arts. 1859 and 1884 CC.
[17] Art. 1102 CC. [18] See Waddams, n. 1 above, 315ff.

aware of the weak position of the mortgagor in the bargaining process. In the case of *dolus*, clauses excluding liability are likewise considered unfair, and they are unenforceable when forming part of a contract.[19] Here, *dolus* clearly runs contrary to good faith as it comprises the giving of wrong information by the one party that leads to a misrepresentation of the clauses or the conditions agreed to, since the other party is unable to know the true extent of the pact.[20] Thus, in such pacts the exclusion of liability results in the unequal position of the parties.

These two cases constitute general examples of cases involving unconscionability in common law.[21] Moreover, they lead us to the concept of imbalance between parties, the main representation in the current Spanish regulations of remedies similar to the doctrine of unconscionability. Perhaps more examples could be found, but the reason for prescription would be the same: to provide the judges with generic remedies in case a contractual clause or pact could, for some reason, be considered contrary to good faith or be deemed unfair. As such they constitute tools for breaking the principle of *pacta sunt servanda*.

1908 Act for the Repression of Usury: The first attempt at regulating in favour of the weaker party

As has been shown in the above analysis of the interpretation of good faith and certain non-unified and special prohibitions, the first real understanding of unconscionability in Spanish law was the presence of certain limits on the freedom of contract – in instances of great imbalance in the bargaining power of the parties. However, this interpretation of good faith is based on the fairness of a legally binding agreement, that is to say, a contract that has been correctly formed. For this reason, we cannot refer to cases of invalidity based on lack of capacity to consent to a contract[22] as cases of unconscionable contracts. In contracts signed with minors or persons with certified mental incapacity the legality of a contract does not depend on its being in conflict with good faith, but rather because it has been entered into with persons who are not legally capable to contract and as such is voidable.

In this context, apart from the prohibitions discussed above, the first Spanish legal text to explore an imbalance between parties that might

[19] Art. 1102 CC. [20] Art. 1269 CC.
[21] Waddams, n. 1 above, 443ff, and 468ff. [22] Art. 1263 CC.

result in a contract being deemed unfair for one or other party was the 1908 Act for the Repression of Usury. This was the first law to protect the weaker party from unfair agreements. Article 1 of the Act stated that the lending of money cannot be considered binding where there is an 'interest notoriously higher than the normal price of money or clearly out of proportion in the circumstances of the case, or leonine [unfairly one-sided]'. This is a general clause setting out an undetermined concept which the court is required to construe; but where the text is innovative is in the second paragraph where a very special meaning dealing with the general idea of the weaker party refers to personal circumstances. In this sense, a lending contract can be deemed invalid because of the special personal circumstances of the borrower, that is 'a distressed situation, inexperience or limited mental faculties'.[23]

In these terms we see a fundamentally new approach closely linked to the absence of consent because of a lack of natural capacity (as is the case with minors and persons of certified mental incapacity). Interestingly, in order to analyse whether the weaker party has understood the exact extent of the contract, the law considers personal circumstances and the possibility of their not having had free will owing to the imbalance. In other words, with no prior judicial intervention to declare insanity and the impossibility of acting without a 'guardian' to represent them in a contract, the court can rule the contract invalid because the weaker party was not aware of the duties that it imposed upon him.

When the Act for the Repression of Usury was brought into force, some scholars claimed that it was overly flexible: that taking into account the personal characteristics of the contractor was too complex a matter for the Spanish legal system, as for all the other continental systems.[24] Further, the Spanish system had no appeal to personal circumstances as a general clause. Thus, the Usury Act was not used as a general clause of unconscionability in either the Spanish system or in the regulation of lending contracts. Wider interpretations of this possibility in relation to good faith were not made, as they were in the German system for

[23] The original text reads:

> Será nulo todo contrato de préstamo en que se estipule un interés notablemente superior al normal del dinero y manifiestamente desproporcionado con las circunstancias del caso o en condiciones tales que resulte aqué l leonino, habiendo motivos para estimar que ha sido aceptado por el prestatario a causa de su situación angustiosa, de su inexperiencia o de lo limitado de sus facultades mentales.

[24] Lacruz, n. 9 above, II–1, 158.

example,[25] and the courts tended to make a more objective construction based on interest payments being out of proportion or clearly excessive than on the subjective approach.

However, the Act for the Repression of Usury can be considered Spain's first consumer law, since it demonstrated an awareness of the imbalance between contracting parties and made it possible for a weaker party to avoid a signed contract.[26] However, it presented the problem of the weaker party in a rather different light to the way in which it was to be defined in the 1980s in Spain's General Consumer Protection Act 1984,[27] as demonstrated below. Today, the problems that have arisen with moratorium interest rates in consumer credits are covered by unfair contract terms.[28] However, the Repression of Usury Act is still in force, after it was ruled not to be unconstitutional,[29] but it is no longer a basic part of the Spanish legal system; control of the imbalance between parties in credit transactions, even those that involve excessive rates of interest, is assumed by consumer law and the regulation of unfair contract terms.

[25] See S. Whittaker and R. Zimmerman, 'Good Faith in European Contract Law: Surveying the Legal Landscape', in S. Whittaker and R. Zimmerman (eds.), *Good Faith in European Contract Law* (Cambridge University Press, 2000) 28–9.

[26] J. Herre, E. Hondius and G. Alpa, *The Notions of Consumer and Professional and Some Related Questions (From the Task Force on Consumers and Professionals)*, in Study Group on a European Civil Code, eds., *Draft Articles*, accessible at: www.sgecc.net/pages/en/texts/index.draft_articles.htm:

> One important addition or alternative is to regulate situations where one party takes advantage of the weaker party's lack of bargaining skill or inexperience. An example of such rules is Art. 4:109 in PECL. This article provides that the weaker party is given the right to avoid the contract or to have the contract adapted where the other party has taken such advantage. Such rules provide important protection in cases where the mandatory rules are not applicable, e.g. because the weaker party is not a natural person.

[27] See *Ley 26/1984, de 19 de julio para la defensa de los consumidores y usuarios* subsequently restructured by Royal Legislative Decree 1/2007, of 16 November, which served a codifying purpose for Spain's main consumer laws, most of which are a development of EU law. However, it is stressed that Spain's first consumer law was enacted before the country joined the EEC on 1 January 1986.

[28] See Judgment of Audiencia Provincial de Lleida, 2a, 25.10.03: Usury Act not mentioned; Judgment of Audiencia Provincial de Cáceres, 2a, 21.01.04: stated that the Usury Act is applicable to other modern lending institutions not regulated in 1908, but applies the standard contract terms Act. See E. Llamas, 'Comentario al art. 10 bis LGDCU', in E. Llamas (ed.), *Ley general para la defensa de los consumidores y los usuarios*, (Madrid: La ley, 2005) 332.

[29] Judgment of the Tribunal Supremo 17–04–1989; 8–09–1991 and 29–09–1992.

Unequal bargaining power, standard terms and consumer law

The imbalance between contracting parties, which has seen the introduction of certain limits on freedom of contract, is particularly relevant in situations of mass contracting, and is changing the rationale whereby the freedom of contract and equality between parties are understood. In this sense, the liberal doctrine of equality between parties assumed that transactions would be conducted with a level of equality that does not exist today, especially in consumer transactions. In order to clarify the approach proposed to unconscionable and consumer contracts, the following section refers to the concept of the consumer as the weaker party, and then analyses how this idea is employed in the fairness control of standard contract terms.[30]

The consumer as non-expert in mass contracting: the institutional role of the weaker party

The weaker party in a consumer transaction is typically considered to be the consumer.[31] Thus, consumer protection is derived from the unequal bargaining power that undermines the ancient dogma of equality. In this sense, as Ramsay has noted, consumer law is facing the materialisation and differentiation of contract law in the twentieth century 'due to the breakdown of the formal system of contract law as an autonomous system of law that assumed a basis of formal equality between contracting parties'.[32] This chapter argues that the concept of the consumer needs to be understood in broader terms than those EU legal definitions based on the non-professional approach, where the consumer is any natural person who is acting for purposes that are outside his trade, business or profession.[33] If we wish to rely on the idea of protecting the weaker party from unconscionable agreements, the consumer has to be considered as a non-expert acting in what we will call mass contracting.[34]

30 Some scholars claim that the new European contract law based on this concept of a weaker party creates a socially oriented contract. See O. Cherednichenko, *Fundamental Rights, Contract Law and the Protection of the Weaker Party* (München: Sellier, 2007) 10 ff. For a discussion of unconscionability as a general principle, see Waddams, n. 1 above, 341.

31 E. Hondius, 'The Protection of the Weak Party in a Harmonised European Contract Law: A Synthesis' (2004) 27 *Journal of Consumer Policy* 245–51.

32 See I. Ramsay, *Consumer Law and Policy*, 2nd edn (Oxford and Portland: Hart Publishing, 2007) 166.

33 See, for example, Art. 1. b Directive 93/13.

34 See I. Barral-Viñals, 'Del consumidor-destinatari final al consumidor – no expert en la contractació en massa' (2007) 2 *Revista Catalana de Dret Privat* 59ff.

Consequently, the consumer needs protection not because he or she is a non-professional, but rather because he or she is a non-expert and therefore can be considered as always being the weaker party, i.e. the one that requires special regulations. This, however, does not sit easily with the freedom of contract as defined in Article 1255 CC. In this sense, Weatherill[35] – when discussing the scope of application of the Unfair Contract Terms Directive – has remarked on what he calls an 'irrational limitation' on consumers. In fact, the remedies for contracts concluded between parties where there is inequality can easily be applied to small business contractors, because, as, this chapter argues, the differential between small and large business contractors may be a good deal wider than that between small trader and consumer.

Moreover, in cases of mass contracting, contracts are standardised and the contractor tends to be a fungible part of the process.[36] A mass contract offered to a fungible contractor is drawn up by a class of experts that depend on their technological background of knowledge. For these two reasons, only one party leads the bargaining process and has an awareness of the necessary information to impose certain conditions[37] in what are standard contract terms. In these cases, the imbalance between the parties and the possibility of protecting the weaker one can render a correctly formed and agreed contract invalid.

In this scenario, consumer law reduces free bargaining power to a formal principle and generates tools that can control the bargaining process and the content of a transaction with a consumer. Clearly, consumer protection rules are turning contract regulation and its interpretation of good faith (e.g. Article 1258 CC) upside down. However, consumer law tends to avoid imbalance by focusing on two principal aspects: lack of information,[38]

[35] S. Weatherill, 'Regulating the Substance of Consumer Transactions', in idem, *EU Consumer Law and Policy* (Northampton, MA: Elgar, 2005) 117.

[36] See L. Díez-Picazo Ponce de Léon, *Derecho y masificación social, tecnología y derecho (Dos esbozos)* (Madrid: Civitas, 1987) 42ff and 95ff.

[37] For the rationale underpinning these ideas, see F. Kessler, 'Contracts of Adhesion: Some Thoughts about Freedom of Contract' (1943) 34 *Columbia Law Review* 629 ff.

[38] In terms of legal remedies, a variety of clauses and information is given to the consumer in the moment prior to the contract, and for that reason is related to the *dolo in contrahendo*. EU legislation uses this process to redress the imbalance in transactions between company and consumer by means of information requirements with three different tools: pre-contractual information requirements, advertisement as an integral part of the offer, and labelling prescriptions, especially in food products. It is generally understood that law tries to re-establish the balance so as to provide the consumer with the characteristics of the goods or service for which he or she is contracting.

and the control of unfair terms. Both types of prescription see the consumer as an institutionally weaker party,[39] but only the regulation of unfair contract terms goes as far as to obtain a review of the contract conditions, and creates the possibility of having standard terms that are not binding owing to their *unfairness* (which is how unconscionability is defined in consumer law).

Following EU prescriptions, the three following tools are used to redress information requirements: pre-contractual information, advertisement as an integral part of the offer, and labelling prescriptions, especially in food products. It is generally understood that the law seeks to redress the balance in order to make known the characteristics of the goods or services that a consumer contracts for. However, in these requirements, the singular claim of a consumer is normally involved with other substantive problems, such as *dolo in contrahendo* (i.e. fault for fraudulent misrepresentation in pre-contractual relations that leaded to a contract), pre-contractual liability, or a finding that the contract is voidable because of misrepresentation or fraud. This aspect resonates once again with the Civil Code and its prescriptions concerning the elements of the contract (Articles 1261, 1300 ff), rather than with the concept of unconscionability.

Consequently, it can be demonstrated that, in Spanish law, the unconscionable nature of a consumer contract is related to the *fairness* of the content of a contract. However, this does not render good faith and unfair contract terms opposites, since Article 85 of the Consumer Protection Act provides an objective meaning of good faith in order to analyse whether a term is unfair or not, and this objective meaning relates to honesty and fairness in contractual relationships.

Standard contract terms and unfairness in consumer contracts

Standard contract terms can be understood as a means of unilaterally determining contract clauses, and as such act as an important limitation on the freedom of contract. Standard terms can imply that, rather than resorting to a bargaining process in order to fix the terms of a contract (free will as provided for in Article 1255 CC), one of the parties – the supplier of the goods or services – fixes them in advance, and so the other

[39] See *Communication from the Commission to the European Parliament, the Council, the Economic and Social Committee and the Committee of the Regions, Consumer Policy Strategy 2002–2006*, COM(2002) 208.

party merely has to accept or reject the offer.[40] This regulation can be approached in one of two ways depending on whether a consumer is involved or not, and only when a consumer is involved is a content review possible.

Standard contract terms in business-to-business (B2B) contracts have controls only for the incorporation and interpretation of clauses, but the law does not permit any review to be made of content. Thus, the standard terms are enforceable provided the adherent has been given the possibility of knowing their content (Article 5) and this is assumed to have occurred when a document containing the standard terms is given to the adherent, or when their content is published at the premises of the supplier if the contract does not generate a document in writing. A further condition for enforcing the standard terms is that they must be drafted in plain, intelligible language and that they must have an interpretation *contra proferentem*, that is to say, the supplier will assume the consequences of any misleading drafting. These then are the few rules applicable to B2B contracts which only deal with the outer appearance of standard terms, i.e. they require that the party to be bound by standard terms is aware that some of the terms in the contract have been preset by the contractor, and where the former is given the opportunity to have this awareness those terms will form part of the contract. Thus, in these cases, there is no fairness control over standard contract terms: there is no way of determining if unequal bargaining power exists, or even whether the party to be bound by standard contract terms knows their exact meaning.

In the case of a consumer transaction, the General Consumer Protection Act 2007 – which amended the text of 1984[41] – contains provisions for consumer contracts regarding content review, when such clauses are deemed unfair (Article 82). An interpretation test of unfairness is contained in the Standard Contract Terms Act, but the content has to be analysed in terms of good faith and not in terms of a significant imbalance between the parties' duties or rights. In this regulatory framework, the control of unfair contractual terms can only be conducted if we are dealing with a consumer transaction. In this instance, it is for the court to rule whether they are enforceable or not, depending on the fairness of the agreement or the particular clause. Thus, a material and substantive analysis can be undertaken and the imbalance between

[40] As stated in Art. 1 Spanish Standard Contract Terms Act 1998.

[41] See n. 27 above.

the parties or the inequality in their respective bargaining powers can render the clause unenforceable. The only condition is that it must relate to a pre-formulated term: the control of standard terms in a contract is limited to the terms that have not been individually negotiated, because there is a suspicion that 'mass-produced' contracts will not be fair to the other party.[42]

Unfair clauses can be pre-formulated, that is to say, clauses that have not been individually negotiated, or practices external to the agreement, related to the execution of the contract. This last term should refer to commercial practices in the execution of the contract, a quite different concept to that of the unfair commercial practices of Directive 2005/29/EC in competition law which Spain has yet to transpose. This unfairness has two central elements: terms contrary to good faith and terms that create a great imbalance between parties. These are general clauses, somewhat more clearly defined than in Article 1258 CC or CCCat, but the system of operation becomes rather complicated because Spanish law recognises five types of clause as being unfair, and a list of clauses that are unfair because they match with the five general types. These general types are extracted from the annex list of the Directive, and can be reduced and freely translated as: a unilateral decision-making power claimed by the supplier; lack of reciprocity; lack of proportionality; failure to comply with consumer rights; and terms against the law. It is readily understood that the last two are largely redundant given that such terms already fall under separate legal controls, even when there is no unfairness. In respect of the list of clauses, it should be noted that a number of new clauses have been included in recent legislative changes. One fascinating example occurring in financial services is described below.

Unfair terms related to financial services: rounding up mortgage interest

The application of content control to financial services under the unfair contract terms (UCT) provisions has been problematic in Spanish law. Consumer associations have widely used the remedy presented in Article 7.2 of the Directive, which was construed in the Spanish system as a new collective action (similar to a class action) in the courts, to decide whether a clause was unfair and to prevent the continued use of such terms (Article 12 of the Standard Contract Terms Act). In Spain, many of

[42] In this sense see Weatherill, n. 35 above, 118.

these terms are related to financial services because of the absence of regulation at the higher levels and so EU directives have been transposed in an attempt to protect consumers of financial services at a time when no general regulation is in place for financial services, which are only partially covered by ministerial instruments known as *órdenes*. In these, for example, we find minor regulations regarding transparency and information rights.[43] For this reason, control of fairness in financial services would be particularly useful in the Spanish system.

The judgment issued by the Audiencia Provincial de Madrid on 10 October 2002 illustrates this point.[44] It is not the first decision in this sense, but it is relevant to the present discussion because it illustrates the added difficulties associated with special contracts of this nature. In this particular instance, a consumer association asked for a term to be deemed unfair as it allowed a bank to round up the interest rate on variable mortgage lending to the next quarter of a decimal. The court declared the terms unfair, prohibited the use of this clause in further credit contracts, and recognised the right to a substantive remedy: refunding the amount charged as a result of the rounding-up practice. Moreover, the court ruled that the decision be included in the National Registry of Standard Terms.

The defendant did not question the material fairness of the clause. He claimed that the control of UCT was limited to aspects unrelated to the essential elements of the agreement, such as the price, and the interest payments that were a part of it; thus, this was not a standard term imposed on the consumers but an individually negotiated clause as a part of the agreed price agreed for the loan. For this reason, any review of the content was not possible. This argument is often advanced by the supplier to avoid the fairness test and normally the courts agree, ruling that interest does not form part of the price, but rather a secondary duty for the debtor.

The second argument is more applicable to the issues under consideration in this chapter: the defendant argued that UCT control was not possible in contractual transactions. These types of transaction are regulated by specific laws in the way that financial contracts are regulated by *ordenes ministeriales*, which ignore any regulations concerning

[43] See I. Barral Viñals, "Credit Cards as Payment Instrument and as a Financial Service in Spain: About the Liability System" (2008) 14 *Journal of International and Comparative Law* 595 ff.

[44] This ruling was followed by others: judgment, Audiencia Provincial de Barcelona, 15_a, 13 July 2005; judgment, Audiencia Provincial de Madrid, 21 February 2006.

the consumer and, hence, any control over unfair terms. According to doctrine, the court insists on the fact that administrative control of the financial services of the Bank of Spain, or similar bodies, should not be confused with material decisions concerning consumer rights reserved to the courts.[45] It is worth focusing on this last argument in order to emphasise the point that the confusing regulatory framework of financial services in Spain cannot be used to obstruct the use of the material tools that consumer law has created, such as the content control of UCT.[46]

These decisions are important in terms of their wider social impact, given that many consumers had this unfair term in their mortgages. Nonetheless, the ruling has had a legal effect as well, because the 2006 Act added a new clause[47] that expressly bans these terms in consumer contracts. The Spanish system seems to be reluctant to use general clauses, even when the courts have validated them, and so it seems likely that the test for fairness in consumer contracts will become a list consisting of fair clauses which can be added to from time to time. However, the primary objective of EU regulation will be undermined by this process:[48] if the list of terms in the Annex of the Directive is a grey rather than a blacklist, then it is the decision-making power of the courts that will be crucial rather than the legislative updating of this list.

Conclusion

The Spanish regulation of standard terms does not comply with the concept of unconscionability in all cases, but only in those instances when a weaker party can be identified, i.e. when the contract is made with a consumer. In all other cases, the law only controls the interpretation and incorporation of clauses, but does not consider whether they are unfair or not. In such cases, in line with the general doctrine governing contracts, only the general principle of good faith can make a contract unenforceable.[49]

[45] See judgment, Audiencia Provincial de Madrid, 11, 21 February 2009 for a development of this argument.

[46] In this sense, financial services are governed by a special regulation in questions of abusive clauses, because exceptions exist in contracts regarding unfair contract terms owing to the type of product, e.g. tradable securities.

[47] See Art. 10bis of LGDCU; now Art. 85ff, text 2007.

[48] See Weatherill, n. 35 above, 119 ff. [49] Art. 1258 CC.

Thus, the only problem that these clauses can present, as de Castro[50] points out, is that no one can consent to standard terms that they are not aware of or do not understand. The contractual agreement should only exist in that part of the contract that can be entirely understood by the party accepting the offer. In other words, when the bargaining process is bilateral, it can be said that both contractors agreed to the conditions as fixed; but when one party fixes them in advance and the other only decides whether he or she agrees to the contract or not, then one party cannot be aware of the exact meaning or extent of the agreement, so the consent can only be partial. This contractual point of view has not been followed by the Standard Contract Terms Act, which only considers the incorporation of control of the clauses, or the General Consumer Protection Act, with its fairness control. It is clear that the point is not whether the consumer has understood the clause and agreed to accept it, but rather the material unfairness that a clause can generate.[51]

Thus there is no general principle that completely reflects the common law concept of unconscionability in the Spanish legal system. However, this chapter has identified several examples, in four main areas, that have the same result:

1. The limitation on the general principle of freedom of contract. In this sense, Article 1255 CC on free will is limited by a number of prohibitions on individual clauses, such as the *pactum commissorium* which is a good example of unconscionability.
2. The general clause of good faith contained in Article 1258 CC also constitutes a means of allowing control over the material consequences of the contract that has been duly formed. This interpretation in terms of trading honesty and the responsible conduct of the parties to an agreement establishes the basis for unfair contract terms as a means of controlling contract content. And even though the parties remain free to incorporate any clause they may wish, all terms are subject to the doctrine of good faith.

[50] F. De Castro, *Las condiciones generales de los contratos y la eficacia de las leyes* (Madrid: Civitas, 1985), 58.

[51] The fact is that Spanish regulations are beginning to incorporate an element of unconscionability without having understood it as a general principle depending on personal circumstances or unequal bargain power. It is for this reason that the courts normally apply EU consumer law in conjunction with the contractual tools contained in the Civil Code. Only the Act for the Repression of Usury adopts the complete set of rules, but it is not applied because it seems quite foreign to the Spanish legal system. Yet, the principle remains.

3. Freedom of contract also has to be reinterpreted in terms of the imbalance between parties that might render certain clauses unenforceable. In this sense, the 1908 Act for the Repression of Usury adopts what might be described as a somewhat common law approach in dealing with the concept of a party who is weaker owing to personal circumstances and which can make a contract void.
4. Finally, this imbalance between parties has been further developed by consumer law, particularly with its control of unfair contract terms, which allows the content of a contract to be revised. In this instance the argument is that the formal equality between parties does not exist and so the freedom of contract that allows the incorporation of almost any term will not hold when its content is unfair; fairness always refers to an objective construction of good faith.

Thus, while not having an articulated concept of unconscionability per se, in terms of equivalence the Spanish system has at its disposal a number of tools that enable it to develop a rather similar concept to that of unconscionability and which lead to similar consequences.

4

Loyalty as a tool to combat contractual unfairness: a French perspective

SÉVERINE SAINTIER

Introduction

French law does not have a general doctrine of unconscionability per se, i.e. as it exists in the American Uniform Commercial Code.[1] Yet, if one considers the concept as an expression of contractual unfairness, then, it is clearly present in French law, not only through various mechanisms in the civil code, but, also through the way the courts have used loyalty as a device to re-establish some balance between the parties. The aim of this chapter is therefore to consider such measures and explore loyalty, as a facet of the wider notion of good faith in order to see how it has developed as a tool to combat contractual unfairness and whether it is still effective in doing so. This will be done in three parts: in the first part, we will consider some of the measures in place in French law which arguably deal with contractual unfairness i.e. *la lésion*, *la cause* and the legislation on consumer contracts.

The second part will concentrate on one specific area, that of pre-contractual fraud, *la réticence dolosive*. The focus on this notion is motivated by the fact that it is an area where the efforts of the courts to use loyalty as a tool to combat unfairness appear to be at their most obvious and therefore the similarities with that aspect of unconscionability at their strongest. Yet, we will also show how this tendency appears to be in retreat in recent judicial developments.[2]

[1] Section 2–302(1) of UCC stipulates: 'If the court, as a matter of law, finds the contract or any clause of the contract to have been unconscionable at the time it was made the court may refuse to enforce the contract, or it may enforce the remainder of the contract without the unconscionable clause, or it may so limit the application of any unconscionable clause as to avoid any unconscionable result.'

[2] *Civ 3ème 17.1.2007 Theuillon* v. *Destemberg*, Bull Civ III, No. 5.

The third part will approach the difficult question of the efficiency of the protection that loyalty provides as a measure to combat unfairness, not only in the context of *la réticence dolosive*, but, again, in the wider context of contract law generally. This more extensive view is necessary following a recent decision of the commercial chamber of the Cour de Cassation which resurrects the old debate of the relationship between good faith/loyalty as a tool to achieve fairness and justice (Article 1134–3 CC) and the principle of sanctity of contract (Article 1134–1 CC).[3] This part will therefore consider the impact of this recent judicial position, which seems to be in line with the policy of the Cour de Cassation,[4] at a time when the European trend appears to be for more protection against unfair practices.[5]

Some existing tools by which French law combats contractual unfairness

As just mentioned, French law does not have a general doctrine of unconscionability. Instead, the civil code deals with certain 'aspects' of contractual unfairness through sporadic mechanisms.[6] For instance, through *la lésion*, the courts have the power to rescind a contract if a gross disproportion between two parties has caused the other to suffer a loss. Although, as a concept, *la lésion* can be used in a wide sense to include any substantive unfairness in a contract's provisions,[7] the way the mechanism of *la lésion*, as defined in the civil code, applies is nevertheless limited in scope and application[8] since it only allows certain

[3] *Cass Com 10.7.2007*, *Fromont* v. *Verdier*, D 2007, J, 2839.

[4] Professor Mazeaud remarks that the Supreme Court, contrary to other EU Member States, appears perenially attached to the sanctity of contract: D. Mazeaud, 'La politique contractuelle de la cour de cassation', in *Libres Propos sur les sources du droit: Mélange en l'honneur de Philippe Jestaz* (Dalloz, 2006) 371–96 at 395.

[5] The Unfair Commercial Practices Directive 2005/29/EC OJ L 149/22 and Article 4.109 PECL for instance.

[6] Spain seems to have a similar approach. For details see I. B. Viñals, *Unconscionability: Freedom of Contract, Unequal Bargaining Power and Consumer Law*, Chapter 3 in this volume.

[7] As remarked by Professor Whittaker in J. Bell, S. Boyron and S. Whittaker, *Principles of French Law*, 2nd edn (Oxford University Press, 2007) 324. An illustration of the pertinence of this remark can be seen in the commentary on the *Theuillon case* (see notes 46–47 below) by Professor Stoffel-Munck that in this instance, the court may have been influenced by the fact that the *lésion* suffered by the seller was not very high: Philippe Stoffel-Munck, D 2007, 1054–5, at 1054, para. 4.

[8] Further restricted in *Civ 1ère, 16.3.2004* and *Civ 1ère, 7.12.2004* both cited in Mazeaud 'La politique contractuelle', n. 4 above, at 376, para 10.

parties[9] to rescind certain types of contract[10] (Article 1118 CC) under strict conditions (the sale price obtained has a value less than the 7/12 of the real value of the property as per Article 1674 CC).

A second and more obvious tool to combat contractual unfairness is that of the consumer legislation on the *clauses abusives* (Article L 132–1 Consumer Code). This legislation, in place since 1978[11] and part of a liberal judicial movement which paid close attention to the inequality of the parties, especially in relation to *clauses pénales* (penalty clauses),[12] is, arguably, the closest French law has to a doctrine of unconscionability. This legislation allows the courts to annul a clause in consumer contracts, which they deem to be unconscionable, i.e. unfair, pursuant to specific guidelines.[13] Originally, the courts could not annul a clause unless it was on a list of clauses deemed unconscionable by decree. However, only one decree was ever enacted and the courts have since held that they possess such an annulment power *contra legem* even if no decree prohibits it.[14] Although the judicial control appears effective, the situation is, however, not perfect. Following the implementation of the EC directive on unfair terms in consumer contracts,[15] penalty clauses inserted in a consumer contract will come under the scrutiny of the

[9] The seller of an immovable who has obtained a far lower price for the sale than its real value (Article 1674 CC); minors (Article 1305 CC) and incapable persons (Article 491-2 CC).

[10] Sale of an immovable property (Article 1674 CC) and contracts entered into for the purpose of apportioning a joint inheritance (Article 887 CC).

[11] Loi 78–23 of 10.1.1978, which has since been amended in 1995 (loi 95–96 of 1.2.1995) to implement the EC Directive 93/13 on unfair terms in consumer contracts and again more recently by Loi 2008–776 of 4.8.2008. The essence of Article L 132–1 Consumer Code, however, remains the same. For detail, see n. 13 below.

[12] In 1975, the Parliament enacted a piece of legislation (Law 9.7.1975) giving more power to the judiciary to control penalty clauses by modifying Article 1152 CC. This was necessary to circumvent the principle of sanctity of contract (Article 1134–1 CC). At the same time, the courts also started to look at *contrats d'adhésion*. Professor Guestin summarises the mood of the time as follows: there was an 'increased demand for good faith in contractual relations': J. Guestin 'The Obligation to Disclose Information', in D. Harris and D. Tallon (eds.), *Contract Law Today* (Oxford: Clarendon Press, 1989) 153. For a critical analysis of the efficiency of the French judicial power in this area, see L. Miller, 'Penalty Clauses in England and France: A Comparative Study' (2004) *International and Comparative Law Quarterly* 79–106.

[13] Article L 132–1 Consumer Code stipulates: 'in contracts concluded between a business and a non-business or consumers, clauses which aim to create or result in the creation, to the detriment of the non-professional or the consumer, of a significant imbalance between the rights and obligations of the parties to the contract, are unfair' (translation obtained from the official website: www.legifrance.gouv.fr). A list of the clauses can also be found on the legifrance website.

[14] *Civ 1ère, 14.5.1991*, D 1991, J, 449.

[15] 93/13 EEC, L 95/29.

consumer code. This is not satisfactory as there are discrepancies between the powers the judges have over general contracts and those they have over consumer contracts.[16] As a result, 'unless the powers are exercised with an eye to compatibility between both areas, divergence between consumer law and general contract principles is conceivable'.[17]

A third tool to combat contractual unfairness is that of *la cause*. Article 1131 CC stipulates that 'an obligation without cause or with a false cause or with an unlawful cause may not have any effect'. Although not originally conceived as a tool to combat contractual unfairness, *la cause* has nevertheless been used for this purpose by the courts, in a variety of ways.[18] Of particular interest in this context is the case law that uses the notion to impose a 'minimum of reciprocity at the inception of bilateral contracts'[19] and the case law on the principle of proportionality.[20]

The former is illustrated by the *Point Club Vidéo* case.[21] In this case, Mr and Mrs Piller, the owners of a small village shop, had decided to open a video club. For that purpose, they entered in a *contrat point club vidéo* with the company DPM. The business failed and the couple tried to get the contract held void for lack of cause. The Cour de Cassation held that, in the circumstances, the contract for the hiring of the video tapes was void for lack of *cause* since its performance according to the economic purpose intended by the parties was impossible, because the obligation of the couple to pay hire charges to the company lacked any real counterpart.[22]

This decision caused some concern: by using *la cause* in such a subjective manner,[23] the Cour de Cassation had gone too far as it was endangering the principle of legal certainty.[24] Such fears appear

[16] Miller 'Penalty Clauses in England and France', n. 12 above, at 104–5. [17] Ibid., at 105.

[18] It appears to have been used by judges as an attempt to re-establish some balance between the parties to consumer credit contracts before the law of 9.7.1975 modifying Article 1152 CC expressly gave them the power to modify manifestly excessive or derisory penalty clauses (see L. Miller n. 12 above and associated text). For a more recent use, see the invalidation of a term in the *Chronopost* affair: *Cass Com 22.10.1996*, D 1997, 121.

[19] Bell, Boyron and Whittaker, *Principles of French Law*, n. 7 above, at 319.

[20] Expression borrowed from Mazeaud, 'La politique contractuelle', n. 4 above, at 384.

[21] *Civ 1ère, 3.7.1996, Sté DPM* v. *Epoux Piller*, Bull Civ I, No. 286; D 1997, J, 500.

[22] Translation from Bell, Boyron and Whittaker, *Principles of French Law*, n. 7 above. In French, 'l'exécution du contrat selon l'économie voulue par les parties était impossible, la cour d'appel en a exactement déduit que le contrat était dépourvu de cause, dès lors qu'é tait constaté le défaut de toute contrepartie réelle à l'obligation de payer le prix de location des cassettes souscrites par M. et Mme Piller . . .'

[23] F. Terré, Ph. Simler and Lequette, No. 342 at 353.

[24] For details of academic papers discussing such cases, in English, see n. 204 and associated text in Bell, Boyron and Whittaker, *Principles of French Law*, n. 7 above, 321.

alleviated by the more recent case of *Hoquet* v. *Sté MDn Multimédia*.[25] In similar circumstances to the *Point Club Vidéo* case, the plaintiff, Mr Hoquet entered into a *contrat point club vidéo* with the defendant. Again, the business was not profitable and when the plaintiff failed to pay the required sum for ten consecutive months, the company sued them for breach. Mr Hoquet counterclaimed that the contract was void for lack of *cause*. The Court of Appeal of Agen rejected his plea and he appealed, unsuccessfully, to the Cour de Cassation.

After reiterating the ratio of the 1996 decision, the Cour de Cassation added that the burden of proof of such an impossibility rested on the party wishing to rely upon it. In this instance, the plaintiff had not established that the contract lacked a *cause* and therefore his claim was rejected. Taking into consideration the circumstances surrounding the case, the court stated that it was the plaintiff himself who had determined the financial objectives of the contract and that, as a shop owner, he was in the best position to do so. The contract was therefore still valid and the plaintiff was consequently bound to perform his contractual obligations. This decision has been welcome as the judicial appreciation as to whether the contract has a *cause* is, once again, objective and by adding the requirement of proof by the party claiming protection, it will be more difficult to establish such a lack of cause.[26]

By using *la cause* as an application of the principle of proportionality, the Cour de Cassation went even further than in the first *Point Club Vidéo* case as exemplified in two decisions[27] where it cancelled an exclusive supply contract for lack of cause on the ground that there was a disproportion between the reciprocal obligations of the parties. In such cases, the court used its annulment power not because of an absence of counterpart, but a disproportion in the parties' reciprocal obligations. The court's intervention to ensure equality between the parties was therefore extensive. However, apart from the impact of the *Hocquet* case, the impact of such decisions is further weakened by a lack of clarity and coherence in the manner of the court's approach to a lack of cause and a false cause.[28]

These three mechanisms are undoubtedly important since they allow the judges to rectify a perceived imbalance in the contract and as such

[25] *Cass Com 27-3-2007*, JCP 2007, II, 10119; D 2007, Pan 2966.

[26] S. Amrani Mekki, D 2007, Pan. 2966–74, at 2970.

[27] *Cass Com 14-10-1997*, Defrenois 1998, 1042 and *Cass Com 8-2-2005*, D 2005, Pan 2841.

[28] S. Amrani Mekki, n. 26 above, at 2971.

deal with contractual unfairness. Yet, such judicial powers are expressly set within certain parameters by the civil code for the *lésion* and by legislation for the *clauses abusives*. In relation to *la cause*, the main problem appears to be a lack of consistency in the use of the notion.[29] The efficiency of such measures to combat unfairness is therefore limited in their scope and application. In such a light, let us turn to loyalty, a facet of the wider notion of good faith, as an illustration of how the French courts combat unfairness at a pre-contractual stage through the concept of *la réticence dolosive*, in order to see whether its scope of application and its efficiency is any wider.

The influence of loyalty on the development of *la réticence dolosive* to combat contractual unfairness

Although unconscionability and good faith are different concepts,[30] they nevertheless share some similarities, one of them being the difficulty in defining them with any precision.[31] Indeed, good faith, as a concept, is present in many civilian systems, yet, none define it with any precision. Similarly, when looking at the relevant parts of texts such as the American Uniform Commercial Code, PECL, the Unidroit principles of commercial contracts and even Directive 93/13 on unfair terms, they all appear to take slightly different stances.[32] In spite of that, all these

[29] See Professor Guestin's comment that it is practically impossible to know what *la cause* refers to: J. Guestin 'Faut il conserver la cause en droit européen des contrats' (2005) 1 *European Review of Contract Law* 396–416, at 396.

[30] For a non-exhaustive list of academic discussion on this, see R. Dugan, 'Standardized Forms: Unconscionability and Good Faith' 14 *New England Law Review* (1979) 711, S. Waddams 'Good Faith, Unconscionability and Reasonable Expectations' (1995) 9 *Journal of Contract Law* 52.

[31] Miller, 'Penalty Clauses in England and France' n. 12 above, 102. Other authors in this volume also mention the difficulty to define the notion with any precision, see chapters by Stephen Waddams, David Capper and Emmanuel Voyiakis. On a similar note but in a commercial law context, Professor Rickett criticises the current tendency of the Australian courts to refer to the notion too readily without proper definition of the notion: C. Rickett, 'Unconscionability and Commercial Law' (2005) 24 *University of Queensland Law Journal* 73–92. See also C. Rickett, *Unconscionability and Commercial Law*, in J. Lowry and L. Mistelis (eds.), *Commercial Law: Perspectives and Practice* (London: Butterworths, 2006) 167–84.

[32] Hence perhaps the difficulty in defining unconscionability with any precision: as Voyiakis remarks in this volume, the problem may be that we are not sure what interest we are trying to protect. He adds that only when this is solved, will we be able to define unconscionability with any precision. For details see Voyiakis, *Unconscionability and the Value of Choice* (Chapter 5 in this volume).

texts share the same aspiration to ensure some balance between the parties, especially when they are not of equal bargaining power, by preventing the other from taking unfair advantage of this inequality.

Such an aspiration is, arguably, also present in the civil law notion of good faith as corroborated by Professor MacKaay, who, in his economic analysis of good faith, contends that one of its defining elements is undue advantage.[33] This aspiration is certainly present in the way the French courts apply the concept of good faith.[34] In fact, and more to the point of this chapter, the desire for 'correcting disparities between the parties'[35] in the name of good faith/loyalty is clearly present in the pre-contractual context of *la réticence dolosive*. Let us for that reason turn to it.

Loyalty as a tool for the courts to combat unfairness in the context of *la réticence dolosive*

French contract law is based on the autonomy of the will (Article 1101 CC); for a contract to be valid, the consent of both parties must therefore be freely given. Accordingly, Article 1109 CC stipulates that 'there is no valid consent where the consent has been given only by mistake, or where it is extorted by duress or induced by fraud'. The one vitiating factor that concerns us for the purpose of this chapter is that of *le dol* (fraud), which can only be a cause of nullity of a contract if 'the artifices by one of the parties are such that it is obvious that without them the other party would not have entered into the contract' (Article 1116 CC). In other words, the *dol* causes the other party to make a mistake.[36]

[33] E. Mackaay 'L'analyse du droit dans les pays civilistes', in B. Deffains (ed.), *Analyse économique du droit dans les pays de droit civil* (Paris/Montréal: Dalloz-Sirey/Editions Thémis, 2008) 11–35. Interestingly, Professor Collins considers unconscionability in similar terms as good faith in France: H. Collins, 'Good Faith in European Contract Law' (1994) 14 *Oxford Journal of Legal Studies* 229 at 250.

[34] The similarity between good faith and unconscionability in France appears at it most obvious when looking at the manner in which France implemented Article 4 of the Directive 93/13 on what amounts to an unfair term: Article L 132–1 Consumer Code does not contain any reference to good faith but simply to the significant imbalance that an unfair term would cause to a party. The EU Commission considers that France has failed to implement this part of the Directive.

[35] Expression borrowed from B. Nicholas, *The French Law of Contract* (Oxford: Clarendon Press, 1992) 104.

[36] Mistake is another vitiating factor within the civil code (Article 1110 CC). Fraud and mistake are closely linked. The link is so strong that Professor Nicholas remarked that instead of separating the *dol* from the mistake, it would be simpler to have two categories of mistake, one caused by a *dol* and one not caused by *dol*: ibid.

Following the lack of explanation in the civil code as to what constitutes an artifice; the task of defining it fell to the judiciary. To the crucial question whether mere silence could be regarded such an artifice, the courts answered in the positive[37] and rapidly linked this to a pre-contractual obligation of disclosure. It is clear that the source for such an obligation was 'the inequality of the parties'[38] which is linked to the liberal movement of the 1970s highlighting an 'increased demand for good faith in contractual relations'.[39] The link between loyalty and the information obligation in the domain of the *réticence dolosive* is so strong that the courts have been described as using loyalty as a legal basis for such obligation.[40] This is indeed clear when we look at how the courts have applied the necessary conditions for a party to be liable for *réticence dolosive*.[41] For instance, when determining the question of legitimate reliance of the victim, the courts paid attention to the nature of the contract and the identity of the parties[42] and tended to be harsher when the victim was not a professional. However, even this condition was significantly weakened in the case of *Plessis* v. *Gas*,[43] where the court held that where there is a *réticence dolosive*, the mistake of the victim is always excusable, i.e. the victim did not have to inform himself, even though, as in this case, the victim was himself a professional.[44] In this case, the court also expressly relied on good faith to find the defendant guilty of a *réticence dolosive* by stating that 'the dol is characterised by the breach of the obligation of loyalty of the contracting party which is constitutive of a *réticence dolosive*'.[45]

[37] *Civ 1ère 19-5-1958*, Bull Civ I, No 251; *Civ 3ème, 15-1-1971*, Bull Civ III, No. 38.

[38] Guestin, 'The Obligation to Disclose Information', n. 12 above, at 153. [39] Ibid.

[40] D. Mazeaud, 'Réticence de l'acquéreur sur la valeur du bien vendu, la messe est dite', D 2007, J 1051 at 1052. Similarly, C. Zimmerman and S. Whittaker, *Good Faith in European Contract Law* (Cambridge University Press, 2000) at 218. See also Professor Mazeaud who states that the *réticence dolosive* is traditionally linked to the obligation to negotiate in good faith: Mazeaud, 'La politique contractuelle', n. 4 above, at 383, para. 16.

[41] The conditions are: (1) the informed party must have the relevant information, or, be deemed to have it, because of his profession or his standing and must know that the information is relevant to the victim; (2) the victim is not only ignorant of that same information but must also have legitimately relied on the other party's knowledge to contract This is loosely based on the classification by Guestin in 'The Obligation to Disclose Information', n. 12 above.

[42] In fiduciary relationships or if one party's profession is such that the trust it brings is heightened, loyalty is more important. Stoffel-Munck, D 2007, n. 7 above, at 1054, para. 3.

[43] *Civ 3ème, 21-2-2001*, D 2001, J, 2702.

[44] The fact that a professional did not have to inform himself was confirmed in *Civ 3ème, 22-6-2005*, CCC 2005, note Leveneur.

[45] In French 'le dol est constitué par le manquement au devoir de loyauté du co-contractant constitutive de réticence dolosive'.

More recently however, the influence of loyalty in this area appears to have weakened. In *Theuillon* v. *Destemberg*,[46] Mr Destemberg, an agricultural worker, who wanted to sell his bungalow, approached Mr Theuillon, an estate agent whose services he had used in the past. In this instance, Mr Theuillon was interested in buying the property for himself and therefore acted in a personal and not a professional capacity when the parties entered into a *promesse de vente*, which Destemberg refused to perform after realising that the price that Theuillon had offered was lower than the market price. Destemberg claimed the *promesse de vente* was null and void for *réticence dolosive*; that Theuillon should have told him that the price the property would have fetched on the open market was higher than the price he had offered. The Court of Appeal accepted his claim on the ground that since Destemberg 'could not himself know the true value of his bungalow',[47] Theuillon, by not telling Destemberg of the real value of his property, was in breach of the obligation of loyalty applicable to all contracting parties, a breach which constituted a *réticence dolosive* under Article 1116 CC. Theuillon appealed. The Cour de Cassation quashed the decision of the Court of Appeal stating 'the buyer, even when a professional, does not owe an obligation of information to the seller with regards to the value of the good purchased'.

This decision confirms and widens the earlier decision of *Clin* v. *Boucher*[48] involving the purchase by Mr Clin of some photos, which he knew to be by a famous photographer, for a price set by Mrs Boucher, which was far lower than what she could have obtained on the open market. Following Mr Clin's failure to disclose what he knew, Mrs Boucher sued him for *réticence dolosive*. The Court of Appeal found in her favour on the ground that she had sold the photos at a *prix dérisoire* (derisory price) compared to the real value of the photos. Mr Clin, through his silence, was in breach of his obligation of good faith, and guilty of a *réticence dolosive* under Article 1116 CC since his silence caused Mrs Boucher to conclude a contract on terms she would not have consented had she known their true value.

The Cour de Cassation quashed the decision of the Court of Appeal, stating that even though fraud can be characterised by the silence of a party, this silence can only be punished if the party in question owes a

[46] *Civ 3ème, 17-1-2007*, Bull Civ III, No. 5. [47] My own translation.

[48] *Civ 1ère, 3-5-2000, Clin v Boucher*, Bull Civ I, No 131; JCP G 2001, II 10510, note C. Jamin.

duty of information to the other. By stating that Mr Clin was guilty through silence when he in fact owed no duty of information as to the value of the photos, the lower court therefore had violated Article 1116 CC.

These two decisions clearly reaffirm that the *réticence dolosive* is directly linked to the obligation of information, i.e. there can only be a *dol par réticence* if the informed party is under an obligation of information. The lack of mention of good faith/loyalty in both cases speaks volumes: the link between loyalty and *le dol* which was prevalent in previous cases is now clearly severed.[49]

Theuillon reopened the debate started by the affair *Clin*. Opinions are divided. Those agreeing with the position of the Cour de Cassation have remarked that in a contract of sale, by nature, the parties have divergent interests. Consequently, the decision is to be applauded precisely for not imposing an obligation to disclose the value of the property since 'the simple asymmetry of information is not sufficient, on its own to impose an obligation of information on the buyer'.[50] Moreover, since the information, in this instance, was freely accessible, there was nothing to disclose.

However, critics of the decision have expressed surprise that, given the circumstances of *Theuillon*, the court did not find the buyer obliged to let the seller know of the value of the bungalow,[51] since the seller's status was much lower than that of the buyer, he being an agricultural worker and his wife unable to work and in receipt of incapacity benefit for years. Others have added that although in this particular case, the buyer was not acting in his capacity as an estate agent since he had bought the house for himself, it was undeniable that the seller, given his lower status, had relied on the 'apparent professional status of the buyer'.[52] The seller had trusted the buyer, he was the weaker party and as such should have been protected.[53] However, the impact of this case must not be overemphasised: although it widens *Clin* by excluding professionals from disclosing information on the value of the goods, it only concerns the seller and not

49 Professor Mazeaud states that 'loyalty is deactivated': Mazeaud, 'Réticence de l'acqué reur', n. 40 above, 1052.

50 Stoffel-Munck, D 2007, J, n. 7 above, 1054–5 at 1055, para. 4.

51 Ibid., 1052. See also S. Amrani Mekki, n. 26 above, 2969.

52 C. Jamin, 'L'acquéreur, même professionnel, n'est pas tenu d'une obligation d'information au profit du vendeur sur la valeur du bien acquis', JCP E *Semaine juridique, entreprise et affaires* (2001), II, 10042.

53 S. Amrani Mekki, n. 26 above, at 2970.

the buyer. As such, the decision does not negate the duty of information of all professionals such as directors of company selling their shares.[54]

Yet, aside from the severance of loyalty from the obligation of disclosure, the decision can also be criticised for fragmenting the unity of *le dol* since there is now a clear distinction between a simple silence and artifices.[55] The former is a narrow category since it can only cause the contract to be held void if the mistake it has caused is *déterminante*, i.e. substantial as per Article 1110 CC; the latter is much wider since it covers cases of mistake on the value of a good.[56] Moreover, whereas in *Clin* v. *Boucher*, arguably all the buyer did was to exploit the mistake of the seller who had simply acquiesced to the price, in *Theuillon*, clearly, Theuillon had actively participated in setting the price, which caused Destemberg to make a mistake. This decision therefore weakens the role of the *réticence dolosive*,[57] which, in terms of case law, represents a serious step-back by fifty years.[58]

This is regrettable and the question is therefore what, if anything, can be done. It has been suggested[59] that the courts should use a different basis than *le dol* and adopt a position similar to that of Article 4.109 of PECL[60] through a common *vice de faiblesse*, something that the second civil chamber of the Cour de Cassation in 2006 appears to have attempted to do in a very little reported decision.[61] In this case, the plaintiff was a young woman who, following her dismissal, hired the defendant, a lawyer to represent her. A few days before the industrial tribunal's hearing, she signed a contract for the fees of the lawyer which stipulated that his fees would be taken from any compensation potentially obtained. The tribunal ruled in her favour and she was awarded damages. When the defendant claimed his fee, she refused to pay him

[54] *Cass Com 27–2–1996 Vilgrain* v. *Alary*, Bull Civ, IV, No. 65; *Cass Com 12–5–2004 Beley v Sté Former et a*, Bull Civ 2004, No 94.

[55] D. Mazeaud, 'Réticence de l'acquéreur', n. 40 above, at 1053, para. 10. [56] Ibid.

[57] S. Amrani Mekki, n. 26 above, at 2969.

[58] D. Mazeaud, 'Réticence de l'acquéreur', n. 40 above, at 1053, para. 10.

[59] S. Amrani Mekki, n. 26 above, at 2970.

[60] Article 4.109 (1) stipulates that a party may avoid a contract if, at the time of the conclusion of the contract: (a) it was dependent on or had a relationship of trust with the other party, was in economic distress or had urgent needs, was improvident, ignorant, inexperienced or lacking in bargaining skill, and (b) the other party knew or ought to have known of this and, given the circumstances and purpose of the contract, took advantage of the first party's situation in a way which was grossly unfair or took an excessive benefit.

[61] *Civ 2ème, 5–10–2006*, D 2007, Jur 2215, note G. Raoul-Cormeil.

and challenged the validity of the contract, claiming that she had not understood and therefore not consented to the fees being deducted from the compensation received. The Rouen Court of Appeal held the contract to be null and void on the ground that her consent had been vitiated as it was neither free nor informed. The lawyer appealed to the Cour de Cassation arguing that the Court of Appeal had not sufficiently characterised which vitiating factor within Articles 1109 and 1110 CC could apply since he was not guilty of fraud nor had he exerted any violence on his client and neither was there any substantial mistake.

The Cour de Cassation rejected his appeal and held that given the circumstances, the consent of Mrs X had indeed not been free; that she was in a state of least resistance due to the fact that she needed to receive the compensation quickly because of her weak financial situation (she was in serious debt) and her physical weakness, a fact proven by medical certificate and a fact that her lawyer was aware of. Such circumstances were therefore sufficient to characterise a vitiating factor (*un vice du consentement*).

The position of the Cour de Cassation is interesting since it does not resort to the traditional vitiating factors in the civil code. Instead, by taking into consideration the victim's weak position as characterised by the specific circumstances surrounding the formation of the contract, to decide that the plaintiff's consent had been vitiated, the court seems to 'create' a new vitiating factor: that of a *vice de faiblesse*. However, as the court fails to explain how this *vice de faiblesse* would work, the decision is consequently disappointing and ultimately limited to its facts.

Adopting a position closer to that of Article 4.109 of PECL is appealing since it would formalise the use of the status of the victim as a basis for more protection. Providing clearer guidelines as to what a weaker party in need of protection is, would in turn avoid having to rely on the judicial resort to loyalty, which, as we are about to see in a wider context of contract law generally, also appears to be in retreat.

The resurrection of the old debate of fairness v sanctity of contract

This debate is clearly not new: although the courts have had the power to intervene on a contract on grounds of fairness and good faith since the creation of the civil code (Article 1134–3 CC), such a power has always been limited by the principle of sanctity of contract (Article 1134–1

CC).[62] The previous part has shown how, in relation to *la réticence dolosive*, the influence of loyalty has weakened following the decision of *Theuillon* v. *Destemberg*. In the case of *Fromont* v. *Verdier*,[63] the commercial chamber of the Cour de Cassation appears to adopt a similarly restrictive position in the wider context of contract law generally.

In the *Fromont* case, the plaintiff, the president of a company[64] whose main object was to run a night club, bought shares from three existing shareholders. Under the terms of the contract, he was bound to give a *complément de prix* (additional sum of money) to the sellers in certain circumstances and the sellers owed him a *garantie de passif* (a protection against a debt appearing after the sale which finds its origin in an event before the sale). In this instance, because of the nature of the main business of the company, there was a possibility that a *redressement fiscal* (fiscal control) could occur, something that the sellers and the buyer were both aware of. The said *redressement fiscal* happened, which caused the debts of the company to increase. The circumstances allowing the sellers to ask for additional funds having materialised, the plaintiff was called upon to pay the additional sum and the plaintiff, in turn, called on the *garantie de passif* which the sellers refused. Litigation then followed.

The Court of Appeal of Paris rejected the plaintiff's claim and held that in the light of the obligation of good faith, he could not possibly require the defendant to perform his obligation since, as a director of the company, he was aware that a fiscal control could occur. The court added that in view of his position within the company, he had deliberately exposed the company to risks which, having materialised, gave rise to the fiscal control which is at the origin of the *garantie du passif*. Good faith therefore prevented him from claiming the *créance* (right to performance of an obligation)[65] that the contract entitled him to.

The Cour de Cassation quashed the decision stating that

> even though the rule whereby contracts must be performed in good faith allows the judge to punish the disloyal use of a contractual prerogative, this does not allow him to attack the substance itself of the rights and obligations legally entered into. The Court of Appeal is therefore in error, for wrongfully applying the second of the above-mentioned texts [Article

[62] See n. 12 above and associated text.

[63] *Cass Com 10-7-2007*, D 2007, AJ 1955; D 2007, J 2844.

[64] In French, the Président du conseil d'administration.

[65] French law classifies the parties according to the contractual obligations they owe to each other as 'creditor' or 'debtor'.

1134–3 CC on good faith] and for refusing to apply the first of the above mentioned texts [Article 1134–1 CC on the sanctity of contracts].[66]

As remarked upon,[67] the vocabulary that the Cour de Cassation used is carefully chosen; the judge can *punish* the disloyal use of a prerogative, but cannot *attack* the substance of the contract. The powers of the judge to interfere with the contract are therefore clearly limited: the judge is the servant of the contract and cannot dictate the way the parties should behave, even in the name of good faith.[68] Some academics have welcomed this decision,[69] but only because it reasserts a well-known principle[70] rather than because it breaks new ground, a point that the Cour de Cassation itself was eager to emphasise in the communiqué it published on its website.[71] This reassertion of the traditional position has been seen as a positive development, because it was felt that good faith gave too much power to the judges to intervene,[72] a power which had allowed them to destabilise the principle of sanctity of contracts.

Praise for the decision is, however, not unanimous. The main criticism is that the vocabulary used is too conceptual;[73] the court makes the distinction between the 'substance of the contract' which cannot be shaped by judicial intervention and the 'contractual prerogatives' which can. Yet, the court fails to define with any precision what such notions are or even what sanctions are applicable.[74] To answer the first

[66] Emphasis added. In French, 'alors que si la règle selon laquelle les conventions doivent être exécutées de bonne foi permet au juge de sanctionner l'usage déloyal d'une pré rogative contractuelle, elle ne l'autorise pas à porter atteinte à la substance même des droits et obligations légalement convenus entre les parties, la cour d'appel a violé, par fausse application, le second des textes susvisés et, par refus d'application, le premier de ces textes'.

[67] L. Aynès, *Revue des Contrats* (2007) at 1108.

[68] H. Houvasse, 'Garantie de passif et force obligatoire du contrôle', *Droit des Sociétés* (2007), Comm 180.

[69] D. Houtcieff, 'Limite du pouvoir de sanction du juge en cas d'usage déloyal d'une pré rogative contractuelle' *JCP G* (2007), II 10154.

[70] *Civ 6–3–1876, Canal de Cramponne*, D. 1876, I, 193 where the court held that 'regardless of how equitable the decision of the judge appears to them, the court cannot modify the contents of the contract' (my own translation). In French 'quelque équitable que puisse leur paraître leur décision, les juges ne peuvent modifier le contenu du contrat'.

[71] Communiqué relatif à l'arrêt No. 966 du 10–7–2007 on the official website: www.courdecassation.fr.

[72] Aynès, n. 67 above.

[73] Philippe Stoffel-Munck, 'Nature et effets du manquement à la bonne foi contractuelle', *D 2007*, 2839–44, at 2839, para 1.

[74] The question is also to know the nature of the sanctions applicable, i.e. contractual or tortuous: D. Mazeaud, *RDC Revue des Contrats* (2007), at 1113.

criticism, it has been remarked that the distinction is clear since it was highlighted by the doctrine some time ago;[75] the 'contractual prerogatives' are attached to the status of the parties of the contract such as the right to terminate the contract, the right to assign it etc. As for the 'substance of the contract', it is what Professor Aynès refers to as 'the bargain' or 'the price' according to Article L 132–1 Consumer Code.[76] Such a substance cannot be touched upon as long as it is *légalement convenu*, i.e. has been freely entered into. The judge can therefore check the manner in which a *créance* was created but cannot attack it. In this case, since the *garantie de passif* had been freely consented to by both parties, the plaintiff could legitimately require the sellers to perform their obligation under it. The sanctity of contract therefore prevented the Court of Appeal from intervening, even in the name of good faith. This point was, once again, emphasised by the Cour de Cassation in its communiqué which stated that 'a bad faith promisee nevertheless remains a promisee and the judge cannot, without attacking the very existence of the obligation itself, exempt the promisor from performing this obligation.'[77]

To the second criticism relating to the sanctions, it has also been remarked that the situation is equally clear. The prerogatives are, in essence, a unilateral power which, if used disloyally, can be sanctioned by preventing the party from using that very power.[78] An illustration of this would be when a party abuses a *clause résolutoire* (termination clause).[79] This very example was cited by the Cour de Cassation in its communiqué in order to show that its decision does not represent a *revirement de jurisprudence* and that the question is therefore settled.

The decision is indeed, in the court's own words, novel (*inédite*)[80] and has undeniably attracted a lot of academic comment since it seems to give sanctity of contract the upper hand. However, whether this decision really marks the end of loyalty as a tool to combat contractual unfairness is not so clear. Let us therefore consider its impact. Again, relying on the

[75] P. Ancel,'Force obligatoire et contenu obligationnel du contrat' *RTDC* (1999) 771–810.

[76] Aynès, n. 67 above.

[77] My own translation. In French: 'le créancier, même de mauvaise foi, reste créancier et le juge ne peut, au seul motif que la créance a été mise en oeuvre de mauvaise foi, porter atteinte à l'existence même de celle-ci en dispensant le débiteur de toute obligation'.

[78] Aynès, n. 67 above, at 1109.

[79] Citing *Civ 1ère 16–2–1999 Van der Schoot* v. *Giraudo*, Juris-Data 1999–000690, Bull Civ I 1999, I, No. 52.

[80] In its communiqué on the official website, www.courdecassation.fr, see n. 79.

court's own words in the communiqué, the main reason for quashing the decision of the Court of Appeal was because of its 'extreme vision of the role of bad faith'. In fact, the alleged bad faith of the plaintiff was that he had exposed the company to the risk of a fiscal control but not that, by his behaviour, he had influenced the consent of the defendant. On this point, again emphasised by the court itself, it is therefore clear that the case law imposing a duty of disclosure, in the name of loyalty, on the director of a company who sells his shares is still valid.[81]

Finally, even if a managing director is not playing fairly in demanding what is owed to him, his *droit de créance* (the right to claim performance of an obligation) must nevertheless be complied with if the obligation is legally formed.[82] What loyalty can redress is not the exercise of a right but the disloyalty accompanying it.[83] To paraphrase, this case appears to be nothing but 'old wine in new bottles'.[84]

Conclusion

This chapter has shown that French law's answer to contractual unfairness is to combat it through specific mechanisms rather than a general doctrine of unconscionability. Such mechanisms, although efficient, are necessarily limited in their scope of application. In a bid to widen the level of protection of some weaker parties, the French judiciary has used loyalty as a tool to impose a pre-contractual information obligation, which, if not complied with, gives rise to liability on the part of the informed party either under the *dol* if the conditions were met, or in tort giving rise to damages. Although this 'moralisation' of *la réticence dolosive*[85] had the advantage of widening the protective net, recent developments have shown that its efficiency relies on an interventionist judicial position (*Theuillon* v. *Destemberg*) which, in its wider context must be carefully balanced with the rule of sanctity of contracts (*Fromont* v. *Verdier*). Although both cases have attracted a lot of attention, their impacts have been quite different.

[81] *Cass Com 27-2-1996 Vilgrain* v. *Alary*, Bull Civ 1996, IV, No. 65; *Cass Com 12-5-2004 Beley* v. *Sté Former et a*, Bull Civ 2004, No. 94.

[82] Stoffel-Munck, 'Nature et effets du manquement à la bonne foi contractuelle', n. 73 above, at 2840, para. 1.

[83] Ibid. at 2841, para. 7.

[84] D. Houtcieff, *Semaine juridique – édition générale* (2007), II, 10154.

[85] Mazeaud, 'Réticence de l'acquéreur', n. 40 above, 1051, para. 4.

In relation to the *Fromont* case, although sanctity of contract prevailed in the instance, the decision itself does not appear to change the essence of the contractual policy which the Cour de Cassation has adopted over the years;[86] good faith/loyalty is therefore still relevant as a judicial tool to combat contractual unfairness. Following the *Theuillon* case however, the role of loyalty is undeniably weaker in relation to *la réticence dolosive*. Moreover, by breaking the bond between loyalty and the obligation of information, *la réticence dolosive* loses its efficiency. This is clearly regrettable.

However, by not imposing an information duty on the buyer and protecting the seller, who, because of the circumstances surrounding the case can be regarded as a typically weaker party deserving of protection, this case highlights, perhaps more importantly, the need to define with precision which interest loyalty/unconscionability seeks to protect.[87] In other words, this case highlights the need to formalise the role that loyalty has played in this area.[88] A possible solution would be to adopt a system not dissimilar to that of Article 4.109 of PECL. Aside from the way this would advance the Europeanisation of contract law, this move would not only solve the schism within *le dol*, but would also, on a wider basis, allow an easier judicial application of unconscionability/loyalty as a concept. Indeed, defining clear criteria would also ensure the respect of the difficult balance between the intervention of the courts and sanctity of contracts. Interestingly though, according to Professor Mazeaud, such a development may not be that far away. He cites a 2002 decision[89] in which the Cour de Cassation appears to have applied the spirit and the letter of Article 4.109 PECL under the guise of economic duress.

[86] Professor Mazeaud states that the values irrigating the contractual policy that the court has been pursuing over the last so many years are: freedom but loyalty, stability but equity and sanctity of contract but justice: Mazeaud, 'La politique contractuelle', n. 4 above, 373, para 6.

[87] Only by doing so, can we then devise a doctrine of unconscionability. See Voyakis, Capper and Waddams in this volume.

[88] As mentioned earlier, the way the courts appreciated the conditions of *le dol* varied with certain circumstances such as the status of the victim, the type of contract etc. See n. 42 above and associated text.

[89] *Civ 1ère, 3-4-2002*, D 2002, 1860, note Gridel. For detail, see Mazeaud, 'La politique contractuelle', n. 4 above, at 394, para. 30.

5

Unconscionability and the value of choice

EMMANUEL VOYIAKIS

Introduction

What is the proper way to justify the doctrine of unconscionability? Should we understand the doctrine as a device by which the state bails people out of poor and uninformed choices they make in their agreements with each other? As a device against some forms of exploitation and in support of individual autonomy? As a redistributive device? As a means for improving efficiency? These perspectives may occasionally overlap in practice, but they are sufficiently distinct in principle. The choice among them will determine not just how the argument in favour of the doctrine ought to be made, but also the range of objections that this argument will need to meet. The aim of this chapter is to explain why making that choice has been a difficult task for contract theory and to offer an alternative justification of the doctrine of unconscionability, which I believe merits independent consideration.

Some threshold difficulties

Compared to the notions of 'duress', 'undue influence' or 'misrepresentation', the notion of 'unconscionability' is harder to unpack. Whereas the former notions give us some immediate glimpse of what is wrong with enforcing an undertaking, e.g. that one party to that undertaking has been put under some sort of illegitimate pressure or has been misled into agreeing, the notion of unconscionability tells us considerably less. On the face of it, all it signifies is that it would be 'against conscience' to insist on enforcing a certain undertaking or, from the point of view of our

I am grateful to Olha Cherednychenko, Peter Jaffey, Holger Sutschet and John Wightman for their comments on earlier drafts. The later part of the chapter rehearses ideas developed more fully in a forthcoming monograph, provisionally titled *Private Law and the Value of Choice* (Hart Publishing: Oxford, 2010).

institutions, to actually enforce it. The problem is not just that this description is too generic – after all, it would be against conscience to enforce an agreement procured by duress, undue influence or misrepresentation – but that it does not give us some hint as to which features of the undertaking make its enforcement illegitimate.

This is not to denigrate the importance of the well-known organising distinction between 'procedural' and 'substantive' unconscionability. It is clear that the legitimacy of enforcing an undertaking may be undermined by flaws either in the process that led to its conclusion, or in the balance between the parties' respective entitlements under the agreement, or both.[1] However, the procedural/substantive distinction does not provide us with a normative criterion that will help us decide in a principled way what counts as a flaw in an undertaking or how serious the flaw must be for courts to refuse to enforce the undertaking as presented to them – I will call this the normative problem. Perhaps the fact that the undertaking was negotiated between parties of vastly different bargaining power should be enough for courts to treat it with suspicion. Perhaps it is also necessary for the party with the greater bargaining power to have acted in a way that makes it responsible for the other party's weakness in the context of their transaction (e.g. A may have encouraged B to rely on A's expertise).[2] Or perhaps nothing short of intentional exploitation will suffice. Different views about the pathology of voluntary undertakings – I outline some well known alternatives in the next section – will lead to different conclusions as to which undertakings are flawed and what ought to be the proper institutional response to their failings.

Here, I think, we can find some explanation of the haziness that surrounds the notion of unconscionability. Duress, misrepresentation and undue influence are clear-cut cases of pathological undertakings, in the sense that any plausible theory of contract law will have to acknowledge that agreements procured by such means should not be enforceable. Things get more controversial when we ask whether *less* dramatic flaws in an agreement (e.g. a great disparity in the parties' respective bargaining power) might justify a similar institutional response. The question then becomes where to draw the line, or how bad things must be for the

[1] See A. Leff, 'Unconscionability and the Code – The Emperor's New Clause' (1967) 115 *U. Pa. L.R.* 485 at 487 (discussing Art. 2–302(1) of the US Uniform Commercial Code).

[2] This is the view taken in *Chesterfield v. Janssen* (1751) 28 Eng Rep 82 at 101, where unconscionability was held to arise 'from the circumstances or conditions of the parties contracting – weakness on the one side, usury on the other, or extortion or advantage taken of that weakness', and more recently in *Boustany* v. *Pigott* (1993) 69 P & CR 298.

state to refuse to take an agreement at face value. The doctrine of unconscionability gives contract lawyers more trouble precisely because it deals with cases that lie at the 'outer reaches' of the pathology of agreements, where the different conceptions of what makes an agreement pathological lead to different practical results.

Closely related, but I think less pressing, is the problem of *taxonomy*. What range of cases should a theory of unconscionability aspire to cover? A quick answer would be: common-law cases that invoke that concept. However, that answer begs two questions. First, it may happen that although courts do not use the language of unconscionability in certain cases, the considerations that they take into account in deciding them are substantially similar to those arising in typical unconscionability cases (restraint of trade clauses are an obvious example). Second, one could plausibly argue that, terminology aside, statutory regimes for the protection of weaker parties to contracts (consumers, employees, insurance holders etc.) raise pretty much the same substantive issues as the typical case of common-law unconscionability. After all, statutes like the Unfair Contract Terms Act 1977 (UCTA) or the Unfair Terms in Consumer Contracts Regulations 1999 (UTCCR) were adopted against the background of the common law and in the light of its shortcomings.[3] The point is not that the typical case of common law unconscionability is identical with the typical case of restraint of trade clauses and the typical case of an unfair or unreasonable term in a consumer contract, but that the taxonomic distinctions between them cannot be taken at face value. Perhaps the received taxonomy reflects some substantive differences in the way the law should treat each class of cases. Perhaps it obscures rather than illuminates the structure of the problems it describes.[4] To resolve that issue, we need to ask first whether the pathology of the agreements addressed by common law and statutory law is similar or different and the answer to that will depend on the way we identify the flaws of those agreements and our theory about how the state should respond to their failings. In short, the taxonomic problem folds back into the normative one.

[3] In the case of the Regulations, against the background of the basic principles common to European contract laws.

[4] See M. Chen-Wishart, *Contract Law* (Oxford University Press, 2nd edn, 2008) at 381: 'one general principle can be more straightforward: for example facts involving lawful pressures may trigger duress and undue influence as much as unconscionable conduct'; S. Waddams, 'Unconscionable Contracts: Competing Perspectives' (1999) 62 *Sask. L.R.* 1, 10.

Five-plus-one accounts of unconscionability

The normative problem is this: we need a principled conception of what counts as a 'flaw' in the content of an agreement, or in the process of its conclusion, and a theory of how the state should respond to such flaws. We can then begin to address the less crucial taxonomic issue, using the notion of unconscionability to capture a group of flawed agreements that cannot be neatly accommodated under the more robust notions of duress, undue influence, misrepresentation and so on.

We are not short of plausible accounts of what might be wrong with the content of an agreement or the process of its conclusion. Each comes with a different view of the general pathology of agreements and, to that extent, each understands the notion of unconscionability in a different way and would include more or fewer agreements within the class of unconscionable contracts. I will outline very briefly what seem to me to be the five strongest contenders.

(1) Those who take the purpose of contract law to be the enforcement of transactions that people enter into voluntarily treat unconscionability as vitiating an agent's *consent* to a transaction and focus on specifying the range of factors that vitiate consent and their effect on the enforceability of a private transaction.[5] (2) Those who see contract law as aiming for corrective justice understand unconscionability as a *wrong* committed by one party to the transaction towards the other and focus their efforts on illuminating the nature of that wrong, be it the wrong of exploitation, of unjustified neglect of the other party's weakness and so on.[6] (3) The fewer theorists who see contract law as aiming to promote and sustain egalitarian distributions think of unconscionability as an effect of *unequal bargaining power* and focus on highlighting the social structures that create such disparities and designing legal principles that temper their effect.[7] (4) Those who see contract law as aiming to enhance individual autonomy treat unconscionability as a placeholder for contracts that limit objectionably an agent's capacity to dispose of her resources in ways that promote her chosen ends and focus on working out which types of agreement impinge more centrally on an agent's capacity for

[5] R. Barnett, 'The Sounds of Silence: Default Rules and Contractual Consent' (1992) 78 *Virginia L.R.* 821; J. Murray, 'Unconscionability: Unconscionability' (1969) 31 *U. Pitt. L.R.* 1.

[6] R. Bigwood, 'Contracts by Unfair Advantage: From Exploitation to Transactional Neglect' (2005) 25 *OJLS* 65; Chen-Wishart, n. 4 above, 378.

[7] A. Kronman, 'Contract Law and Distributive Justice' (1980) 89 *Yale L.J.* 472; H. Collins, *Regulating Contracts* (Oxford University Press, 2003), Chapter 11.

autonomous action.[8] (5) Finally, those who see the aim of contract law as being the pursuit of efficiency treat unconscionability as signifying the range of agreements that the state ought not to enforce in principle if it is to achieve the best *cost-benefit* balance in private agreements and try to work out the economics required to flesh out this conception.[9]

Each of those theories has a different view of what counts as a 'flawed' or pathological agreement. Whereas corrective justice theories will regard garden-variety consumer contracts as pathological only when a business has used its superior bargaining power in a wrongful manner against the consumer, distributive justice theories will say that the disparity of bargaining power between businesses and consumers is itself enough warrant for the law to treat consumer contracts with suspicion, to the extent that this disparity can be attributed to an unjust distribution of resources.[10] Some autonomy theorists will disagree with both views: they will say that the less an agreement impinges on an agent's capacity to lead an autonomous life, the slimmer the justification for the law to refuse to enforce agreements that the agent has entered into.[11]

Note, furthermore, that all five theories purport to set normative standards for the law as a whole. They do not place emphasis on the taxonomic differences between common law and statutory means of addressing flawed agreements. Under any one of those theories, we have to submit the common law doctrine of unconscionability or restraint-of-trade clauses, as well as the statutory protections of consumers, employees or insurance holders to similar normative tests.

All the same, theoretical discussion leaves one with a palpable sense that none of the five theories has a perfect fit with our intuitions as to

[8] S. Shiffrin, 'Paternalism, Unconscionability Doctrine and Accommodation' (2000) 29 Phil. & Pub. Aff. 205; D. Kimel, *From Promise to Contract: Towards a Liberal Theory of Contract* (Hart Publishing: Oxford, 2003) 126–35.

[9] F. Buckley, 'Three Theories of Substantive Unfairness' (1990) 19 *Hofstra L.R.* 33; R. Korobkin, 'Bounded Rationality, Standard Form Contracts and Unconscionability' (2003) 70 *U. Chi. L.R.* 1203.

[10] Jules Coleman takes the more nuanced view that when the injustice of the background conditions is too great or widespread, it may force us to rethink whether we ought to enforce voluntary transactions made under these conditions: J. Coleman, *The Practice of Principle* (Oxford University Press, 2001) 33: 'While the set of holdings that can be secured by a practice of corrective justice need not coincide exactly with holdings that should exist according to the best theory of distributive justice, holdings must nevertheless satisfy certain minimum conditions of moral legitimacy in order for us to speak of protecting them by a practice of corrective justice.' See also J. Coleman, *Risks and Wrongs* (Cambridge University Press, 1992) 304.

[11] Shiffrin, n. 8 above, 249.

which agreements are flawed and what the state ought to do about them. The discrepancy can come in any of three forms: either the theory says that there is nothing wrong with an agreement that we have reason to regard as pathological, or it fails to capture the character of our reasons for regarding it as pathological, or it fails to match what intuition suggests as the appropriate legal remedy.

Consent theories have received the worst press in that regard. Despite its surface appeal, the idea that unconscionable agreements are agreements that an agent did not enter into 'freely' or 'voluntarily' seems to have surprisingly little explanatory value.[12] The reason, I think, is that the contrast between a free or voluntary choice and a constrained choice is misplaced as a standard of our responsibilities for the agreements we enter into. Many of our choices take place under tight constraints, but this fact does not always affect our responsibility for having chosen one way or another or the enforceability of our undertaking. My choice to accede to the robber's demands in order to save my life may not make me responsible to pay the demanded ransom, but my choice to agree to pay my surgeon for a life-saving operation clearly does. We could, of course, try to distinguish between the two cases by saying that my consent to paying the surgeon is 'genuine' whereas my consent to paying the ransom is not, but this would only illustrate that the mere appeal to the notion of consent is unable to explain the difference.

Corrective justice theories are problematic for an apparently different reason. There is a host of agreements that can legitimately be regarded as pathological even though no wrong has been committed between the parties to it.[13] Consumer contracts are an obvious example here. The business that inserts an exclusion or limitation of liability clause into its standard form contract is not automatically wronging the consumer, in the sense that the business cannot be held responsible for many important limitations to the consumer's bargaining power (e.g. that the consumer is not in a position to negotiate; that going elsewhere would entail greater transaction costs etc.). If agreements can be pathological without the commission of a wrong, then corrective justice can at best offer only part of the normative story we are after.

The difficulty with distributive theories is somewhat trickier to state, since there persists some confusion as to what theories are actually

[12] S. Smith, *Contract Theory* (Oxford University Press, 2004) 323–39; Waddams, n. 4 above, 2–3.

[13] Ibid.; Smith, n. 12 above, 322–3.

claiming. It is often thought, for example, that distributive theories hold that the aim of contract law should be to promote and sustain just distributions of wealth.[14] The objection to this aspiration leaps from the page: regulating contracts is not a good way to redistribute wealth, if only because it exposes the task of redistribution to the risk of people deciding not to enter into agreements.[15] I think that the point of distributive theories is quite different, though. Their basic insight is that the core function of the law is to distribute sets of options, some taking the form of material resources (mainly distributed by tax laws) and others taking the form of rights; entitlements to require the enforcement of voluntary transactions are a subset of those rights. In that sense, contract law is not so much a tool for changing distributive shares but is itself part of the larger pattern of distribution of options and opportunities across society. What distributive theories claim, to my mind very plausibly, is that the distribution of contract rights must be sensitive to the distribution of other rights and resources across society, with a view to ensuring that on the whole agents are treated under some measure of equality. Consumers and employees need special protection in their agreements with businesses and employers in order to redress the inequality of bargaining power that market economies create between capital-possessing businesses and employers, on the one hand, and labour-producing consumers and employees, on the other. If our economy worked differently, e.g. producing smaller disparities in bargaining power, contract rights would probably not need to include such strong protections for these groups.

A more serious difficulty for distributive theories, I think, is that there are several contract rights that we would *not* want to be sensitive to the larger patterns of distribution. In fact, one might even say that there is a group of contract rights that people should have irrespective of issues of social (distributive) justice. If I put Bill Gates at gunpoint to get him to buy my book, I cannot invoke the fact that he is the beneficiary of a grossly unjust distribution to justify the enforcement of our agreement. Of course, any law allowing or prohibiting enforcement will have distributive consequences by virtue of its generality, but it seems to me that the notion of egalitarian distribution plays little role in explaining why

[14] Ibid., 137–8. A variation of this conception treats unconscionability as a 'welfare' mechanism: E. Posner, 'Contract Law in the Welfare State: A Defense of the Unconscionability Doctrine, Usury Laws and Related Limitations on the Freedom of Contract' (1995) 24 *J. Leg. St.* 283.

[15] Smith, n. 12 above, 137; Waddams, n. 4 above, 13–16.

I should not be able to have it my way with Bill Gates. It seems enough that any principle allowing enforcement of our agreement would license people to force others into making certain choices by putting them at gunpoint.

Autonomy theories have much more intuitive appeal because they begin from a very attractive general idea, characteristic of liberalism, namely that the law should allow people to be the authors of their lives and to use their talents and resources to further their chosen ends. One important upshot of the ideal of autonomy is that it discourages paternalist conceptions of contract law, in which the state bails people out of bad bargains they have struck by treating their judgement about the value of their bargain as inferior.[16] Beyond that point, though, the appeal to autonomy – like the appeal to all abstract ideals – is only as good as one's practical conception of what that value requires or allows.[17] In that regard, some influential autonomy-based accounts of the pathology of agreements seem to me rather conservative in their reach. In her important contribution to the debates about unconscionability, Seana Shiffrin has tried to develop a non-paternalist and autonomy-based account of unconscionability. She argues that the main question for the theory of unconscionability is to specify the circumstances under which the law may legitimately refuse to assist exploitative behaviour between individuals. In her view, given that 'a state committed to the equal status of all its citizens should forbear from siding with and lending its force to the citizen who acts contrary to this notion', the state has a general reason to refuse to assist the exploiters' project.[18] Moreover, Shiffrin notes, exploiters cannot invoke their autonomy as an objection to the state's refusal to assist their effort, to the extent that market transactions do not tend to impinge on the core of their autonomy rights, as would 'activities that involve intimate uses of the body, the exercise of conscience, or other behaviors that are central to one's sense of self'.[19]

The first of those two points strikes me as overly conservative. True, the presence of exploitation is certainly sufficient warrant for the state to refuse to enforce an agreement. But it does not follow that exploitation should be *necessary* for the state to treat an agreement with suspicion, or that businesses, employers or insurers who insert certain terms in their

[16] On paternalist justifications of unconscionability, see Shiffrin, n. 8 above, 208ff.

[17] Dori Kimel uses the idea of autonomy to reach an account that does not differ significantly from the one I outline in the following section.

[18] Shiffrin, n. 8 above, 250. [19] Ibid., 249.

favour in standard form contracts are thereby 'exploiting' their clients. In particular, it is not clear why the complaints of consumers, employees or insurance holders must derive their normative force from the language of exploitation. A consumer can reasonably object to a principle that allows businesses to insert wide exclusion of liability clauses into their standard contracts without necessarily having to show that she was thereby 'exploited' (I will say more on what I take to be the true character of the consumer's complaint in the next section). Perhaps Shiffrin worries that the more we extend the state's powers in relation to contracts that are not outright exploitative, the harder it might be to resist the charge of paternalism, i.e. the charge that the state is second-guessing people's poor transactional choices. That is a legitimate worry, but it looks more like a challenge that the defence of more extended state powers would have to meet than an outright reason for thinking that no such defence can succeed. At any rate, there is no *a priori* reason to assume that the appeal to autonomy cannot be made compatible with a more active regulatory role for the state.[20]

Finally, efficiency theories seem less suited than other alternatives as accounts of the reasons we have for regarding some agreements as 'flawed' and for allowing the state to refuse to enforce them or, at least, not to take them at face value. The basic reason is that these utilitarian theories make little space for the idea that people have a strong interest not only in what will happen but also in being able to have what will happen depend on their *choices*, even when the exercise of this ability leads to sub-optimal results. Rights, including contract rights, should in this sense be regarded as not wholly dependent on cost-benefit or efficiency considerations. At the same time, it is hard to deny that such considerations *do* play a role in justifying contract doctrine. For example, I think that a business could very plausibly object to a principle requiring it to negotiate individually with every consumer on the ground that the transaction costs entailed by such a principle would negate much of the value of mass-production and mass-retail enterprise. More generally, one does not need to be a utilitarian to recognise that protecting an agent's rights may involve serious costs for other agents and that difficult judgements may often be required to gage the level of protections that are reasonably acceptable to both rights-holders and other parties. So even if efficiency theories will not do as general accounts of the pathology of agreements and the attitude the state should take towards them, they

[20] See Kimel, n. 8 above, 129–31.

feature certain insights about the relevance of costs that any alternative theory would need to incorporate.

The picture, so far, looks like this: there are several appealing theories, each with strong aspects, but none of them seems to provide a compelling and unifying account of what agreements are 'flawed' and how the state should respond to them. How should we proceed?

One group of authors urges us to acknowledge that the range of reasons bearing on these questions cannot be captured by a single theory.[21] In this 'pluralist' conception, the best of the available theories can claim to account successfully for at least part of those reasons, each plugging the gaps left by the others. Corrective justice theories work reasonably well in contexts where wrongdoing is present; distributive theories explain how inequalities in bargaining power can justify state intervention even when there is no wrong; autonomy theories are useful in ruling out paternalist accounts and articulating some limits to state intervention; and efficiency theories can explain the relevance of cost considerations.

It seems to me that the pluralist conception runs against two difficulties. The first is that, since the five theories purport to occupy the same justificatory space, any attempt to accommodate them would have to say more about their relationship and the many contexts in which they generate conflicting prescriptions. The suggestion that each theory can be made to work 'in its own domain' can be misleading. For example, if we hold that consumer transactions are in the domain of distributive justice, we are not simply saying that corrective justice principles do not apply to those contracts, but that distributive justice concerns *override* those of corrective justice in the given context, since the former finds flaw in a transaction that the latter regards as normal. If this is correct, the pluralist conception must be governed by a principle that regulates which theory is fit for each context, or which kind of considerations are overriding in each situation. Embracing many theories at once does not, therefore, rid us of the task of finding a unifying normative principle for the pathology of agreements.

The second difficulty is that the pluralist conception may give received theories too much credit. I think that the assumption that the chief problem of received theories is their insufficient *breadth* is too charitable, since these theories may have trouble capturing the character of our

[21] Smith, n. 12 above, 364 ('no single justification can apply to all such contracts'); Waddams, n. 4 above, 16–17.

reasons even in cases that they are supposed to be best suited for. We may, for example, be able to give a reasonably good intuitive account of some central examples of flawed agreements without invoking notions like consent, wrongs, egalitarian distribution or efficiency. This fact may not guarantee that these scattered intuitions will hang together as a neat 'sixth' theory, but it should give us enough incentive to seek some alternative framework.

The value of choice

To sum up: the notion of unconscionability does not give any direct clue about what might be wrong with the agreements that it concerns. A theory of unconscionability must therefore draw on a principled conception of what makes an agreement between individuals pathological and of the proper attitude of the state towards such agreements. That conception will be much broader than the common-law doctrine of unconscionability, but this is a source of worry only if you think that the taxonomic distinctions between common law and statutory law – as well as those between various aspects of the common law – are somehow intrinsically important. Should it turn out that we need to retain these distinctions, I have suggested that we might use unconscionability as the notion that 'mops up' any pathological agreements that more robust doctrines like those of duress, undue influence or misrepresentation leave unaccounted for.

In the previous section I tried to illustrate the difficulties contract theory has had in developing a satisfactory normative account of what constitutes a pathological agreement and what the state ought to do about it. In this section I will outline an alternative account (the 'value of choice' account, based on T. M. Scanlon's work on choice and responsibility[22]), which I believe can combine some of the more appealing aspects of existing theories by putting them at the service of an independent and normatively attractive central idea.

I begin from what might seem an unlikely starting point. I think that the well-publicised weaknesses of consent theories should not blind us to two important senses in which those theories set normative debates about contract on the right track. First, consent theories oppose paternalism and favour a liberal approach to the role of the state in relation to private agreements. By enforcing voluntary agreements, the state

[22] T. M. Scanlon, *What We Owe To Each Other* (Harvard University Press, 1998), 251ff.

respects an agent's capacity to act on her own conception of the good, withholding judgement as to the correctness of that conception. Second, the distinction between 'genuine' and 'non-genuine' consent, for all its paltriness, alerts us to the fact that what the state ought to respect is not *all* outward expressions of assent, but only expressions of assent that are the result of actions for which the agent can legitimately be held accountable.

There is, however, a sense in which the idea of 'consent' is too crude to reflect the depth of these intuitions. For a start, the notion of 'consent to an agreement' seems to me very clumsy. We consent to other people's plans; to a medical operation; to a directive. The description of our acts in these contexts as instances of 'consent' implies that we take a positive attitude towards the acts, plans or intentions of some *other* agent or agents. It also implies that although it is up to us to choose whether to take a positive or negative attitude, the *object* of our attitude (the suggestion, the operation, the law) has been formed independently of our own choices. Someone else proposes, suggests, intends or requires; our part is to decide whether or not we will go along.[23] You would never say that you decided to consent to your own suggestion or that you decided to consent to a plan you thrashed out jointly with your friend. Now, many contracts, not least consumer contracts, are formed on a similar 'are you in or are you out?' basis. The business determines the content of the contract and our choice is whether or not to enter into it. However, this is hardly a general or essential feature of private agreements. Many agreements are negotiated in ways that allow the choices of both parties to affect not only whether there is an agreement but also what the agreement says. Saying that the parties to such agreements, which are still the textbook example of a contract, decide to consent to their own agreement sounds rather odd. So rather than consent, I think we should take the essential feature of contracting to be the more general and flexible idea that an agent's eventual responsibilities under an agreement must depend on that agent's *choices*. Choice, not consent, seems more fitting as the core notion of a non-paternalist account of contract law.

An advantage of putting the notion of choice in the driving seat is that this makes for a natural connection between our theory of contract law

[23] In that regard, it is no accident that consent theories have been most effective in a context where the content of our choices is heavily circumscribed, namely political obligation. The content (some say even the normative force) of the political duties we have is only very indirectly dependent on our choices.

and our intuitions about moral responsibility. The connection can in turn help to flesh out the significance of choice in the context of agreements and the role of the state in relation to them.

A crude summary of our intuitions about responsibility would be that people should only be held accountable for their choices, not their circumstances. The summary is crude for two reasons. First, our circumstances always 'frame' the choices we face and affect the value these choices have for us.[24] I can be held accountable for not paying for the bike I bought because, normally, being able to buy or not to buy the bike is a choice I have reason to value. By contrast, I am not accountable for having chosen to sell you my home for fear that you would carry out your threat to harm my family, because there is nothing valuable in being forced to choose in these circumstances between one's home and the safety of one's family. Although I get to choose in both contexts, my choice in the second context is not something I have reason to value. To that extent, I have good grounds to reject any moral or legal principle that would take the second choice as a basis for holding me accountable.

Second, the fact that an agent's choices may be 'framed' by circumstances does not always entail that framed choice will lack value for that agent. It is sometimes legitimate to hold people accountable for framed choices made in tough conditions. I sold my car for pittance because I needed the money urgently; knowing nothing about art, I decided to trust your (honest but mistaken) statement that my Mondriaan was a fake worth only a few pounds. As in the duress example, my choices here were constrained or 'framed' by my circumstances. However, they were still valuable to me: a person in need of a quick access to resources has reason to want to be able to offer especially appealing terms to third parties able to provide them, while a person who knows nothing about art has reason to want to be able to rely on the honest opinion of more knowledgeable people who happen to offer their (in my example, free) assistance. We can even imagine examples in which a choice has value for an agent *only* when it is very tightly framed. Suppose that there is a dangerous epidemic and people are advised to inoculate themselves against it. You rush to the pharmacist for the vaccine and he tells you that you can choose from about sixty different varieties. Given the urgency of the situation and your lack of expertise, you are most likely to find that a more restricted set of options, e.g. giving the pharmacist a

[24] I take the notion of 'framing' from A. J. Julius: see A. Julius, 'Basic Structure and the Value of Equality' (2003) 31 *Phil. & Pub. Aff.* 321, 324–6.

summary of your health and having him whittle down the options to a choice between two or three varieties of the vaccine, would be much better for you. When it comes to choice, less can be more.[25]

Taking these points into account, we could reformulate the relationship between choice and responsibility along the following lines. The choices we make are almost always framed, in some way or another, by circumstances beyond our immediate control. However, framed choice may still attract responsibility, so the challenge is not to distinguish between framed and unframed choice, but between cases of legitimate and illegitimate framing (the point is well and widely understood in contract doctrine on duress and undue influence). That distinction, as I have suggested, would need to turn on whether the framed choice is a choice that the choosing agent has reason to value. I therefore propose that we endorse the following 'value of choice' principle:

> It is legitimate to hold agents accountable for their choices in a given context, if those choices were made from within a *range of options* and under *conditions* that agents could not reasonably reject as a ground of being held accountable.

Formulated differently, the 'value of choice' principle holds that agents can object to being held accountable for their choices when these choices were framed in ways that exclude options that agents can reasonably want to have available, or conditions that agents have reason to want to obtain, for their choices to make them accountable.[26]

I believe that the 'value of choice' principle not only accounts for the range of cases that lend existing theories their appeal, but also gives us better insight into the pathology of those cases. For a start, it seems to me that what corrective justice theories (as well as some autonomy theories) classify as wrongs are basically instances where one agent has framed the options and/or conditions of another agent's choice in such a way that it would be illegitimate to hold the choosing agent accountable within that setting. For example, a victim of exploitation can object to a principle that allowed the enforcement of her choice to assent to an undertaking, as long as she has had to make that choice from within an objectionably

[25] For a discussion of contexts where choice has no value for an agent, see A. Voorhoeve, 'Scanlon on Substantive Responsibility' (2008) 16 *J. Polit. Philos*. 184. See also Kimel, n. 8 above, 128–31; J. Raz, *The Morality of Freedom* (Oxford University Press, 1986) 380–2.

[26] The last proviso is important. We are not asking the speculative question of what options and conditions the agent would like to have available, but the moral question of what options and conditions she could reasonably require for her choice to make her accountable.

constrained range of options or under objectionable conditions. Furthermore, that complaint seems to me good enough to bar enforceability. It is not necessary to invoke the *further* (possibly true) fact that duress is also a wrong, since agents can reasonably object to any principle that holds them accountable for choices they make in the context of a private transaction, if the principle is not sensitive to the range of options that agents can reasonably want to be available to them or the conditions that they can reasonably want for their choices to generate enforceable commitments. The lesson we ought to draw from corrective justice theories is not so much that wrong-doing bars enforceability, but the more general idea that the value of agents' choices in the context of a private agreement can depend on the way parties to the agreement treat each other.

Second, it seems to me that the main intuition of distributive theories can be usefully reformulated as a point about the value of framed choice. An agent's choices can be framed not just by the conduct of the other party to the transaction, but also by the social structures in which the transaction between the parties takes place. A consumer's choices are limited not so much because of the behaviour of the business towards him/her, but because of the position that each occupies in the conditions of market economy. For example, the structure of markets and modern economies of scale make it reasonable for businesses to want to minimise their transaction costs by using standard term agreements. Consumers may benefit from this standardisation, but they also have reason to insist that the standard terms not exclude options and alternatives that they reasonably want to have open to them (e.g. to be able to sue for fraud or certain forms of negligence) or for certain conditions before their choices become enforceable (e.g. 'change of mind' or 'cooling-off' periods for distance transactions). Described in the abstract, these points concern the society-wide distribution of costs and options in the context of which business-consumer transactions takes place. However, the enforceability of those transactions does not depend on whether the distribution itself is just, but on the effects of whatever pattern of distribution exists on the value of the parties' respective choices. This explains why it may be legitimate to enforce a transaction between a business and a consumer while accepting that the social structures that create such big disparities in their bargaining power may be unjust.

Furthermore, the 'value of choice' account can give us useful insights into the relationship between the pathology of agreements and the attitude that the state ought to take towards them. In particular, the value of choice principle can explain why sometimes the more appropriate legal remedy for a pathological agreement will not be to refuse to enforce it, but to keep the agreement 'alive' and provide weaker parties with more choices and alternatives *within* it, than they would be able to secure through market negotiation. Examples of such cases include issues of health and safety, working conditions, dismissal and restraint of trade in the context of employment contracts; regulations on the exclusion of liability, the right of termination and the interpretation of consumer contracts (including contracts of insurance) and so on. In these contexts, the argument for 'affirmative' rather than 'negative' measures turn on three basic features on the situations they regulate. First, that the inequality of bargaining power between the parties constrains the choices and alternatives of one side. Second, that the value of being able not to enter into the transaction in these circumstances is considerably smaller for the weaker party than for the stronger party. For example, the respective value for employees and consumers of being able to refuse work or to refuse to buy basic consumer goods is smaller than the value for the employers of being able to turn potential employees away or the value for businesses of being able to turn away customers, insofar as the ability to find decent work and to buy basic consumer goods affects more people's life prospects and more profoundly so. Third, that neutralising the influence of such constraints on the value of the weaker party's choice may actually require affirmative measures, such as minimum wage legislation, that work to *modify* the terms of the 'live' transaction instead of rendering it unenforceable. The point is that if we refused to enforce employment contracts entered into under the influence of objectionable constraints, we would not be enhancing the value of the employees' choice at all. In fact, we would be reducing that value even further.

To sum up: under the 'value of choice' principle I have proposed, an agreement counts as 'flawed' or pathological, and the state ought to treat it with suspicion, when an agent could reasonably reject the set of alternatives that she has had to choose from, or the conditions under which the choice was presented to her, as a basis for being held accountable. The value of the choice for the agent may depend on a variety of considerations, including the conduct of the parties to an agreement towards each other and the social structures within which the agreement is concluded.

Figuring out whether the 'value of choice' principle demands that an agent be held accountable for her choices in the context of an agreement will require substantive judgements in each particular situation. The purpose of the principle – indeed, of all principles – is not to substitute such particular judgements but to guide them. The 'value of choice' principle fulfils this role by asking us to decide whether an agent should be held accountable for her choices on the basis of two specific questions. Did the choice include options that the agent could reasonably want to have available for her choice to be binding? And did the choice take place under conditions that the agent could reasonably want to obtain for her choice among the available options to make her accountable?

The proposed account does not allow an agent to deny responsibility under an agreement on the mere ground that she struck a particularly bad bargain, or on the ground that the agent was not knowledgeable enough on the subject-matter of the transaction. It only allows this when the agent could reasonably reject the range of available options or the conditions in which she had to choose among them as a basis for being held accountable. Having said that, I think it is an advantage of the 'value of choice' principle that it avoids oversimplifying the issue. Under the principle, determining whether an agent is responsible for her choices in the context of an agreement will require us to open up legal analysis to research on the social, economic and political structures shaping people's choices and on people's cognitive capacities and their biases in situations of choice among multiple alternatives. With regard to the latter, there is a wealth of recent research that not only illuminates the mental process and psychology of choice, both in market and non-market settings, but also calls into question traditional assumptions about what Susan Hurley called 'the primacy of private responsibility'.[27] In particular, it is becoming increasingly clear that many choices that traditional conceptions regarded as centrally determined by reasons accessible to an agent, and for which those conceptions held the agent responsible, are in fact pervasively influenced by a wide variety of factors that lie beyond the agent's cognitive control. Kahneman and Tversky give the following examples:

> A physician, and perhaps a presidential advisor as well, could influence the decision made by the patient or by the President, without distorting or suppressing information, merely by the framing of outcomes and

[27] S. Hurley, 'The Public Ecology of Responsibility' available at www.bristol.ac.uk/philosophy/hurley/papers/Responsibility.doc. An example of this conception of responsibility can be found in the famous dictum in *Printing & Numerical Registering* v. *Sampson* (1875) LR 19 Eq 462 at 465: 'If there is one thing which more than another public policy requires, it is that men of full age and competent understanding shall have the utmost liberty of contracting, and that their contracts, when entered into freely and voluntarily, shall be held sacred and shall be enforced by courts of justice.'

> contingencies. Formulation effects can occur fortuitously, without anyone being aware of the impact of the frame on the ultimate decision. They can also be exploited deliberately to manipulate the relative attractiveness of options . . . Lobbyists for the credit card industry insisted that any price difference between cash and credit purchases be labeled a cash 'discount' rather than a credit card 'surcharge' . . . Because losses loom larger than gains, consumers are less likely to accept a surcharge than to forego a discount.[28]

Discussing cognitive anomalies in social settings, Hurley further reports:

> Many cognitive anomalies are influenced by statements found in the socio-cultural environment, including those carried by various media. It seems natural to suppose, with Descartes and Mill, that comprehending a statement comes first and is neutral between accepting and rejecting it. But experiments show that people tend initially to accept a statement they comprehend even when explicitly told it is false. They must go through a further cognitive process of disbelieving it, so that it is not used in making decisions. This further process can be blocked by cognitive load or time pressure.[29]

These insights into the framing effect of social contexts and the limits of our cognitive capacities should lead us to reconsider our conception of which agreements are purely 'bad bargains' – for which an agent should be held responsible – and which have been rendered pathological in the sense of having been significantly influenced by factors outside the agent's substantive responsibility. At the same time, these insights set a normative measure for the regulation of private agreements and the variety of responses that the state can take to their pathology. One can think of many contexts, from online transactions to the provision of consumer credit and other financial services, in which information about the cognitive aspects of an agent's choice can affect our view of the value of that choice for the choosing agent. For example, one should expect that the collapse of the sub-prime mortgage market in the United States will precipitate more detailed research into the framing effect of certain market and advertising practices on the choices of mortgage holders. It is possible that many of those mortgage agreements were simply bad bargains that people should bear responsibility for. However, there are

[28] D. Kahneman and A. Tversky, *Choices, Values and Frames* (Cambridge University Press, 2000) 11.

[29] Hurley, n. 27 above, 9. Hurley here draws on D. Gilbert *et al.*, 'You Can't Not Believe Everything You Read' (1993) 65 *J. Pers. Soc. Psychol.* 221–33.

indications that many mortgage-holders' choices were framed by social structures and market practices beyond their control and insidiously affecting the value of their options.[30] To the extent that this is true, the 'value of choice' principle would require a considered regulatory response to address the effect of these framing factors before drawing conclusions about the proper limits of the responsibility of individual borrowers.

Conclusion

The fact that the notion of unconscionability does not tell us immediately what is wrong with the agreements it concerns may, after all, be a virtue. Lacking a surface explanation, we are required to look deeper and confront directly a couple of complex questions in contract theory: when should we regard an agreement as pathological and how should the state respond to such agreements?

I have tried to explain why contract theory has had difficulty coming up with satisfactory general answers to these questions – a difficulty also attested by some confusion over the significance of common-law taxonomy. I have pointed to some important weaknesses in available theories and given some reasons why the effort to combine them under a 'pluralist' conception is unlikely to fare much better.

I have then proposed an alternative account, the 'value of choice' account, which I believe is sufficiently distinctive to merit independent consideration. Under this account, an agreement is pathological – and the state should not take it at face value – if an agent's choices in relation to it were made from within a range of alternatives or under conditions that the agent could reasonably reject as grounds for being held so accountable. In turn, the value of choice for an agent will depend not just on how that agent has been treated by other parties to the agreement (the focus of corrective justice and, in part, autonomy theories) but also on the cost of the alternative options (the focus of efficiency theories) and on the social structures within which the choice was made (the focus of distributive theories). If successful, the proposed account could manage to accommodate the attractions of existing theories while putting them at the service of a unifying and morally appealing liberal idea. Furthermore,

[30] See P. Krugman, 'A Catastrophe Foretold', *New York Times*, 26 October 2007, at www.nytimes.com/2007/10/26/opinion/26krugman.html (on institutional failures) and 'Enron's Second Coming?', 1 October 2007, available at www.nytimes.com/2007/10/01/opinion/01krugman.html (on aggressive marketing practices).

it would explain why there are cases in which the best response to a pathological agreement is not to refuse to enforce it, but to modify its terms.

Finally, I have tried to give a glimpse into how research on unconscionability would proceed under the 'value of choice' account: circumspection about the significance of common-law taxonomy and the distinction between common law and statutory law; less emphasis on establishing exploitation or other forms of wrongdoing; more emphasis on the structures that frame people's choices, especially in consumer, employment and insurance agreements; and more openness to research about the cognitive capacities of agents and the entrenched biases of human rationality.

6

From individual conduct to transactional risk: some relational thoughts about unconscionability and regulation

JOHN WIGHTMAN

1. Introduction

In this volume, Stephen Waddams presents a powerful argument that it is impossible to establish an overall rationale which justifies the scope and content of the law of unconscionability.[1] Commentators have particularly focused on wrongdoing by the defendant and absence of consent by the claimant,[2] but it seems these factors, either singly or together, do not provide an adequate basis for the outcomes produced by the application of unconscionability.[3]

In this chapter, the concern is not with the issue of doctrinal rationale, but rather with what I argue is an important but neglected dimension of unconscionability. This is the element of transactional risk – specifically, characteristics of particular kinds of transaction which, in interaction with the conduct of the parties, create unusual risk for one party. The

[1] Unless the context indicates otherwise, I adopt the wider usage of unconscionability which treats it as an umbrella that includes not just the unconscionable bargain doctrine in English law but also a range of doctrines that may result in a contract being set aside where there is overreaching behaviour, including vitiating factors such an undue influence, unconscionable dealing, duress and fraudulent misprepresention. The focus is confined to the issue of whether a contract should be set aside, and thus omits consideration of the use of unconscionability to deprive terms of effect, as under s. 2–302 of the Uniform Commercial Code.

[2] See especially P. Birks and C. N. Chin, 'On the Nature of Undue Influence', in J. Beatson and D. Friedmann, *Good Faith and Fault in Contract Law* (Oxford: Clarendon Press, 1995), arguing that impaired consent underlies the doctrine of undue influence. I use 'claimant' throughout to refer to the party who is claiming that the contract should be set aside, despite the fact that, in some litigation, they will be a defendant, e.g. in the non-commercial surety cases.

[3] Stephen Waddams (Chapter 2 in this volume) argues that other factors such as unjust enrichment and distributive justice have to be invoked.

claim is that transactional risk is a variable which is useful in revealing both some fundamental distinctions between different strands of unconscionability doctrine, and also in clarifying important similarities between some strands of unconscionability and the legislative regulation of transactions.

The approach adopted here draws on the relational contract theory developed by Ian Macneil. Although some of the situations where unconscionability is applied concern long-term relationships of the kind where relational theory is usually applied, in this instance the relevance of relational contract theory to transactional context stems from its wider engagement with the role of the social matrix within which all contractual relations – not just long-term ones – take place.

I explore the role of context, and attempt to pin down the role of transactional risk, by contrasting the orthodox approach to unconscionability – labelled the individual conduct model – with a model based on contractual risk. Under the orthodox approach, the claimant has to establish the presence of a specific vitiating factor, while, under the contractual risk approach, the law singles out risk factors the presence of which place the burden on the defendant of justifying the transaction. Three kinds of contractual risk are identified: (1) that based on some personal characteristic of the claimant, e.g. who is 'poor and ignorant', or is a minor; (2) that deriving from a relationship between the parties, as where there is a relationship of trust and confidence in a case of two-party undue influence; and (3) that based on the nature of transaction. The example of the non-commercial surety is used to illustrate the latter approach, and it is argued that this is distinctive: by relaxing the requirement of some overreaching behaviour on the part of the defendant, it imposes a responsibility for protection of the claimant without wrongdoing having to be shown. Once this break with the rest of unconscionability is recognised, transactional risk can be seen to have affinities with some regulatory techniques, as well as some pre-classical doctrine. The chapter concludes by outlining some implications of a focus on transactional risk. But first, it is necessary to identify the relevant aspects of Macneil's relational theory and how they shape the ensuing analysis.

2. Macneil's relational theory and the critique of neo-classical contract law

There are two aspects of Macneil's theory which are especially relevant to an exploration of the transactional context of unconscionability.

The overall approach I am adopting is informed by the idea of relational contract theory as a method which applies to all contracts, not just long term ones; and more specifically, his critique of neo-classical contract law is of value in understanding the way in which unconscionability doctrines have responded to context. Each of these are considered in turn.

a) The implications of relational theory beyond long-term contracts

The relational theory which Ian Macneil developed has often been treated by other scholars as applying primarily to long-term contracts, particularly the way in which these relations are adjusted and preserved over time;[4] this view stems in part from a focus on his widely known construction of the discrete/relational continuum. This distributes exchange relationships according to how far they display discrete or relational characteristics. A discrete contract, (sometimes called 'one shot') is one where the parties' interaction is limited, confined by a clear specification of performances from the outset, and thus demarcated from the other transactions or relations in which the parties are engaged. His example was 'the purchase of gasoline on the New Jersey turnpike by someone who rarely uses the road'.[5] A relational contract is one where the relationship is long-term or open-ended (e.g. employment, some supply contracts), and where performance is not wholly specified from the outset but is adjusted as the circumstances unfold.

The problem with this widely known but simplified picture is that it conveys the impression that exchanges at the discrete end of the continuum are not relational in any sense, and that relational contract theory has no application to them. However, Macneil's work also emphasises the relational character of discrete exchanges; he also pointed out that even the purchase of petrol in the New Jersey turnpike example is only possible because of the social institutions and practices which make such

4 It is this impact that has been seen as most influential: see Jay Feinman, 'Relational Contract Theory in Context' (1999) 94 *Northwestern University Law Review* 737 and 'The Reception of Ian Macneil's Work on Contract in the USA', in D. Campbell (ed.), *The Relational Theory of Contract: Selected Works of Ian Macneil* (London: Sweet and Maxwell, 2001).

5 'Contracts: Adjustment of Long-Term Economic Relations under Classical, Neoclassical, and Relational Contract Law' (1978) 72 *Northwestern University Law Review* 854, 857.

a glancing exchange so effective.[6] Picking up on these different emphases, David Campbell, has persuasively argued that discrete contracts must be seen as 'relationally constituted';[7] he makes clear that 'relational' has been used by Macneil in two different senses. One meaning of relational refers to an exchange which is longer term, or non-discrete, and thus denotes particular kinds of contract. The other meaning of 'relational' refers to the fact that all contracts are dependent upon the social institutions and practices which constitute them. It is this second, wider, meaning of relational which I argue is fruitful in focusing analysis of the role of transactional context in relation to unconscionability.

Macneil's primary focus was the practice of exchange rather than the law, and he developed ten 'common contract norms', which were seen both as descriptive of observable contract behaviours, and as attaining normative character by virtue of repeated usage.[8] These norms are not intended as a prescription of specific norms which ought to apply to exchanges generally, but they vary in their application according to context, and the location of the transaction type on the relational/discrete continuum. However, anyone attempting to apply Macneil's whole theory to a specific aspect of contract law faces the problem that it is complex and highly elaborate, containing many neologisms; it has not been widely applied by others in its totality. Moreover, the utility of the detail of the common contract norms for the analysis of particular aspects of contract law – as opposed to the social practices of exchange – has been doubted.[9]

Although there are problems in applying Macneil's whole theory to a specific context, I believe the fundamental orientation of relational theory sheds valuable light on the nature of unconscionability as an idea. Thus, whilst not pursuing an analysis in terms of the common contract norms, I believe there are three key insights of relational theory which can inform an analysis of unconscionability.

[6] The relational dimensions were emphasised in 'Values in Contract: External and Internal' (1983) 78 *Northwestern University Law Review* 340, 345: 'even a transaction deliberately chosen for its discreteness is deeply embedded in a wide range of interconnected relations'.

[7] 'The Relational Constitution of the Discrete Contract', in D. Campbell and P. Vincent Jones (eds.), *Contract and Economic Organisation* (Aldershot: Dartmouth, 1996).

[8] See generally I. Macneil, *The New Social Contract: An Inquiry into Modern Contractual Relations* (Yale University Press, 1980).

[9] D. Campbell, 'Ian Macneil and the Relational Theory of Contract', in Campbell, *Relational Theory of Contract* n. 4 above.

First, the place of consent and agreement in the relational approach is much more modest than that encountered in most of the case law which makes up the common law of contract. The concepts of classical contract law maximise the extent of obligation which can be expressed as deriving from consent, including even standard form contracts and many implied terms: Macneil effectively reverses this presumption and sees consent as explaining relatively few of the norms which contract law expresses. Thus the common contract norm of 'effectuation of consent' is concerned with giving effect to the consent of the parties; this gives consent a very limited scope, arguing that almost any contract will have more complicated consequences than anyone can possibly have in mind at once. He sees the adoption by contract law of an objective approach to agreement as an example of using consent-based language to express and justify norms which are not derivable from explicit consent.

In adopting a subjective interpretation of consent, Macneil is not arguing that parties should only be bound by an obligation to which they have subjectively consented: rather, many contractual obligations simply cannot be derived from consent. Macneil's view amounts to a kind of consent scepticism, so that in addressing unconscionability, one needs to be cautious in attributing consequences to either the presence *or* absence of consent.

Second, the corollary of the decentring of consent is a recognition that most norms are socially derived; a recognition, Macneil argued, that was obscured by the role of consent: 'the dominant role of consent in classical jurisprudence has put intellectual barriers in the way of communicating a broader analysis of the subject than appears in that jurisprudence.'[10] Norms may derive from the nature of the parties' evolving relationship, the practices of a particular market sector, or from society in general, including norms imposed by law. In legal terms such norms may be expressed through the various kinds of implied term, the contextual interpretation of written terms, and the law, including unconscionability, controlling permissible advantage taking. The potential content is enormous, and although such norms may well require cooperation between the parties, this is not (as is commonly thought) a necessary feature of a relational approach.[11]

Third, the method of a relational approach is not rooted in doctrine. It does not aim to elucidate doctrine, in the sense of clarifying it by removing

10 Macneil, *New Social Contract*, n. 8 above, 47.

11 See Macneil, 'Contracting Worlds and Essential Contract Theory' (2000) 9 *Social and Legal Studies* 431, 433 for an emphatic expression of this point.

inconsistency, and neither does it attempt to find an alternative, better rationale of the law. The relational method was described by Jay Feinman as resembling 'policy analysis',[12] thus embracing an explicit linking between norms, rules, and outcomes. Although it would be wrong to characterise doctrinal analysis as wholly deductive, there is an expectation in that tradition of legal analysis that external considerations (most obviously 'policy') are a last analytical resort: coherence is sought as far as possible within the existing legal sources. In contrast a relational approach is open in attempting to identify the relevant norms in a context, and in assessing how the law may express these. One consequence of this approach is that, when the role of law in a specific context is addressed, a relational approach potentially encompasses the whole of the law relating to exchanges in that context. This includes not just private law beyond contract, but all forms of regulation of the subject matter of the exchanges in question.

Taken together, these relational elements generate an approach which focuses primarily on the transactional context: once the norms governing exchanges are traced to origins which are social rather than individual, it seems unavoidable that the overall context is taken into account. Although this approach is engaged with doctrine, it is in a sense emancipated from it: doctrine remains an object of analysis, but does not confine the method to be employed in analysing it. In addition, a relational approach also has a generalising dimension: as well as the focus on particular contexts, it can also raise its gaze and address the operation of the law in exchanges more generally. This generalising dimension enables relational analysis to address both doctrine and instrumental regulation, without being confined by the method associated with each.

b) Unconscionability and the critique of neo-classical contract law

Macneil saw unconscionability as a feature of neo-classical contract law. This was his term for the law which superseded classical law in the second half of the twentieth century,[13] and which, while retaining

[12] 'Relational Contract Theory in Context', n. 4 above, 743.

[13] This terminology was coined with reference to American law, and both classical and neo-classical law are tied to landmarks in contract scholarship. Thus, classical law is associated with Williston's treatise (first edition 1920–2) and the first Restatement of Contracts, while neo-classical is associated with Corbin's treatise (first edition, 1950), the second Restatement (1962–1979), and the Uniform Commercial Code (1952–). English law has arguably followed a similar trajectory, although it lacks equivalent way-markers.

individual autonomy at its core, adapted where the classical law account of contracting departed most obtrusively from the reality of contracting practice; in American law this adaptation was partly achieved through using doctrines such as unconscionability and good faith. For Macneil, the primary problem with neo-classical contract law is that its doctrines and principles, being based in the classical law, provide an explanation of contractual obligation as rooted in consent and agreement which fails to recognise the extent to which many contractual obligations are based in norms which are socially derived.

A consequence of the dominance of consent and agreement as organising principles was, in Macneil's view, that unconscionability was 'peripheral' and 'hovered around the edges' of the neo-classical law.[14] In a sense, unconscionability was stranded; it was difficult to confine within the agreement-based conceptual structure of neo-classical law, yet there was no alternative body of principle which provided a more hospitable means of expression.

Some aspects of unconscionability are easier to square with agreement-based concepts than others. The modern development of unconscionability in American law has included not only procedural but also substantive unconscionability, although it is the former which is accommodated most readily within agreement-based concepts. Procedural unconscionability takes account of defects in the bargaining process; these are expressed as vitiating factors, and typically involve wrongdoing by a defendant which can be treated as undermining the consent of the claimant, thus bringing unconscionability under the umbrella of the conceptual structure of the neo-classical law. In contrast, substantive unconscionability refers to unfairness in the content of terms, and not some defect in the process of contract formation. Some cases under the unconscionability provision of the Universal Commercial Code (UCC) have adopted a predominantly substantive approach, although this use of unconscionability has remained controversial amongst commentators; the fault line seems to be whether it is legitimate to treat substantive unfairness as sufficient on its own for unconscionability to be used to overturn a contract.[15]

[14] 'Relational Contract Theory: Challenges and Queries' (1999) 94 *Northwestern University Law Review* 877, n. 113.

[15] See the contrasting views in four of the leading articles: A. Leff, 'Unconscionability and the Code – The Emperor's New Clause' (1967) 115 *University of Pennsylvania Law Review* 485; M. Ellighaus, 'In Defense of Unconscionability' (1969) 78 *Yale Law Journal* 757; R. Epstein, 'Unconscionabilty: A Critical Reappraisal' (1975) 18 *Journal of Law and Economics* 293; M. Eisenberg, 'The Bargain Principle and its Limits' (1982) 95 *Harvard Law Review* 741.

As a matter of principle, this fault line seems fundamental: on it depends the degree of advantage taking which the law permits in market relations, i.e. whether the parties merely have to abstain from overreaching behaviour, or whether they must go further and refrain from striking terms which appear unfair (at least with benefit of hindsight), despite the absence of overreaching behaviour.[16] However, although the principle at stake seems stark enough, in application the distinction can become muddied. This is because the fact of a glaring imbalance in the parties' respective obligations, instead of being seen as a sufficient reason on its own to set a contract aside, may be treated by a court as *evidence* of impaired consent by the claimant or overreaching behaviour by the defendant (or indeed both).[17] Given the gravitational force which concepts of consent and agreement can arguably exert on neo-classical contract law, it would hardly be surprising if concerns grounded in substantive unfairness more readily find expression in the more orthodox concepts which define procedural defect.

One consequence of the tendency of the neo-classical law to ground the rules where possible in the classical concepts is that reference to the wider transactional context has been muffled. If a purely procedural notion of unconscionability is adopted, it seems inevitable that the rules will focus on the acts of wrongdoing by the defendant which result in an undermining of the consent of the claimant, and in principle the presence or absence of these elements does not depend on the particularities of the kind of transaction in question. However, at the level of application, these tests can create practical difficulty. For example, establishing whether a claimant's will was overborne, or whether the defendant had exerted undue influence, involves assessing actual mental states of the parties, which of course is an inherently problematic exercise.

One response to the difficulty of proof is to treat the substantive fairness of the transaction as a practical indicator of procedural unconscionability.

[16] Those arguing that procedural unconscionability is essential have also had to reckon with a substantial body of mainly older case law where unconscionability was used to set aside transactions on grounds that were substantive rather than procedural. Much of this case law concerns gifts or transfers were the parties are not at arm's length, and this seems to have led to this body of law being marginalised in modern discussions of the application of contract to ordinary market transactions. The classic study is L. Sheridan, *Fraud in Equity* (London: Pitman, 1957); see R. W. Clark *Inequality of Bargaining Power* (Toronto: Carswell, 1987) 248.

[17] See below *Credit Lyonnais* v. *Burch* [1997] 1 All ER 144.

Another response to this difficulty is to make it easier in certain circumstances to establish that consent had been interfered with by the defendant's wrongdoing. The most well-known example of this is where undue influence is presumed by virtue of a pre-existing relationship of confidence, as a result of which the burden is then on the defendant to show that undue influence was not present. Although this just involves a switch in the burden of proof rather than any change in governing principle, I argue below that in fact it is an example of a distinctive approach to the question of unconscionability which has much wider significance. It is characterised by the way in which the heightened risks to the claimant, posed by features of the contractual context, become the reason for the law to adopt a different approach to assessing the validity of a contract. Moreover, this approach is more explicit in taking account of contextual factors, and I argue that the special rules which spread within and beyond the neo-classical law to handle contractual risk are an important way in which the law has taken context into account when addressing unconscionability issues.

3. Two models of unconscionability

The individual conduct model and the contractual risk model contain contrasting approaches adopted by the law when assessing the validity of a transaction on grounds of actual or suspected unconscionability; they can be applied to regulation which affects private rights, as well as judge-made law. The essence of the distinction can be stated shortly. In the individual conduct model, a contract is presumed from evidence (e.g. signature) and the claimant then has to establish that the specific conduct of the parties meets the requirements of the general doctrines regarding vitiating factors. In the contractual risk model, the law places the burden on the defendant to establish the legitimacy of the transaction by showing that certain additional requirements have been met. These requirements stem from a perception of increased risk to parties in the claimant's position, and so result in a focus on risk in a category of situations, rather than just on the parties' conduct in the specific case; by fulfilling these requirements the defendant can show that the risk has not eventuated in the specific case. Three kinds of contractual risk recognised by the law are identified: personal characteristic risk, relational risk, and transactional risk. All of these result in an increased role for context compared with the individual conduct model, although this is greatest in the case of transactional risk.

The models are presented as ideal types, in that they are intended to describe the different techniques in a pure form. They are not intended to be descriptive of all doctrines or rules, some of which display elements of both individual conduct and contractual risk.[18] The account of the individual conduct model is relatively brief, mainly because it reflects orthodox understandings about how unconscionability doctrine is applied. After noting the key features of both models, the rest of this chapter is devoted to explicating and exploring the transactional risk model.

(a) *Individual conduct model*

This is the mainstream approach to unconscionability. In this model, the validity of the contract is put into question by the claimant seeking to prove the elements of doctrinal principles such as duress, misrepresentation, actual undue influence, unconscionable bargains, or unconscionable dealing. The focus can be either on the conduct of the defendant in engaging in some form of overreaching, or on the quality of the consent or agreement of the claimant: it thus includes both 'claimant sided' and 'defendant sided' approaches.[19]

In Macneil's terms, this approach to unconscionability is neo-classical, in that it sees the vitiating factors as reasons to qualify the normal expectation that parties will be bound by what they appear to agree. The departure from the governing principle of deriving the obligations from the agreement of the parties is confined to those situations where the specified conduct is demonstrated to be present; other situations remain undisturbed.

The focus on the conduct means that it is primarily a procedural conception of unconscionability which is in play; where some procedural defect in terms of consent or wrongdoing is alleged, the burden of proof lies on the party claiming that the contract is not fully binding. However, pursuing Macneil's insight about the minimal role of consent, there is another way of describing how the law on contract formation interacts with the burden of proof. The adoption of the objective approach to agreement means that the law does not require 'real' consent, in some subjective sense, to be proved. The rules of contract formation and

[18] For an example which displays elements of both, see the discussion below of *Commercial Bank of Australia* v. *Amadio* (1983) 151 CLR 447.

[19] See Birks and Chin, 'On The Nature of Undue Influence', n. 2 above, for discussion.

incorporation of terms prescribe what must be proved to establish a contract and its terms; a signature, although not necessary as a general rule, will almost invariably be sufficient. Although accounts of the law of contract do not usually regard it in this way, the presence of signed terms effectively creates a presumption that they represent the parties' agreement.[20] In general, neo-classical contract law requires vitiating factors to be established by proof of relevant individual conduct in specific circumstances; given the basic indicators such as signature, a binding contract is assumed unless there is evidence to the contrary.

Although the requirement that the claimant establish the presence of some vitiating factor is the standard approach, it is not the only one present within the law.

(b) Contractual risk model

The contractual risk model is based on the perception that in particular circumstances the degree of risk to the claimant is such that it is justified to require the defendant to demonstrate the legitimacy of the contract. Instead of the claimant having to establish specific evidence which leads to the contract being set aside, the defendant has to establish positive reasons why the contract should stand. This means that rules which adopt this approach are typically composed of two stages. Stage one involves defining some special category of contracts with features that create unusual risks for one party. Stage two is that enforceability by the party who would benefit from that risk is made conditional on specific requirements being met by that party. It is thus a reversal of the position in the individual conduct model, where a contract is presumed unless the claimant establishes the presence of a vitiating factor. Under the contractual risk model, there is effectively a presumption of no contract which has to be displaced by showing that the requirements have been met.

In switching the presumption about whether a contract is valid, the law is responding to the fact that the reasons for withholding validity are disproportionately associated with certain characteristics, with the result

[20] Scrutton LJ's famous dictum in *L'Estrange* v. *Graucob* to the effect that a party is bound by terms they have signed unless there is vitiating factor assumes that the burden is on the signer to prove the presence of a such a factor ([1934] 2 KB 394, 403); Maugham LJ referred to a presumption that a 'formal contract' contains the terms (404). The parol evidence rule – at least when it applies – reinforces this by providing that, if the contract is put into writing, oral evidence cannot be adduced to qualify those terms.

that a category of transactions where there is heightened risk are picked out for different treatment. I argue that is possible to identify three kinds of contractual risk which the law recognises as justifying a more favourable response (from the claimant's point of view). These are (a) personal characteristic risk, where the risk stems from the characteristics of particular categories of individuals; (b) relational risk, where the risk stems from a pre-existing relationship between the parties, and (c) transactional risk, where the risk stems from the nature of the transaction in question.

This focus on risk almost inevitably entails a greater focus on context: arguably, risk is inherently contextual. The relevance of context to risk stems from the fact that the idea of risk is about what may happen, not about what has happened in an individual case. The perception of risk of an adverse outcome in any specific instance depends upon perceiving that instance as part of a category of instances which together share characteristics which result in the heightened risk of an adverse outcome. Context is thus relevant in identifying these characteristics, although the context which is relevant is not the specific context of a particular transaction in dispute, but rather the category of transactions of which it is part.

(i) Personal characteristic risk

This kind of risk is where the law responds to the fact that the claimant falls into a specific category of persons who are taken to have characteristics which justify relaxing to some degree the classical assumption i.e. that a person to is to treated as bound by transactions to which they appear to agree. The clearest example of this is the law on contractual capacity as it applies to minors.

The law on minors' contracts is structured by a general presumption that a contract is not enforceable against a minor; this is subject to exceptions. The main exception is the sale of necessaries, where a supplier can claim a reasonable sum for goods that count as necessaries and for which the minor had a requirement when they were supplied.[21] Also, a contract of employment will be only be binding on the minor if it is for their overall benefit.[22] The evidential burden of satisfying all these qualifying conditions is on the party seeking to enforce the contract against the minor. This is an example of contractual risk

[21] Sale of Goods Act 1979, s. 3(3).

[22] E.g. *Chaplin* v. *Leslie Frewin (Publishers)* [1966] Ch 71.

which is seen as attaching to the whole category of minors' contracts, and which is perceived to stem from assumptions about the general characteristics of a category of persons (inexperience, lack of judgment or foresight etc.).

Note that the law, even when enforcing a minor's contract, is not concerned with the individual conduct of the parties in the making of the contract: it makes no difference whether, in a particular case, the supplier was guilty of wrongdoing, or whether the minor was mature for their years and capable of independent judgment. The test is wholly substantive; i.e. were the goods or services necessary for this minor, and was the contract of services for their overall benefit?

It may be objected that the law on minors contracts has nothing to do with unconscionability; it is, after all, categorised as an issue about capacity. However, although the legal categorisation is different, the underlying issue is the same. Minors are treated differently because of concerns about their competence to contract, and it precisely this concern which underlies some of the rules on unconscionability. Thus, in the case of mental impairment, the claimant has to show that the defendant knew of the disability *and* that this disability prevented them from understanding the transaction.[23] This falls squarely within the individual conduct model, and provides a clear contrast with the treatment of minors. The contrast thus lies in the legal technique which has been selected to handle the different category, rather than in the motivating concern for depriving a contract of effect.

The treatment of minors is not an example that the law has widely followed. The elderly, like mental patients, are not treated as an equivalent category and (unless they fall within the other two categories of risk) must prove the necessary elements of an unconscionable bargain, actual undue influence etc. However, the case law stemming from *Fry* v. *Lane*[24] on 'poor and ignorant persons' is an instance of a categorisation of personal characteristics which, in combination, with other factors, throws a burden of proof on the defendant. In *Fry* v. *Lane*, the claimants, who were to receive an interest under a will on the death of the testator's widow, sold the interest to the defendant. They were 'poor persons in a humble position', had no independent advice, and the sale was at an undervalue. When the widow died, they contested the transaction, and Kay J held that, where the sale is at an undervalue, 'the

[23] The leading modern authority is *Hart* v. *O'Connor* [1985] AC 1000.

[24] (1887) 40 Ch D 312.

circumstances of poverty and ignorance of the vendor, and absence of independent advice, throw upon the purchaser, when the transaction is impeached, the onus of proving . . . that the purchase was fair, just, and reasonable.'[25]

Compared with minors' contracts, this principle requires the claimant to establish more primary facts before the burden is shifted; in the case of minors the simple fact of minority is sufficient. However, once the three factors are established, the burden shifts so that the claimant does not have to prove any overreaching conduct on the part of the defendant, nor that they did not understand the specific transaction.

(ii) Relational risk

This kind of risk arises where the nature of the pre-existing relationship between the defendant and claimant was such that there is a risk that the claimant will be disadvantaged; although this kind of risk may overlap on particular facts with personal characteristic risk, its nature is nonetheless distinct.

The central example of relational risk is presumed undue influence. There are two conditions which must be met for this presumption to arise. The first is that a relationship of trust and confidence exists between the parties: this may arise automatically i.e. because the relationship has been recognised as such by the law (e.g. solicitor/client) or it may be proved by the claimant on the specific facts. The second is that the transaction must be either a 'manifest disadvantage' to the claimant, or at least 'call for explanation'.[26] Once the claimant has established these, the defendant must show that the transaction was not procured by their undue influence. There have been two main categories of situation where the doctrine has been applied. One is where the trust placed in the defendant stems from an established professional relationship, such as solicitor/client; the other is where the defendant has some close relationship with the claimant based on family or friendship. In both sorts of case, the rationale for the rule is based on risk: because the defendant is in a position to influence the claimant in relation to (for example) the disposal of property, he must demonstrate that a transaction with

[25] Ibid., 322.

[26] The latter term was favoured in *Royal Bank of Scotland* v. *Etridge (No. 2)* [2001] UKHL 44.

him, which is disadvantageous to the claimant, was not tainted by such influence.[27]

The context where the law on undue influence has been most often argued in recent times is that of three-party undue influence, i.e. those cases involving the guarantee of a bank loan where a non-commercial surety provides security for the debt of another. Although this application of undue influence continues to involve relational risk, I argue that it has also introduced a further dimension of risk which stems from the nature of the transaction – called here transactional risk.

(iii) Transactional risk

Transactional risk arises where the nature of the transaction itself creates an increased risk that the claimant will suffer disadvantage. On its own, this is, of course, a very large category, and its scope depends on how increased risk is measured. However, it becomes manageable if we confine the focus to those situations where the law adopts a contractual risk approach, and it is plausible to suppose that transactional risk is at least one of the factors responsible for requiring the defendant to establish the legitimacy of the transaction. Although the main example explored below is that of the non-commercial surety, it is also apparent both in pre-classical contract doctrine and in modern examples of legislative regulation.

Possibly the earliest instance of the law singling out a species of transaction because of its inherent risk was that of catching bargains. These were typically loans where the borrower agreed to pay back a much larger sum when they received an anticipated inheritance, or when an interest in remainder came into possession; the transaction could also be framed as a sale of the future interest. From the late seventeenth century courts of equity refused to enforce such transactions with expectant heirs unless full value was given in return, and this protection was extended to contracts anticipating interests in remainder.[28] The burden of proof was on the person dealing with the expectant to establish there was full value.

[27] Mindy Chen-Wishart has argued that the debate between claimant-sided and defendant-sided theories is sterile, and that a relational analysis offers a better understanding. She sees the norms of the pre-existing relationship as the basis of undue influence: 'they trigger implicit relational norms about how people in such relationships treat each other': 'Undue Influence: Beyond Impaired Consent and Wrongdoing towards a Relational Analysis', in A. Burrows and A. Rodger (eds.), *Mapping the Law* (Oxford University Press, 2006).

[28] For detailed account of the development see Clark, *Inequality of Bargaining Power*, n. 16 above, Ch. 1, and Sheridan, *Fraud in Equity*, n. 16 above, 132–45.

Catching bargains were treated differently because of the risks that were perceived to be posed to one side: it seems that the risk was seen to lie in a combination of an heir being poorly off, in 'necessitous circumstances',[29] and the fact that it was an expectancy which was being pledged in return, not something which was immediately available to the heir.[30] The feature of a person in need selling a future interest was seen as the basis of the extension to remainders,[31] and it was when Romilly MR attempted to extended the rule yet further to apply to interests in possession that the rule was changed by the Sale of Reversions Act 1867.[32] This provided that 'no purchase made bona fide and without fraud or unfair dealing of any reversionary interest in real or personal estate shall hereafter be opened or set aside merely on ground of undervalue'. Although this section was initially interpreted in a restrictive way,[33] it meant that heirs and those with an interest in remainder were no longer treated as a special category where the defendant had to establish that the sale was not at an undervalue.

Examples from modern legislative regulation include contracts that are subject to 'cooling off' periods. The cooling off period has become a widely used regulatory technique in consumer protection, and has been applied to contracts concluded off trade premises, distance selling, sale of timeshares, and sale of extended warranties on domestic electrical goods.[34] The usual technique adopted is to require that, after a contract has been signed, the consumer is given written notice of their right to cancel the contract within the prescribed period. The consumer not only has the right to cancel within that period, but may cancel at any time if they did not receive the written notice of their right to cancel at the required time.

[29] Clark, n. 16 above, 3–5, citing Lord Hardwicke in *Barnardiston* v. *Lingood* (1740) 2 Atk 133.

[30] The catching bargain cases suggest that eighteenth and nineteenth century judges were aware of the irrationally low value that could be placed on future benefits. This phenomenon is now labelled 'hyperbolic discounting' in behavioural economics; see discussion below.

[31] *Gowland* v. *De Faria* (1810) 17 Ves 20 per Grant MR.

[32] *Webster* v. *Cook* (1867) 2 Ch App 542, where the sale was of a life interest in possession; Romilly was reversed on appeal.

[33] *Earl of Aylesford* v. *Morris* (1871) 8 Ch App 484.

[34] Consumer Protection (Cancellation of Contracts Concluded away from Business Premises) Regulations 1987; Consumer Protection Distance Selling Regulations 2000; Timeshare Regulations 1997; Supply of Extended Warranties on Electrical Goods Order 2005.

A much more robust form of regulatory protection is visible in the provisions for the execution of a compromise agreement by an employee. If an employee's agreement to forego employment protection rights is to be effective, strict requirements must be met, including the provision of independent advice by an advisor who has indemnity insurance, and who comes within the categories of advisor prescribed in the legislation.[35]

In both the catching bargain example and these regulatory examples, the law has not created a presumption of wrongdoing which can be rebutted: it simply specifies the legal consequences which will flow from certain facts. As a result, there is no enquiry into the reality of consent or whether wrongdoing was present. Although the policy behind cooling off periods has been explained in terms of combating high pressure selling, the legal rules take no account of whether, in an individual case, such behaviour actually occurred. Thus, in these instances of transactional risk, the law is concerned with the *risk* of disadvantage in a category of transactions, rather than with whether that risk eventuated in a specific case.

These examples of transactional risk are ones where the legal tests employed have been decoupled from the question of the reality of consent or wrongdoing; they provide a contrast with the leading example of relational risk, where it remains open to the defendant to rebut a presumption of undue influence. Here, although the law is adopting a contractual risk approach, in that the defendant must surmount additional hurdles to justify the transaction, it remains possible in theory for the defendant to retrieve the position by adducing the appropriate evidence.

Despite this contrast with the modern law of undue influence and the fact that the examples have been drawn from either pre-classical doctrine or modern legislation, transactional risk can be seen as an important dimension in the development of modern doctrine. This is evident in the treatment of non-commercial sureties, explored in some detail below.

4. The treatment of non-commercial sureties: the emergence of transactional risk from undue influence

The development of the special rules for non-commercial sureties marks a significant departure in the modern approach to unconscionability. This departure can be seen as a shift of emphasis from one kind of

[35] Employment Rights Act 1996, s. 203.

contractual risk to another: from relational risk to transactional risk. To explain and develop this point, some detailed analysis of the evolution of the position reached in *Royal Bank of Scotland* v. *Etridge (No. 2)*[36] is necessary.[37]

(a) The approach in Barclays Bank *v.* O'Brien *and* Royal Bank of Scotland *v.* Etridge (No. 2)

The fact pattern in the non-commercial surety cases is well known. A principal debtor (usually the husband) runs a business which needs to borrow money from a bank. The debtor wishes a friend or relation (usually the spouse) to provide security for the loan in the form of a charge over property, typically the family home. Later, when the business has failed, the bank takes legal proceedings to realise the security by having the property sold. This is resisted by the surety, claiming that he/she was pressurised by the debtor to sign the charge, or that the facts were misrepresented.

The 1980s saw a steady increase in reported decisions, leading to the House of Lords' decision in *Barclays Bank* v. *O'Brien*[38] in 1994. In *O'Brien*, Lord Browne-Wilkinson framed the issue as one of achieving a balance between two purposes; the need to enable the wealth in owner-occupied homes to be used as collateral for business loans, and the need to protect sureties from undue influence that may arise within an intimate relationship, especially when the husband faces acute financial problems. In doctrinal terms, this was achieved by adapting the equitable principles of undue influence and the doctrine of notice.

The decision in *O'Brien* did not stem the flow of appeal cases and the issue was revisited by the House of Lords in *Etridge*. It was held that if the surety could establish (a) that the transaction was one which called for explanation, and (b) he/she placed trust and confidence in the principal debtor, then an evidential presumption of undue influence was raised which, if not rebutted, would enable the surety to treat the transaction with the lender as voidable unless the lender took certain steps. If the

[36] [2001] UKHL 44.

[37] For an interesting discussion of the surety situation in terms of risk and moral hazard, see R. Mackenzie, 'Vulnerable Providers of Security, Risk Management and Moral Hazard: Independent Legal Advice after *Barclays Bank v O'Brien, Massey v Midland Bank plc* & *Clark Boyce v Mouat*', in R. Baldwin, and P. Cane (eds.), *Law and Uncertainty: Risks and Legal Processes* (Kluwer, 1997) 313.

[38] [1994] 1 AC 180.

lender relied on independent advice, then the provision of the advice had to comply with requirements that were set out in some detail.[39]

The ruling in *Etridge* effectively amounts to a code of conduct with which a lender will need to comply if they wish to be able to rely with confidence on the security provided by a surety being realisable. Although the cases in *Etridge* all concerned spouses, it was also held that the code applied not just to those in an intimate relationships, but to *all* non-commercial sureties: it was not practical to expect lenders to detect when there was a risk of undue influence in particular cases, and it was difficult, without the risk of arbitrary exclusion, to define a subset of non-commercial sureties.[40]

The decision in *Etridge* received a mixed response; although it was welcomed as providing a clearer statement of what was expected of lenders and advisors, some critics felt it did not go far enough in protecting potentially vulnerable sureties. The focus here, however, is not directly on the merits of the ruling itself, but rather on the form which this development of the law on undue influence has taken.

(b) *The distinctiveness of the* Etridge *solution*

The position reached in *Etridge* marked a significant departure from the relational risk approach in two-party undue influence; two features of this departure merit emphasis here. First, the requirement that undue influence (or other wrong) must be committed by the other party to the contract was relaxed. Instead, once the court has concluded, with the assistance of an evidential presumption in appropriate cases, that undue influence was committed by the third party (the principal debtor), then the focus is on the circumstances in which this undue influence will affect the validity of the transaction with the lender. Although this was a radical step, it was achieved by using an old conceptual mechanism: the doctrine of notice. The adoption of this approach in *O'Brien* had been widely

[39] These steps were: (a) the lender had to explain to the surety that they would need written confirmation from a solicitor that the surety had had the proposed transaction explained fully to them; (b) the solicitor must then explain their role in providing advice; (c) the solicitor must explain the possible consequences, including an assessment of the financial position of the principal debtor, for which purpose he must be supplied with information by the lender; (d) the solicitor must emphasise that the surety has a free chioce; (e) with the surety's agreement, the solicitor then confirms in writing to the lender that these steps have been taken (see *Etridge (No. 2)* [2001] UKHL 44, 65 per Lord Nicholls).

[40] Ibid., para. 87.

criticised as inappropriate, and Lord Nicholls recognised that it was a clear departure from its established meaning.[41]

In one sense, speaking of 'notice' of the wrongdoing tends to preserve the notion that undue influence is operating in the usual way; the notice element is just transferring the effect from principal debtor to lender. However, this way of putting it is, so to speak, going round two sides of a square when, in effect, the law has taken the diagonal path. The *Etridge* approach imposes a contractual responsibility on defendants when they have not themselves committed an act which amounts to a vitiating factor: a responsibility to guard against the possibility of wrongdoing by another. This aspect does not seem to have been remarked upon, and it may be that the use of a doctrine which, in other circumstances, defines illegitimate advantage taking by a defendant has helped to obscure the degree of novelty involved. In any event, it is extremely unusual for the judge-made law of contract to impose an obligation on one party to protect another where there is neither wrongdoing by the defendant nor a pre-existing or fiduciary relationship between the parties.

The second distinctive feature is the focus on a detailed specification of the steps a lender needs to take to avoid being affected by any wrong-doing by the principal debtor. In the two-party undue influence cases, the party in whom the other placed trust and confidence is typically unable to rebut the presumption because there was nothing resembling independent advice; judges have not spelt out, in those cases, what precisely must be done. However, in *O'Brien*, Lord Browne-Wilkinson spelt out what should be done: the lender had to meet the surety on their own, explain the effects of the transaction, and recommend that they seek legal advice. In *Etridge* it was recognised that lenders were reluctant to hold such meetings, and, to avoid any doubt of the sort that followed *O'Brien*, even more detailed steps were set out, describing precisely how the surety should receive advice from a solicitor.

Although the spelling out of the detailed steps may appear as a fleshing out of the idea of independent advice in two-party cases, its legal significance is different. Where the steps are taken by the lender, they

[41] Ibid., paras. 38–41. The doctrine was applied beyond its original meaning in relation to the purchase of defective title, where a purchaser with actual or constructive notice of a defect in the title takes the property subject to it. In contrast, in the surety context there is no issue of title, and the presence of notice determines whether the surety transaction is affected by the wrongdoing of the third party. Also, when the lender is put on enquiry, the steps are not designed to elicit information, but rather are intended to minimise the risk that a wrong is committted.

do not rebut the presumption of undue influence: they simply determine whether the lender is affected by the undue influence on the part of the principal debtor which has, as a matter of evidence, already been established. In contrast, in two-party cases, effective independent advice will have the effect of rebutting the presumption.

These two departures only seem explicable on the basis that the courts have responded to transactional risk, i.e. risks which are inherently part of the non-commercial surety relationship. The *Etridge* solution means that the surety arrangement can be set aside even where the defendant lender has no knowledge of undue influence by the principal debtor, and cannot be said to be at fault for not having such knowledge. It is therefore unavoidable that the scope of the defendant's responsibility for guarding against risks they have not themselves created will be defined in terms in which wrongdoing by the lender does not figure.

Once the protection required by the law against transactional risk goes beyond the avoidance of wrongdoing by the defendant, it also becomes inevitable that the law articulates what it expects to be done to avoid the risk; this means that the law's primary identification of contracting behaviour is at the level of transaction type to which the special requirements apply. The law here is being applied to a routine commercial transaction, which is in contrast to two-party undue influence, where the transactions are either gifts, or aberrant cases of contracts where the relationship of trust and confidence is used for commercial advantage, e.g. within a family, or between solicitor and client.

It is instructive to compare these distinctive features of *Etridge* with the approach adopted by the High Court of Australia to effectively the same fact pattern. In *Commercial Bank of Australia* v. *Amadio*,[42] the majority of the court applied the doctrine of unconscionable dealing where an elderly couple, with limited understanding of written English, had executed a mortgage securing the debts of their son's company. Although the charge was to be for an unlimited amount and time, the son had told them it was confined to $50,000 for a duration of six months; the bank became aware of this. Applying *Blomley* v. *Ryan*,[43] the court held that, if the parents could show they were subject to a special disability which was evident to the bank, the burden was then on the bank to show why it was not unconscionable to enforce the charge;

[42] (1983) 151 CLR 447.

[43] (1956) 99 CLR 362, where the sale of a farm by its elderly owner when intoxicated was set aside.

the court found for the parents. Even though the switch of the burden is characteristic of the contractual risk approach, individual conduct seems to be the main trigger, in particular the fact that the disability was evident to the defendant.[44] The result thus offers a sharp contrast with *Etridge*, where knowledge is irrelevant to the defendant's liability.[45]

(c) *The attenuated role of wrongdoing*

It was suggested above that the novelty of relaxing the requirement of wrongdoing by the defendant may have been obscured to a degree by the application of the language of undue influence in relation to the conduct of the principal debtor. Although it remains formally necessary for the claimant to establish undue influence by the principal debtor, it is striking how attenuated this requirement has become.

After *O'Brien*, it sometimes seemed that pleading undue influence was little more than a formality. Lawyers acting for sureties would argue that because (a) there was an intimate relationship between surety and principal debtor, and (b) the surety relied on the principal debtor for all financial decisions, a presumption of undue influence by the principal debtor was thereby raised.[46] Given that the principal debtor (i.e. typically the husband) could easily find it is his interests to confirm that the surety had indeed placed trust and confidence in him, the lender who had not taken the required steps (or met their object in some other way) would find it very difficult to adduce evidence to prove a negative, i.e. that undue influence was not present.[47] Peter Birks, writing between the decisions in *O'Brien* and *Etridge*, saw the allegation of undue influence in the pleadings as a formulaic 'recitation' which 'resembled the dead words of the old forms of action'.[48] He argued that the principle that was emerging from the case law was simply that the transaction could be set aside unless the lender took the prescribed safeguards, and that this could

[44] Personal characteristic risk was one factor in the finding of a special disability; Deane J referred to the claimants' age, limited English, as well as the circumstances in which the document was presented for signature, and lack of understanding of the document (477).

[45] The court was unable to consider the implications of undue influence by the son as this was not contained in the pleadings.

[46] It was argued that the manifest disadvantage element was met because the suretyship was one-sided.

[47] See *Barclays Bank* v. *Boulter* [1997] 2 All ER 1002.

[48] 'The Burden on The Bank', in F. Rose (ed.), *Restitution and Banking Law* (Oxford: Mansfield Press, 1998) 196.

and should be stated without any reference to undue influence or the doctrine of notice.[49]

The House of Lords in *Etridge* expressed some concern about the readiness with which undue influence was presumed in some circumstances, and emphasised that the surety transaction must be one 'calling for explanation', and that any 'presumption' of undue influence was purely evidential. However, the ease with which undue influence could be established was explicitly geared to the degree of apparent substantive unfairness: 'the greater the disadvantage to the vulnerable person, the more cogent must be the explanation before the presumption will be regarded as rebutted.'[50] An example of how easy it will be to raise (and difficult to rebut) the presumption in a case of serious disadvantage is the Court of Appeal's decision (expressly approved by the House of Lords) in *Credit Lyonnais* v. *Burch*.[51] There, a young employee provided an unlimited guarantee of her employer's business debts, secured on the equity in her flat (her only asset), and the court readily concluded there was undue influence by the principal debtor, despite the lack of any specific evidence that the employee relied on her employer in such matters.[52]

Undue influence is normally regarded as a procedural test which is triggered when a threshold of substantive unfairness is crossed (either 'manifest disadvantage', or a transaction 'calling for explanation'). But it seems at least arguable that, when applied to the conduct of the third party in the surety transaction, the crucial issue is the degree of substantive unfairness. At least in the more egregious cases (like *Burch*), it seems the law after *Etridge* is not far from the position advocated by Birks, i.e. whether the contract is set aside should depend on whether the defendant lender has taken the prescribed safeguards. To the extent this is true, it becomes a purer form of the transactional risk approach.

(d) Transactional risk and regulation

It has already been noted that the transactional risk approach is detectable in some instances of legislative regulation, and it is striking that the *Etridge* solution resembles regulation in some key respects.

49 Ibid., 195.

50 *Royal Bank of Scotland v Etridge (No. 2)* [2001] UKHL 44, 24 (Lord Nicholls).

51 [1997] 1 All ER 144.

52 Millett LJ held that a relationship of trust and confidence could be inferred from the mere fact of the transaction; ibid., 154.

The ruling is designed to be pre-emptive, setting out how adverse consequences, unwelcome to both lender and putative surety, can be avoided. A consequence of the pre-emptive nature of the ruling is that there is a break with the orthodox way in which private law doctrine is engaged with a set of facts. Typically, rules of contract law are specified in general terms which then have to be applied to specific facts *ex post*, i.e. at a point in time after the events in question have occurred. Where lawyers advise clients (usually commercial) about how to plan their transactions to avoid undesirable consequences, it will involve a process of predicting how a court would apply law in the various possible scenarios that might arise – aptly described by Macneil as 'looking forward to the court's looking backward'.[53] The result of *O'Brien* and the *Etridge* is to substantially change this process. The focus of the ruling is *ex ante*: it sets out how the process of entering the transaction should be carried out in order to avoid it being tainted by undue influence or other wrong. This short circuits the usual process, in that lenders, and solicitors retained by sureties, are told what they need to do directly, without it having to be deduced from a prediction of how the court would apply a general doctrine to the facts of a particular case.

This *ex ante* approach also characterises regulation that engages directly with the enforceability of a transaction. Cooling off periods, or the rules about compromise agreements, all provide a detailed focus on how these categories of transactions are to be made. Arguably, a precondition of this *ex ante* focus is identication of risk across a category of transactions.

5. Some implications of transactional risk

The foregoing analysis has identified transactional risk as a factor in the law's treatment of the validity of contracts. Some implications of the argument remain to be explored, although space constraints mean that I can do little more than outline some of those implications here; further analysis of these issues will be pursued in a separate article.

(a) The nature and incidence of transactional risk

So far, the discussion of transactional risk has treated it as a feature of particular kinds of transaction where the law has placed the burden on

[53] *Contracts: Exchange Relations and Transactions* (1978), in Campbell, *Relational Theory of Contract*, n. 4 above, 356.

the defendant of establishing that the contract is legitimate. Although this is sufficient for the purposes of establishing transactional risk as a category, it raises the question of the nature of transactional risk: what is it about particular types of transaction that results in the law effectively flipping the presumption, so that the defendant has to establish its legitimacy? If these features can be clarified, it then becomes possible to begin to identify other transactions where it may be argued that the law should adopt a similar approach. Three possible approaches are outlined below.

The first approach is to attempt to identify elements which are common to the various contexts where transactional risk has already been identified. An analysis of the instances discussed in this chapter suggests that three elements figure prominently. The strongest common feature is that, whilst benefit to the claimant from the transaction may be immediate, the claimant's own performance is postponed into the future: this figures in the non-commercial surety cases, catching bargains, and in some of the contracts subject to cancellation within cooling off periods. The second element is a degree of transactional complexity which makes it more than usually difficult for the claimant to make an informed judgement about what is in their interests. Combined with the element of futurity, this may mean, as in the non-commercial surety example, that the precise performance that will be required of the claimant may be contingent on uncertain events the occurrence of which is difficult to calculate at the time of entering the transaction. The third element is a clear disparity between the parties in terms of their experience of entering such transactions. Given the elements of complexity and futurity, claimants are at a disadvantage in the process of negotiation because they are likely to be (at least initially) unaware of the existence or nature of pitfalls which are well understood by defendants.

These features mean that 'one shot' players will find it especially difficult to make sound judgements in the absence of independent advice. Without such advice, there can be something approaching a trap which requires parties to tread very carefully. This creates the clear opportunity for defendants (or a third party) to take advantage of the fact that claimants may not be in a position to act in their best interests.

The problem with this sort of approach to identifying the risk associated with certain transaction patterns is that, even if it is agreed that the selected features do seem to correlate with transactional risk, it still lacks any theoretical view of *why* these features should result in the law exacting these additional requirements. One theoretical account, which in some respects looks well suited to assessing transactional risk, is that offered by behavioural economics. When applied to law, this approach departs from traditional law and economics because it sees the role of law as doing more than responding to the familiar sources of market failure such as transaction costs, lack of competition or lack of information. It takes seriously the idea that individuals' ability to act rationally in their own interests can frequently be attenuated by common cognitive and behavioural traits. This has resulted in a large literature which attempts to establish experimentally the various systematic biases to which people may be subject when entering transactions. Examples include framing, which is the tendency for the way a decision is presented to affect the choice that is made, and hyperbolic discounting, which is the tendency to undervalue future opportunities or consequences compared with those available more immediately.

Because these biases relate to the nature of choices, and how they are presented, some transaction patterns will be more likely to trigger them; they can thus be treated as identifying a form of transactional risk. Commentators have argued on this basis for regulatory reforms involving devices such as cooling off periods, default rules, or enhanced informational requirements.[54]

Although behavioural economics offers a sophisticated analysis of some sources of transactional risk, its nature as ultimately a part of neo-classical economics means that its normative orientation remains limited.[55] Even where choice is subject to biasing effects, consent in some de-biased form remains the touchstone. In particular, behavioural economics is not oriented to address the larger normative question of what obligations are owed when an organisation that is very familiar with the pitfalls (and opportunities for exploitation) of a particular transaction routinely deals with parties who are traversing those pitfalls for the first time; this is ultimately a question about the form of exchange morality which is to be expressed in the law. Nevertheless, a question that deserves

[54] The literature is voluminous, see especially: C. Sunstein and R. Thaler, 'Libertarian Paternalism is not an Oxymoron' (2003) 70 *University of Chicago Law Review* 1159, and C. Camerer *et al.* 'Regulation for Conservatives and the Case for Assymetric Paternalism' (2003) 151 *University of Pennsylvania Law Review* 1211. Useful overview: Iain Ramsay, *Consumer Law and Policy* (Oxford: Hart Publishing, 2007) 71.

[55] A key limit stems from the imperative within neo-classical economics to address a serious concern about paternalism; see e.g. the critique of libertarian paternalism in G. Mitchell, 'Libertarian Paternalism is an Oxymoron' (2005) 99 *Northwestern University Law Review* 1245.

exploration is how far the biases identified by behavioural economics can inform the application of a contractual morality which is not confined by the presuppositions of neo-classical economics.

In contrast, it is also possible to use relational theory, my starting point for the focus on contractual risk in general and transactional risk in particular, to construct a very different analysis of the issue of transactional risk. Relational theory emphasises the importance of norms that are derived from the parties' own transactional context; these can include the parties' own established understandings, and the practices of a community of regular contractors of which they are part. There has been an increasing recognition among commentators on English law that contract law can reflect these implicit dimensions of contractual relationships through existing doctrine, notably implied terms and the contextual interpretation of written terms.[56] In similar vein, I have argued that the implicit understandings in contracting communities can play a key role in 'taming' the operation of standard form contracts.[57] The claim is that this occurs through the shaping and dissemination of understandings about how terms will be treated in practice – e.g. which terms are meant seriously, how disputes over them will be resolved. These understandings not only provide the context for resolving issues about performance, but also provide the background against which contracts are made; although express agreement can settle the details of a particular transaction, the understanding of and agreement to complex standard forms does not derive so much from individual consent at each moment of formation but from the acquired familiarity with how the form is treated by other contracting parties.

If contextual norms and practices play this role in rendering standard forms workable pieces of self-regulation by a contracting community, they critically depend on the existence of the social processes constituted by regular mutual economic interaction. Once one turns to the features of transactional risk noted above, it is striking that we are dealing with a very different picture. The transactions are of significant complexity, but, because the claimants are not part of a contracting community, there are great disparities in familiarity and experience; one party is typically

[56] See D. Campbell and H. Collins, 'Discovering the Implicit Dimensions of Contracts', in D. Campbell, H. Collins and J. Wightman (eds.), *Implicit Dimensions of Contract* (Oxford: Hart, 2003).

[57] J. Wightman, 'Beyond Custom: Contract, Contexts, and the Recognition of Implicit Understandings', ibid., 143, 168–171.

ignorant of the whole nature of the transaction until they are presented with it for the first time. Seen in this way, it is the *absence* of implicit or background understandings which prevents the inexperienced party participating fully in the formation of the contract.

This presents a contrast with the way that behavioural economics diagnoses transactional risk. There, the focus is on biases in decision-making which stem from cognitive or behavioural traits which get in the way of rational choice. The relational analysis suggests that there would be serious problems in expecting inexperienced contractors to participate fully in the agreement of the contract *even if the cognitive and behavioural biases were removed.*

Thus, although we may be able to identify in broad terms the features that are associated with transactional risk, it seems that how one pins down the precise source of that risk depends on how one regards the foundation of contractual obligation, especially the role ascribed to consent.

(b) *Transactional risk and rationales of unconscionability*

Does adopting a transactional risk approach have implications for the grounds on which a contract is to be set aside? The fact that the overall contractual risk model is defined in terms of legal technique (rather than substantive reasons) suggests that the model is not *inherently* confined to expressing particular sorts of justification for setting a contract aside.

One possibility is that the choice of technique is a purely practical matter, which does not register any change in justifying principle, but merely strikes a balance about whether it is better to have a rule which is under- or over-inclusive in its application.[58] However, it is only possible to describe a rule as under- or over-inclusive by reference to the policy or principle which is claimed to underlie it. It thus possible that, where a new rule , based upon a transactional risk approach, ends up protecting claimants in more situations, it may be explicable on the basis that this extra protection is not the inevitable (but unwanted) by product of an over-inclusive rule, but rather the desired outcome which is justified by a principle more protective of the claimant. For example, the solution in

[58] For example, in his critique of unconscionability, Richard Epstein recognised that having a general rule that minors contracts were not enforceable against the minor was over-inclusive, but justified on the basis that it was the least costly overall: 'Unconscionabilty: A Critical Reappraisal' (1975) 18 *Journal of Law and Economics* 293, 300–1.

Etridge means that, where a lender fails to take the appropriate steps, a contract will be set aside if undue influence by the principle debtor is established, irrespective of whether the lender knew or ought to have known of the undue influence. In contrast, in the equivalent Australian case of *Commercial Bank of Australia* v. *Amadio*, where the individual conduct approach predominated, actual or constructive knowledge of the disability wrongdoing had to be proved.

This example suggests that a transactional risk approach is capable of reflecting rationales of unconscionability which are more protective of claimants than the procedural concerns of the individual conduct approach; in the case of the non-commercial surety, this is possible because a standard test of the prescribed steps is applied, detached from any issue about what the defendant knew or should have know in an individual case. However, it is nevertheless the case that the transactional risk approach – at least in the modern instances – takes a procedural view of the question of validity, albeit of a different kind to that associated with the neo-classical law. In the case of both non-commercial sureties and cancellation rights within cooling off periods, the right of defendants to enforce the contract is dependent on them taking steps which are intended to give the claimant an opportunity to reconsider the advisability of the transaction; they thus appear concerned directly with the reality of the claimant's consent. Although the thinness of this kind of protection can be criticised on the basis it offers insufficient protection in some cases, it seems typical of modern instances of the transactional risk approach. In contrast, the old catching bargain cases included the requirement that the defendant show they had paid 'full value' for the expectancy, and thus adopted a substantive test.

In summary, the transactional risk approach is neutral in terms of the reasons it may express for setting a contract aside. It contains both the potential to express norms which are merely a reflection of the overwhelmingly procedural concerns of the neo-classical law, but can also, as the case of the non-commercial surety shows, provide more protection by removing the need to prove knowledge or wrongdoing on the part of the defendant. The degree of protection, together with its underlying rationale, thus remains contestable within the transactional risk approach.

6. Conclusion

The purpose of this chapter has been to develop the idea that an approach based on contractual risk is visible in the law of unconscionability, and to identify a distinctive form of that risk – transactional risk – which is instantiated in the law on non-commercial sureties, and which is also apparent more generally, including in regulation. I have also attempted to explore, albeit in outline, possible ways in which the nature of transactional risk can be identified. However, the discussion of transactional risk has been confined to the situations where it appears to be a factor in the law requiring the defendant to establish the legitimacy of the transaction in ways that go beyond the simple assertion that the claimant entered the contract.

Although the focus on transactional risk has been confined for the purposes of the analysis above, it is clear from the insights of both behavioural economics and relational theory that the problems stemming from transactional risk are not confined to those cases where it registers most clearly in the law. An outstanding question is how far an approach based on the individual conduct model can cope satisfactorily with risks which are associated with a particular transaction type; I plan to explore this question further.

7

An economic perspective on legal remedies for unconscionable contracts

QI ZHOU

1. Introduction

The doctrine of unconscionability has been widely adopted in the law of contract by many jurisdictions.[1] It is a legal redress for a party who makes an unfair contract. In general, a contract is held to be unconscionable when the court believes that it contains one or more contractual terms which are substantially unfair to one party. A typical example is an add-on clause in a consumer credit sale which provides that all of the goods previously purchased by the buyer from the seller will be used as security for the debts incurred with the current purchase, and that a single default by the buyer could permit the seller to repossess all of the goods. Such a contractual term may be unenforceable in both the UK and the US, although the legal rules are based upon different grounds. In the US it contravenes Section 2–302 of the Uniform Commercial Code (UCC) and is treated as an unconscionable term. In the UK there is no doctrine of unconscionability in general contract law, but the legal consequence is the same for a different reason; the term violates Regulation 8 of the Unfair Terms in Consumer Contracts Regulations 1999. The same result can probably be reached in Germany for a breach of Article 138 of the German Civil Code (BGB).

The remedy for unconscionable contracts also varies from jurisdiction to jurisdiction. In the US, when a contract is held to be unconscionable, the court can declare that it is void *ab initio* and unenforceable, or replace

[1] Section 2–302 of the Uniform Commercial Code in the US, Article 1674 of Code Civil in France, Article 138 of BGB in Germany. Although there is no doctrine of unconscionability adopted in general English contract law, similar rules can be found in the law in relation to consumer transactions, e.g. Article 8 of the Unfair Terms in Consumer Contracts Regulations 1999.

the unconscionable term with a reasonable one.[2] English courts adopt similar remedies for unfair terms in consumer contracts, but have no power to replace the unconscionable term.[3] In German contract law, if a contract is held unconscionable in breach of Article 138(2) of the BGB, the whole contract is void *ab initio*.[4] In France, if a consumer contract contains an unconscionable term, the contract is avoidable rather than void *ab initio*; the consumer can rescind the contract in accordance with L132–1 of the Consumer Code. The same remedy can also be found in the UNIDROIT Principles of International Commercial Contracts.[5]

In brief, there are three contract law remedies adopted for unconscionable contracts: (1) invalidation of the whole contract; (2) judicial modification of the unconscionable term; and (3) rescission. Besides these three contractual remedies, there is a fourth option: damages in tort law. Although this has not been adopted by any main jurisdictions in the world, as a theoretical speculation, the law could make the overreaching party liable for writing the unconscionable contract and award damages to the aggrieved party.

Scholars of law and economics have produced a large amount of literature on the efficiency characteristics of the doctrine of unconscionability for the purpose of answering the normative question of whether or not it is efficient to have the doctrine in contract law. For example, Posner argues that the doctrine of unconscionability is economically justified for deterring welfare opportunistic behaviours, which cannot be avoided by traditional public laws.[6]

[2] Section 2–302 of the UCC provides: 'If the court as a matter of law finds the contract or any clause of the contract to have been unconscionable at the time it was made the court may refuse to enforce the contract, or it may enforce the remainder of the contract without the unconscionable clause, or it may so limit the application of any unconscionable clause as to avoid any unconscionable result.'

[3] Article 8 of the Unfair Terms in Consumer Contracts Regulations 1999 provides: '(1) An unfair term in a contract concluded with a consumer by a seller or supplier is not binding on the consumer. (2) The Contract shall continue to bind the parties if it is capable of continuing in existence without the unfair term.'

[4] Article 138(2) of BGB provides: 'In particular, a transaction by which a person exploits the position of constraint in which another person finds himself, or the inexperience, lack of discernment or substantial weakness of will of that other person, in order, for his own benefit advantage in return for the provision of a service which is markedly disproportionate to such provision, is void.'

[5] Article 3.10 of the UNIDROIT Principles provides: 'A party may avoid a contract or an individual term of it if, at the time of the conclusion of the contract, the contract or term unjustifiably gave the other party an excessive advantage.'

[6] E. Posner, 'Contract Law in the Welfare State: A Defence of the Unconscionability Doctrine, Usury Laws, and Related Limitations on the Freedom of Contract' (1995) 24 *Journal of Legal Studies* 283–319.

In contrast, Epstein claims that the cost to society of the doctrine exceeds the benefits; it is inefficient to afford the party a legal remedy if the contract was voluntarily concluded in the absence of fraud, mistake or duress.[7] Without further evidence offered by empirical research, theoretical debates continue and there is no answer to the question.[8]

Another stream in law and economics scholarship sidesteps the normative questions and focuses on the design of legal standards for the doctrine of unconscionability. Writings in this stream assume that the doctrine is economically justified; they are interested in the question of how an efficient legal standard can be designed for it. Korobkin applies a behavioural law and economics approach to the topic, suggesting that the doctrine of unconscionability should be adjusted to correct the contracting parties' bounded rationality.[9]

However, from an economic perspective, there are three crucial questions in relation to the doctrine of unconscionability. First, is the doctrine justified on the grounds of efficiency? Secondly, how can an efficient legal standard for unconscionable contracts be designed? Thirdly, how should the law choose legal remedies? Current scholars of law and economics have perhaps given too much of their attention to the first two questions, with little discussion of choice of remedies.[10] Yet the third question is of equal importance in practice. This chapter addresses the last question. Drawing upon the assumptions that the law of contract should embrace the doctrine of unconscionability and that the legal standard for unconscionable contracts is efficient, it explores the main economic features of each possible private law remedy for unconscionable contracts and offers some theoretical insights into choosing the most cost-effective remedy.

[7] R. Epstein, 'Unconscionability: A Critical Reappraisal' (1975) 18 *Journal of Law and Economics* 293–315; also see, A. Schwartz, 'A Reexamination of Nonsubstantive Unconscionability' (1977) 63 *Virginia Law Review* 1053–83, at 1070; R. Epstein, 'Unconscionability: A Critical Reappraisal' (1975) 18 *Journal of Law and Economics* 293–315, at 304.

[8] In one empirical study, Ostas showed that the US courts seem to follow economic reasoning when hearing unconscionable contract cases: D. Ostas, 'Predicting Unconscionable Decisions; An Economic Model and an Empirical Test' (1991) 29 *American Business Law Journal* 536–84.

[9] R. Korobkin, 'Bounded Rationality, Standard Form Contracts, and Unconscionability' (2003) 70 *The University of Chicago Law Review* 1203–95.

[10] Recently some scholars have switched their attention to legal remedy; e.g. R. Craswell, 'Property Rules and Liability Rules in Unconscionability and Related Doctrines' (1993) 60 *The University of Chicago Law Review* 1–65; O. Ben-Shahar, 'How to Repair Unconscionable Contracts' (2008) *Michigan Law Working Papers*, No. 07–023, available at www.ssrn.com/abstract=1082926.

The chapter proceeds as follows. Section 2 outlines the main economic arguments supporting and opposing the doctrine of unconscionability to provide some background knowledge for the economic analysis in the rest of the chapter. In section 3, a deterrence model of private law remedies is briefly presented. The model is applied to the analysis of two economic features of each possible remedy for unconscionable contract, viz. deterrence and impact on the incentive to trade. Section 4 concludes the chapter.

2. Economic debates on the doctrine of unconscionability

Traditional economic analysis suggests that self-interest equals public interest. This idea can be dated back to Adam Smith's famous argument of the 'invisible hand', which claims that when individuals pursue their own self-interest, they thereby promote the public interest.[11] Based upon this economic reasoning, it is argued that the law should enforce all voluntary contracts concluded by competent and informed persons, regardless of their distributional consequences.[12] In a perfectly functioning market with complete information, all contracts are efficient; there is no need for legal intervention in private contracting processes.[13] Assume that there are two types of seller of a homogeneous good: the first charges a high price with a long-term quality warranty, while the second charges a lower price with a short-term quality warranty. If buyers have an identical preference for a long-term warranty, all of them will patronise the first type of seller. Contracts concluded between them will be Pareto-efficient.[14] This drives the second type of seller either to offer a long-term warranty or to leave the market. Consequently, only sellers offering the long-term warranty can survive in the market, and all of the contracts are efficient. On the other hand, if buyers have different preferences, some preferring a long-term warranty while others do not, both types of seller will exist in the market, and buyers can patronise different sellers in accordance with their own preference. The contracts concluded are also Pareto-efficient. Therefore, there is no need for legal intervention in private contracting processes.

[11] R. Malloy, *Law in a Market Context*, 1st edn (Cambridge University Press, 2004) 27.

[12] A. Schwartz, 'The Enforceability of Security Interests in Consumer Goods' (1983) 26 *Journal of Law and Economics* 117–62, at 117.

[13] R. Craswell, 'Passing on the Costs of Legal Rules: Efficiency and Distribution in Buyer-Seller Relationships' (1991) 43 *Stanford Law Review* 3618–98, at 363.

[14] For discussion of Pareto efficiency and its implications, see J. Coleman, *Market, Morals and the Law* (Cambridge University Press, 1988) 95–132.

The above reasoning draws upon a crucial assumption that the buyer is competent to process information correctly in order to maximise his self-interest;[15] but not infrequently, this assumption proves false in reality. Scholars of behavioural law and economics have convincingly proven that the ability of human beings to process information is imperfect. In particular, when faced with complicated information or when receiving a huge amount of information in a short time, a person is more likely to make judgements against his self-interest.[16] If the party is incapable of appreciating the legal effects of some contractual terms, not only is the contract actually concluded against his true will, but he becomes more vulnerable to exploitation by the other party. Given the bounded nature of human rationality, many contracts concluded voluntarily are thus not truly Pareto-efficient.

Take consumer credit sales as an example. In today's world nearly all consumers can purchase goods on credit. However, while this brings great benefits for them, enhanced access to credit can induce more irrational consumer behaviour, such as excessive borrowing, thereby giving sophisticated sellers an opportunity to exploit consumers' bounded rationality. The short-term satisfaction to the consumer of raising a loan may not be good from a long-term perspective, as excessive borrowing may leave him in a serious financial predicament in the future. His present short-term happiness is outweighed by the future disutility. More importantly, from the standpoint of society as a whole, excessive borrowing without control may lead to severe macroeconomic problems.[17]

It is reasonable to assume that a self-interested firm rarely takes this problem into account. It has only two concerns. First, it will hope that consumers will borrow as much as possible in order to maximise the profit from sales. Secondly, it will strive to minimise the risk of default on repayment by consumers. If the seller is effectively insured against buyers' default, it will prefer a credit buyer to a cash buyer, because it can charge the former a higher price than the latter. The profits to the seller derive not only from the sale of goods, but also from the interest on the loan.

[15] Korobkin, 'Bounded Rationality', n. 9 above, at 1208.

[16] For general discussion of behavioural law and economics and its applications to contract law, see C. Jolls, C. Sustein and R. Thaler, 'A Behavioural Approach to Law and Economics' (1998) 50 *Stanford Law Review* 1471–550; M. Eisenberg, 'The Limits of Cognition and the Limits of Contract' (1995) 47 *Stanford Law Review* 211–59.

[17] The credit crunch in current global financial markets is an obvious example.

Some often-used techniques against default on repayment by consumers are add-on clauses, penalty clauses and disproportional deposits.[18] All share the feature that setting a draconian penalty deters consumers from defaulting on the repayment in order to secure the seller's profit from credit sales. In a recent paper, Korobkin has forcefully demonstrated that individual buyers are often insensitive to such clauses.[19] They are often incompetent to judge the value of these contractual terms correctly, and even ignore the existence of such terms in the contract, usually agreeing to them without a second thought. It follows that the contracts actually concluded by them are not Pareto-efficient.

It can easily be demonstrated that there is a conflict between the public interest and the seller's private interest in this context. The law should deter sellers from behaving to maximise their self-interest when this impairs the public interest. The doctrine of unconscionability can come into play to achieve this. By invalidating the contract or the unconscionable term, the doctrine undermines the seller's guarantee against the risk that the buyer will default on repayment, thereby reducing his expected profit from the credit sale, rendering cash sales more profitable. As a consequence, firms will have less incentive to offer credit sales. The less credit available the harder it becomes for consumers to borrow, which in turn reduces excessive borrowing. The doctrine overcomes – or at least weakens – one party's incentive to exploit the other party's bounded rationality.[20]

However, the doctrine of unconscionability also has an adverse effect: undermining parties' incentive to trade. The disincentive is mainly attributable to two factors. The first is the problem of adverse selection facing sellers,[21] which is particularly manifest in consumer credit sales. There is usually an information asymmetry between the seller and the buyer. The former is unable to distinguish buyers who will default from those who will not. The add-on clause or equivalent is a practical solution to the problem. By setting a severe penalty for default on the repayment, the seller can put off those buyers who would be likely to default into abstaining from purchasing on credit. Therefore, he can

[18] *Williams* v. *Walker-Thomas Furniture Co.*, 350 F. 2d 445 (D.C. Cir. 1965); Epstein, 'Unconscionability' n. 7 above, at 306; S. Waddams, 'Unconscionability in Contracts' (1976) 39 *Modern Law Review* 369–93.

[19] R. Korobkin, 'Bounded Rationality', n. 9 above, (2003) 70 at 1231.

[20] Posner, 'Contract Law in the Welfare State', n. 6 above.

[21] G. Akerlof, 'The Market for "Lemons": Qualitative Uncertainty and the Market Mechanism' (1970) 84 *Quarterly Journal of Economics* 488–500.

expect with confidence that the buyers accepting the penalty will repay the loan.[22] If the law forbids the seller to do so, it impairs the enforceability of repayment. Two consequences may follow: the seller will either not offer any credit sales, or may increase the price to cover the risk. The latter certainly undermines honest buyers' incentive to trade. These buyers will not default, so they are willing to accept a penalty clause in return for paying a lower price. The doctrine of unconscionability leads the seller to charge them a higher price. In brief, the doctrine of unconscionability can undermine the incentives of both parties.

Secondly, the doctrine creates an opportunity for right-holders to abuse their legal rights. The argument supporting the doctrine is based upon the assumption that all consumers have the same level of competence and are unable to process complicated information correctly. In fact, this is not true. The rationality of consumers varies: some are more rational than others. Some empirical research on consumer behaviour has already shown that it is not true that consumers, particularly poor ones, are incompetent or less rational than the average of ordinary people in society.[23] Some sophisticated consumers might use the doctrine to escape from a bad bargain. Without an appropriate mechanism to control this kind of opportunistic behaviour, the doctrine will generate considerable costs both for society and for individual contractors. For society, frivolous litigation generates unnecessary administrative costs, which will be passed on to taxpayers, while the individual contractor will take more precautions against the risk of opportunism from the other party. The increase in the precautionary cost will reduce his expected profit and therefore undermine his incentive to transact.

If we take for granted that the doctrine of unconscionability should be adopted in contract law for correcting allocative efficiency resulting from parties' bounded rationality, then the question remaining is how we can effectively avoid unconscionable contracts, while at the same time minimising the party's disincentive to trade. In the next section, I will build a simple deterrence model of private legal remedies, then examine the deterrence effect of each possible private law remedy on unconscionable contracts and their impact on the parties' incentive to trade.

22 For general discussion on solutions to adverse selection see B. Patrick and M. Dewatripont, *Contract Theory*, 1st edn (The MIT Press, 2005) 47–99.

23 Schwartz, 'A Reexamination of Nonsubstantive Unconscionability', n. 7 above, at 1079; J. White and F. Munger, 'Consumer Sensitivity to Interest Rates: An Empirical Study of New-car Buyers and Auto Loans' (1971) 69 *Michigan Law Review* 1207–58.

3. Economic analysis of legal remedies

The traditional economic analysis sees individual behaviour as the result of a cost-benefit calculation. It is assumed that the person will assess the expected costs and benefits of a proposed act and will decide whether or not to act on the basis of this balancing. A legal remedy is then simply seen as an instrument by which the cost of the behaviour for the person can be increased. Thus, to deter a person from behaving in a certain way, the law could use the legal remedy to increase the cost to him of that behaviour, so that he could no longer profit from doing so.[24] Based upon this theory, we could create a deterrence model of legal remedy for unconscionable contracts:

$$Dq \geq G \tag{1}$$

Here, $\boldsymbol{D}$ represents the private legal remedy for unconscionable contracts; $\boldsymbol{q}$ stands for the probability of private legal enforcement. In reality, the enforcement is imperfect, so, $\boldsymbol{q} < 1$, but >0. $\boldsymbol{G}$ is the contracting party's profit from writing the unconscionable term. If this inequality is held, the party will be unable to make a profit from writing the unconscionable term. Therefore, the remedy creates an effective deterrence. Now let us apply this model to the analysis of each of the possible private legal remedies, viz. damages, invalidation of contract, rescission and judicial modification of the unconscionable term.

(a) The remedy of damages

The remedy of damages can be defined as a sum of financial compensation paid by the wrongdoer to the victim for his wrongdoing. Although the main jurisdictions in the world have not adopted it as a legal remedy for an unconscionable contract concluded in the absence of any tortious behaviour, e.g. fraud or negligent misrepresentation, it is still a plausible option in the theoretical analysis. Compared with other remedial alternatives, the deterrence of damages is more effective. In theory, such deterrence will always be effective, even if the

[24] Q. Zhou, 'A Deterrence Perspective on Damages for Fraudulent Misrepresentation' (2007) 19 *Journal of Interdisciplinary Economics* 83–96, at 88; G. Becker, *The Economic Approach to Human Behaviour*, 1st edn (The University of Chicago Press, 1976).

legal enforcement of a private law remedy is imperfect, as is normally the case in reality. This is because there is no upper limit for setting the level of damages, ***D***. If the probability of legal enforcement is imperfect ($q<1$), ***D*** can always be increased to achieve $Dq > G$ by setting $D \geq \frac{G}{q}$.

To illustrate, suppose that the seller could make a profit of £100 from including an unconscionable term in the contract, viz. ***G***=£100, and that legal enforcement is perfect, $q= 1$. The law could effectively overcome the party's incentive to include the unconscionable term by setting damages at £100, thereby eliminating the profit from the unconscionable term. If the legal enforcement is imperfect, $q < 1$, the effective deterrence can only be achieved by setting ***D*** higher than the profit, so that $D \geq \frac{G}{q}$. For example, let us assume that $q = 0.85$. After ***D*** is discounted by ***q***, ***Dq*** is £85 ($0.85 \times 100 = 85$), which is less than ***G***, £100. This indicates that the seller can still make a net profit of £15 after being sanctioned by damages. To create an effective deterrence, ***D*** ought to be increased to at least £117. Only by this means can the seller's net profit be reduced to nil.[25] This analysis has two implications. First, there are two ways to enhance deterrence: we could either increase the level of legal sanction, ***D***, or improve the legal enforcement, ***q***. When both strategies are plausible, we should choose the one with the lower administrative cost. Secondly, in the case of imperfect legal enforcement ($0 < q < 1$), damages can always be adjusted to achieve effective deterrence by setting $D \geq \frac{G}{q}$, because there is no upper limit for the level of ***D***. As will be seen later, all of the other remedial alternatives have an upper limit for ***D***, which therefore cannot be set in excess of this limit to achieve effective deterrence in the case of imperfect legal enforcement.

The main pitfall of the remedy of damages is the strong adverse effect on the incentive to trade. But this disadvantage should not be exaggerated. In theory, there is only one way to achieve effective deterrence without undermining the parties' incentive to trade, which is to set ***Dq*** higher than the profit from the unconscionable term but less than the profit from an identical contract without the unconscionable term. This would be possible under the remedy of damages. By way of illustration, consider the following example.

A seller could make a profit of £800 *ex ante* from his contract with a buyer. If he includes a penalty clause, his profit *ex ante* increases to £1,000 because the risk of the buyer's breach is reduced, so the seller

[25] If $q= 0.85$, and G= 100, $G/q= 117$, so D should be set at 117.

can make a profit of £200 (£1,000- £800=£200) from the penalty clause. Assuming that the legal enforcement is perfect (***q***= 1), the remedy of damages can effectively overcome the seller's incentive to include the penalty clause by setting ***D***=£200 to eliminate the seller's profit from the clause, but at the same time it does not undermine the seller's incentive to trade, as he can still gain £800 from trading with the buyer.

But the problem of disincentive to trade will become serious if we relax our assumption. Assume this time that ***q***= 0.125; now, to achieve effective deterrence, we must set ***D***=£1600 in order to make ***Dq***=£200, the gain from the penalty clause. In this case, if the contract is held unconscionable, the seller will suffer a loss of £800 from contracting with the buyer. His incentive to trade is certainly undermined.

This example shows that as long as ***Dq*** is lower than the party's profit from the contract without the unconscionable term, the remedy of damages has no effect on his incentive to trade. In addition, the problem of disincentive can be mitigated by improving the legal enforcement, ***q***, so that the level of damages decreases, but without undermining the deterrence.

Another challenge to the remedy of damages is how to prevent the abuse of the legal remedy. If damages were adopted, there would be an inevitable question to be answered: whether or not the aggrieved party is allowed to claim damages in combination with another contract law remedy, for example that of rescission. Damages will always motivate the protected party to abuse the legal right, regardless of the answer to this question.

Of course, allowing the claim for both remedies overcompensates the aggrieved party for the loss resulting from the unconscionable contract. This in turn will motivate him to make both claims. The overcompensation will undermine the other party's incentive to trade by increasing his *ex ante* liability cost. The same problem applies where the law allows the aggrieved party to claim only one remedy. If he can still make a gain from the contract, even though it is unconscionable, he will preserve the contract and simultaneously claim damages. This would be a case where the seller includes a penalty clause in the contract, but the buyer does not breach it. It is reasonable to assume that after performing the contract, the self-interested buyer would have a strong incentive to claim damages from the seller.

(b) Invalidation of contract

Invalidation of contract in this chapter is used to denote that the contract becomes void *ab initio*, that is to say, if one or more terms in the contract is held unconscionable, the court will treat the contract as never having been in existence. This is a radical contract law remedy. Declaring a contract void *ab initio* not only poses the danger of uncertainty in the law, but also confers a considerable judicial power on courts.[26] Compared to the remedy of damages, the deterrence of invalidation of contract is less effective. Three remarks should be noted.

First, if legal enforcement were perfect ($q=1$), the invalidation of contract would create the same degree of deterrence as damages. Once the contract is declared void *ab initio*, neither party can realise its expected interest from the contract. Therefore, D, the liability cost to the party under the remedy of invalidation of contract, equals his expected profit from the unconscionable contract, which is measured as his expected profit from the transaction and the extra profit from including the unconscionable term, G. Therefore, the deterrence of invalidation of contract is effective, because if $q=1$ and $D>G$, Dq always exceeds G.

Secondly, the deterrence of invalidation of the contract is still effective in the case of imperfect legal enforcement ($q<1$), if $q \geq \frac{G}{D}$.[27] This implies that so long as the reduction in the probability of legal enforcement is not less than the ratio of the overreaching party's expected profits from the unconscionable term to the expected profit from the unconscionable contract, the deterrence is still effective.

Thirdly, if $q < \frac{G}{D}$, the deterrence of invalidation of the contract is ineffective and the deterrence can be enhanced only by improving the legal enforcement, q. Unlike the remedy of damages, under the invalidation of contract D is fixed: it equals the party's expected profit from the unconscionable contract. Therefore, the deterrence cannot be improved by increasing D. This is why, in terms of deterrence, damages are a preferable remedial alternative to the invalidation of contract, when legal enforcement is poor.

Turning to the issue of disincentive to trade, it can be shown that the disincentive under the remedy of invalidation of contract is very moderate relative to the remedy of damages. Under the former remedy, there is no chance for the aggrieved party to abuse his legal right. Where the contract is void *ab initio* for the reason of unconscionability, there was never a legally binding contract between the parties. Even where the

[26] B. Markesinis, H. Unberath and A. Johnston, *The German Law of Contract: A Comparative Treatise*, 2nd edn (Hart Publishing, 2006) 248.

[27] The deterrence is effective when $Dq \geq G$. Rearranging the inequality in terms of q, we get $q \geq \frac{G}{D}$.

contract has been partially performed, either party could claim the return of the value which he has transferred to the other party on the ground of restitution. This eliminates the chance for the aggrieved party to adopt a 'wait and see' strategy in order to escape from the bad bargain.

(c) *The remedy of rescission*

Rescission as a remedy for unconscionability has been adopted by French contract law and the UNIDROIT Principles of International Commercial Contracts. From a legal perspective, there is a fundamental difference between the rescission of a contract and its invalidation. If the contract is rescindable, there is a valid contract until the contract is rescinded. Conversely, if the contract is invalid, it is void *ab initio*, meaning that there was never a legally enforceable contract. From an economic perspective, the implications drawn from the analysis of the deterrence of invalidation of contract apply equally to the remedy of rescission. There is no need for repetition.

It can be said, however, that rescission is a more effective deterrent than invalidation of contract. Compared to the remedy of invalidation, the liability cost to the overreaching party, ***D***, is the same: it equals the party's expected profit from the unconscionable contract. Nonetheless, it is reasonable to assume that ***q***, the probability of legal enforcement, is higher under the remedy of rescission. There is no chance for the aggrieved party to abuse the legal right under the remedy of invalidation of contract. In contrast, under the remedy of rescission, the law confers on the aggrieved party the right to decide whether or not to rescind the contract when it is unconscionable. This gives him a chance to escape the bargain by using the doctrine of unconscionability. The increase in the chance of abusing the legal right in turn raises the probability of legal enforcement. Consequently, deterrence is enhanced.

Another advantage of rescission over invalidation of contract is that it gives the parties a second chance to reach a Pareto-efficient agreement. If the contract is voidable rather than void *ab initio*, the overreaching seller still has a chance to realise his expected profit from the contract by offering a price reduction to compensate the aggrieved buyer for waiving the right of rescission. The remedy of rescission thus increases the bargaining power of the aggrieved party. As long as the modification of the contract is Pareto-efficient, both parties will agree on it.

Therefore, if the party himself has an information advantage over the court in deciding what is best for him, the remedy of rescission is preferable to invalidation of contract; otherwise, the latter is better than the former.[28] But this argument should be accepted with some caution. As noted in section 2, the economic justification for the doctrine of unconscionability is that it compensates for the aggrieved party's bounded rationality. If that party's incompetence prevented him from making the right decision at the time of concluding the contract, it is not inappropriate to suspect his competence to make a Pareto-efficient modification later.

Moreover, it is also reasonable to predicate that rescission generates more uncertainty than invalidation of the contract, because of the increase in the possibility of abuse of the legal remedy by the aggrieved party. Accordingly, the disincentive to trade would be greater where rescission rather than invalidation is the available remedy .

(d) Judicial modification of the unconscionable term

When judicial modification of the unconscionable term is adopted as the remedy for unconscionable contracts, the court will either invalidate only the unconscionable term and enforce the remainder of the contract, or replace it with a reasonable term, which is normally the default rule in contract law. For example, if an agreed damages clause is deemed as a penalty by the English court, it is invalid. The default damages rule in the law of contract will apply.

The deterrence of this remedy is effective when legal enforcement is perfect. Because under this remedy the court will invalidate the unconscionable term or replace it with a reasonable term, it eliminates the party's profit from the unconscionable term. Thus the liability cost, $\boldsymbol{D}$, equals $\boldsymbol{G}$ when $\boldsymbol{q}=1$, $Dq \geq G$ can be held. However, if legal enforcement is imperfect, as it normally is in reality ($\boldsymbol{q}<1$), $\boldsymbol{Dq}$ will be smaller than $\boldsymbol{G}$, so it will be ineffective in deterring the party from including the unconscionable term in the contract. Unlike the remedy of damages, the remedy of judicial modification cannot increase the level of $\boldsymbol{D}$ to achieve effective deterrence. Therefore, it can be said that this remedy offers ineffective deterrence in reality.

The remedy of judicial modification creates only a faint disincentive to trade. Under this remedy, the overreaching party can always make a profit

[28] R. Craswell, 'Property Rules and Liability Rules', n. 10 above.

Table A

	Damages	Rescission	Invalidation of contract	Judicial modification
Deterrence	strongest	strong	moderate	low
Disincentive	strongest	strong	moderate	low

from the contract, because it is enforceable even if the unconscionable term is invalid. In addition, given that the probability of legal enforcement is always low in reality, the party's *ex ante* profit from the unconscionable term may be positive. Thus, the party's incentive to trade diminishes only slightly.[29]

The deterrence and the disincentive to trade of each possible legal remedy for unconscionable contracts are summarised in Table A. It can be seen that at one end of the spectrum, damages is the most effective remedy in terms of deterrence, but it also has the greatest adverse effect on incentive to trade. At the other end of the spectrum, judicial modification has the least adverse effect on incentive, but is also the least effective remedy in terms of deterrence. There is a positive correlation between deterrence and disincentive to trade: the greater the deterrence, the higher the level of disincentive. There is thus no remedy which can both effectively deter unconscionable contracts and incur no disincentive to trade.

4. Conclusion

In this chapter, I have applied the law and economics analytical framework to the study of private legal remedies for unconscionable contracts. The analysis is based upon two assumptions: that the objective of the doctrine is to correct the allocative inefficiency caused by the parties' bounded rationality, and that it is efficient to afford the private law remedy for a party who has entered into an unconscionable contract. I have shown that there are two fundamental economic issues to examine in relation to the legal remedy, viz. deterrence and the disincentive to trade. From an economic perspective, the choice of appropriate remedy for unconscionability among the remedial options is dependent upon the emphasis of the lawmaker. If the lawmaker intends to focus on

[29] Ben-Shahar, 'How to Repair Unconscionable Contracts' n. 10 above.

effective deterrence, damages are obviously the preferable option, while if the major concern is the disincentive to trade caused by the doctrine of unconscionability, then judicial modification is the most suitable choice. If, however, the lawmaker seeks to achieve some level of compromise, both invalidation of contract and rescission are plausible alternatives.

PART II

Conceptualising unconscionability in financial transactions

8

Usury and the judicial regulation of financial transactions in seventeenth- and eighteenth-century England

WARREN SWAIN AND KAREN FAIRWEATHER

> The true spirit of usury lies in taking an unjust and unreasonable advantage of their fellow creatures.[1]

The extent to which similar principles applied to loan transactions which fell outside the ambit of the usury laws, under the guise of unconscionability and related doctrines, was a question of great importance from the late seventeenth century.[2]

The usury laws: the changing face of statutory regulation

John Baxton described usury as 'lending for gaine',[3] the 'gaine' meaning the additional sum paid to the lender above the amount of the loan.[4] His definition pre-dated the seventeenth century. It was derived from the canon law[5] applied by the ecclesiastical courts, which had largely

Durham Law School.

[1] *Earl of Chesterfield* v. *Janssen* (1750) 2 Ves Sen 125, 142 (Burnett J).

[2] This study excludes mortgages, on which see ch. 2 by Stephen Waddams in the current volume and R. W. Turner, *The Equity of Redemption* (Cambridge University Press, 1931).

[3] *The English vsurer; or Vsury condemned, by the most learned and famous diuines of the Church of England* (London: John Morton, 1634), at 1.

[4] Baxton, *The English vsurer*, at 2.

[5] The canon law on this point was derived from the mid-twelfth century text Gratian's *Decretum*, on which see P. Landau, 'The Development of Law', in D. Luscombe and J. Riley-Smith (eds.), *The New Cambridge Medieval History* IV (Cambridge University Press, 2004) 113, 128–9. On the ecclesiastical jurisdiction, see R. H. Helmholz, *The Oxford History of the Laws of England: vol. I, The Canon Law and Ecclesiastical Jurisdiction from 597 to the 1640s* (Oxford University Press, 2004), at 378–82; R. H. Helmholz, 'Usury and the Medieval English Church Courts' (1986) 61 *Speculum* 364.

policed these transactions in the Middle Ages.[6] In canon law, usury, any usury, was totally prohibited.[7] Money lending continued unabated but those who wanted to avoid the risk of religious sanction were required to go to the trouble of disguising the true nature of the transaction.[8]

By the late sixteenth century the old consensus was starting to collapse. In Thomas Wilson's *A Discourse Upon Usury*, published in 1572, a preacher, a lawyer, a merchant and a doctor of civil law debate the merits of usury. In the eyes of the preacher, usurers were little better than common criminals:

> I will wyshe some penall lawe of death be made against those usurers, as well as agaynste theeves or murtherers, because their offence hurtheth more universallye and toucheth a greater number.[9]

By the end of the discussion, the more pragmatic lawyer and merchant are convinced by the force of the preacher's argument. The reality was rather different.

First the ecclesiastical courts were emasculated[10] and then a statute of 1571 was widely interpreted as removing the prohibition on usury at common law.[11] Loans with a rate of interest below ten per cent were treated as perfectly legal, whether falling within the traditional definition of usury or not.[12] Two hundred years later, the new distinction, between 'moderate' and exorbitant profit' was captured by William Blackstone.[13] The former was lawful interest, the latter was usury.

[6] The role of the common law increased over time but it was not unimportant even in the Middle Ages: G. Seabourne, *Royal Regulation of Loans and Sales in Medieval England* (Woodbridge: The Boydell Press, 2003) 25–69.

[7] For the intellectual background to the medieval debate on usury, see D. Wood, *Medieval Economic Thought* (Cambridge University Press, 2002) 159–80.

[8] For examples of the ecclesiastical courts attempting to tackle evasion, see Helmholz, 'Usury', n. 5 above, 371.

[9] R. H. Tawney (ed.), T. Wilson, *A Discourse Upon Usury 1572* (London: Bell and Sons, 1925) 232.

[10] J. H. Baker, *An Introduction to English Legal History*, 4th edn (London: Butterworths, 2002) 130–2.

[11] For a wealth of detail on the statute, see N. Jones, *God and the Moneylenders* (Oxford: Basil Blackwell, 1989).

[12] The earliest authorities were not all one way: A. W. B. Simpson, *A History of the Common Law of Contract* (Oxford University Press, 1996) 514–15.

[13] W. Blackstone, *Commentaries on the Laws of England* (Oxford: Clarendon Press, 1766), vol. II, at 456–7.

There was some resistance, particularly amongst religious writers, to the new order.[14] But even staunch advocates of prohibition were prepared to concede that it was difficult to enforce.[15] There was a growing, if sometimes grudging, acceptance that money lending was a fact of life essential to economic progress.[16] John Benbrigge made the point that:

> To speak of abolishing usury is idle; All states have ever had it, in one kind, or rule, or other , so as that opinion must be sent to Utopia.[17]

Francis Bacon, who had himself suffered at the hands of moneylenders, accepted that:

> Since there must be borrowing and lending, and men are so hard of heart as they will not lend freely, usury must be permitted.[18]

At the same time the whole character of money lending was changing. Professional moneylenders became increasingly common[19] and lending more sophisticated, all underpinned by a growing body of literature on the mathematics of interest rates.[20]

With the prohibition removed, attention shifted to the appropriate level of lawful interest, which by 1713 had fallen to five per cent.[21] Some

[14] Anon., *A Brief Survey of the Growth of Usury in England* (London, 1671) 2; Anon., *The death of usury* (Cambridge: John Legatt, 1594); T. P. *The case of usury further debated* (London: Jonathan Robinson, 1684).

[15] W. Burton, *A Sermon Preached in the Cathedral Church of Norwich the XX1 Day of December 1589 Sig. Hi-ii*, cited by Jones, *God and the Moneylenders*, n. 11 above, at 168.

[16] J. Appleby, *Economic Thought and Ideology in Seventeenth Century England* (Princeton University Press, 1978) 63–72, 87–93. On the expanding economy of the sixteenth and seventeenth centuries, see C. G. A. Clay, *Economic Expansion and Social Change: England 1500–1700: vol.* ɪɪ, *Industry, Trade and Government* (Cambridge University Press, 1984), ch. 8.

[17] J. Benbrigge, *Usura Accommodata* (London: Nathaniel Brookes, 1646) 1.

[18] For a similar view, see R. Fenton, *A Treatise of Usurie* (London: William Aspley, 1611); M. Mosse, *The Arraignment and Conviction of Usurie* (London: Thomas Man, 1595).

[19] There were some professional lenders prior to the late sixteenth century but much of the lending was more of a small scale activity between friends and neighbours. For details, see C. Muldrew, *The Economy of Obligation* (Basingstoke: MacMillan, 1998), ch. 8; M. McIntosh, 'Money Lending on the Periphery of London' (1988) 20 *Albion* 557.

[20] C. G. Lewin, *Pensions and Insurance Before 1800: A Social History* (East Linton: Tuckwell Press, 2003), ch. 7.

[21] Lawful interest fell in stages: (1623–1624) 21 Jac I c. 17 (8%), (1660) 12 Car II c. 13 (6%); (1713) 12 Ann st. 2 c. 16 (5%). A number of writers advocated reducing interest rates as a way of encouraging the economy: T. Culpeper, *A tract against the high rate of usury* (London: Christopher Wilkinson, 1668); J. Child, *Brief Observations Concerning Trade*

moneylenders, no doubt, kept within the new law.[22] Others reacted as they had done to the prohibition, by attempting to disguise the real nature of their loans. Mark Ord writing in the early nineteenth century grumbled that:

> After a long contest between the usurer and the legislature, the ingenuity of the former hath prevailed over the authority of the latter; for the legislature have never yet been able to extirpate the practices of usurers, to get extravagant interest.[23]

Methods of statutory avoidance were both varied and extensive.[24] In the early nineteenth century, Robert Comyn listed fifteen types of loan transactions which fell outside the statutes.[25]

The difficulty for the courts was, as the political theorist Robert Filmer observed, that there was often little in substance to separate loans that fell within the statutes and those that did not.[26] In these circumstances, it is perhaps unsurprising that attempts to counter evasion produced mixed results. *Richards* v. *Brown*[27] provides a good snapshot of the kind of tensions which could arise when a judge like Lord Mansfield, reputed to be sensitive to the needs of merchants, came up against commercial morality. The parties had entered into an annuity agreement. In his evidence the borrower quoted the lender's statement that: 'he never lends money but by way of annuity'. Lord Mansfield underlined the passage in his notebook.[28] In the face of this apparently strong evidence and the very evident pecuniary desperation of the borrower, the first instinct of a streetwise jury at Guildhall, possibly themselves merchants, was to hold that the loan fell outside the statute. Only when the matter

and Interest of Money (London: Elizabeth Calvert, 1668). These views were not shared by everyone as was evident in Thomas Culpeper's reply to his critics: T. Culpeper, *A Short Appendix to the Late Treatise Concerning the Abatement of Usury* (London: Christopher Wilkinson, 1668).

22 P. Temin and Hans-Joachim Voth, 'Banking as an Emerging Technology: Hoare's Bank, 1702–1742' (2006) 13 *Financial History Review* 149, 176 provides evidence that Hoare's Bank reduced their rate of interest to 5% after 1713.

23 M. Ord, *Essay on the Law of Usury*, 2nd edn (London: 1804) 82–3, cited by S. Campbell, 'The Economic and Social Effect of the Usury Laws in the Eighteenth Century' (1933) 16 *Transactions of the Royal Historical Society 4th Series* 197, 205.

24 Anon., *A Common Law Treatise of Usury* (London: John Wickins, 1710).

25 R. Comyn, *A Treatise on the Law of Usury* (London: R. Pheney, 1817), ch. 2.

26 R. Filmer, *Quæstio quod liberica* (London: Humphrey Mosely, 1653), Preface.

27 (1778) 2 Cowp 770.

28 Lord Mansfield's note is reproduced in J. Oldham, *The Mansfield Manuscripts and the Growth of English Law in the Eighteenth Century* (London: The University of North Carolina Press, 2004), vol. I, 649.

was put to the jurors a second time and pressure applied by Lord Mansfield did they find the transaction usurious.[29]

Yet the problem went much deeper than persuading mercantile juries that a given transaction was usurious. Both Lord Hardwicke and Lord Mansfield pronounced on the wrongfulness of statutory evasion[30] but the traditional way in which usurious transactions were identified proved to be a major obstacle to achieving their objectives. In *Murray* v. *Harding*, Blackstone J explained: 'I do not know an instance where the principal is bona fide hazarded, that the contract has been held to be usurious.'[31] Provided the transaction involved a hazard, so that there was no guaranteed return of the principal, and no mention of a loan, and sometimes even if there was,[32] it was difficult to show that the usury laws had been compromised.[33] One possible escape route, which had proved popular with the ecclesiastical courts but which brought no guarantee of success, was to look beneath the surface of the transaction to the intent of the parties. Lord Mansfield was particularly taken with the rhetoric of intention:

> The question is, what was the substance of the transaction, and the true intent and meaning of the parties? For they alone are to govern, and not the words used.[34]
>
> It is impossible to wink so hard, as not to see, that there was no idea between the parties of any thing but a loan of money.[35]

It is doubtful whether this was an effective way of shoring up statutory regulation. One of Lord Mansfield's contemporaries was not convinced, complaining that the 'laws in force against usury have been notoriously eluded'.[36] By the eighteenth century, one device, perhaps more than any other came to encapsulate the problem.

29 Ibid., 651.

30 Lord Hardwicke: *Lawley* v. *Hooper* (1745) 3 Atk 278, 279; *Searle* v. *Carpenter* (1754) Amb 243. Lord Mansfield: *Floyer* v. *Edwards* (1774) 1 Cowp 112, 114–15; *Richards* v. *Brown* (1778) 2 Cowp 770, 776–7; *Jestons* v. *Brooke* (1778) 2 Cowp 793, 796; *Lowe* v. *Waller* (1781) 2 Doug 736, 740.

31 (1773) 2 Wm Bla 859, 865. De Grey CJ made a similar point at 863.

32 *Murray* v. *Harding* (1773) 2 Wm Bla 859, 864 (De Grey CJ): 'Communication concerning a loan has sometimes infected the cases and turned a contract into usury. But then the communication must be mutual. Application for a loan is not such a case, provided the party applied to refuses a loan but treats for an annuity.'

33 M. Ord, *Essay on the Law of Usury* (London: E. Brook, 1797) 68–9.

34 *Richards* v. *Brown* (1779) 2 Cowp 770, 776.

35 *Lowe* v. *Waller* (1781) 2 Doug 736, 740.

36 Anon., *Reflections on Usury* (London: R Faulder, 1783) 13.

Annuities for the life of the seller: a case study in statutory avoidance

The annuity for the life of the seller[37] was labelled a 'public nuisance' by a Parliamentary Committee[38] but it was relatively simple to draw up and proved to be enormously popular.[39] A lender (the buyer) offered a borrower (the seller) a capital sum (the principal). In return the borrower undertook to pay a sum of money each year (the annuity) for the rest of his life. The period taken to repay the principal (the years' purchase) was usually set at six years.[40] The number of years' purchase represented the price. To take a simple example, A sells an annuity of £1,000 a year for his own life to B at six years purchase. In return B pays £6,000 to A. The lender's profit (or interest) came from the annual payments beyond six years which he hoped to receive. The hallmark of an annuity for the life of a seller was that a typical borrower could only offer fairly poor security such as a bond, personal property or a life estate and was unable to repay the whole sum in one go.[41]

One future and one current Lord Chancellor were both scathing about this type of annuity. Thomas Erskine wrote that:

> There is no honest trade so lucrative as to allow a profit on money borrowed by annuity at 6 years' purchase, and therefore there can seldom be one of that sort sold but upon some sudden emergency, or some very

[37] An invaluable guide is provided by Sybil Campbell, 'Usury and Annuities of the Eighteenth Century' (1928) 44 *Law Quarterly Review* 473. These devices seem to have been around from at least the early eighteenth century. W. Bohun, *The Practising Attorney: or Lawyer's Office* (London, James Crokatt, 1724) 386 contains an example. For an example of one of the common newspaper advertisements for this sort of transaction, see Anon., *Reflections*, n. 36 above, 5. Annuities for the life of the buyer on the other hand were attended 'with little mischief' and for the benefit of both parties, see T. Erskine, *Reflections on gaming, annuities, and usurious contracts*, 3rd edn (London: T. Davies, 1776) 24.

[38] *Report From The Committee Appointed To Take Into Consideration The Laws now in being against Usury, And The present Practice of purchasing Annuities for the Life of the Grantor* (London, 1777). Anon., *Reflections*, n. 36 above, at 10 'where one annuity is bought at seven or eight years purchase, ten are bought at six'.

[39] Campbell, 'Usury and Annuities', n. 37 above, provides evidence from the Close Rolls of the popularity of annuities.

[40] *Report From The Committee*, at 4. Some were even shorter where the security was less good or the borrower was in poor health, ibid., at 5.

[41] R. Withy, *A Practical Treatise Upon The Law of Annuities* (London: J. Butterworth, 1800) 2.

> pungent distress, which this scandalous contract palliates for a moment, to rivet it closer and to confirm it for ever; like the medicines of a quack, or the bottle of a drunkard, which rock the senses for an hour to awake an idiot or a cripple.[42]

Lord Hardwicke, complained that, 'I really believe in my conscience, that ninety-nine in a hundred of these bargains are nothing but loans turned into this shape to avoid the statutes of usury.'[43] From the lender's point of view, the beauty of an annuity for the life of the seller was that, provided that it was carefully drafted, it had all the advantages of a loan without any of the drawbacks.[44] The interest charged was above the legal maximum but on the face of it there was a risk, so the transaction was not usurious.[45] The seller agreed to make an annual payment rather than simply to repay the principal. As a result, if the seller died before any payment was made, the buyer recovered nothing.[46] In truth there was rarely much of a hazard. The ready availability of life insurance by the eighteenth century saw to that.[47] By insuring the life of the seller, buyers were usually protected in the event of an early death.[48] Lord Hardwicke observed that 'everybody knows, that this casualty of losing the Principal is secured by insuring the life, upon which the annuity depends'.[49] The courts were largely untroubled by this practice:

> So many Annuities however have been established by the courts, in which such insurances have been known to subsist, that we must conclude, that this circumstance does not of itself render the transaction usurious.[50]

42 Erskine, *Reflections*, n. 37 above, 27.

43 *Lawley* v. *Hooper* (1745) 3 Atk 278, 279.

44 Attorneys were important not just in drafting these agreements but as brokers. This may be one reason why this legally watertight way of avoiding usury was so popular: C. W. Brooks, *The 'Lower Branch' of the Legal Profession in Early Modern England* (Cambridge University Press, 2004) 196–7.

45 For an example, see Campbell, 'Usury and Annuities', n. 37 above, 479.

46 *Roberts* v. *Tremayne* (1616) Cro Jac 507 (though not in the context of an annuity).

47 On the growth of life insurance see: Lewin, *Pensions*, n. 20 above, 325–31; Oldham, *Mansfield Manuscripts*, vol. I, n. 28 above, 474–8. For some minor practical problems, see Withy, *Annuities*, n. 41 above, 17.

48 There was a small risk that the life insurance would be invalidated or if the borrower left the jurisdiction it became difficult to realise the security see, Campbell, 'Usury and Annuities', n. 37 above, 478–80.

49 *Lawley* v. *Hopper* (1745) 3 Atk 278, 280.

50 F. Plowden, *A Treatise Upon the Law of Usury and Annuities* (London: J. Butterworth, 1797) 274.

Rather feeble attempts at statutory intervention failed to regulate annuities for the life of the seller.[51] In the end it was, perhaps, this device more than any other which contributed to the death of the statutory restrictions on usury in the nineteenth century. In the meantime, and in the absence of a very effective scheme of statutory regulation, equity had an important role to play in regulating financial transactions.

Why equity intervened and early attempts at relief

The subject of loan transactions continued to generate strong views beyond the confines of legal London. One early eighteenth-century polemicist carped that:

> The scandalous practice of usury, ought to be an abomination to every honest person, and common interest of money may sometimes be a grievance.[52]

Loans also left a mark on the mercantile literature of the seventeenth and eighteenth centuries.[53] Hogarth's rake would have felt at home in some of the authorities.[54] High levels of borrowing amongst the aristocracy were not uncommon.[55] The trappings of status at the dawn of a consumer society did not come cheap.[56] It was easy to lose large sums of money at the gaming table.[57] Agricultural depressions which blighted the

[51] Campbell, 'Usury and Annuities', n. 37 above 484–5; Anon., *Reflections*, n. 36 above, ii-iii, 9–10. R. Hannay, *Defence of the Usury Laws* (Edinburgh: William Blackwood, 1823) 45 described this legislation as 'useless'.

[52] Anon, *Law quibbles. Or, a treatise of the evasions, tricks, turns and quibbles, commonly used in the profession of the law, to the prejudice of clients, and others* (London: Thomas Corbett, 1724) 28.

[53] D. Defoe, *The Complete English Tradesman in Familiar Letters* (London: Charles Rivington, 1726) xiv, 'the tragic stories of tradesmen undone by usury are so many, and the variety so great'. For examples, see Anon., *A Gentleman's Assistant*, 2nd edn (London: Thomas Bever, 1709); S. Howard, *Every tradesman his own lawyer* (London: W. Stratford, 1794).

[54] Hogarth painted *A Rake's Progress* in 1734. Ironically the main protagonist Tom Rakewell, who loses his fortune, inherited his great wealth from a moneylender father. For details on the painting, see C. Riding, *Hogarth* (London: Tate, 2006) 86–93.

[55] L. Stone, *The Crisis of the Aristocracy 1558–1641* (Oxford University Press, 1965), ch. 9.

[56] On the rise of consumer society amongst the upper reaches of society: M. Berg, *Luxury and Pleasure in Eighteenth-Century Britain* (Oxford University Press, 2005).

[57] For a discussion of the legal consequences of the eighteenth-century gambling mania, see W. Swain, 'Da Costa v. Jones', in C. Mitchell and P. Mitchell (eds.), *Landmark Cases in the Law of Contract* (Oxford: Hart, 2008), ch. 4.

eighteenth century would have depleted income.[58] In these circumstances, it was easy to see how the fears of Thomas Lodge, that usurers 'inriche themselves mightelye by others misfortunes, but also eate our English Gentrie out of house and home',[59] might be realised. But it was not just the spendthrift who found it difficult to borrow at low rates of interest. A series of financial crises combined with high government borrowing threatened the private credit market throughout the eighteenth century.[60] The relatively low level of lawful interest may have made the problem worse. As some lenders became more circumspect,[61] borrowers were pushed into the arms of more unscrupulous lenders charging punitive rates of interest.[62]

In the event that a debtor was sued for failure to repay his loan, it was open to him to plead usury.[63] If successful, then the contract was rendered void.[64] If the contract fell outside the usury laws, he was in a vulnerable position at common law. In the absence of other grounds to avoid the contract, such as illegality or fraud, then the agreement stood. A debtor who stopped paying was likely to be liable for the full value of the loan. There is no compelling evidence to suggest that juries were prepared to mitigate the damages awarded where the price paid was out of proportion to the value received, for example in the typical transaction where hidden interest was payable.[65]

58 G.E. Mingay, 'The Agricultural Depression 1730–1750' (1956) 8 *Economic History Review* 323. Though at the same time improvements in agricultural methods increased profitability, see J. Rule, *The Vital Century* (London: Longman, 1995) 47–55.

59 *An alarum against vsurers* (London: S. Clarke, 1584).

60 T. S. Ashton, *An Economic History of England in the 18th Century* (London: Methuen, 1959) 29; J. Hoppit, 'Financial Crises in Eighteenth-Century England' (1986) 39 *The Economic History Review* 39. The biggest crisis of course was a result of the South Sea Bubble: see J. Hoppit, *A Land of Liberty? England 1689–1727* (Oxford University Press, 2002) 334–5. Government debt was enormous. By 1820 it was twice national income: G. Clark, 'Debt, Deficits, and Crowding Out: England, 1727–1840' (2001) 5 *European Review of Economic History* 403. The Government paid higher rates of interest than permitted under the usury statutes, which, combined with better security ensured that it was a desirable borrower: W. Beawes, *Lex Mercatoria* (London: R. Baldwin, 1792) 411.

61 P. Temin and Hans-Joachim Voth, 'Interest Rate Restrictions in a Natural Experiment: Loan Allocation and the Change in the Usury Laws in 1714' (2008) 118 *The Economic Journal* 743.

62 Jeremy Bentham made this very point in his famous *Defence of Usury; Shewing the Impolicy of the Present Legal Restraints on the Terms of Pecuniary Bargains* (London: T. Payne, 1787) 29.

63 W. Tidd, *The Practice of the Court of King's Bench in Personal Actions*, 2 vols. (London: Thomas Whieldon, 1794), vol. I, 374.

64 *Loyd* v. *Williams* (1771) 3 Wils KB 250.

65 J. Barton, 'The Enforcement of Hard Bargains' (1987) 103 *Law Quarterly Review* 118.

The Court of Chancery was less forgiving when it came to financial transactions which fell outside the wording but not the spirit, of the usury laws. The nineteenth-century writer Hugh Bellot summarised the position before 1750:

> The reports of cases . . . are very meagre, and it is difficult to ascertain whether they proceeded on any uniform principle; but it may be assumed that the policy of the Court of Chancery was to relieve against what were called catching bargains, which were transactions looked upon as evasions of the usury laws then in force and which transactions were very narrowly watched.[66]

Equitable relief consisted of little more than a series of common situations loosely bound together by some shared themes. Most of the authorities are concerned with attempts to evade the usury laws, many involved heirs and some raised the issue of inadequacy of value. There is no consistent terminology. The word 'unconscionable' does not always appear. All of the authorities are concerned with some sort of unfairness.

Where the transaction fell within the statutes of usury, there was no difficulty in Chancery granting relief.[67] Those transactions which had a whiff of usury but fell outside the statutes were more troublesome. The early cases typically involve a sale of goods which was a popular way of evading the usury laws before annuities became fashionable.[68] A borrower approached a lender or intermediary. The lender then agreed to sell the borrower goods at a grossly extravagant price on credit using a bond. The borrower sold the goods and generally received a fraction of what he paid. The lender's profit, provided he could recover on the bond, amounted to the difference between the price paid by the borrower and what he could have got for the goods if he sold them himself.

In *Fairfax* v. *Trigg*, Lord Nottingham poured opprobrium on these arrangements:

> This court ought to discountenance and relieve against all corrupt traffic between the shopkeepers and young gentleman who are usually drawn in and entangled with such kind of bargains.[69]

66 H. Bellot and R. Willis, *The Law Relating to Unconscionable Bargains with Money Lenders* (London: Stevens and Hayes, 1897) 35.

67 *Lawley* v. *Hooper* (1745) 3 Atk 278, 279–81; *Earl of Chesterfield* v. *Janssen* (1750) 2 Ves Sen 125, 142–4, 147–8, 150–1, 153–5; *Spurrier* v. *Mayoss* (1792) 4 Bro CC 28, 30.

68 For details on this method of evasion, see A Barrister, *Legal Recreations or Popular Amusements*, 2 vols. (London: J. Bew, 1792), vol. i, 410.

69 (1676) [581] (1961) 79 *Selden Society* 448.

The usual measure of relief, he explained, was to reduce the sum owing to the 'true and real' value of the goods sold. The party seeking relief on this occasion was simply described as a student in Lincoln's Inn. In the early reported authorities most are described as heirs.[70] Sheridan treats these authorities as the origin of equitable jurisdiction over young heirs.[71] The judgments provide few clues about why relief was granted. Chancery judges may have been motivated by a desire to prevent evasion of the usury laws, dislike of sales at an exorbitant price, a desire to protect young heirs, or a mixture of all three. It is not difficult to imagine why so many of these cases involve young heirs as well as naiveté. The borrowers in these transactions lacked ready cash. Their only valuable asset was their future inheritance. It was only on inheriting that they would be able to pay the money back. This sort of scenario was sometimes obvious on the face of the agreement. In *Bill* v. *Price*, for example, several young heirs bound themselves to pay severally and jointly upon the death of their fathers.[72]

Loans disguised as sales were not the only method of avoiding usury which caught the attention of Chancery judges in the 1680s. The post-obit bond usually provided the borrower with an immediate payment. In return he promised that on the death of his father or other relative he would repay a much larger sum. The risk of death before inheritance ensured that the post-obit bond fell outside the ambit of the usury laws. Lord Nottingham, on giving relief on a post-obit bond, warned that 'no family can be safe if this is suffered'.[73] The case before him was a strong one: in addition to a post-obit bond the agreement involved a sale at an exorbitant price in which the plaintiff had agreed to purchase various items which he planned to sell and clear his debts.

In Lord Nottingham's opinion, 'this infamous kind of trade and circumvention ought by all means to be suppressed'.[74] Lord Keeper North, who heard the next stage of the litigation, adopted a less paternalistic line. He recognised that it was a 'hazardous bargain' but in the absence of 'proof of any fraud' the claim was dismissed.[75] When the case came on a third time, Lord Chancellor Jeffreys sought to discharge Lord Nottingham's decree, with the observation that the bargain was

[70] *Bill* v. *Price* (1686) 1 Vern 467; *Lamplugh* v. *Smith* (1688) 2 Vern 77; *Whitley* v. *Price* (1688) 2 Vern 78; *Wiseman* v. *Beake* (1690) 2 Vern 122.

[71] L. A. Sheridan, *Fraud in Equity: a Study in English and Irish Law* (London: Pitman, 1957) 143.

[72] (1686) 1 Vern 467. [73] *Anon.* (1680) [1089] (1961) 79 *Selden Society* 868. [74] Ibid.

[75] *Barny* v. *Beak* (1682) 2 Chan Cas 136.

unconscionable.[76] As this litigation demonstrates, there were plainly differences of opinion between Chancery judges about the appropriateness of intervention. Lord Keeper North seems to have been particularly adverse to granting relief. In *Batty* v. *Lloyd*, he said that:

> One that is necessitous must sell cheaper than those who are not. If I had a mind to buy of a rich man a piece of ground that lay near mine, for my convenience, he would ask me almost twice the value: so where people are constrained to sell, they must not look to have the fullest price.[77]

In a statement that resonates even today, he makes the point that those whose finances are in a poor state of repair should not be able to expect to negotiate a favourable arrangement with a lender and to expect the law to bail them out when everything comes unstuck. *Wiseman* v. *Beake*, a few years later, represents the opposing position. The plaintiff was a long way from being a young heir. He was a forty-year-old proctor in Doctors' Commons.[78] He was still granted relief. Although the agreement was described as a 'contrivance'[79] and 'fraud',[80] there is nothing to suggest that this was anything other than a perfectly standard post-obit bond. The tensions generated by these two extreme positions would bubble to the surface in the eighteenth century, particularly in cases of financial transactions at an undervalue.[81]

Irrespective of the precise format, what all these transactions had in common was that one party, in urgent need of ready cash, was prepared to enter into a highly disadvantageous agreement.[82] *Nott* v. *Hill* is a good early example. The plaintiff, who was entitled to the estate tail, sold his expectancy at a considerable under value.[83] Lord Nottingham, in setting the agreement aside, expressed himself in quite broad terms:

> Put the case Hill had given him £30 to have five times so much on the father's death, should not the court relieve in such a case? Here you have five times the value in land . . . He said, by the Civil Law a bargain of double the value shall be avoided, and wish'd it were so in England.[84]

[76] *Berney* v. *Pitt* (1686) 2 Vern 14. [77] (1682) 1 Vern 142.

[78] Doctors' Commons was a court practising civil law dealing in admiralty and matrimonial matters. A proctor was equivalent to an attorney in the common law.

[79] (1698) 2 Vern 121, 122; (1698) 2 Freeman 111. [80] (1698) 2 Freeman 111.

[81] Even within the same hearing: *Keen* v. *Stuckeley* (1721) Gilb Rep 155.

[82] On hard bargains more generally, see Barton, 'Hard Bargains', n. 65 above

[83] The estate tail was a very typical form of dynastic landholding see, A. W. B. Simpson, *A History of the Land Law*, 2nd edn (Oxford University Press, 1986) 90–1.

[84] (1682) 2 Chan Cas 120.

As in *Batty* v. *Lloyd*, Lord Keeper North once again refused to set the agreement aside.[85] But when the executor of the original defendant tried to get specific performance of the agreement, he was not sympathetic:

> A contract which carries an equity to have it decreed in specie ought to be without all objection . . . and the practice of purchasing from heirs was grown too common, and therefore he would not in any sort countenance it.[86]

Refusal of specific performance had less drastic consequences than setting the contract aside because the plaintiff was still left with a remedy at law.[87]

It is dangerous to draw many firm conclusions about under value from the earliest cases. Part of the difficulty in making sense of these authorities is that many different factors may have influenced the outcome. In the seventeenth century, in particular, the reasoning is not fully set out. There are examples of agreements that appear to be set aside for inadequacy of value but they are not strong authorities[88] and others where equity came to the opposite conclusion.[89] When inadequacy was combined with some other factor the courts were more responsive. Evidence of fraud was particularly helpful.[90] In the absence of fraud, an 'unreasonable advantage made of a necessitous man' could be enough to tip the balance.[91] As demonstrated by *Nott* v. *Hill* itself, an heir dealing with his expectancy who sold at an under value was also likely receive a favourable hearing.

Earl of Chesterfield v. *Janssen*: structuring relief in equity

By the middle of the eighteenth century a clearer picture was beginning to emerge. This came about, in part, as a result of *Earl of Chesterfield* v. *Janssen*.[92] In their commentary, White and Tudor, the authors of *A Selection of Leading Cases in Equity*, wrote that:

[85] (1683) 1 Vern 167. [86] *Johnson* v. *Nott* (1684) 1 Vern 271.

[87] At common law they could bring an action for debt or damages. In *Nott* v. *Johnson* (1687) 2 Vern 25, Lord Chancellor Jeffreys held that the agreement should be set aside, thereby restoring Lord Nottingham's original position.

[88] In *Fawcet* v. *Bowers* (1693) 2 Vern 287 no explicit reasoning was provided. In *Francis Pawlett* v. *Pleydell* (1679) [935] (1961) 79 *Selden Society* 739, Lord Nottingham said that he saw no reason for Chancery to interpose, but the parties agreed a compromise.

[89] *Hobert* v. *Hobert* (1683) 2 Chan Cas 159.

[90] *Ardglasse* v. *Muschamp* (1684) 1 Vern 237.

[91] *Cole* v. *Gibbons* (1734) 3 P Wms 290, 294. [92] (1750) 2 Ves Sen 125, 1 Atk 301.

> *Chesterfield* v. *Janssen*, is a case of very frequent reference, celebrated ... above all for the learned judgment of Lord Hardwicke himself, in which he has so admirably classified the different species of fraud against which equity will give relief.[93]

Relief was rationalised on the basis that it was the job of Chancery to protect against fraud. That Lord Hardwicke should single out fraud is not very surprising. Fraud was one of the three traditional heads of Chancery jurisdiction.[94] Lord Hardwicke set down five heads of fraud. Three are particularly relevant in this context:

> Fraud apparent from the intrinsic nature and subject of the bargain itself; such as no man in his senses and not under delusion would make on the one hand and no honest and fair man would accept on the other;
>
> Fraud, presumed from the circumstances and condition of the parties contracting ... it is wisely established in this court to prevent taking surreptitious advantage of the weakness or necessity of another: which knowingly to do is equally against conscience as to take advantage of his ignorance;
>
> the last head of fraud, on which there has been relief, is that, which infects catching bargains with heirs, reversioners, or expectants in the life of the father.

A few years later, in a letter to his friend, Lord Kames, Lord Hardwicke would claim that 'fraud is infinite' and that 'no invariable rules can be established'.[95] Whether fraud by this time, even in equity, was as broad as Lord Hardwicke's remarks suggest is perhaps doubtful.[96] Ironically his classification would contribute to the growth of 'invariable rules', which by the nineteenth century would change the face of equitable relief.[97] A flavour of what was going on can be gleaned from two late eighteenth-century statements, one from a legal writer and one from a judge. In an

93 F. T. White and O. D. Tudor, *A Selection of Leading Cases in Equity*, 2 vols. (London: W. Maxwell, 1849), vol. I, 410.

94 H. Rolle, *Un Abridgement des plusieurs cases et resolutions del Common Ley* (London: A. Crooke, 1668) 374; E. Coke, *The Fourth Part of the Institutes of the Laws of England* (London: W. Lee, 1644), 84; D. E. C. Yale (ed.), *Lord Nottingham's Manual of Chancery Practice and Prolegomena of Chancery and Equity* (Cambridge University Press, 1965) 191.

95 P. Yorke, *The Life and Correspondence of Philip Yorke, Earl of Hardwicke*, 3 vols. (Cambridge University Press, 1913), vol. II, 550–5.

96 M. Lobban, 'Contractual Fraud in Law and Equity, *c*1750–*c*1850' (1997) 17 *Oxford Journal of Legal Studies* 441, 448–50.

97 J. Newland, *A Treatise on Contract Within the Jurisdiction of Courts of Equity* (London: Butterworth, 1806); G. Jeremy, *A Treatise on the Equitable Jurisdiction of the High Court of Chancery* (London: J. Clarke, 1828).

editorial note to his 1793 edition of Ballow's *A Treatise of Equity*, John Fonblanque explained:

> Even in cases of fraud, which from their nature must be almost infinitely various in their circumstances, courts of equity constantly proceed upon some clear and established principle sufficiently comprehensive to meet the circumstances of the particular case to which it is applied, and not upon a vague, arbitrary, and indefinite power.[98]

Lord Thurlow made a very similar point:

> The Court will not correct a contract, merely because a man of nice honour would not have entered into it; it must fall within some definition of fraud; the rule must be drawn so as not to affect the general transactions of mankind.[99]

Admiration for clear definitions was in tune with the intellectual climate of the period.[100] Precedent was also becoming more important in Chancery.[101] As the categories of relief became fixed the process probably killed off for good the prospect of an overarching doctrine of unconscionability. But in the meantime there was still a good deal that remained to be settled. Lord Hardwicke's first category[102] would prove particularly problematic.[103] The pre-1740 cases were largely one way. Inadequacy of price was not enough to achieve relief by either setting the

98 (London: Whieldon and Butterworth, 1793), vol. i, Book 1, Chapter 1§3 (k).

99 *Fox* v. *Mackreth* (1788) 2 Bro CC 400, 420.

100 The new more scientific method in legal writing evident in the works of Blackstone was continued by writers such as John Joseph Powell in his *Essay Upon Contracts and Agreements* (London: J. Johnson, 1790).

101 The rise of precedent, began under Lord Nottingham and quickened during Lord Hardwicke's tenure: D. E. C. Yale, *Lord Nottingham's Chancery Cases Vol. 1* (1954) 73 *Selden Society* xxxvii-cxxiv; C. Croft, 'Lord Hardwick's Use of Precedent in Equity', in T. G. Watkin (ed.), *Legal Record and Historical Reality* (London: Hambledon, 1989) 121–55; D. Lieberman, *The Province of Legislation Determined: Legal Theory in Eighteenth-Century Britain* (Cambridge University Press, 1989) 81–3.

102 The first category mentioned above. It is the second category in Lord Hardwicke's original scheme after actual fraud.

103 M. Horwitz, 'The Historical Foundations of Modern Contract Law' (1974) 87 *Harvard Law Review* 917; M. Horwitz, *The Transformation of American Law 1780–1860* (Harvard University Press, 1977), ch. 6 ; A. W. B. Simpson, 'The Horwitz Thesis and the History of Contracts' (1979) 46 *University of Chicago Law Review* 533; P. Atiyah, *The Rise and Fall of Freedom of Contract* (Oxford University Press, 1979) 169–77; J. Gordley, *The Philosophical Origins of Modern Contract Doctrine* (Oxford University Press, 1991) 147–58.

contract aside or refusal of specific performance.[104] In the early 1740s, some remarks by Lord Hardwicke seem to suggest that the position had changed. But, significantly, these comments were made in the context of claims which involved more than just inadequate price.[105] Matters reached a head in 1749 when he announced that specific performance might be refused solely on the basis of an inadequate price.[106] These developments had obvious significance for loan transactions, but the cases were still not all one way. In what were both apparently straightforward annuity cases, specific performance was refused in one and granted in the other.[107]

In the seventeenth century fraud was usually understood to be something distinct from inadequacy of price. It was just one of a number of factors that the courts took into account, like being an heir or taking advantage of weakness, albeit a particularly strong one. By the middle of the eighteenth century, fraud had come more to the fore. In *Lawley* v. *Hooper*, Lord Hardwicke explained that 'wherever they have found the least tincture of fraud in any of these oppressive bargains, relief hath always been given'.[108] This did not mean that Lord Hardwicke was any more likely to set aside contracts than his predecessors.[109] From around 1780 something extraordinary began to happen. In *Gwynne* v. *Heaton*[110] Lord Thurlow held that whilst mere 'inadequate consideration' was not alone sufficient to merit setting a contract aside, where there was an 'inequality so strong, so gross, and manifest, that it must be impossible to state it to a man of common sense, without producing an exclamation at the inequality of it',[111] then the situation was different. *Gwynne* v. *Heaton* can be explained on the basis that the plaintiff was an

[104] Barton, 'Hard Bargains', n. 65 above, 124–6.

[105] *Barnardiston* v. *Lingood* (1740) 2 Atk 133 (expectant heir); *Buxton* v. *Lister* (1746) 3 Atk 383 (misrepresentation).

[106] *Underwood* v. *Hitchcock* (1749) 1 Ves Sen 279.

[107] Refused: *Vaughan* v. *Thomas* (1783) 1 Bro CC 556. Granted: *Lord Carbery* v. *Weston* (1757) 1 Bro PC 429. One reason for the different outcome may arise from the fact that the annuity in the former was sold at five years' purchase and in the latter at seven years' purchase. Six years, purchase was generally accepted to be the market price. The annuity in *Vaughan* v. *Thomas* was therefore below the normal market price.

[108] (1745) 3 Atk 278, 279.

[109] *Lawley* v. *Hooper* (1745) 3 Atk 278; *Nichols* v. *Gould* (1752) 2 Ves Sen 422.

[110] (1778) 1 Bro CC 1. [111] Ibid., 9.

heir.[112] *Heathcote* v. *Paignon*[113] went one stage further. The plaintiff was not an heir and Lord Thurlow expressly found 'no evidence of distress'. The annuity was still set aside on the basis that:

> There is such inadequacy as to shew that the person did not understand the bargain he made, or was so oppressed that he was glad to make it, knowing its inadequacy, it will shew a command over him which may amount to fraud.[114]

The line between inadequacy of value as a ground to set an agreement aside and inadequacy of value as evidence of oppression sufficient for an agreement to be set aside is a fine one particularly where, as here, it was the only evidence before the court.[115] Because fraud must still be present[116] there were two great advantages. Superficially, at least, it allowed an escape from Lord Thurlow's fear that 'if the court should take such a ground as to rest the case upon the market price, every transaction of this kind would come into the court of equity'.[117] There is probably a good deal of truth in the remarks of one Irish Lord Chancellor:

> Inadequacy of price is not of itself sufficient, but the Court has got at it by indirect means – it has been astute, as it is said to infer fraud from inadequacy, so as to raise it indirectly into a ground for relief.[118]

At the same time this approach retained a degree of flexibility given that each particular instance turned on whether or not there was a fraud. The way in which specific performance operated told a similar story. In *Day* v. *Newman*, Arden MR had refused specific performance on the grounds of inadequacy of price whilst admitting that there was 'no pressure of circumstances whatever'.[119] Later judges clarified his position.

112 The plaintiff, who had entered into an annuity because he was destitute, having been 'turned out of doors' by his father for marrying a servant, could count himself lucky to come before Lord Thurlow. A man who co-habited with a bar-maid who bore him three daughters, might be expected to have some sympathy for the plaintiff's plight.

113 (1787) 2 Bro CC 167. 114 Ibid., 175.

115 In most situations there was additional evidence.

116 *Speed* v. *Philips* (1796) 3 Anstr 732, 736; *Moth* v. *Atwood* (1801) 5 Ves Jun 845.

117 (1787) 2 Bro CC 167, 175. For similar statements, see *Nichols* v. *Gould* (1752) 2 Ves Sen 422, 423, 28 ER 270; *Griffith* v. *Spratlay* (1787) 1 Cox 383, 388. For a much later judgment along similar lines, see *Bower* v. *Cooper* (1843) 2 Hare 408, 410: 'The court would treat men's contracts with great levity, if on such a state of circumstances it should refuse to carry them into execution.'

118 *Drought* v. *Eustace* (1828) 1 Mol 328, 335 cited by Sheridan, *Equity*, n. 71 above, 130.

119 (1788) 2 Cox 77, 82.

It was made clear that inadequacy of price was only relevant as evidence of fraud.[120]

Heirs continued to be treated as a special group particularly worthy of protection.[121] This paternalistic attitude, was as much about protecting family property as individual heirs,[122] and is particularly evident in sales of reversions.[123] After *Gowland* v. *De Faria*[124] which involved a sale of an annuity using a reversion as security, this strict position, was arguably relaxed. Provided the purchaser could show that they had given a fair price the transaction stood.[125] Sailors dealing with prize money were also seen as a special case.[126]

The end of the usury laws

A Select Committee Report of 1818 painted a gloomy picture:

> That it is the opinion of this Committee, that the Laws regulating or restraining the rate of Interest have been extensively evaded, and have failed of the effect of imposing a maximum on such rate; and that of late years, from the constant excess of the market rate of interest above the rate limited by law, they have added to the expense incurred by borrowers on real security, and that such borrowers have been compelled to resort to the mode of granting annuities on lives, a mode which has been made a cover for obtaining higher interest than the rate limited by law, and has further subjected the borrowers to

120 *Collier* v. *Brown* (1788) 1 Cox 429; *White* v. *Damon* (1802) 7 Ves Jun 31; *Coles* v. *Trecothick* (1804) 9 Ves Jun 234, 246, Lord Eldon: 'Unless the inadequacy of price is such as shocks the conscience, and amounts in itself to conclusive and decisive evidence of fraud in the transaction, it is not itself a sufficient ground for refusing specific performance.'

121 *Barker* v. *Vansommer* (1782) 1 Bro CC 149 (sale); *Darley* v. *Singleton* (1810) Wight 25 (post-obit bond).

122 Newland, *Contract*, n. 97 above, 436. These concerns were sometimes openly expressed: *Twistleton* v. *Griffith* (1716) 1 P Wms 312, 313; *Cole* v. *Gibbons* (1734) 3 P Wms 290, 293; *Walmesley* v. *Booth* (1741) 2 Atk 27, 28; *Baugh* v. *Price* (1752) 1 Wils KB 320, 322; *Davis* v. *Duke of Marlborough* (1819) 2 Swan 108, 140.

123 *Coles* v. *Trecothick* (1804) 9 Ves Jun 234, 246. 124 (1810) 17 Ves Jun 20.

125 The process of establishing a fair value caused a split between those who favoured using actuarial and market values: *Headen* v. *Rosher* (1824) M'Cle & Yo 89. This approach was later abandoned: Sale of Reversions Act (1867) 31 & 32 Vict. c. 4.

126 *Baldwin* v. *Rochford* (1748) 1 Wils KB 229; *Taylour* v. *Rochford* (1751) 2 Ves Sen 281; *How* v. *Weldon* (1754) 2 Ves Sen 516. Prize money consisted of the proceeds from cargo captured from enemy ships: E. Roscoe, *A History of the English Prize Court* (London: Lloyds, 1924) 52.

> enormous charges, or forced them to make very disadvantageous sales of their estates.[127]

Little more than a quarter of a century later the usury laws would be repealed.[128] Imperfect though judicial regulation undoubtedly was, there is little doubt that without the intervention of Chancery in the seventeenth and eighteenth centuries, the situation for borrowers would have been very much worse.

127 *Select Committee on Usury Laws* (1818) (376) vi 137 19th Century House of Commons Sessional Papers.

128 Usury Laws Repeal Act (1854) 17 & 18 Vict. c. 90.

9

Protection of the vulnerable in financial transactions – what the common law vitiating factors can do for you

DAVID CAPPER

Introduction

This collection of essays is concerned with the protection of the vulnerable in financial transactions, and specifically examines the role of unconscionability in those transactions. We should understand 'financial transactions' in a broad sense, as any contract involving valuable assets and requiring significant expertise in assessing the wisdom of entering into it. We should understand vulnerability in a broad sense too. A clear picture of this is presented by the Australian doctrine of unconscionable dealing which makes much use of the concept of 'special disadvantage', described by Kitto J in *Blomley* v. *Ryan* as 'illness, ignorance, inexperience, impaired faculties, financial need or other circumstances' that affect a person's ability to conserve their own interests.[1] Unconscionability in this context and other contexts relevant to this chapter consists of taking unfair advantage of vulnerability.[2]

This chapter will examine the grounds upon which the common law may be prepared to rescind or grant other relief to a vulnerable contracting party because of some occurrence in making the contract. These grounds are commonly referred to as 'vitiating factors'. Five are commonly recognised – mistake, misrepresentation, duress, undue influence, and unconscionable dealing. In turn these can be sub-divided into two classes – mistake and unfair influence. Mistake contains the vitiating factor of 'mistake' itself as well as misrepresentation as a form of induced mistake. Unfair influence consists of all the others.

[1] (1956) 99 CLR 362, at 415.

[2] For a magisterial study of unconscionability see S. M. Waddams, 'Unconscionability in Contracts' (1976) 39 *Modern Law Review* 369.

An important question running through much of this chapter is the extent to which relief for the vulnerable depends on the unconscionable conduct of the other party, or whether relief is related solely to the adequacy of the vulnerable party's consent. The view expressed here is that the defendant's unconscionable conduct is a necessary precondition for the grant of relief for two interconnected reasons. First, as Professor Enonchong has pointed out, the common law does not disappoint contractual expectations unless the party to be disappointed has done something to make those expectations less than fully legitimate. In part this rests upon the objective theory of contracts – it is not what a party subjectively agreed to that matters but what he or she may reasonably be taken as agreeing to.[3] Secondly, as Professor Bigwood has argued, contracting parties are entitled to promote their self-interest and the only limitation on this is that they must observe the rules of the bargaining process.[4] The need for unconscionable conduct does not mean that protection for the vulnerable is weak because, as the argument below will demonstrate, unconscionable conduct is a highly context-specific concept and can consist of passive acceptance of benefits when the defendant knows or should know that the other party is vulnerable.

One subject which this chapter will not tackle in any detail is remedies. This is certainly not because this subject lacks importance but only because considerations of space render it impossible to do justice to it. For the most part it will be assumed that if the claimant demonstrates that the contract has been vitiated then the relief granted will be rescission.[5]

The chapter now proceeds to examination of the vitiating factors in turn to see what protection they may be able to provide vulnerable

[3] N. Enonchong, *Duress Undue Influence and Unconscionable Dealing* (London: Sweet and Maxwell, 2006) 349–50.

[4] R. Bigwood, 'Contracts by Unfair Advantage: From Exploitation to Transactional Neglect' (2005) 25 *Oxford Journal of Legal Studies* 65. See also R. Bigwood, 'Conscience and the Liberal Conception of Contract: Observing Basic Distinctions Part II' (2000) 16 *Journal of Contract Law* 191, at 220.

[5] There are some very difficult and important issues about rescission which cannot be explored in this chapter. E.g. on whether rescission is the act of the innocent party or the decision of the court, see J. O'Sullivan, 'Rescission as a Self-Help Remedy: A Critical Analysis' (2000) 59 *Cambridge Law Journal* 509–43; on whether rescission can be partial, see J. Poole and A. Keyser, 'Justifying Partial Rescission in English Law' (2005) 121 *Law Quarterly Review* 273; on rescission generally, see D. O'Sullivan, S. Elliott and R. Zakrzewski, *The Law of Rescission* (Oxford University Press, 2008).

parties, beginning with the first of the two factors concerned with entering into a contract subject to mistake.

Mistake

In broad terms non-induced mistake takes two forms, one where both parties are mistaken (common mistake) and the other where only one party is mistaken (unilateral mistake). In English law a common mistake has to be so fundamental that it makes the contract void and this test is virtually impossible to satisfy.[6] Until relatively recently there was a parallel doctrine of mistake in equity which made a contract voidable but this doctrine was effectively buried by the Court of Appeal in *The Great Peace*.[7] Although two doctrines originating at common law and in equity are difficult to justify there is a strong argument to be made for two doctrines recognising mistakes preventing contract formation (void contracts) and those creating defective contracts (voidable contracts) that should sometimes be rescinded.[8] In some parts of the common law world this is the position,[9] but seemingly not in England. Where it is, the basis for relief seems to be that once the mistake is discovered it is unconscionable for the defendant to bind the other party to the contract.[10] In this context unconscionability bears a different meaning to where the defendant procured the contract by unconscionable conduct and this probably militates against over-readiness to grant relief. Since unconscionability operates in this different way common mistake is less clearly related to the problem of vulnerability than other vitiating factors.

Unconscionability has more of a role to play in unilateral mistake. The common law has reached the position where A can rescind where B enters into the contract knowing that A is mistaken about a crucial aspect of the contract, or where B at least clearly should know of A's mistake.[11] On several occasions the remedy for unilateral mistake has been the rectification of a written contract into the one A believed the writing

[6] Consider, for example, *Bell* v. *Lever Bros* [1932] AC 161.
[7] [2002] EWCA Civ 1407; [2003] QB 679.
[8] A. Burrows, 'We Do This at Common Law but That in Equity' (2002) 22 *Oxford Journal of Legal Studies* 1, at 6; D. Capper, 'Reconfiguring Mistake in Contract Formation', in M. Bryan, *Private Law in Theory and Practice* (Routledge Cavendish, 2006) 119.
[9] See Capper ibid. [10] Ibid.
[11] *Taylor* v. *Johnson* (1983) 151 CLR 422.

reflected.[12] It must be emphasised that where the contractual negotiations are at arm's length, the mistaken party has had expert legal advice but between itself and the advisers the mistake has been carelessly missed, there will be no relief.[13] There is no vulnerability that is unconscionably exploited in such cases.

Vulnerability in the context of unilateral mistake as to identity is extremely complicated. The scenario evoked here is where the owner of a car (O) is dispossessed by a rogue (R) who fraudulently misrepresents his identity. Before O discovers the fraud R sells the car to a third party (T) who buys in good faith without notice that O is the true owner. According to a majority of the House of Lords in *Shogun Finance Ltd* v. *Hudson* the contract between O and R will be void if O intended to contract with the person R said he was and nobody else. If the contract is void R will acquire nothing which can be sold to T and O can repossess the car. This will be very hard on T who will probably have to try and recover from R the sum paid to R to buy the car. If O intended to contract with the person he or she dealt with (whoever this was) the O-R contract will be voidable for fraudulent misrepresentation. As T's good faith purchase intervenes before O can rescind T gets to keep the car and O has to try and recover damages from R.[14] It is very difficult for O to demonstrate that the identity of R as the person he said he was mattered so much that the contract would only have been made with him. Hence most 'identity fraud' cases like this are resolved in T's favour. The complicating feature in our context is that both O and T

[12] Rectification has been recognised as a legitimate remedy in *A. Roberts and Co Ltd* v. *Leicestershire County Council* [1961] Ch 555; *Riverlate Properties Ltd* v. *Paul* [1975] Ch 133 (relief denied because the lessee could not have been expected to know of the lessor's mistake); *Thomas Bates and Son Ltd* v. *Wyndham's (Lingerie) Ltd* [1981] 1 WLR 505; *Commissioner for the New Towns* v. *Cooper (GB) Ltd* [1995] 2 All ER 929; *George Wimpey UK Ltd* v. *V.I. Construction Ltd* [2005] EWCA Civ 77, [2005] BLR 135 (relief denied because the defendant's behaviour was not unconscionable). Professor Burrows and Professor McLauchlan have offered two contrasting perspectives on what rectification means in the context of unilateral mistake: see A. Burrows, 'Construction and Rectification', in A. Burrows and E. Peel (eds.), *Contract Terms* (Oxford University Press, 2007) 77; D.W. McLauchlan, 'The "Drastic" Remedy of Rectification for Unilateral Mistake' (2008) 124 *Law Quarterly Review* 608.

[13] *The Nai Genova* [1984] 1 Lloyds Rep 353; *George Wimpey UK Ltd* v. *V.I. Construction Ltd*, n. 12 above.

[14] [2003] UKHL 62, [2004] 1 AC 919. For analysis of this issue see C. MacMillan, 'Rogues, Swindlers and Cheats: The Development of Mistake of Identity in English Contract Law' (2005) 64 *Cambridge Law Journal* 711; D.W. McLauchlan, 'Mistake of Identity in Contract Formation' (2005) 21 *Journal of Contract Law* 1.

are vulnerable to R, so that the construction of a legal rule for the protection of the vulnerable is a most difficult task. In general, it is submitted that the loss should fall on O as the person better placed to avoid the loss.[15]

Misrepresentation

To rescind a contract on the ground of misrepresentation one must prove that the other party made a false pre-contractual statement of fact which induced the first party to enter into the contract.[16] Contract textbooks usually distinguish between three types of misrepresentation – fraudulent, negligent, and innocent – but if the first party wishes only to rescind the contract it is not generally necessary to distinguish between these types. Section 2(2) of the English Misrepresentation Act 1967 does allow the court to award damages in lieu of rescission in a case of non-fraudulent misrepresentation – negligent or innocent – if it thinks it would be equitable to do so having regard to the nature of the misrepresentation and the effect granting or refusing rescission would have on each party. Here it may be important to distinguish negligent from purely innocent misrepresentation. There is a statutory right to damages under section 2(1) for misrepresentations made without reasonable ground for believing in the truth of the statement made, and section 2 (3) requires any liability under section 2(2) to be taken into account in assessing damages under section 2(1). There are also two common law torts under which damages may be claimed for false statements causing loss, whether a contract is entered into or not. The tort of deceit applies to any dishonest statement[17] and, provided any losses can be causally linked to this recovery, is not limited by remoteness.[18] Negligent misstatement applies where a special relationship is created between the statement maker and another under which the former assumes responsibility to take reasonable care in the making of the statement.[19] This summary

[15] See Capper, n. 8 above, 145–50.

[16] These propositions are taken from J. Cartwright, *Misrepresentation Mistake and Non-Disclosure*, 2nd edn (London: Sweet and Maxwell, 2007) 2.02–03.

[17] The most frequently cited definition seems to be from the speech of Lord Herschell in *Derry* v. *Peek* (1889) 14 App Cas 337, at 374: 'fraud is proved when it is shewn that a false representation has been made (1) knowingly, or (2) without belief in its truth, or (3) recklessly, careless whether it be true or false.'

[18] *Smith New Court Securities Ltd* v. *Citibank NA* [1997] AC 254.

[19] *Hedley Byrne & Co Ltd* v. *Heller & Partners Ltd* [1964] AC 465.

masks a welter of fascinating issues but space is not available to explore them further.[20]

There is clearly much potential for the protection of the vulnerable in the principles sketched above. Many inaccurate pre-contractual statements can lead to rescission of the contract provided they have sufficient materiality. A damages remedy may be available in addition to or as an alternative to rescission. But does relief depend upon the unconscionable conduct of the defendant or is it afforded on the ground of the claimant's defective consent? The relief available probably does not much depend upon the answer to this question, but as the argument of the restitution scholars who favour the consent thesis rests in part upon misrepresentation it is convenient to consider it here.

This argument begins with the proposition that a contracting party who seeks only to rescind a contract and not to claim damages on any of the grounds above is only asking for the reversal of an unjust enrichment and not compensation for any wrong.[21] The argument is taken further by James Edelman who points out that what is unconscionable about non-fraudulent misrepresentations is that the misrepresentor seeks to enforce the contract *after* he discovers its inaccuracy.[22] *Ex post facto* unconscionability, it is argued, does not impact upon the making of the contract, only upon whether it should be enforced. All that went wrong at the time of making the contract was that the claimant's consent was vitiated by the morally innocent misinformation supplied by the defendant.

At a micro level this argument may be answered with the proposition that in contractual negotiations one should get the facts right and that it is unconscionable to get them wrong when one knows that the other party could thus be led into making the contract. In another dictum of Jessel MR in *Redgrave* v. *Hurd* his Lordship said:

> A man is not to be allowed to get a benefit from a statement which he now admits to be false. He is not to be allowed to say, for the purpose of civil

[20] For a very useful recent study of the remedy of damages for misrepresentation see J. Poole and J. Devenney, 'Reforming Damages for Misrepresentation: the Case for Coherent Aims and Principles' (2007) *Journal of Business Law* 269.

[21] P. Birks, 'Undue Influence as Wrongful Exploitation' (2004) 120 *Law Quarterly Review* 34; P. Birks, *Unjust Enrichment*, 2nd edn (Oxford: Clarendon, 2005) 176–8.

[22] J. Edelman, *Gain-Based Damages* (Oxford: Hart, 2002) 53. See also the following dictum of Jessel M. R. in *Redgrave* v. *Hurd* (1881) 20 Ch D 1, at 12–13: 'Even assuming that moral fraud must be shewn in order to set aside a contract, you have it where a man, having obtained a beneficial contract by a statement which he now knows to be false, insists upon keeping that contract. To do so is a moral delinquency: no man ought to seek to take advantage of his own false statements.'

> jurisdiction, that when he made it he did not know it to be false; he ought to have found that out before he made it.[23]

At a macro level the arguments are even stronger. We will see when we get to undue influence that the unconscionability basis for relief is even stronger than for misrepresentation. The argument of the restitution scholars begins from misrepresentation but is essentially made in the undue influence context. Were the common law to take the position that rescission for undue influence rests upon unconscionable conduct but that rescission for misrepresentation rests upon defective consent, Occam's razor[24] would be wielded. Neither is there much logic in the proposition that unconscionable conduct is required if the claimant seeks damages for misrepresentation but not if she only wants release from the contract. More fundamental still are the arguments presented in the introduction to this chapter, that depriving a contracting party of its expectation requires proof that it did something to deserve this.

Duress[25]

Where a contracting party is coerced by the other party into making a contract the contract may be rescinded. Three kinds of illegitimate pressure are recognised by the common law – duress to the person, duress of goods, and economic duress. Duress to the person consists of making threats to kill or threats of violence towards a contracting party or a member of his or her family.[26] Duress to goods largely takes the form of detention or threatened detention of the claimant's goods unless money is paid or some other benefit transferred.[27] Economic duress seems to be relied on most often when a party claims it was coerced into agreeing to some contractual alteration[28] either by a threat to break the contract or to do some lawful act.[29] But duress, particularly

[23] Ibid., at 12.

[24] Entia non sunt multiplicanda praeter necessitatem: never multiply entities beyond necessity.

[25] The summary of the law below is reliant upon Part 1 of Professor Enonchong's book cited in note 3. The problems with the doctrine were clearly identified in E. McKendrick, 'The Further Travails of Duress', in A. S. Burrows and A. Rodger (eds.), *Mapping the Law: Essays in Memory of Peter Birks* (Oxford University Press, 2006) 181.

[26] *Barton* v. *Armstrong* [1976] AC 104.

[27] Enonchong, n. 3 above, at 5–008.

[28] *DSND Subsea* v. *Petroleum Geo-Services* [2000] BLR 530.

[29] *CTN Cash and Carry Ltd* v. *Gallaher Ltd* [1994] 4 All ER 714; *Attorney General for England and Wales* v. *R* [2003] UKPC 22, [2004] 2 NZLR 577. As these cases show lawful act duress is particularly difficult to establish.

economic duress, has struggled to attain true theoretical coherence.[30] Five aspects of the doctrine have proved especially troublesome. First, there is the problem of achieving a clear concept of what is illegitimate pressure in the commercial context where contracting parties are prima facie entitled to exert lawful act pressure to obtain the best contractual terms they can. Secondly, doubt exists as to whether a threat to break a contract is always illegitimate pressure.[31] Thirdly, duress clearly cuts across other categories of relief, especially actual undue influence and unconscionable dealing discussed in the following sections, to the point where it is often difficult to see what additional protection it offers to vulnerable parties. Fourthly, there is the vexed question of what effect must the duress have on the mind of the coerced party. Initially the view was expressed that the will of the innocent party is 'overborne' by the duress to the point where he or she cannot give a meaningful consent.[32] This view was trenchantly criticised by Professor Atiyah[33] and others[34] on the ground that it would prevent contract formation altogether. The orthodox view of today is that duress taints consent in a sense similar to undue influence and unconscionable dealing. As Lord Scarman put it, the classic case of duress is 'not the lack of will to submit but the victim's intentional submission arising from the realisation that there is no other practical choice open to him'.[35] Fifthly, there seems to be authority for the proposition that different causative tests apply to different forms of duress – duress to the person seemingly has just to be 'a' cause of the decision to enter into the contract,[36] whereas other forms require a 'but for' test. These problems significantly reduce the utility value of duress in the present context.[37] In addition to this duress tends to operate outside of the relational contexts where vulnerable people are in most need of protection. It is to these relational contexts that we now turn.

30 For one attempt to give it this, see S. A. Smith, 'Contracting Under Pressure: A Theory of Duress' (1997) 56 *Cambridge Law Journal* 343.

31 Dyson J was in some doubt about this in *DSND Subsea Ltd* v. *Petroleum Geo-Services ASA* [2000] BLR 530.

32 *Pao On* v. *Lau Yiu Long* [1980] AC 614, at 635.

33 P. S. Atiyah, 'Economic Duress and the Overborne Will' (1982) 98 *Law Quarterly Review* 197.

34 *Crescendo Management Pty Ltd* v. *Westpac Banking Corporation* (1988) 19 NSWLR 40, at 45–6, per McHugh JA.

35 *Universe Tankships* v. *ITF* [1983] AC 366, at 400.

36 *Barton* v. *Armstrong* [1976] AC 104 (PC).

37 For another sceptical view of economic duress see the decision of the New South Wales Court of Appeal in *ANZ Banking Group* v. *Karam* [2005] NSWCA 344, [2005] NSWLR 64.

Undue influence

It remains customary to distinguish two kinds of undue influence – actual and presumed. *Actual* undue influence, as the name implies, is an influence which is both *undue* and actually proved. *Presumed* undue influence is an evidential inference drawn from a relationship between persons and the nature of a transaction arising out of that relationship. What this explanation shows is that there are not two kinds of undue influence, but one kind which can be established in two different ways.[38] Most of the controversy surrounding undue influence is concerned with presumed undue influence so most of the discussion in this section will be devoted to that. It will also be necessary to analyse the operation of undue influence and other vitiating factors in the context of surety debt, where a person in an emotional relationship with a borrower executes a charge over his/her property or the borrower and the surety's joint property to support a loan to the borrower. But first an important issue concerning actual undue influence must be revisited.

Actual undue influence

Since there is an obvious similarity between duress and actual undue influence it has been suggested that the two should be merged into one. The restitution scholars, from whose views this chapter has already parted company, have suggested that actual undue influence cases should be treated as duress.[39] The difficulty with this argument is that it is inseparably linked to the other argument, refuted below, that presumed undue influence is concerned with the claimant's defective consent and not the defendant's unconscionable conduct. But as presumed undue influence is nothing more than undue influence that exists as a matter of inference from primary facts it cannot be separated from actual undue influence. As was argued above in the context of duress,

[38] See *Royal Bank of Scotland* v. *Etridge (No. 2)* [2001] UKHL 44, [2002] 2 AC 773, at [93] (Lord Clyde).

[39] P. Birks and N. Y. Chin, 'On the Nature of Undue Influence', in J. Beatson and D. Friedmann (eds.), *Good Faith and Fault in Contract Law* (Oxford University Press, 1995) 57, at 63–5. Without explicitly supporting subsuming actual undue influence into duress Professor Burrows has also questioned whether both doctrines are necessary; see Burrows, n. 8 above, 6.

there is a surfeit of categories here but the one which should go is duress.[40]

Presumed undue influence

The presumption of undue influence arises from a combination of (a) a relationship of trust and confidence, or of ascendency and dependence, between two persons, and (b) a transaction which calls for an explanation. The presumption arising from proof of these matters is evidential rather than legal. The court may draw the inference that the defendant did not behave fairly to the other party so that the defendant will be at risk of an adverse finding[41] unless he produces evidence that the claimant entered into the transaction after 'full, free and informed' thought.[42] The usual way of doing the latter is by showing that the claimant had the benefit of independent advice, but in two-party undue influence cases this advice must *emancipate* the claimant from the undue influence and not just explain the nature of the transaction.[43]

The issue to be addressed now is one already averted to, whether presumed undue influence is concerned with the vulnerable party's consent or the unconscionable conduct of the defendant. The 'consent' thesis usually begins with reference to the seminal decision of the Court of Appeal in *Allcard* v. *Skinner* where Cotton LJ said:

> the court interferes, not on the ground that any wrongful act has in fact been committed by the donee, but on the ground of public policy, and to prevent the relations which existed between the parties and the influence arising therefrom being abused.[44]

Although this dictum dismisses the idea that any wrongful act has been proved it seems also to imply that a prophylactic approach is taken lest confidential relationships be abused. This is confirmed if reference is made to another dictum in the same case, this time from Bowen LJ:

[40] This appears close to the view of Dr Devenney and Professor Chandler: see J. Devenney and A. Chandler, 'Unconscionability and the Taxonomy of Undue Influence' (2007) *Journal of Business Law* 541, at 553–5.

[41] See *Etridge (No. 2)*, n. 38 above, at [14] per Lord Nicholls.

[42] *Zamet* v. *Hyman* [1961] 1 WLR 1442, at 1446, per Lord Evershed MR.

[43] *Etridge (No. 2)*, n. 38 above, at [20] per Lord Nicholls; *Hammond* v. *Osborn* [2002] EWCA Civ 885, at [50], per Ward LJ; *Jennings* v. *Cairns* [2003] EWCA Civ 1935, at [38], per Arden LJ.

[44] (1887) 36 Ch D 145, at 177. The consent thesis is broadly supported by Charlotte Smith in her essay on this case in C. Mitchell and P. Mitchell, *Landmark Cases in the Law of Restitution* (Oxford: Hart, 2006) 183.

> it is of essential importance to keep quite distinct two things which in their nature seem to be different – the rights of the donor, and the duties of the donee *and the obligations which are imposed on the conscience of the donee by the principles of this Court*.[45]

What this means is that the defendant has obligations imposed upon him by the nature of the parties' relationship and also carries an evidential burden of proving that he was not in breach of those duties. If he is in breach he has not committed a wrongful act for which he may be sued but he is liable to suffer the loss of the transaction he cannot show to have been procured without undue influence.[46]

Recent English case law clearly demonstrates that relief from a transaction vitiated by presumed undue influence is based upon the defendant's unconscionable conduct in the sense described in the previous paragraph. The *Etridge* framework alone demonstrates this through its equation of undue influence proved by the presumption with actual undue influence proved by the claimant's evidence.[47] Two post-*Etridge* Privy Council decisions remove any doubt that may have lingered after *Etridge*. In *Attorney General for England and Wales* v. *R* a member of the SAS failed to establish that his agreement to a confidentiality clause was vitiated by the presumed undue influence of his commanding officer.[48] Lord Hoffmann, delivering the majority judgment of the Board, said that 'undue influence is based upon the principle that a transaction to which consent has been obtained by unacceptable means should not be allowed to stand'.[49] In

[45] Ibid., at 189 (emphasis added). Both dicta were in the context of gifts but they apply with equal force to contracts.

[46] There have been instances where claimants have been awarded equitable compensation instead of rescission in undue influence cases; see, e.g. *Mahoney* v. *Purnell* [1996] 3 All ER 61; *Jennings* v. *Cairns* [2003] EWCA Civ 1935. This has been criticised on the ground that equitable compensation should be treated as damages and the latter may only be awarded for wrongs, i.e. torts or breaches of contract. See P. Birks, 'Unjust Factors and Wrongs: Pecuniary Rescission for Undue Influence' (1997) 5 *Restitution Law Review* 72. Professor Burrows would also prefer it if equitable compensation awards were treated as damages: see Burrows, n. 8 above, at 7–16. This chapter does not need to address the question whether monetary relief should only be awarded for 'wrongs' in the sense used in this footnote. Even if it should, it does not damage the thesis presented here that unconscionable conduct is required before relief from undue influence can be justified.

[47] Importantly Lord Nicholls in *Etridge* specifically said that 'undue influence has a connotation of impropriety. In the eye of the law, undue influence means that influence has been misused' [2001] UKHL 44, at [32].

[48] See *Attorney General for England and Wales* v. *R*, n. 29 above.

[49] Ibid., at [21]. In the next paragraph Lord Hoffmann went on to explain that in presumed undue influence the evidence may raise a rebuttable presumption of unacceptable means.

National Commercial Bank (Jamaica) Ltd v. *Hew* Lord Millett described undue influence as 'one of the grounds on which equity intervenes to give redress where there has been some unconscionable conduct on the part of the defendant. It arises whenever one party has acted unconscionably by exploiting the influence to direct the conduct of another which he has obtained from the relationship between them.'[50] Particularly clear on the kind of unconscionable conduct in vogue here is the decision of the Court of Appeal in *Hammond* v. *Osborn*.[51] The deceased was an elderly bachelor in poor health befriended by the defendant. She prepared two meals a day for him and did his shopping. She was also authorised to draw on his current account for the payment of bills and accessories. The friendship developed to the point where the deceased gave her almost all his money (*c.* £300,000), with some of which she bought a house for herself. The deceased received no independent advice and his estate was left with a £50,000 bill for capital gains tax on his disposals. He still retained his house and his pension but he had little to rely on if his circumstances were to change. The presumption of undue influence was raised and the defendant failed to rebut it. The Court of Appeal made it clear that her conduct was not reprehensible and steered clear of unconscionability rhetoric in its judgments. But it is perfectly clear that the acceptance of such an extravagant gift without the insistence that the donor take independent advice about the effect this would have on his finances and alternative ways of showing his appreciation for the defendant's support, was unconscionable conduct.[52]

So presumed undue influence is not a claimant-sided form of relief as the restitution scholars have contended. But neither is it entirely a defendant-sided form of relief. In truth what is required is both defective consent on the part of the claimant and unconscionable conduct by the defendant which procured that consent.[53] Since the concept of unconscionable conduct analysed here is at least similar to Professor Bigwood's theory of transactional neglect it is capable of providing powerful protection for vulnerable persons.[54] In fact this may even be more extensive

[50] [2003] UKPC 51, at [29]. [51] [2002] EWCA Civ 885.

[52] An essentially similar approach was taken in *Jennings* v. *Cairns* [2003] EWCA Civ 1935, *Niersmans* v. *Pesticcio* [2004] EWCA Civ 372, *Macklin* v. *Dowsett* [2004] EWCA Civ 904, and *Goodchild* v. *Bradbury* [2006] EWCA Civ 1868. See also the support given to this concept of unconscionable conduct in Devenney and Chandler, n. 40 above, at 560.

[53] D. Capper, 'Undue Influence and Unconscionability: A Rationalisation' (1998) 114 *Law Quarterly Review* 479.

[54] See Bigwood, n. 4 above.

protection than a purely consent-based system because, in order to protect the security of contracts, it might be necessary to restrict relief to cases where there was no meaningful consent at all, not just a vitiated consent. This chapter's conception of undue influence is essentially similar to Mindy Chen-Wishart's extremely thoughtful study resting upon the defendant's abuse of relational norms.[55]

Third party undue influence

Over the last two decades the English courts have developed principles to deal with the phenomenon of a person in a close emotional relationship with a borrower standing surety for a loan from a bank and executing a charge over her property or the borrower and the surety's joint property to secure that guarantee. The problem which the courts have been trying to address is the borrower procuring the surety's support through undue influence or some other unconscionable behaviour. The surety will have a right to set aside the guarantee if the bank is sufficiently affected by the borrower's unconscionable conduct.

The law is currently summarised in the seminal decision of the House of Lords in *Royal Bank of Scotland* v. *Etridge (No. 2)*.[56] Since the risk of unconscionable conduct by the borrower is perceived to be high the bank is obliged to ensure that the surety is independently advised in all cases where it knows that the relationship between the borrower and the surety is non-commercial. This will normally be the case and this is not altered by the surety being a director or shareholder in the borrower's company unless that position is a very significant one. However if it appears that the loan is joint this will only be treated as a suretyship transaction if the bank knows that this is the true position.[57] If there was unconscionable

[55] M. Chen-Wishart, 'Undue Influence: *Beyond* Impaired Consent and Wrongdoing towards a Relational Analysis', in A. Burrows and A. Rodger, n. 25 above, at 201; M. Chen-Wishart, 'Undue Influence: Vindicating Relationships of Influence' (2006) 59 *Current Legal Problems* 231. In my opinion this is by some distance the best work on the nature of undue influence.

[56] See n. 38. For analysis see M. Oldham, 'If at First . . . Undue Influence and the House of Lords' (2002) 61 *Cambridge Law Journal* 29; M. P. Thompson, 'Wives, Sureties and Banks' (2002) *Conveyancer and Property Lawyer* 174; S. Wong, 'Revisiting *Barclays Bank v. O'Brien* and Independent Legal Advice for Vulnerable Sureties' (2002) *Journal of Business Law* 439; D. O'Sullivan, 'Developing *O'Brien*' (2002) 118 *Law Quarterly Review* 337; A. Phang and H. Tjio, 'The Uncertain Boundaries of Undue Influence' (2002) *Lloyd's Maritime and Commercial Law Quarterly* 231.

[57] The loan appeared joint in *Chater* v. *Mortgage Agency Services Number Two Ltd* [2003] EWCA Civ 490 so the lender was unaffected.

conduct by the borrower and the bank fails to have the surety independently advised the surety may have the guarantee set aside.[58]

The role of the independent adviser is different in three-party 'undue influence' cases than in two-party cases. In two-party cases the independent adviser must emancipate the weaker party from the undue influence but in three-party cases needs only to explain the nature of the transaction to her.[59] This goes beyond giving a formal explanation of the nature of the documents to be signed and requires advice as to the state of the borrower's account and the economic risks the surety is running. The bank must put the adviser in possession of this information and to do this must obtain the borrower's consent to its release, otherwise the transaction cannot proceed. On completion of the necessary interview with the surety the adviser must then certify that the surety has been independently advised and at this point the bank's security would generally be safe. The advice is at a lower level in three-party cases because the bank is not the party alleged to be guilty of unconscionable conduct so the 'reasonable steps' required to protect itself from losing the guarantee are necessarily of a lower level. Where the bank is aware of information suggesting that the surety is the victim of unconscionable conduct it must supply this information to the adviser and it is probable in these circumstances that the adviser will have to emancipate the surety from the effects of that conduct or withdraw from the transaction.[60] However, it is not otherwise the role of the adviser to veto the transaction, even if it seems seriously unwise. An adviser may also act for the borrower because insistence on a separate adviser for the surety would increase transaction costs, but the adviser should withdraw if it seems that there is a serious conflict of interest.

Subject to one caveat, it is submitted that the current procedure maintains a reasonable balance between the interests of the bank and the surety. Although it has been shown that the surety's problem is more a matter of protecting the emotional relationship with the borrower than

[58] Note that it is the bank's responsibility to have the surety independently advised. The guarantee was set aside in *Greene King Plc* v. *Stanley* [2001] EWCA Civ 1966 because it was the borrower who arranged advice for the sureties.

[59] This protection is similar to that offered to surety wives under the principle of *Yerkey* v. *Jones* (1939) 63 CLR 439; *Garcia* v. *National Australia Bank Ltd* (1998) 194 CLR 395.

[60] Fiona R. Burns, 'The Elderly and Undue Influence Inter Vivos' (2003) *Legal Studies* 251, at 278–9; O'Sullivan, n. 56 above, 349. This probably means situations as egregious as *Credit Lyonnais Bank Nederland NV* v. *Burch* [1997] 1 All ER 144.

the latter's unconscionable conduct,[61] it is difficult to expect more of the independent advice than what is currently provided. But it is open to question whether the bank should retain the benefit of the guarantee where it fails to have a surety in a non-commercial relationship with the borrower independently advised and there was no unconscionable conduct by the borrower. It is true that all through the development of this principle a solution has been sought to the problem of borrower unconscionable behaviour which affects the bank. So if the risk of borrower misbehaviour does not materialise it might be said that there is no reason to avoid the guarantee. But it would not expect too much of banks to make them accountable for what they should do anyway and it would offer sureties some protection against the myriad of problems they face when asked to execute these guarantees.[62] Indeed this is in substance the position according to the Australian principle of *Yerkey* v. *Jones*,[63] applicable certainly to surety wives but potentially ripe for extension to other persons in vulnerable emotional relationships.

Unconscionable dealing

The last vitiating factor potentially offers most protection to the vulnerable because it applies in circumstances of relational inequality where the stronger party can be shown to have acquired an economic advantage through unconscionable conduct.[64] The two main elements of the doctrine are relational inequality and the defendant's unconscionable conduct. Substantive unconscionability is an evidentiary factor which assists in establishing unconscionable conduct in cases where the latter is not overt, but the relational inequality and substantive terms strongly suggest that the transaction could only have been produced this way. The principal advantages of this doctrine from the vulnerable's perspective are that the relational inequality need not be squeezed into a box like the relationship of confidence and trust found to exist between the employer

[61] B. Fehlberg, *Sexually Transmitted Debt* (Oxford University Press, 1997).

[62] These views are also developed in D. Capper, 'Banks, Borrowers, Sureties and Undue Influence – A Half-Baked Solution to a Thoroughly Cooked Problem' (2002) 10 *Restitution Law Review* 100.

[63] (1939) 63 CLR 649; reaffirmed in *Garcia* v. *National Australia Bank Ltd* (1998) 194 CLR 395.

[64] The legal framework is set out in more detail in D. Capper, 'Unconscionable Bargains', in N. Dawson, D. Greer and P. Ingram (eds.), *One Hundred and Fifty Years of Irish Law* (SLS, 1996) 44; N. Bamforth, 'Unconscionability as a Vitiating Factor' (1995) *Lloyd's Maritime and Commercial Law Quarterly* 538; Capper, n. 53 above.

and employee in *Credit Lyonnais Bank Nederland NV* v. *Burch*,[65] and the unconscionable conduct can take the form of passive receipt of benefits in circumstances where the stronger party knows that the weaker is labouring under significant disadvantage.[66] Where the latter applies, the obligation of the defendant is almost like a duty to take reasonable care to ensure that the claimant fully understands the implications of the transaction and thus fully consents to it.

Unconscionable dealing is a relatively unfamiliar ground of relief in England. Courts in Ireland and the major Commonwealth jurisdictions are much more familiar with it.[67] Its application in England recently has been conservative to say the least. In *Portland Building Society* v. *Dusangh* the Court of Appeal found nothing unconscionable in the grant of a 25-year repayment mortgage by a 72-year-old gentleman born in India to support a loan to his son to enable the latter to set up a Spar supermarket business.[68] Simon Brown LJ said: 'I simply cannot accept that building societies are required to police transactions of this nature to ensure that parents (even poor and ignorant ones) are wise in seeking to assist their children.' In *Jones* v. *Morgan* the Court of Appeal did not think it unconscionable for a stockbroker to lend an unsophisticated farmer £105,000 at 15 per cent interest charged on land the farmer was trying to convert into a nursing home, together with a 50 per cent share in any company or organisation which came to run the nursing home.[69] These decisions have relied much upon a dictum of Browne-Wilkinson J in *Multiservice Bookbinding Ltd* v. *Marden* that 'one of the parties to [the contract] has imposed the objectionable terms in a morally reprehensible manner, that is to say, in a way which affects his conscience'.[70] In their apparent insistence

65 [1997] 1 All ER 144.

66 As examples of passive receipt unconscionability see *Rooney* v. *Conway* [1982] 5 NIJB (Hutton J); *Bridgewater* v. *Leahy* (1998) 194 CLR 457.

67 See Capper, n. 64 above.

68 [2000] 2 All ER (Comm) 221, [2000] EWCA Civ 142. The decision is criticised in L. McMurtry, 'Unconscionability and Undue Influence: An Interaction?' (2000) *Conveyancer and Property Lawyer* 573.

69 [2001] EWCA Civ 995. The farmer was not well served by his solicitor but it is not clear that this should make a decisive difference. The transaction was set aside, but because of a clog on the equity of redemption. For critical commentary see J. P. Devenney, 'A Pack of Unruly Dogs: Unconscionable Bargains, Lawful Act (Economic) Duress and Clogs on the Equity of Redemption' (2002) *Journal of Business Law* 539.

70 [1979] Ch 84, at 110; quoted with approval by Peter Millett QC in *Alec Lobb (Garages) Ltd* v. *Total Oil (Great Britain) Ltd* [1983] 1 WLR 87, at 94. Significantly Browne-Wilkinson J later said (at 111) that where no explanation was provided for an unreasonable or unusual stipulation the court might infer that unfair advantage had been taken.

that unconscionable conduct involves some form of imposition the English courts have not only ignored authority from other jurisdictions but have also disregarded the historical antecedents of unconscionable dealing in the *Fry* v. *Lane* line of cases.[71] This view of unconscionable dealing is very firmly defendant-sided,[72] but analysis of the cases throughout the common law world demonstrates that both claimant-sided and defendant-sided elements are crucial to this doctrine.

Were the English courts to return to the true nature of unconscionable dealing much more protection of the vulnerable would be afforded. Their reluctance to embrace it fully is probably explicable in terms similar to the hesitation surrounding its proposed merger with undue influence.[73] This is the 'fear of opening the floodgates of discretion'.[74] But can it seriously be argued that undue influence, if retained as a separate doctrine, is truly capable of securing these floodgates? What is the meaning of 'relationship of trust and confidence' or 'ascendency and dependence'? What is a transaction that 'calls for explanation'? Retaining it as a separate doctrine presents the additional problem of trying to distinguish it from unconscionable dealing, as the *Burch* case graphically illustrates.[75] The certainty argument actually supports merger of these doctrines. Furthermore, the problems identified with duress above would support the more comprehensive merger of doctrines advocated by Justice Phang.[76]

Conclusion

Five vitiating factors offer vulnerable persons a patchwork quilt of protection from entering into financial transactions they would do better to avoid. As duress, undue influence and unconscionable dealing focus more on relationships open to abuse, these are the doctrines most likely

[71] (1889) 40 Ch D 312, at 322, where Kay J said: 'The result of the decisions is that where a purchase is made from a poor and ignorant man at a considerable undervalue, the vendor having no independent advice, a Court of Equity will set aside the transaction.' For further elucidation of this point see Devenney and Chandler, n. 40 above, and Devenney, n. 69 above.

[72] In line with the views of Birks and Chin, n. 39 above, who distinguish unconscionable dealing from the claimant-sided undue influence in this way.

[73] Capper, n. 53 above.

[74] Phang and Tjio, n. 56 above, at 242.

[75] See n. 65 above. This case should have been pleaded as an unconscionable bargain. As there was no way the Court of Appeal was going to uphold the guarantee it had to squeeze the case into undue influence.

[76] A. Phang, 'Undue Influence – Methodology, Sources and Linkages' (1995) *Journal of Business Law* 552.

to be invoked. Common mistake does not arise in specifically relational contexts, so the deep problems in that doctrine need not detain us for long. Unilateral mistake and misrepresentation can arise in vulnerability contexts, but sufficiently frequently in others that the immense problems, particularly with misrepresentation, are better left to another occasion. Of the three remaining vitiating factors duress is the least useful and cuts across other categories so much that merger with undue influence and unconscionable dealing is where its future should lie. Undue influence has done the bulk of the work in protecting the vulnerable, at least in England, but it overlaps with unconscionable dealing so much that problems of inclusivity and delineation arise, to the extent that coherent doctrine is something the common law still seeks. That coherence can be found if undue influence and unconscionable dealing (together with duress) are merged together into one doctrine. The third-party undue influence scenario of today would then become one of third-party unconscionable dealing. This would not necessarily involve any change to the principles applying in that area, but if the argument presented above, that the bank should lose the benefit of a guarantee where it fails to have the surety independently advised when it should, were accepted, this could be rationalised as unconscionable conduct by the bank.

10

Borrowers as consumers: new notions of unconscionability for domestic borrowers

SARAH NIELD

Introduction

The classic situation in which unconscionable bargains and the wider doctrine of oppressive and unconscionable terms developed was where an impecunious borrower took a loan to ease his plight. Originally it was an heir to a landed estate who mortgaged his expectant interest to secure that loan,[1] but it is now the domestic borrower who mortgages his or her home to fund either a loan for its purchase or to secure other liabilities. It is in this latter context that this chapter will consider the current statutory protections that have overshadowed the original equitable jurisdiction and introduced new notions of unconscionability to English law.

The idea of the statutory protection in this context is not new. Laws against usury, which initially outlawed and later controlled interest rates, date from the Middle Ages and were only abolished in the mid-nineteenth century.[2] Statutory protection continued to control moneylenders[3] but, as credit has become part of everyday life, there has been an overhaul of the statutory landscape governing the supply and control of credit to domestic borrowers.[4] This legislation has abandoned the broad discretionary jurisdiction that justified intervention on the grounds of unconscionability

1 *Earl of Aylesford* v. *Morris* (1872–73) LR 8 Ch App 484.

2 The laws against usury were finally abolished by the Usury Laws Repeal Act 1854.

3 See, for example, Moneylenders Act 1900.

4 The Consumer Credit Act 1974 was passed following the recommendations of the Committee on Consumer Credit, Cmnd 4596, 1971 (Crowther Committee). It was subject to major review by the Government White Paper *Fair Clear and Competitive: The Consumer Credit Market in the 21st Century* (Cm 6040, 2003). After a number of scandals, in particular the collapse of Barings Bank, the Financial Services and Markets Act 2000 introduced independent regulation of the financial services industry by the Financial Services Authority. First legal mortgages of homes came under the regulatory umbrella of the Financial Services Authority in 2004.

and in its place has developed a complex web of statutory provisions and regulatory responsibilities, which protect the impecunious borrower as a consumer. It is not intended in this chapter to examine each of these measures in detail but to look to the broad sweep of this new statutory landscape. In so doing three broad themes will be considered, namely the regulatory control of the market, controls over the borrower/lender relationship and the routes that provide redress to domestic borrowers.

The statutory overview

The statutory landscape operates at these three levels. At the regulatory level the Financial Services and Markets Act 2000 (FSMA) and Consumer Credit Act 1974 (CCA) provide a divided regime for the control of the secured domestic lending market. Regulatory control operates through the Financial Services Authority (FSA) where the lending falls within the FSMA, and the Office of Fair Trading (OFT) where the lending is governed by the CCA. Domestic mortgages are also recognised as consumer products, with the borrower entitled to protection under the Unfair Terms in Consumer Contract Regulations and the Consumer Protection from Unfair Trading Regulations. Additional control of the borrower/lender relationship is provided by sections 140A–D of the CCA, but only where the borrowing falls within that statute.

A domestic borrower in dispute with a lender has various routes to redress. They may take advantage of the dispute resolution services of the Financial Services Ombudsman (FSO). They may also have legal rights of action where the mortgage breaches the rules laid down by the FSMA or CCA. Particularly significant in this respect is the right to bring a claim for breach of statutory duty under the FSMA and the potential unenforceability of non-compliant CCA mortgages. Last, but by no means least, is the possibility of asking the court to delay enforcement of the lenders' rights to enforce their security, notably their right to take possession, provided by section 36 of the Administration of Justice Act 1970 as amended (AJA) and the newly introduced Pre-action Protocol for Possession Actions based upon Mortgagee Arrears (the Protocol).[5]

[5] See www.civiljusticecouncil.gov.uk.

The divided market

The first task for the aggrieved borrower is to work out exactly what protection and redress may be available to him or her. The FSMA governs Regulated Mortgage Contracts,[6] being first legal mortgages of the borrower's home entered into after November 2004. However, CCA protection is more difficult to work out.[7] To avoid dual regulation, mortgages regulated by the FSA[8] and mortgages made to certain institutional lenders[9] are excluded and so the CCA generally covers the equitable or second mortgage market. The focus is on mortgages made by individuals,[10] although high net worth borrowers can elect to forgo protection.[11] Originally CCA protection was limited to loans not exceeding £25,000 but this ceiling has been removed as from April 2008.[12] Second or equitable mortgages in excess of £25,000 entered into prior to April 2008 continue to be unregulated.

There is thus a dual regulatory system, overseen by the FSA in respect of Regulated Mortgage Contracts and the OFT for CCA regulated mortgages. It is difficult to see the justification for this split, which appears to be a result of history and industry influence rather than rational policy. At the time of the enactment of the CCA in 1974 first legal mortgages of the home were not the object of regulation. They were primarily made by building societies that were thought to be already sufficiently regulated by voluntary industry codes of conduct. It was the second mortgage market, granted largely by finance companies to borrowers needing to consolidate debts or raise additional finance, which was the target of regulation. Even then regulation was limited to smaller loans not exceeding £25,000, a ceiling which became unrealistic as house prices soared. The deregulation of the home finance market led to pressure for independent regulation and in 2004 the industry reluctantly succumbed to what was perceived to be the lesser evil of FSA regulation.[13] Regulation is thus split according to the type of loan not the type of borrower. Yet there

[6] See SI 2001/544 Article 61 (as amended).

[7] See S. Brown, 'The Consumer Credit Act 2006: Real Additional Mortgagor Protection' (2007) *Conveyancer and Property Lawyer* 325.

[8] S. 16(6C) CCA. [9] S. 16(1) CCA.

[10] S. 8 CCA, although some business loans e.g. to a sole trader or small partnership are regulated, see s. 16B.

[11] S. 16A CCA and SI 2007/1168.

[12] S. 2 CCA. The £25,000 ceiling still applies to business loans.

[13] See Council of Mortgage Lenders' policy paper, 'Mortgage Regulation – Background', available at www.cml.org.uk/cml/policy/issues/271.

is evidence that it is the sub-prime borrower that is most in need of protection, although sub-prime borrowing spans the regulatory divide.[14] It is thus not surprising that there have been calls, both by lenders and by those representing borrowers, for a single regulatory system,[15] and that the Treasury is now actively exploring this possibility.[16]

Other distinctions and similarities

It should be noted at this point that other distinctions exist between Regulated Mortgage Contracts and CCA mortgages. Remedial responses differ where a mortgage fails to comply with the regulatory regime to which it is subject. Loans by unlicensed lenders are prima facie unenforceable under both regulatory regimes[17] but the protection afforded to a borrower with a non-compliant CCA mortgage is wider than to a borrower under a Regulated Mortgage Contract which falls foul of the rules prescribed by the FSMA. A non-compliant CCA mortgage is prima facie unenforceable[18] but a breach of the rules governing Regulated Mortgage Contracts merely leads to monetary redress through an action against the lender for breach of statutory duty.[19]

A further and particularly significant distinction relates to the court's jurisdiction to intervene: the court's ability to delay possession proceedings, under the AJA and the Protocol, as well as to control unfair terms and practices under general consumer regulation, is common but the court has wider jurisdiction to control enforcement and mortgage terms under the CCA. The court may do so either upon enforcement, under

[14] See for instance Citizens Advice, *Set Up to Fail: CAB Clients' Experience and Secured Loan Arrears Problems* (December 2007), available at www.citizensadvice.org.uk and FSA Mortgage Effectiveness Review 2006 available at www.fsa.gov.uk.

[15] The Council of Mortgage Lenders has called for regulation of the secured credit market solely through the FSA – see Council of Mortgage Lenders' Response to the Consumer Credit Directive available at www.cml.org.uk. Citizens Advice has called for a new regulatory body for home mortgages – see *Set up to Fail*, n. 14 above.

[16] See Treasury, Mortgage Regulation (December 2010), available at www.hm-treasury.gov.uk.

[17] A loan by an unlicensed lender under the CCA is unenforceable save by order of the OFT – see s. 40(1) CCA and a loan by an unlicensed lender under the FSMA is unenforceable save by order of the court – see ss. 26 and 28 FSMA. The unlicensed lender is also subject to criminal liability.

[18] See ss. 65, 92, 105 and 126 CCA. The court may order enforcement and is given a wider discretion in exercising its jurisdiction in the light of the prejudice caused to the borrower and the culpability of the lender. If enforcement is ordered the court may impose conditions or vary or amend terms – see ss. 127, 135 and 136 CCA.

[19] S. 150 FSMA.

section 136, and more generally under sections 140A–C. There is no similar jurisdiction in relation to Regulated Mortgage Contacts.

The FSO, FSA and OFT do work closely together to share information and coordinate action. For instance, the FSO reports the nature of common complaints and any unfair terms or practices it uncovers to the FSA and OFT. However, these measures smack of papering over the cracks of an illogical division of regulatory responsibility, not to mention the inefficiencies and increased costs that must result.[20]

Market regulation

Recent decades have seen big changes in the mortgage market and its regulation. Building societies, once the major source of home finance, have been deregulated and banks have entered the market with many building societies choosing to become banks answerable to their shareholders rather than their members. Increased competition saw a dramatic rise in the availability of credit, checked only by the global credit crunch. Total mortgage debt grew from 50 to 80 per cent of Gross Domestic Product during the decade from 1997 to 2007 with in the region of 11.7 million mortgages securing loans exceeding £½ trillion.[21] Governments have largely stood back from state provision of housing and encouraged home ownership through relatively cheap and easily available mortgage finance as well as shared ownership schemes that have enticed those on low incomes into the housing market.[22] As house prices increased, the equity created also encouraged greater consumption, funded again by secured credit. The effect of these policies is now being felt with the restriction of credit triggering a steep recession.

Market regulation has focused upon compliance with processes from initial qualification to the market through to continuing accountability by the monitoring of compliance with industry benchmarks of good practice in which the market forces of choice and competition are allowed to operate.[23]

[20] M. Oldham, 'Mortgages', in L. Tee, *Land Law, Issues, Debates, Policy* (Cullompton: Willan Publishing, 2002) 169.

[21] See the Turner Review, n. 16 above.

[22] L. Whitehouse, 'The Home-owner: Citizen or Consumer', in S. Bright and J. Dewar (eds.), *Land Law Themes and Perspectives* (Oxford University Press, 1998).

[23] See for instance I. Ramsay 'Consumer Law, Regulatory Capitalism and the New Learning in Regulation' (2006) 28 *Sydney Law Review* 9 and P. Cartwright, 'Consumer Protection in Financial Services: Putting the Law in Context', in P. Cartwright (ed.), *Consumer Protection in Financial Services* (London: Kluwer Law International, 1999).

The avowed aim is encapsulated by the mantra of 'responsible lending and responsible borrowing'. The 'decentred regulatory approach' of the mortgage market and the twin goals of responsible lending and responsible borrowing are evident in the FSMA and CCA. The objectives of both pieces of legislation are, on the one hand, to support responsible lending through licensing and compliance with codes of conduct which epitomise responsible lending practices and, on the other hand, responsible borrowing by encouraging consumer choice through the power of information.

Before the credit crunch, competition was promoted by a dazzling array of mortgage products with lending at record levels to a wide range of borrowers. With the assistance of standardised comparative information, some borrowers were able to exercise choice by switching to the lender offering the most attractive terms.[24] However, the provision of information is only part of the story. Borrowers also need to be able to evaluate that information in the light of their financial resources but the legislation provides no mechanisms to ensure that they are able to do so. The financial education of borrowers is a policy aim and there is a host of OFT and FSA leaflets to provide guidance but these are loose measures which depend upon the willingness and ability of vulnerable borrowers to use them effectively. Evidence from both the FSA[25] and the Citizens Advice Bureau[26] suggest that certain borrowers, particularly those in the sub-prime market, did not shop around and were unable to assess their financial position to make viable funding choices.

Patently, lenders have failed to lend responsibly.[27] Lenders were prepared to offer 100 per cent plus mortgages[28] and have used higher and higher multipliers of borrowers' incomes to set lending ceilings.[29] Lenders were also lax in checking the borrowers' ability to pay and were too keen to accept self-certification.[30] Lenders further stand accused of failing to bring home to borrowers the risks and consequences of default associated with their borrowing when evidence suggests that

[24] See FSA, Mortgage Effectiveness Review 2006, available at www.fsa.gov.uk.

[25] FSA, Mortgage Effectiveness Reviews of 2006 and 2008, available at www.fsa.gov.uk.

[26] *Set Up to Fail*, n. 14 above.

[27] It is now evident that the attraction of both reduced exposure and the profits generated by the securitisation of their mortgage investments encouraged lenders to lend irresponsibly.

[28] The proportion of 100 per cent plus mortgages almost doubled from 3.9 per cent in 2005 to 7.4 per cent in 2007: see the Turner Review, n. 16 above.

[29] The proportion of mortgages securing loans exceeding 3.5 of income rose from 20 per cent in 2005 to 30 per cent in 2007: see the Turner Review, n. 16 above.

[30] *Set up to Fail*, n. 14 above; also FSA, Mortgage Market Review (October 2009), available at www.fsa.gov.uk.

many borrowers, particularly within the sub-prime market, do not understand the mortgage basics of variable repayments and the possibility of repossession if those payments are not met.[31]

Control and monitoring of lenders operates through the tried and tested formula of licensing. Lenders must be licensed by the OFT under the CCA and the FSA under the FSMA. Under both statutory regimes a loan by an unlicensed lender carries the stigma of criminal liability[32] and the loan itself is unenforceable except, in the case of a Regulated Mortgage Contract, when the court is persuaded to order enforcement in the light of the culpability of the lender,[33] or, in the case of a CCA regulated loan by order of the OFT.[34]

Monitoring by both the FSA and the OFT is ongoing with both regulators able to investigate licence holders, and with powers to warn and to revoke, vary, impose conditions on and refuse to renew licences if they find anything untoward.[35] The stick is not the only influence on behaviour; market codes and benchmarks of good practice under both regimes also hold out the carrot to influence lenders' behaviour. Yet, evidence suggests that this decentred regulation has fallen short.[36]

FSMA – Principles, codes and the MCOB

Any permission to carry on mortgage business is subject to the statements of principle, codes of practice[37] and rules made by the FSA.[38] The statements, codes and rules represent three tiers of regulatory guidance. The statements of principle set out the overarching ethos governing the conduct of mortgage business. The codes of practice provide examples of the types of activity that, on the one hand comply with and on the other hand breach the relevant principles, but it is the rules that set out the detailed regulations.[39]

A breach of the principles or the codes of conduct does not provide any right of action to the borrower. Enforcement is solely through disciplinary action by the FSA.[40] A breach of the rules may trigger an

[31] Ibid. [32] S. 23 FSMA and s. 36 CCA. [33] Ss. 26 and 28 FSMA. [34] S. 40(1) CCA.
[35] See ss. 32–33A–E CCA and Part IV FSMA.
[36] *Set Up to Fail*, n. 14 above, and Mortgage Market Review, n. 30 above. [37] S. 64 FSMA.
[38] S. 138 FSMA.
[39] Ss. 8–10 FSMA. In preparing the principles, codes and rules, the FSA is required to consult with bodies representing the mortgage industry and consumers.
[40] Ss. 64(8) and 66 FSMA.

action by the borrower for breach of statutory duty, although the enforceability of the mortgage is unaffected.[41]

The rules regulating mortgage business are set out in that part of the FSA handbook entitled *Mortgages: Conduct of Business* (MCOB).[42] The MCOB regime adopts a 'cradle to grave' approach which governs the whole course of the borrower's relationship with the lender. There are rules governing the marketing of mortgage products[43] and the provision of information through all stages from the first visit of a potential borrower, through to the pre-application illustration of the available loan terms[44] and the mortgage offer itself,[45] with continuing requirements for information on the actual grant of the loan and periodically during the mortgage term.[46] Further rules call upon the lender to lend responsibly in the light of a prospective borrower's ability to pay.[47] If the borrower should fall into arrears, there are rules which regulate how the lender should respond.[48]

The rules are intended to meet the overarching statement of the principles which call upon lenders 'to pay due regard to the interests of its customers and treat them fairly',[49] 'to pay due regard to the information needs of its clients, and communicate information to them in a way which is clear, fair and not misleading',[50] and to 'take reasonable care to ensure the suitability of its advice and discretionary decisions for any customer who is entitled to rely upon its judgment'.[51]

The twin principles of responsible lending and responsible borrowing are enshrined within a lender's duty to provide information to the borrower in an intelligible and prescribed form, which should enable borrowers to compare different mortgage products and make informed choices about which mortgage best suits their needs. The most significant piece of information is the pre-application illustration, known as the Key Facts Illustration which the borrower must be given time to consider.[52] This illustration must be in the prescribed form to facilitate comparison between different mortgage products. It must contain details

[41] S. 150 FSMA. [42] http://fsahandbook.info/FSA/html/handbook/MCOB.
[43] http://fsahandbook.info/FSA/html/handbook/MCOB/3.
[44] http://fsahandbook.info/FSA/html/handbook/MCOB/5.
[45] http://fsahandbook.info/FSA/html/handbook/MCOB/6.
[46] http://fsahandbook.info/FSA/html/handbook/MCOB/7.
[47] http://fsahandbook.info/FSA/html/handbook/MCOB/11.
[48] http://fsahandbook.info/FSA/html/handbook/MCOB/13. [49] MCOB, Principle 6.
[50] MCOB, Principle 7. [51] MCOB, Principle 9.
[52] http://fsahandbook.info/FSA/html/handbook/MCOB/2/4. The borrower must also be given time to consider the mortgage offer.

of (inter alia) the type of mortgage, the overall cost of the mortgage, the monthly repayments, any arrangement fee and any charges imposed for early repayment.[53]

There is a danger that this presentation of information becomes a mere formulaic process. The information that is provided is repetitious and largely confined to the financial implications of the mortgage. Thus, although the borrower is provided with information, the rules are short on any process to try and bring home to the borrower the implications of that information to his or her particular circumstances. The borrower is expected to borrow responsibly but may simply not be in a position to make responsible choices.[54]

Lenders 'must be able to show that before deciding to enter into, or making a further advance on, a regulated mortgage contract . . . account was taken of the customer's ability to repay'.[55] This assessment is to be made against the lender's written policy which is to look primarily to the level of the borrower's actual or reasonably anticipated income. This assessment is made from the lender's perspective; it does not provide for a judgement which is communicated to, or which may assist, the borrower in making his or her decision to borrow. The principle of responsible lending overlooks the fundamental tension that the primary pressure on mortgage advisors is to meet lending targets so healthy returns to shareholders can be maintained. It is not to protect the borrower beyond being able to demonstrate adequate compliance with regulatory standards so the lender's licence is not placed in jeopardy.

CCA – Prescribed processes and unenforceability

Mortgages falling within the CCA are also subject to comprehensive rules covering the whole process from advertisement, through to creation of the mortgage and its enforcement in the event of default.[56] This cradle to grave approach is similar to, but more proscribed than, the requirements governing FSA regulated mortgages. Furthermore, the consequences of non-compliance are more far-reaching.

[53] http://fsahandbook.info/FSA/html/handbook/MCOB/5 and MCOB 10 which details how the APR is calculated.

[54] See findings contained in FSA's Mortgage Reviews of 2006 and 2008 available at www.fsa.gov.uk and *Set Up to Fail*, n. 14 above.

[55] MCOB, 11.3.1.

[56] See s. 55 CCA (pre-mortgage information), ss. 77, 77A and 78 (information to be provided during the mortgage) and ss. 76, 86B–86E, 87 and 88 (information on default).

Where the CCA goes further is in prescribing the form and execution of the agreement[57] and the supporting mortgage.[58] In addition, the process of completing the mortgage is regulated. The borrower must be supplied with a copy of the mortgage and given a cooling-off period to consider his or her position before the mortgage can be executed.[59]

The consequence of failing to provide requisite information or to comply with the rules governing form and execution is that the mortgage cannot be enforced except by order of the court.[60] The court is given a wide discretion whether or not to enforce the agreement or mortgage, in the light of the prejudice caused to the borrower and the culpability of the lender. If enforcement is ordered, the court may impose conditions and amend or vary the terms of the mortgage.[61]

There is no equivalent to the MCOB handbook to govern CCA mortgages although the OFT may issue regulations and guidance to its licensed lenders.[62] They have been accused of failing to provide adequate, comprehensive and current guidance or to put in place an effective monitoring and compliance strategy.[63] There is some evidence that the OFT are acting to rectify these omissions, although their measures may smack of shutting the stable door after the horse has bolted. The OFT's General Guidance on Fitness of Licensed Lenders was updated in January 2008[64] and now requires further information to enable the OFT to assess a lender's fitness to undertake sub-prime lending. The OFT has also announced that it will take into consideration any breach of the FSA rules and principles, in particular irresponsible lending, when making licensing decisions or taking enforcement action. Consultations have been initiated on Second Charge Lending,[65] Irresponsible Lending[66] and the OFT's Financial Services Strategy.[67] Finally, not before time,

[57] S. 60 CCA. [58] S. 105 CCA.

[59] Unless the mortgage is for bridging finance or to purchase of land: see CCA ss. 58 and 61. See also ss. 62, 64, 67 and 68 regarding execution of the credit agreement.

[60] See also ss. 65, 92, 105, 126 and 127 CCA. [61] See ss. 135 and 136 CCA.

[62] Ss. 26 and 33A–E CCA. [63] *Set Up to Fail*, n. 14 above.

[64] Consumer Credit Licensing, General Guidance for Licensees and Applicants on Fitness and Requirements, OFT 969 (January 2008), available at www.oft.gov.uk.

[65] Second Charge Lending, OFT Guidance for Brokers and Lenders, OFT 1105con (July 2009), available at www.oft.gov.uk.

[66] Irresponsible Lending, OFT 1012 (August 2008) and OFT 1107con (July 2009), available at www.oft.gov.uk. The OFT's final guidance on Irresponsible Lending is anticipated by March 2010.

[67] Financial Services Strategy, OFT1077con (April 2009), available at www.oft.gov.uk.

the OFT has announced plans to update its guidelines on Non-Status Lending. The current guidelines are over a decade old.[68]

The Turner Review

Although not the sole cause of the credit crunch, it is evident that irresponsible lending and questionable mortgage funding models have played their part, whilst the consequences of the restriction in credit are likely to hit borrowers particularly hard with forecasts suggesting that the number of mortgage repossessions will rise to 53,000 this year.[69] In October 2008 the Government initiated a review by the FSA into the regulation of financial services, focusing upon the causes and remedial responses to the credit crunch. The FSA's Turner Review was published in March 2009.[70] The review concluded that previous FSA supervision had placed an over-reliance on market regulation and the self-correcting potential of a free market in mortgage products. However, the belief that borrowers were best served by an unfettered and transparent market in which they could be relied upon to make responsible borrowing choices best suited to their needs has proved misplaced. Likewise, the hope that lenders, in the conduct of their business, would conduct a proper evaluation of risk to make responsible lending decisions has too often been dashed.

As a result the FSA have announced that their approach to mortgage regulation will be more intensive and intrusive. It will look not just to compliance with the processes found in the MCOB, but also to an evaluation of lenders' business models and their associated risk. The FSA will also focus upon the technical ability of a lender's key personnel as well as their past probity. The FSA's recommendations do not stop there. They are actively considering the possibility of product regulation with stipulated loan to value and loan to income ratios potential targets. Mortgage regulation is thus at a crossroads: reliance on pure market regulation stands discredited and ahead is the certainty of greater oversight by regulatory bodies.

[68] Non-status Lending, Guidelines for Lenders and Brokers, OFT 192 (November 1997), available at www.oft.gov.uk.

[69] There were 46,000 mortgage repossessions in 2009. See mortgage repossession statistics and forecasts available at www.cml.org.uk.

[70] Available at www.fsa.gov.uk.

Unfair terms, practices and relationships

Equity only limits the freedom of the parties to contract on whatever terms they choose where oppressive and unconscionable conduct has been reflected in the resulting terms of the parties' bargain. Unreasonableness is not enough.[71] Statutory protection of consumers through the Unfair Terms and Practices Regulations sets a lower standard of good faith and fair dealing where freedom of contract is illusory because lenders are able to dictate terms and insist upon the use of standard terms and conditions. Borrowers may benefit from this consumer-based protection. After some initial hesitation, it is clear that the Unfair Term Regulations do apply to contracts affecting land, including mortgages entered into by individuals when acting as consumers rather than in a business capacity.[72] Thus they may regulate the fairness of terms governing domestic mortgages, whether regulated under the FSMA or CCA. One would expect the reach of the Unfair Practices Regulations to be similarly construed.

In addition, there is the jurisdiction under sections 140A–C of the CCA, that is borrower specific but provides redress only to individual borrowers falling within the CCA and is not available to borrowers under FSA regulated mortgages. They must rely on the MCOB which, whilst based upon the overall principle of treating the borrower fairly, is short on specific rules on the fairness of terms or providing the borrower with a judicial route prohibiting unfair terms or practices.[73]

Unfair Terms Regulations

The impact of the Unfair Terms Regulations (UTR)[74] in striking down unfair terms,[75] and the role of the OFT in acting as a 'consumer watch-dog'

[71] *Kreglinger* v. *New Patagonia Meat and Cold Storage Co Ltd* [1914] AC 25; *Knightsbridge Estates Ltd* v. *Bryne* [1939] Ch 441; *Cityland & Properties (Holdings) Ltd* v. *Drabrah* [1968] Ch 166; and *Multiservice Bookbinding Ltd* v. *Marden* [1978] Ch 84.

[72] *Newham LBC* v. *Khatun* [2004] EWCA Civ 55 and *Evans* v. *Cherry Tree Finance Ltd* [2007] CLY 766.

[73] MCOB 12 requires early repayment charges and default charges to be a genuine pre-estimation of the lender's loss and any charges, including interest rates, not to be excessive.

[74] SI 1999/2083 which amends and replaces the original regulations in SI 1994/3159. The regulations were enacted in pursuance of the Unfair Terms in Consumer Contracts Directive, 93/13/EEC. The OFT has issued a guidance note on the regulations: see Unfair Contract Terms Guidance, OFT 311 (September 2008), available at www.oft.gov.uk.

[75] Under Reg. 8 UTR an unfair term is not binding.

shaping standard terms in consumer contracts, is well known.[76] The OFT may take action on complaints made by consumers and consumer organisations and restrain the use of unfair terms, through both informal undertakings and formal proceedings.[77] Their tactics appear to work, with OFT bulletins full of reports of terms that have been altered and so triggering a ripple effect on other lenders with similar terms and conditions. But prevention is often better than cure and the OFT's guidance upon its interpretation of and approach to the Unfair Terms Regulations is thus of particular value.[78] There is also more specific OFT guidance on Calculating Fair Default Charges on Credit Card Contracts,[79] which has wider implications for similar default charges found in mortgages.

The focus of the requirement of fairness is upon standard terms and conditions which are not individually negotiated by the lender and the borrower.[80] The core terms of the contract are excluded from the requirement for fairness but must be expressed in plain intelligible language.[81] Core terms are those terms which relate to the main subject matter of the contract or the adequacy of the consideration.[82] The House of Lords in *Director General of Fair Trading* v. *First National Bank Plc*[83] has made it clear that core terms should be restrictively construed.[84] In the context of a mortgage, core terms should be limited to the amount of the loan and the initial level of interest chargeable; supplementary provisions resulting in additional charges following default should be subject to scrutiny.[85]

'Plain and intelligible language' is an explicit requirement which affects all terms including the core terms.[86] The terms must be capable of being understood by ordinary members of the public and any uncertainty is to be construed in favour of the borrower.[87] These requirements present a challenge given the inherent complexity of mortgages, yet in *Office of Fair Trading* v. *Abbey National Plc*[88] the court was unimpressed by arguments that complexity should affect the standard.

[76] See, for instance, S. Bright, 'Winning the Battle Against Unfair Contract Terms' (2000) 20 *Legal Studies* 331.

[77] Other bodies, including the FSA and the National Consumer Council, are also given power to initiate action see UTR, regs. 10–15.

[78] This guidance was initially issued in February 2001 and was updated in September 2008 – see n. 74 above.

[79] Calculating Fair Default Charges in Credit Card Transactions, OFT 842 (April 2006), available at www.oft.gov.uk.

[80] UTR, reg. 5(2). [81] UTR, reg. 6(2). [82] Ibid. [83] [2001] UKHL 52.

[84] See also *Office of Fair Trading* v. *Abbey National Plc* [2009] UKSC 6.

[85] Ibid. and *Falco Finance Ltd* v. *Gough* [1999] CCLR 16. [86] UTR, reg. 7(1).

[87] UTR, reg. 7(2). [88] [2008] EWHC 875.

The comprehensibility of the result is important and it is no excuse that a reasonable attempt to explain complex subject matter has been made if a lay man would still fail to grasp its meaning. The aim of comprehensibility is also supported by the prohibition on terms which a borrower has no real opportunity to consider before the mortgage is completed.[89]

The test of unfairness found in regulation 5(1) encompasses both a lack of good faith and a significant imbalance in the rights and liabilities of the parties which operates to the detriment of the borrower. Schedule 2 of the Unfair Terms Regulations illustrates the test by setting out a non-exhaustive 'grey list' of terms which potentially may be regarded as unfair. Of particular significance to mortgages is paragraph (e) which provides that a term 'requiring any consumer who fails to fulfill his obligation to pay a disproportionately high sum in compensation' is potentially unfair. It has been used to good effect on differential interest rates payable following default, excessive interests rates and early repayment sanctions.[90] Paragraphs (j) and (k) address a lender's right to vary the terms of any loan, although under paragraph 2 (b) the ability of a lender to vary interest rates is accepted in principle.[91] The grey list's focus is upon substantive fairness but the good faith requirement also adds an element of procedural fairness in how the loan is negotiated and the lender/borrower relationship subsequently conducted.[92]

The message is clear, that lenders must make sure that their standard terms and conditions meet the standards of fairness required by the legislation and illustrated by the OFT's guidance.[93] Furthermore, lenders must ensure that the implications of those terms are brought home to

[89] See Sch. 1, para. 1(i).

[90] *Falco Finance Ltd* v. *Gough* [1999] CCLR 16. See also Unfair Contract Terms Bulletins available at www.oft.gov.uk.

[91] The OFT has issued guidance calling for variations to be made against some measures and to be notified to the borrower who should be able to withdraw from the mortgage: see Unfair Contract Terms Bulletin 9 available at at oft.gov.uk. See also the impact of implied terms governing variation in *Paragon Finance Plc* v. *Nash* [2001] EWCA Civ 1466.

[92] See for instance *Director General of Fair Trading* v. *First National Bank* [2001] UKHL 52 at para. 17, per Lord Bingham; H. Collins 'Good Faith in European Contract Law' (1994) 14 *Oxford Journal of Legal Studies*, 229; H. Beale, 'Legislative Control of Fairness: The Directive on Unfair Terms in Consumer Contracts', in J. Beatson and D. Friedman (eds.), *Good Faith And Fault In Contract Law* (Oxford: Clarendon Press, 1995) 231.

[93] See generally J. Simmonds, 'Bankers' Documents and the Unfair Terms in Consumer Contracts Regulations 1999' (2002) 17 *Journal of International Business Law* 205.

borrowers. The indications are that some, but not all, lenders have received and understood that message and acted accordingly.[94]

Unfair Practices Regulations

The Unfair Practices Regulations (UPR)[95] came into force on 26 May 2008, implementing the Unfair Commercial Practices Directive.[96] These regulations, which again are enforceable by the OFT as part of their regulatory armory, introduce a general duty upon traders not to trade unfairly[97] and seek to ensure that they act honestly and fairly towards customers by prohibiting misleading actions,[98] omissions[99] and aggressive commercial practices.[100] Certain specific practices contained in the schedule to the regulations are always considered unfair and the OFT has issued joint guidance, with the Department of Business Enterprise and Regulatory Reform.[101] It is anticipated that these regulations, like the Unfair Terms Regulations, will apply to the practices of lenders when dealing with individual borrowers, although it is too early to gauge their impact.

Sections 140A–C Consumer Credit Act

Sections 137–140 of the Consumer Credit Act 1974 empowered the court to reopen consumer credit agreements where they found that the payment terms were 'grossly exorbitant' or where the agreement 'otherwise grossly contravene[d] ordinary principles of fair dealing'. These tests were notoriously difficult to satisfy,[102] so it came as no surprise when they were revised by the Consumer Credit Act 2006. The new provisions are far wider in their approach and operate at two levels. First, they provide a means of redress to individual borrowers and also a further opportunity for regulatory oversight by the OFT.[103]

[94] The FSA's Report on Fairness of Terms in Consumer Contracts June 2008, available at www.fsa.gov.uk, found that some lenders, particularly smaller lenders, are unaware of the need to comply with the UTRs.

[95] SI 2008/1277. [96] Directive 2005/29. [97] UPR, Reg. 3. [98] UPR, Reg. 5.

[99] UPR, Reg. 6. [100] UPR, Reg. 7.

[101] See Guidance on the UK Regulations Implementing the Unfair Commercial Practices Directive May 2008, available at www.oft.gov.uk.

[102] See *A. Ketley Ltd* v. *Scott* [1980] CCLR 37; *Davies* v. *Direct Loans* [1986] 1 WLR 823; and *Paragon Finance plc* v. *Nash* [2002] 1 WLR 685.

[103] See s. 140D CCA.

The terms of section 140A are wide and enable the court to consider all matters that they consider relevant including the particular circumstances of the creditor and borrower, the terms of the agreement and the lender's behaviour and practices throughout the mortgage term to determine whether 'the relationship between the creditor and debtor arising out of the agreement . . . is unfair'. The burden of proof is upon the lender to establish that the relationship is not unfair.[104] The redress available is also far-ranging. The court may order the reimbursement of sums paid by the borrower, the alteration of the mortgage terms or the setting aside, either in whole or in part, of any duty imposed upon the borrower.[105]

The court is yet to offer its interpretation of unfairness in this context. In the meantime, the OFT have made clear that they will use their own interpretation of the fairness standards under sections 140A–C through their licensing, monitoring and enforcement powers.[106] Here their guidance under the Unfair Terms Regulations provides valuable pointers with the added advantage that core terms, for instance excessive interest rates, may be scrutinised. The OFT may also review the ways in which lenders enforce their rights and remedies under their mortgages, including the imposition of default charges and exercise of their right to take possession before the borrower has been given an adequate opportunity to clear arrears. Lending practices before the mortgage may also be reviewed with irresponsible lending and the sale of mortgage payment protection insurance as possible targets.[107]

Borrower redress

A borrower under a FSA regulated mortgage can bring proceedings for breach of statutory duty based upon a breach of the MCOB rules and a borrower under a CCA regulated mortgage may challenge the enforceability of a non-compliant mortgage or can seek redress under sections 140A–C. However, adversarial court proceedings may be an unrealistic route for an individual borrower. Fortunately, other routes to redress exist.

[104] S. 140B(9) CCA. [105] S. 140B(1) CCA.

[106] In pursuance of their duties under s. 140D CCA, see *Unfair Relationships*, OFT 854 (May 2008), available at www.oft.gov.uk.

[107] See S. Brown, 'The Consumer Credit Act 2006: Real Additional Mortgagor Protection' (2007) *Conveyancer and Property Lawyer* 325.

Financial Services Ombudsman

The FSA handbook requires a regulated lender to have in place a complaints handling process which complies with the requirements set out in the handbook.[108] A borrower's first step is thus to resolve their complaint directly with the lender. Their next step is then to approach the FSO which provides an alternative means of resolving disputes.[109]

The FSO may consider complaints made by borrowers under both FSMA and CCA mortgages. Any award that they make is based upon what is fair, just and reasonable, rather than upon the application of strict rules, and is enforceable against the lender in the same way as a court judgment.[110] By contrast an unsatisfied borrower may continue to pursue his or her claim through the courts.

The FSO provides a practical route to resolve relatively small and straightforward disputes. It has the advantage of being free at the point of entry and, with speedier and less formal methods of working, more accessible to many borrowers. The misselling of endowment mortgages and mortgage payment protection insurance and excessive charges for default and early redemption have been the major source of complaints.[111] The FSO has also noted an increase in complaints on the comprehensibility of mortgage terms.[112]

Enforcement of mortgages

The fairness or otherwise of loan terms rarely becomes an issue until default by the borrower prompts enforcement by the lender. Reference has already been made to the need for the lender, under both an FSA regulated mortgage and mortgages governed by the CCA, to periodically inform the borrower of the amount owing under the mortgage,[113]

[108] http://fsahandbook.info/FSA/html/handbook/DISP.

[109] The FSO is set up under Part XVI of the FSMA. See generally P. Morris and R. James 'The Financial Ombudsman Service: A Brave New World in "Ombudsmanry"' (2002) *Public Law* 640 and E. Ferran, 'Dispute Resolution Mechanisms in the UK Financial Sector' (2002) 21 *Civil Justice Quarterly* 135.

[110] S. 229 FSMA.

[111] Misselling of endowment mortgages accounted for 49% of complaints made to the FSO in 2006/2007.

[112] See FSO Annual Review 2006/2007 and regular issues of the Ombudsman News available at www.financial-ombudsman.org.uk/publications/ar07.

[113] MCOB 7.5 and ss. 77, 77A and 78 CCA.

including arrears,[114] and to give notice of any default prior to any enforcement action.[115] The borrower should thus be aware of his or her repayment record and any arrears and default charges.[116]

The primary enforcement route is for a lender to seek possession and then exercise their power of sale to recoup the sums owing from the sale proceeds. The CCA requires the lender to obtain a court order to obtain possession,[117] which most lenders, in any event, will wish to pursue to avoid the risk of criminal sanctions.[118] The fact remains that the lender's right to possession is an inherent right flowing from section 87(1) of the Law of Property Act 1925 and, unless expressly so limited, is not prima facie dependent on default. The dynamics of proceedings can thus immediately put the borrower on the back foot with little or no hope of challenging the grant of the possession order itself. Instead the onus is upon the borrower to apply to adjourn the proceedings or delay the arrival of the bailiff by seeking a stay of enforcement of the possession order.

The primary jurisdiction of the court in this regard is found in the well-known provisions of section 36 of the AJA. This valuable jurisdiction allows the borrower time to repay the sums he or she owes under the mortgage. It can be employed to effectively reschedule the amount owing over the entire term of the mortgage where the borrower can satisfy the court that he has an adequate income stream.[119] Less well known is the jurisdiction of the court under sections 129 and 136 of the CCA.[120] Under section 129 the court may make a time order allowing time for the repayment of a CCA regulated loan and under section 136 the court is given a general jurisdiction when making an order to amend the mortgage terms.[121]

But the preference must be to avoid the trauma and expense of enforcement proceedings in the first place. MCOB 13 sets out the rules

[114] MCOB 7.5.8, 7.5.9 and 13.4 and ss. 86B and 86C CCA

[115] See MCOB 13.4.5 and ss. 86E and 87 CCA.

[116] Borrowers who for some reason are not resident at the mortgaged property may be unaware of enforcement action: see *Ropaigealach* v. *Barclays Bank* [2000] QB 263.

[117] See s. 126 CCA.

[118] Under the Criminal Law Act 1977 or the Protection from Eviction Act 1977.

[119] See *Cheltenham & Gloucester Building Society* v. *Norgan* [1996] 1 WLR 343. The court's jurisdiction is more circumscribed where the loan and arrears are to be discharged from the proceeds of sale of the mortgage property: see *Bristol & West Building Society* v. *Ellis* (1997) 73 P&CR 158.

[120] Borrowers' ignorance of these provisions was noted by the House of Lords in *Director General of Fair Trading* v. *First National Bank Plc* [2001] UKHL 52.

[121] For instance the running of interest, ibid.

to which lenders regulated by the FSA are expected to adhere. There is the overarching principle that lenders must treat borrowers in arrears fairly and have in place a policy which requires the lender to enter into a constructive dialogue with the defaulting borrower to try and reschedule the arrears rather than proceed immediately to repossession.[122]

Research suggests that MCOB 13 is not being applied consistently by lenders with some lenders resorting to legal action at an earlier stage than others, particularly against sub-prime borrowers.[123] The result is increased pressure on defaulting borrowers and also an increase in the enforcement costs that they must shoulder. The response has been to introduce a pre-action protocol.[124] This Protocol replicates MCOB 13 and thus effectively transfers monitoring MCOB 13 compliance from the FSA to the court, which may penalise a non-complying lender by withholding their costs of action. The Protocol also extends the reach of MCOB 13 to all mortgage possession actions, whether or not sought under FSA regulated mortgages.

However, there are worrying reports that some lenders are trying to avoid taking possession proceedings with a number of routes being exploited. First, a lender may sell without obtaining possession. In these circumstances the mortgage is discharged and the interest of the borrower is overreached, vesting instead in the balance of the proceeds of sale (if any).[125] The purchaser can then seek possession based upon their unencumbered ownership of the borrower's home which the court has no jurisdiction to delay.[126] Secondly, worried borrowers may be tempted to escape their financial worries by handing their homes back to their lenders. Many borrowers simply do not appreciate that they may be given time to clear their arrears or that they remain liable under their covenant to repay any shortfall between their outstanding debt and the sum realised from the sale of their home.[127] There has also been a growth in companies offering sale and lease back arrangements whereby they agree to buy the borrower's home, often at a much reduced price,

[122] In October 2008 the Council of Mortgage Lenders issued its industry guidance on compliance with MCOB 13: see www.cml.org.uk.

[123] See *Set Up To Fail*, n. 14 above and FSA, Mortgage Effectiveness Review Arrears Findings (August 2008), available at www.fsa.gov.uk.

[124] The introduction of the Protocol was brought forward to 19 November 2008: available at www.civiljusticecouncil.gov.uk.

[125] S. 2(1)(iii) and s. 88 or s. 89 Law of Property Act 1925.

[126] *Horsham Properties Group Ltd* v. *Clark* [2008] EWHC 2327.

[127] Although the lender must sue for recovery within the relevant limitation period: see *Wilkinson* v. *West Bromwich Building Society* [2005] UKHL 44.

and arrange to lease it back to the borrower on terms which offer little security and the prospect of rising rents. There are plans for this exploitative practice to come under FSA regulation.[128]

Conclusion

As the above review demonstrates there is a comprehensive and detailed statutory framework governing loans which are secured by a first or second mortgage over the borrower's home. These provisions now overshadow any equitable protection based upon unconscionability and instead look to concepts of fairness within a regulated credit market overseen by independent monitoring bodies. A significant problem however is that there is not one regulatory framework but two, although calls to rationalise the framework now appear to be the subject of serious consideration.

Borrower protection is predicated upon viewing the borrower as a consumer who is able to make responsible borrowing decisions within a competitive market. Responsible borrowing is underpinned by access to standardised information in the hope that borrowers will make informed comparisons between different mortgage products and ultimately borrowing decisions best suited to their needs. But evidence suggests that borrowers are often in no position to make responsible borrowing choices simply because they have no choice or are ill equipped to make prudent choices.

Lenders are likewise charged with lending responsibly. Responsible lending is supported by market benchmarks of lending behaviour which are monitored through regulatory accountability and alternative dispute mechanisms but with the ultimate sanction of court intervention. But lenders have patently failed to lend responsibly, particularly to sub-prime borrowers. The fundamental principles of responsible borrowing and responsible lending have thus already faltered and are now being tested to the full by the credit crunch and the attendant increase in repossessions.

The bottom line is that the treatment of the borrower as a consumer is dependent upon the health of the mortgage market. When the mortgage market sneezes, borrowers catch a cold. Unfortunately, it has become all too evident that the mortgage market has suffered from serious flaws which regulation failed to detect and address before it was too late. The

[128] See FSA Consultation Paper, Regulating Sale and Leaseback: An Interim Regime (February 2009), available at www.fsa.gov.uk.

fundamental question is setting the parameters of market forces when the product being peddled is of such import and carries such long term consequences for many borrowers.[129] Whitehouse, writing a decade ago, warned against treating borrowers as consumers where the product is a mortgage secured against their home.[130] Her premonition is in danger of turning to reality.

[129] The FSA published more concrete proposals to curb irresponsible lending in its Mortgage Market Review (n. 30 above). These proposals herald a significant regulatory shift away from responsible borrowing, based upon information disclosure. Instead, lenders are called upon to take greater responsibility for prudent lending by assessing affordability against verifiable evidence of the borrower's disposable income. More controversial product regulation may then prove unnecessary.

[130] Whitehouse, n. 22 above.

11

Conceptualising and understanding fairness: lessons from and for financial services

PETER CARTWRIGHT

Introducing fairness

'Fairness' is at the heart of many requirements placed on suppliers when dealing with their consumers. Some measures use the term 'fair', while others use similar expressions like 'reasonable'. Frequently the requirements are placed on all sectors; sometimes they are more limited. They may have their basis in statute, in the common law, in regulatory guidance or in codes of practice. Traders wishing to comply with their obligations must negotiate a complex web of requirements.

The requirement to be fair plays a particularly prominent role in the regulation of financial services firms' (hereafter 'firms') dealings with their consumers. An examination of this subject is particularly apt for a number of reasons. First, the Financial Services Authority (FSA) has recently set much store by its 'Treating Customers Fairly' (TCF) Initiative. TCF forms an important part of the FSA's efforts to place more emphasis on 'principles-based regulation'. Secondly, recent statutory developments have imposed new fairness obligations on firms when dealing with consumers. These initiatives increase the already complex and fragmented regulatory framework in the UK.

The purpose of this chapter is to consider the meaning(s) of fairness in the context of the relationship between firms and consumers. It begins by examining the principal general statutory provisions on fairness, and then moves on to those provisions dealing specifically with financial services. Next, the main part of the chapter examines the key elements of fairness. It suggests that by isolating these elements, while recognising the potential for overlap between them, we can better understand when firms are acting fairly towards consumers.

This chapter forms part of a research project funded by the ESRC and the Financial Services Research Forum. I am grateful to both for their support.

The chapter does not examine the role of common law and equity because of the extent to which they are considered elsewhere. It uses the term 'consumer' rather than 'customer', except when referring specifically to TCF. In most situations the terms will be synonymous. In this chapter a consumer is considered to be a private individual who deals with business in a private capacity, and thus reflects the commonly understood meaning of the term.[1]

General statutory provisions on fairness: unfair terms

Rather than examine every legal regime that adopts a test of fairness, this part considers the principal general statutory regimes that have implications for financial services. Where unfair terms are concerned, there are two main pieces of legislation. First, the Unfair Contract Terms Act 1977 (UCTA) is concerned primarily with contractual terms that purport to exclude or restrict liability. UCTA makes certain terms void and subjects others to a test of reasonableness. Section 3 covers contracts made on standard terms (including with other businesses), and contracts made with consumers (whether or not on standard terms). It provides that, as against the other party, a firm cannot exclude or restrict any liability of his in respect of the breach, or claim to be entitled to render a contractual performance substantially different from that which was reasonably expected of him, except in so far as the term satisfies the requirement of reasonableness. Secondly, the Unfair Terms in Consumer Contracts Regulations 1999 (UTCCR)[2] provide a method of challenging unfair terms, which have not been individually negotiated, in contracts between suppliers (here 'firms') and consumers.[3] The UTCCRs provide that 'core provisions' (those which relate to the definition of the main subject matter of the contract, or to the adequacy of the price or remuneration) cannot be challenged, provided they are expressed in clear language. For example, an interest rate in a loan will presumably be a core term.[4]

[1] For an examination of the possible meanings of 'consumer' in this context see P. Cartwright, 'Consumer Protection in Financial Services: Putting the Law in Context', in P. Cartwright (ed.), *Consumer Protection in Financial Services* (Dordrecht: Kluwer, 1999) 3–6.

[2] SI 1999/2083, implementing Directive 93/13/EEC. [3] UTCCR, Regulation 5(1).

[4] By contrast, a term which provides for default interest to be paid until the time that the borrower repays will not be a core term. See *Director General of Fair Trading* v. *First National Bank Plc* [2002] AC 481. Furthermore, the FSA has stated that it believes interest rate variation clauses are not core terms. This is because they relate to varying rather than

Schedule 2 provides an indicative and non-exhaustive 'grey list' of terms which may be regarded as unfair.

Regulation 5(1) states that 'a contractual term which has not been individually negotiated shall be regarded as unfair if, contrary to the requirement of good faith, it causes a significant imbalance in the parties' rights and obligations arising under the contract, to the detriment of the consumer'. Well before the advent of the Regulations, Bingham LJ famously equated the civil law concept of good faith with 'playing fair', 'coming clean' and 'putting one's cards face up on the table'.[5] In *Director General of Fair Trading* v. *First National Bank Plc*, Lord Bingham argued that openness required 'that the terms should be expressed fully, clearly and legibly, containing no concealed pitfalls or traps' and that the requirement of significant imbalance is met if a term 'is so weighted in favour of the supplier as to tilt the parties' rights and obligations under the contract significantly in his favour'.[6] Some terms on the grey list are of particular relevance to financial services, such as those which might seek to 'enable the seller to alter the terms of the contract unilaterally without a valid reason that is specified in the contract'.[7] The FSA has provided some guidance on such terms.[8]

Where firms breach legislation such as the UTCCR, this may provide evidence that other obligations, such as TCF are also breached. As Davidson observes: 'the drafting of fair contractual terms in standard form documentation is an important manifestation of fair customer treatment at the product design stage of the product life cycle'.[9] The FSA has also noted the close relationship between unfair terms and TCF.[10]

General statutory provisions on fairness: fairness and commercial practices

As well as tackling unfair terms, the law controls unfair practices. The Consumer Protection from Unfair Trading Regulations 2008 (CPR)

setting the price. See FSA, *Fairness of Terms in Consumer Contracts: Statement of Good Practice* (FSA, 2005) para. 1.9

5 *Interfoto Picture Library Ltd* v. *Stiletto Visual Programmes Ltd* [1989] QB 433 at 439.

6 [2001] 3 WLR 1297 at 1308.

7 UTCCR, Schedule 2 (1)(j).

8 See FSA, *Fairness of Terms in Consumer Contracts*, n. 4 above.

9 J. J. Davidson, *The UK Financial Services Authority's 'Treating Customers Fairly' Initiative and its Potential for Application in the Australian Financial Services Industry* (CCCL Research Paper, July 2006).

10 FSA, *Fairness of Terms in Consumer Contracts*, n. 4 above.

concern unfair practices which distort the economic behaviour of average consumers so that they take transactional decisions that they would not otherwise have taken.[11] There are four main categories of unfair commercial practices: the 31 specific practices that are always unfair; misleading practices (covering both actions and omissions); aggressive practices; and those unfair under the general prohibition.

Under Article 3(9), Member States are permitted to impose requirements that are more restrictive or prescriptive than the usual test where financial services are concerned. However, as any such requirements must go at least as far as the Directive, the provisions of the Directive apply as minimum standards.[12] The Directive has been taken into account in preparing documents such as the FSA's latest Conduct of Business Sourcebook (COBS)[13] and the Banking Code 2008.[14] The details of the CPR are considered in more detail later.

Fairness and financial services

A number of regimes focus specifically on financial services:

Unfair relationships and consumer credit

Consumer credit regulation falls under the Consumer Credit Act 2006 and is principally the responsibility of the Office of Fair Trading (OFT). Under s. 140A a court can make an order in relation to a credit agreement if it finds that the relationship between the creditor and the debtor is unfair because of one or more of the following:

(a) any of the terms of the agreement or of any related agreement;
(b) the way in which the creditor has exercised or enforced any of his rights under the agreement or any related agreement;
(c) any other thing done (or not done) by, or on behalf of, the creditor (either before or after the making of the agreement or any related agreement).

Subsection (2) then states that in deciding to make a determination under s. 140A, the court shall have regard to 'all matters it thinks

[11] SI 2008/1277; the CPR implements Directive 2005/29/EC.
[12] In most other sectors, the Directive imposes maximum harmonisation.
[13] Available at http://fsahandbook.info/FSA/html/handbook/COBS.
[14] Available at www.bankingcode.org.uk/pdfdocs/PERSONAL_CODE_2008.PDF.

relevant'. It has been noted that 'the statutory provisions do not identify any badges of unfairness or, indeed, supply any meaningful criteria for identifying an unfair credit relationship'.[15] However, this does allow for maximum flexibility. Furthermore, the OFT has recently issued guidance on the exercise of its powers, while consciously not defining what is an unfair relationship.[16] It is clear that unfairness may involve both contract terms and business practices, and that account could be taken of, among other things: whether terms are unfair under the UTCCR; whether costs are excessive; whether FSA rules, TCF outcomes or codes of practice have been breached; and whether adverse findings have been made by the Financial Ombudsman.[17]

Fairness and self-regulation: the Banking Code

Like consumer credit, much retail banking is not the responsibility of the FSA: '[t]echnically, the FSA has "switched off" Principle 6 ("Treating Customers Fairly") with respect to deposits, except for a review of the way that banks handle complaints.'[18] The Banking Code, however, does govern elements of the relationship between banks and their customers. This voluntary code is aimed at setting good standards of banking practice, and is enforced on subscribers by the Banking Code Standards Board (BCSB). The latest (March 2008) version of the Code states:

> We promise we will treat you fairly and reasonably when providing you with products and services covered in this Code. We will keep this promise by meeting all of the key commitments shown below . . .

An overall fairness objective similar to this was recommended by the Code's Independent Reviewer.[19] This followed calls by the FSA and the BCSB independent directors who had described the absence of such an obligation as 'anomalous'. There are concerns with the wording. In particular, the inclusion of the words 'we will keep this promise by'

[15] House of Lords EU Committee 36th Report of Session (2005–6), *Consumer Credit in the EU* (HL 210–1) para. 192.

[16] OFT, *Unfair Relationships* (OFT Guidance, May 2008). [17] Ibid. ch. 4.

[18] T. Huertas, 'The Future of Retail Banking in the UK' (speech to the IEA 10th Anniversary Conference, 6 June 2007). Available at www.fsa.gov.uk/pages/Library/Communication/Speeches/2007/0606_th.shtml). The FSA does, however, have responsibility for prudential matters.

[19] 2007 Independent Review of the Banking Codes (available at: www.bba.org.uk/content/1/c6/01/15/40/Independent_Code_Review_2007.pdf).

appears to limit the ambit of the obligation. Furthermore, with the exception of the undertaking to 'lend responsibly' the Code says little about substantive fairness. For example, in relation to charges, the obligations only concern informing consumers about charges or changes to charges, and say nothing about the fairness of those charges. Indeed, a good deal of the Code concerns what banks expect of consumers, rather than what consumers are entitled to expect of their banks. From the perspective of consumers, further development of the Code would be desirable. It is notable that a large number of the independent reviewer's recommendations were rejected by the Code's sponsors.

Fairness and the Financial Ombudsman Service

The Financial Ombudsman Service (FOS) is now the principal means of redress for consumers when dealing with firms. Ombudsmen have received the approval even of those who are critical of most consumer protection initiatives.[20] According to the FSA Handbook the Ombudsman will determine a complaint 'by reference to what is, in his opinion, fair and reasonable in all the circumstances of the case'. In determining this, the Ombudsman will 'take into account the relevant law, regulations, regulators' rules and guidance and standards, relevant codes of practice and, where appropriate, what he considers to have been good industry practice at the relevant time'.[21]

The Ombudsman's flexibility here is considerable. James and Morris cite 'the capacity to transcend strict legal rules and draw upon a range of extra-legal standards in a manner which usually operates to the benefit of the consumer' as one of the major strengths of the system.[22] Fairness, according to James 'represents the essence of the ombudsman function – the requirement to do justice in the individual case, free from the constraints of formal precedent and taking a common sense approach'.[23] The Chief Ombudsman has argued that the test encompasses

[20] See, for example, G. J. Benston, *Regulating Financial Markets: A Critique and Some Proposals* (London: Institute of Economic Affairs, 1998) 122.

[21] DISP 3.8.1 R. (the FSA's Dispute Resolution Handbook), available at http://fsahandbook.info/FSA/html/handbook/DISP.

[22] R. James and P. Morris, 'The New Financial Ombudsman Service in the UK', in C. Rickett and T. Telfer (eds.), *International Perspectives on Consumers' Access to Justice* (Cambridge University Press, 2003) 184.

[23] R. James, 'Reform of the Complaints Process in Financial Services – the Public and the Private' (1998) *Public Law* 201, 206.

considerations of wider public policy or the general public good.[24] Concerns have been expressed about lack of certainty and precedent.[25] However, the Ombudsman does pay close attention to how previous cases have been decided, and decisions will act as persuasive precedents: '[w]e are not bound by the doctrine of precedent, but we do aim for consistency.'[26] This consistency is ensured by the use of lead cases, and the communication of this provided by tools such as bulletins, reports and briefing notes.

The matters that the Ombudsman takes into account when making decisions are also important to consider. Sometimes, cases can be decided swiftly on the basis of existing laws, codes and regulatory guidance, but the Ombudsman can go beyond these. This flexibility is important. As Nobles argues 'while considerations of justice and the need for good administration point to the need for ombudsmen to decide matters on a consistent basis, they also need the ability to depart from usual practice where appropriate'.[27]

Fairness and the FSA: treating customers fairly (TCF)

Since its creation, the FSA has had regard to broad principles, as well as detailed rules, in exercising its powers. The FSA's 'Principles for Businesses', for example, are designed to encapsulate what the Authority expects. They concern the following: integrity; skill, care and diligence; management and control; financial prudence; market conduct; customers' interests; communications with customers; conflicts of interest; customers' relationships of trust; customers' assets; and relations with regulators. Despite such principles having long been important to the FSA, obligations have traditionally been heavily rule-based. However, the FSA is increasingly moving from rules to principles.[28] According to the FSA this means 'where possible, moving away from dictating through detailed, prescriptive rules and supervisory actions

[24] W. Merricks, 'The Jurisprudence of the Ombudsman' (paper delivered at Conference on 'Insurance Contract Law: Winds of Change', St John's College Cambridge, 6 April 2001).

[25] See Lord Ackner, *Report on a Unified Complaints Procedure* (London: Personal Investment Authority, 1993) para. 93, cited in James and Morris, n. 22 above, 185.

[26] Merricks, n. 24 above.

[27] R. Nobles, 'Rules Principles and Ombudsmen: Norwich and Peterborough Building Society v Financial Ombudsman Service' (2003) 66 *Modern Law Review* 781, 789.

[28] See FSA, *Principles-based Regulation: Focusing on the Outcomes that Matter* (April 2007) and J. Black, M. Hopper and C. Band, 'Making a Success of Principles-based Regulation' (2007) 1 *Law and Financial Markets Review* 191.

how firms should operate their business'.[29] An important part of this move is TCF.[30] The most relevant of the Principles for Businesses here are Principle 6 ('[a] firm must pay due regard to the interests of its customers and treat them fairly') and Principle 7 ('communication with customers') which states that 'a firm must pay due regard to the information needs of its customers and communicate information to them in a way which is clear, fair and not misleading'.

TCF is illustrative of 'meta regulation', where the regulator sets out in broad terms what it wants firms to achieve, and firms are charged with making this part of their culture.[31] Using regulation to influence organisational culture has long been discussed by academics and TCF is a particularly good illustration of it in practice.[32] Briault has stated that the initiative seeks to ensure that customers are treated fairly in all parts of their business and throughout a product's life cycle, namely 'product design, marketing and promotion, sales and advice, after sales information, and complaints handling'.[33]

It is helpful to consider the different views that may exist of what it means to treat customers fairly from the perspectives both of the FSA and of consumers. These are set out and considered in more detail below.

The Financial Services Authority's view of treating customers fairly

The FSA has identified six 'consumer outcomes' which relate to the product life cycle, and which are central to its idea of TCF:

1. Consumers can be confident that they are dealing with firms where the fair treatment of customers is central to the corporate culture.
2. Products and services marketed and sold in the retail market are designed to meet the needs of identified consumer groups and are targeted accordingly.

[29] FSA, *Principles-based Regulation*, n. 28 above, para. 1.2.

[30] See Black *et al.*, n. 28 above; Davidson, n. 9 above; and J. Edwards, 'Treating Customers Fairly' (1996) 14 *Journal of Financial Regulation and Compliance* 242.

[31] C. Parker 'Meta Regulation: Legal Accountability for Corporate Social Responsibility', in D. McBarnet, A. Voiculescu and T. Campbell (eds.), *The New Corporate Accountability: Corporate Social Responsibility and the Law* (Cambridge University Press, 2007).

[32] See, for example, I. Ayres and J. Braithwaite, *Responsive Regulation* (New York: Oxford University Press, 1992).

[33] C. Briault, 'More Principles-based Regulation and Treating Customers Fairly' (speech to ASIC Summer School, 7 March 2007), available at www.fsa.gov.uk/pages/Library/Communications/Speeches/2007/0307_cb.shtml.

3. Consumers are provided with clear information and are kept appropriately informed before, during and after the point of sale.
4. Where consumers receive advice, the advice is suitable and takes account of their circumstances.
5. Consumers are provided with products that perform as firms have led them to expect and the associated service is both of an acceptable standard and as they have been led to expect.
6. Consumers should not face unreasonable post-sale barriers imposed by firms to change a product, switch provider, or make a complaint.

Consumer views of treating customers fairly

The FSA commissioned research to help it to understand consumers' perceptions and views of what constitutes fairness in their dealings with firms.[34] The final report identified a set of principles which, the authors suggest, provide a summary framework of the consumer perspective on fairness. These were:

1. Give the customer what they have paid for.
2. Do not take advantage of the customer.
3. Offer the customer the best product you can.
4. Do your best to resolve mistakes as quickly as possible.
5. Show flexibility, empathy and consideration in dealing with customers.
6. Exhibit clarity in all customer dealings.

These principles emerged following 'a good deal of guidance and facilitation on the part of the moderator' and 'would not tend to occur spontaneously in discussions with consumers'.[35] Nevertheless, they provide a useful insight into what consumers regard as fair or unfair, and how this might differ from how the FSA views the same issue.

Towards understanding fairness

It is clear that there are different ways of conceptualising fairness. Fairness may focus on procedure (such as behaving in a fair way) or substance (such as ensuring a fair outcome). Regulation may control

[34] FSA, 'Treating Customers Fairly: The Consumers' View' (FSA Consumer Research 38: June 2005).
[35] Ibid., 36.

terms and/or practices, and be of general or limited application. Content may be found in statute, case law, regulators' and ombudsmen's rules, or self-regulatory codes. The headings below suggest a framework, or taxonomy, within which fairness can be considered. This is not the only way to examine the issues, but may help to focus attention on some key themes.

Information

Information is central to an examination of unfairness in the context of financial regulation.[36] In the economic concept of the perfect market, all players (including consumers) have perfect information about the nature and values of commodities traded.[37] In such an environment perfect competition is possible. Although perfect information may be a chimera, it may not be too ambitious to aim for well-informed and knowledgeable consumers. Cruickshank argued that knowledgeable consumers: 'provide the best incentive to effective competition', arguing that 'with the right information, consumers can take responsibility for their own financial well-being, shop around and exert the pressures on suppliers which drive a competitive and innovative market'.[38]

Most consumers find themselves in a position of information asymmetry in relation to firms, and this provides one of the principal justifications for financial regulation.[39] Although the market provides some incentives for suppliers to disclose information demanded by consumers, such disclosure does not always occur in practice.[40] There are several reasons for this. For example: many financial products are credence goods, the characteristics of which cannot be judged until long into the future; firms are under incentives only to provide information that they

[36] J. Vickers, 'When is Trading Unfair?' (speech to the David Hume Institute, Edinburgh, 26 April 2001), available at http://oft.gov.uk/news/speeches/2001/04014.

[37] Other characteristics of the perfect market include numerous buyers and sellers, free entry and exit and an absence of externalities: see I. Ramsay, *Rationales for Intervention in the Consumer Marketplace* (OFT, 1984) para. 3.3.

[38] *Competition in UK Banking: A Report to the Chancellor of the Exchequer* (the Cruickshank Report) (London: Stationery Office, March 2000), Executive Summary, para. 50.

[39] The other being the need to avoid systemic risk; see H. Davies, 'Why Regulate?' (Henry Thornton lecture, City University Business School, 4 November 1998), Available at www.fsa.gov.uk/Pages/Library/Communication/Speeches/1998/SP19.shtml

[40] See OFT, *Consumer Detriment under Conditions of Imperfect Information* (OFT Research Paper 11, prepared by London Economics, August 1997).

believe will be profitable; rivals and third parties may not be under incentives to correct the information provided by the firm; and some types of information (in particular relating to quality) cannot be as effectively communicated as other types (such as price). This can lead to focal point competition, with firms focusing only on specific factors.[41]

Information asymmetry and disclosure

Where information cannot be provided, regulation can do little. However, where firms are merely reluctant to provide information, regulation may provide a solution. For example mandatory disclosure may help markets to function, 'augmenting the preconditions of a competitive marketplace rather than substituting regulation for competition'.[42] Disclosure regimes exist in a number of areas, and have been championed by commentators from different perspectives.[43] However, they are not universally admired. Benston, for example, cites two main arguments against mandatory disclosure. First, he argues that while information asymmetry exists in financial services markets 'the potential market failures ... apply with equal or greater force to many products and services that are not regulated'.[44] Secondly, he asks why a government agency 'is more likely than suppliers to determine what information consumers would find useful for making "informed" decisions'.[45] Recently, a report by the National Consumer Council and the Better Regulation Executive argued that while information requirements were sometimes beneficial, the majority of them were not producing the desired outcomes.[46] One difficulty with replying on disclosure is that it is not clear that consumers are particularly good at making what might be described as 'rational' decisions, even when they have what appears to be relevant information. Research in behavioural economics has revealed a wide range of biases that characterise consumer decision making. Such biases have been summarised by Ramsay as including: hyperbolic

[41] For a fuller discussion, see OFT Research Paper 11 (*ibid.*) and (in relation to banking) P. Cartwright, *Banks, Consumers and Regulation* (Oxford: Hart Publishing, 2004) ch. 3.

[42] S. Beyer, *Regulation and its Reform* (Cambridge MA: Harvard University Press, 1982) 151.

[43] See, for example, D. Llewellyn, *The Economic Rationale for Financial Regulation* (FSA Occasional Paper 1, April 1999).

[44] Benston, n. 20 above, 60. [45] Ibid.

[46] Better Regulation Executive and National Consumer Council, *Warning: Too Much Information can Harm* (Interim Report, July 2007).

discounting; over-optimism; framing effects; availability and anchoring.[47] It is not possible to do justice to the findings here, but it should be noted that they counsel against a heavy reliance on information remedies.

With the FSA's move to principles-based regulation, mandatory disclosure will still have a role. According to the FSA's *Consumer Outcomes*: firms should ensure that '[c]onsumers are provided with clear information and are kept appropriately informed before, during and after the point of sale'.[48] There may be some areas where it is appropriate for detailed disclosure requirements to be set out.

Consumers recognise the relevance of information to fairness. When consumers argue that firms should 'give the customer what they have paid for' it seems that this 'focuses on the supplier's obligation to ensure that the customer's understanding of what they have purchased and the reality of the product being sold coincide'.[49] Consumers perceive the necessity of both providing information and ensuring understanding. This is linked to the issue of 'expectation' discussed below. Consumers also ask firms to 'exhibit clarity in all consumer dealings'. Firms fail to achieve this if they do not disclose information that would have been helpful, something that disclosure regimes help to address. Provisions that prohibit misleading omissions are also beneficial here.[50] However, an equally important factor in exhibiting clarity is ensuring that misleading information is not provided.

False and misleading information and the vulnerable consumer

It may appear obvious that firms should ensure, and the law should require, that false and misleading information is not supplied. False information distorts the market and, where provided knowingly, is also socially objectionable.[51] However, most provisions go further: they do not require proof of knowledge, and they cover misleading as well as false information. But how do we decide whether information is misleading?

Information is liable to be interpreted in different ways. As Sunstein observes, 'almost all substantive advertisements will deceive at least some

[47] I. Ramsay, *Consumer Law and Policy* (Oxford: Hart Publishing, 2007) 71–84.

[48] FSA, *Principles-based Regulation*, n. 28 above.

[49] *Treating Customers Fairly*, n. 34 above, 36.

[50] See Consumer Protection from Unfair Trading Regulations, Regulation 6.

[51] See D. Cayne and M. J. Trebilcock, 'Market Considerations in the Formulation of Consumer Protection Policy' (1973) 23 *University of Toronto Law Journal* 396.

of the people in the light of the exceptional heterogeneity of listeners and viewers'.[52] This creates difficulties in designing appropriate regulatory provisions. Regulation 5(2) of the CPR states that a practice is a misleading action where it contains false information and is therefore untruthful in relation to specific matters, or if it or its overall presentation in any way deceives or is likely to deceive the average consumer in relation to any of those matters (even if it is factually correct) and 'it causes or is likely to cause the average consumer to take a transactional decision he would not have taken otherwise'.

The average consumer test involves an objective standard. Regulation 2(2) confirms this by stating that, in determining the effect of a commercial practice on the average consumer where the practice reaches or is addressed to a consumer or consumers, account shall be taken of 'the material characteristics of such an average consumer including his being reasonably well-informed, reasonably observant and circumspect'. However, in two situations the test is varied. First, where the practice is aimed at a 'clearly identifiable group of consumers' the average consumer is the average member of that group. In some cases this may make a difference, for example where practices are aimed at overindebted consumers, or consumers with only a basic grasp of English. Secondly, Regulation 2(5) makes it clear that, where there is a clearly identifiable group of consumers who are particularly vulnerable to either the practice or to the underlying product 'because of their mental or physical infirmity, age or credulity in a way which the trader could reasonably be expected to foresee', then 'average consumer' means an average member of that group, provided that the practice will materially distort only the economic behaviour of that group. This is without prejudice to 'the common and legitimate advertising practice of making exaggerated statements which are not to be taken literally'.

It is unclear which groups are particularly vulnerable for those reasons. The young (and perhaps the elderly) might sometimes be particularly vulnerable because of their age. Those with impaired sight or hearing may sometimes miss relevant information. One might therefore see this as a duty on traders to ensure that such consumers have all the information they need. However, where it comes to mental infirmity and credulity, the test becomes more difficult to use. With 'mental infirmity' it is difficult to find an 'average' person against whom to judge the effect

[52] C. Sunstein, *Free Markets and Social Justice* (New York: Oxford University Press, 1997) 284.

of the practice. In the case of credulity, are there clearly identifiable groups of particularly credulous individuals?

As noted above, the Regulations deal with misleading omissions as well as actions. According to Regulation 6(1), a commercial practice is misleading if, in its factual context, among other things 'the commercial practice omits material information . . . and it causes or is likely to cause the average consumer to take a transactional decision he would not have taken otherwise.' This is potentially very wide. Wilhelmsson suggests that it 'almost gives the court a *carte blanche* to decide what information should be given in which type of commercial practice'.[53]

We can conclude from this that an important element of fairness is providing customers with clear information and keeping them appropriately informed. But difficulties remain in identifying precisely what this means in practice. The FSA's recent publication *Treating Customers Fairly: Measuring Outcomes* presents a mixed picture of how far firms have progressed. It stated that, while there were improvements in some areas, 'there is a lot more to do before information from firms to consumers could generally be considered to be fair and clear'. [54]

Suitability

There are, perhaps, three linked elements to suitability to consider here: suitability of advice, of products, and of targeting. Advice might also be linked to information (considered above). It is also important to think about the requirements placed upon different sorts of supplier.

The TCF Outcomes state that firms should ensure that 'where consumers receive advice the advice is suitable and takes account of their circumstances'. This is relevant to Principle 9 of the 'Principles for Businesses', which states that '[a] firm must take reasonable care to ensure the suitability of its advice and discretionary decisions for any customer who is entitled to rely upon its judgement'. Where consumers have obtained a recommendation, the advice has to reflect their needs, priorities and circumstances. The FSA has recently placed great emphasis on the essential legal requirement that a firm must 'act honestly fairly and professionally in line with the best interests of its

[53] G. Howells, H. Micklitz and T. Wilhelmsson, *European Fair Trading Law* (Aldershot: Ashgate, 2006) 152.

[54] FSA, *Treating Customers Fairly: Measuring Outcomes* (Nov. 2007) 5, available at www.fsa.gov.uk/pubs/other/tcf_outcomes.pdf.

clients'.[55] Consumers view this as an important aspect of fairness. The call to 'offer the customer the best product you can' suggests that consumers see it as unfair for firms not to recommend to consumers the most appropriate product for them. If this is so, consumers' wishes go further than the FSA's requirements, imposing a requirement of suitability well beyond the current regime. It would be difficult to impose such a requirement on firms.

Suitability of advice is closely linked with suitability of products and of targeting. The TCF Outcomes state that firms should ensure that 'products and services are designed to meet the needs of identified consumer groups and are targeted accordingly'. This goes well beyond any relationship based upon advice. It may be unfair to develop products that are not appropriate for those at whom they are targeted. For example, payment protection insurance has been marketed to consumers who would not have been able to claim on the insurance.[56]

As well as arguing that firms should offer customers the best product they can, consumers also suggested that an element of unfairness was that of 'taking advantage' of the consumer. Designing and targeting products inappropriately could be a clear example of this. While taking advantage 'probably requires defining as much as fairness',[57] it seems to reflect the asymmetry of information and power. Although the FSMA includes the general principle that consumers should take responsibility for their decisions, it is clear that firms also must take responsibility to avoid improperly taking advantage of their consumers. It should be noted that the concept of 'responsible lending', which forms part of the obligations of the Banking Code, and can also be taken into account by the OFT when deciding if there has been an unfair or improper credit practice, contains echoes of suitability.

Treating Customers Fairly: Measuring Outcomes suggests that there is a considerable amount of work to be done in this area. It states that the FSA has seen specific products where there is evidence of unsuitable advice and adds that its broader work has shown common weaknesses in firms' advice processes. The FSA adds that this increases the risk of misselling.[58] The main initiative in this area was the Retail Distribution Review (RDR). The aim of this, according to the FSA, was:

[55] See for example FSA, *Retail Distribution Review – Interim Report* (April 2008), 14, available at www.fsa.gov.uk/pubs/discussion/rdr_interim_report.pdf.

[56] Huertas, n. 18 above. [57] FSA 'Treating Customers Fairly', n. 34 above, 37.

[58] N. 54 above, 5.

> for more consumers to have sufficient confidence in the market to want to use its products and services more often. To achieve this, we need an industry that more clearly acts in the best interests of its customers and treats them fairly.[59]

The FSA published a feedback statement as part of the RDR in November 2008 which sets out proposals for consultation.[60] The FSA intends full implementation by the end of 2012. It is not possible to go into detail on these here, but proposals include clarifying the different types of service, changing rules and disclosure in relation to remuneration and providing clarity of guided sales.[61] The proposed changes are not as radical as those originally mooted.

Pressure

It was noted above that one element of unfairness identified by consumers was 'taking advantage' and that this concept reflects in part the power asymmetry that may exist between firms and consumers. Firms could take advantage of consumers by placing them under inappropriate pressure. This can take a variety of forms, from refusing to leave a customer's home when asked, to making persistent demands for payment. It overlaps potentially with information-based unfairness too, as a firm may find it easier to apply pressure where consumers lack information (for example on their rights). A number of provisions protect consumers against inappropriate pressure. One obvious such provision is that found in Regulation 7(1) of the CPR which deals with aggressive commercial practices:

> A commercial practice is aggressive if in its factual context, taking account of all its features and circumstances –
> (a) it significantly impairs or is likely significantly to impair the typical consumer's freedom of choice or conduct in relation to the product concerned through the use of harassment, coercion or undue influence; and
> (b) it thereby causes or is likely to cause the typical consumer to take a transactional decision he would not have taken otherwise.

Perhaps the key question is: how far can traders go to persuade consumers to act in the way(s) they want? Commercial practices are

[59] N. 55 above, para. 1.

[60] FSA *Retail Distribution Review Including Feedback on DP 07/1 and the Interim Report* (FSA, November 2008), available at www.fsa.gov.uk/pubs/discussion/fs08_06.pdf.

[61] Ibid.

generally concerned with persuading the consumer to act in a particular way. Advertising is largely about 'preference manipulation'. As Howells observes, it will be interesting to see 'which sales techniques aimed at manipulating the consumer's will are permitted, and which are deemed illegitimate'.[62] Certain provisions are specifically banned by the Regulations, including 'creating the impression that a consumer cannot leave the premises until a contract is signed', and 'conducting personal visits to the consumer's home, ignoring the consumer's request to leave or not to return, except in circumstances and to the extent justified to enforce a contractual obligation'. Reference should also be made to the unfair relationships provisions of the Consumer Credit Act 2006 which permit account to be taken of business practices such as the use of inappropriate pressure.[63] This area of law is not well developed, and needs to be viewed alongside common law and equitable notions such as duress and unconscionability.[64]

Expectation

It is important for all players in the marketplace to think about the expectations of other players.[65] It has been argued that 'programmes of consumer protection serve the ethical purpose of protecting the legitimate interests of consumers'.[66] In our discussion, attention should focus on the expectations that consumers [are entitled to] have of firms. Where the TCF Outcomes are met: 'Consumers are provided with products that perform *as firms have led them to expect* and the associated service is both of an acceptable standard and *as they have been led to expect*' [emphasis added].

Firms may generate expectations in different ways, such as by their advertising, or through the advice process. Where firms have led consumers reasonably to expect particular performance it might be unfair if the products do not provide that. There is, however, a problem in judging

[62] Howells *et al.*, n. 53 above, 184. [63] Ibid.

[64] See C. Twigg-Flesner, D. Parry, G. Howells and A. Nordhausen, *An Analysis of the Application and Scope of the Unfair Commercial Practices Directive* (Report for the Department of Trade and Industry, May 2005) 55–66.

[65] See for example FSA, *Reasonable Expectations: Regulation in a Non-zero Failure World* (FSA, September 2003), and the criticisms of it in P. Cartwright, 'Reasonable Expectations, (Un)reasonable Assumptions and Banking Regulation' [2006] *Lloyds Maritime and Commercial Law Quarterly* 82.

[66] R. Bradgate, R. Brownsword and C. Twigg-Flesner, *The Impact of Adopting a Duty to Trade Fairly* (DTI, July 2003) 2.

whether the consumer's expectation was a reasonable one. Where firms create an image of trust and reliability, perhaps it is reasonable to expect them to be held to the expectations they create. Ramsay, for example, demonstrates how firms emphasise trust and confidence by their advertising and suggests that: 'it does not seem far-fetched to argue that these images and stories may raise consumer expectations that they will be treated fairly.'[67]

Further difficulties arise where the expectation was not generated by the firm, but by others. Should firms be especially guarded where a particular viewpoint is common, but misconceived? The TCF Outcomes refer to consumers being provided with products that perform as firms have led them to expect and state that the associated service should be 'both of an acceptable standard and as they have been led to expect'. Even if this means 'as they had been led to expect by the firm', any meanings given to what has been said cannot be divorced from the surrounding environment of consumer understanding and expectation. It is important here to remember that different responsibilities will be placed upon different players in the supply chain. For example, we would expect different things of a core product provider from what we would expect of an intermediary. The FSA has produced regulatory guidance to address these issues, and they remain important to the Retail Distribution Review.[68]

There is no suggestion that firms should be held responsible simply on the basis that the product has not performed as well as was hoped. Performance risk is an inherent characteristic of many financial products. As Huertas points out:

> fairly sold products that produce bad financial outcomes for consumers are part and parcel of and [sic] efficient market for retail financial services, not a cause for regulatory intervention. Unfair treatment of consumers is.[69]

Treating Customers Fairly: Measuring Outcomes found several areas where false expectations were created. The paper concluded that when coupled with the 'disappointing' findings on information and advice this suggested that 'consumers may often not experience the specific product

[67] I. Ramsay, *Advertising, Culture and the Law* (London: Sweet and Maxwell, 1996) 18.

[68] See in particular 'The Responsibilities of Providers and Distributors for the Fair Treatment of Customers' (RPPD) Annex of the Providers and Distributors Regulatory Guide Instrument (FSA 2007/41).

[69] N. 18 above.

and services features or standards they expect'.[70] It seems that this is an area where more work is needed.

Discrimination

Consumers may face different types of discrimination. They might be denied access to products or only allowed access to products on less favourable terms as a result of factors such as race, colour, gender or disability. We know that non-white groups have lower consumption of many financial products, compared with white groups, but this may largely be explained on the basis of social background.[71] The law prohibits certain forms of discrimination. For example, s. 20 of the Race Relations Act 1976 states that: 'it is unlawful for any person concerned with the provision (whether for payment or not) of goods, facilities or services to the public or a section of the public to discriminate against a person who seeks to obtain those goods, facilities or services.' In its Discrimination Law Review, the Government stated:[72]

> In general, anyone providing a service (or supplying goods or making available facilities or premises) to the public should not be able to pick and choose which section of the public he or she will serve. However, there may be good reasons for allowing differential treatment in particular cases.

Some forms of discrimination are patently unfair. Others may be easier to justify (such as charging a person more for life insurance because of their medical history or even gender). There are provisions in sex and disability discrimination legislation that allow insurers to justify less favourable treatment if it is based on actuarial or other statistical data or information on which it is reasonable to rely. The Gender Directive required this to be tightened further.[73] It is also lawful to charge consumers different rates for loans depending on the risks they are deemed to pose. We know too that firms routinely offer financial products on less

[70] N. 54 above, 22.

[71] A. Herbert and E. Kempson, *Credit Use and Ethnic Minorities* (London: Policy Studies Institute, 1996). There is evidence of discrimination on the grounds of race and gender in the retail motor car market in the USA: see I. Ayres, 'Fair Driving: Gender and Race Discrimination in Retail Car Negotiations' (1991) 104 *Harvard Law Review* 817.

[72] Department for Communities and Local Government, *Discrimination Law Review* (Consultation Paper) para. 2.4, available at www.communities.gov.uk/documents/corporate/doc/325335.doc.

[73] Council Directive 2004/113/EC.

favourable terms to those with whom they already have a long-term contractual relationship. For example, new borrowers may get better terms than existing borrowers. This is a form of discrimination, and it may appear unfair to the loyal customer, but it is doubtful that it will ever fall foul of the law.

The focus of anti-discrimination efforts will inevitably be on those particularly invidious forms of discrimination (such as on grounds of race) that are so difficult to justify. This is dealt with by race relations legislation in the UK. In the USA, the Community Reinvestment Acts require financial institutions to disclose information about the extent to which they serve particular social groups, and impose upon institutions an obligation to meet the credit needs of the community.[74]

There are ways in which discrimination against consumers may, apparently paradoxically, be advantageous for those consumers. The selling of inappropriate financial products to consumers has long been a cause for concern. In particular, commentators have called for lenders to engage in more responsible lending. As noted above, measures are now in place to address this.

Post-sale conduct and redress

Consumer law has frequently focused on the pre-contractual behaviour of firms, but post-sale behaviour is also deserving of attention, especially where long-term contracts are involved. The TCF Outcomes state that 'Consumers should not face unreasonable post-sale barriers imposed by firms to change a product, switch provider, or make a complaint.' Webster suggests that post-sale barriers may be 'cultural, contractual or competitive' and that 'ultimately, the consumer must feel confident that they are able to switch providers without incurring excessive penalties'.[75] One example given of a post-sale barrier is that of mortgage exit administration fees. Here the FSA has worked out a Statement of Good Practice with the Council of Mortgage Lenders.[76]

Where complaints handling is concerned, the FSA sets minimum standards. Complaints are generally the first stage in obtaining redress,

[74] See I. Ramsay and T. Williams, 'Racial and Gender Equality in Markets for Financial Services', in Cartwright (ed.), n. 1 above.

[75] K. Webster, 'Treating Customers Fairly and Fairness in Contract Terms' (speech to the Council of Mortgage Lenders, 18 July 2007), available at www.fsa.gov.uk/pages/Library/Communication/Speeches/2007/0718_kw.shtml

[76] Ibid.

and consumer law has long emphasised the barriers faced by consumers in obtaining this. Markets only work effectively where consumers can hold firms to account for their actions by switching providers, communicating dissatisfaction and obtaining recompense. However, obtaining redress will be prohibitive for consumers because of 'transaction costs', particularly enforcement costs.[77] Taking advantage of consumers' difficulties here is a clear example of unfairness.

It is sometimes difficult to judge when the post-sale conduct of firms amounts to imposing 'unreasonable' barriers or 'taking advantage'. Conduct that appears unfair to consumers may sometimes be legitimate, such as seeking repossession where a consumer is in arrears. However, firms may sometimes behave unfairly in enforcing their legal rights. The Banking Code, for example, recognises the importance of dealing sympathetically with these issues, and a failure to do so might be regarded as unfair. One element of fairness identified by consumers is to: 'show flexibility, empathy and consideration in dealing with customers.' According to the Report on consumers' views of fairness 'the respondent perception of fairness is that a degree of discretion should be used and each situation judged separately with the provider giving the customer the benefit of the doubt'.[78] This applies even where a firm might be within its rights to enforce specific terms.

A related element of unfairness identified by consumers was that of not resolving mistakes as quickly as possible. The Report on consumers' views of fairness found 'a view that providers are quick to charge customers for their mistakes but less ready to pay out in recognition of their own errors'.[79] It is important to recognise here the role of the Financial Ombudsman Service in the resolution of disputes. The breadth of the Ombudsman's discretion means that he is able to take into account the post-sale conduct of firms.

Conclusions

This chapter argues that fairness pertains to the information consumers are given, the suitability of the products and advice they receive, the pressure they face, the extent to which their expectations are generated and met, the discrimination they endure, and the extent to which they

[77] See e.g. I. Ramsay, 'Consumer Redress Mechanisms for Poor-Quality and Defective Products' (1981) 31 *University of Toronto Law Journal* 117.

[78] N. 49 above, 38. [79] Ibid., 37.

can complain, switch, and sue post-sale. However, it recognises that the nature of unfairness is so multi-faceted, and so indeterminate, that providing a perfect taxonomy is impossible.

One point that the FSA has made constantly is that the attitude of a firm may be a good indicator of whether it takes fairness seriously. The FSA talks about the 'culture' of the firm being important, such that 'Consumers can be confident that they are dealing with firms where the fair treatment of customers is central to the corporate culture.'[80] The FSA has emphasised that TCF should be driven by senior management, and built into the firm's operations and processes. For example, if a firm does not take training seriously, and has a rewards structure based heavily on commission, that may lead to problems for consumers. The FSA now has a supervisory tool for assessing TCF culture in firms (taking into account the following factors: leadership; strategy; decision making; controls; recruitment; training and competence and reward). Firms that can show they take TCF seriously can expect less intrusive supervision. Attitude and culture perhaps transcend the elements of fairness identified. Thus, although it may never be possible perfectly to define fairness, if we can distil its essence, we may be able better to ensure that consumers are truly treated fairly.

[80] For a discussion of the possible meanings of culture in the context of TCF and its relationship with ethics, see J. Edwards 'Treating Customers Fairly' (2006) 14 *Journal of Financial Regulation and Compliance* 1358.

12

Open the box: an exploration of the Financial Services Authority's model of fairness in consumer financial transactions

TONI WILLIAMS*

Introduction

The first global financial crisis of the twenty-first century has fuelled extensive debate about the regulation of financial markets and transactions.[1] Although much of this debate so far has focused on the inter-firm and intra-group dealings among financial firms that the crisis has exposed as sites of systemic risk, the catalytic effects of the insecurities and vulnerabilities experienced by sub-prime borrowers in the US and by Northern Rock savers in the UK has given new prominence to the regulation and governance of personal financial transactions. Responding to the urgency of the perceived need to strengthen consumer confidence in banks, European jurisdictions moved swiftly to shore up depositor compensation funds, increase coverage limits and eliminate co-insurance requirements, apparently with little regard to the moral hazard consequences of such measures.[2]

Other consumer-oriented proposals for the new regulatory order include financial product safety regulation, additional information sharing and disclosure measures, further development of responsible lending standards, and the activation of the self-protective capacities of financial

* My thanks to Iain Ramsay for insightful comments and suggestions.

[1] See for example, A. Turner, *The Turner Review: A Regulatory Response to the Global Banking Crisis* (London: FSA, 2009); P. Gowan, 'Crisis in the Heartland' (2009) 55 *New Left Review* 5–29 and sources cited therein.

[2] International Association of Deposit Insurers, *Core Principles for Effective Deposit Insurance Systems* (Basel: IADI, 2008); A. Demirgüç-Kunt and E. Detragiache, 'Does Deposit Insurance Increase Banking System Stability? An Empirical Investigation' (2002) 49 *Journal of Monetary Economics* 1373–406; G. Hoggarth, P. Jackson and E. Nier, 'Banking Crises and the Design of Safety Nets' (2005) 29 *Journal of Banking & Finance* 143–59; Council Directive (EC) 2009/14 amending Directive 94/19/EC on deposit-guarantee schemes as regards the coverage level and the payout delay [2009] L 68/6.

consumers through financial education and advice and, where possible, carefully crafted default rules.[3]

Many such proposals build on the regulatory foundation that has been laid by the Financial Services Authority (FSA), the UK's main market regulator of consumer financial markets and products. Despite operating for most of its short life in an environment that celebrated 'light-touch' regulation, the FSA has nonetheless created an innovative model of fair dealing in consumer financial transactions. This model blends the neoliberal project of constituting financial markets as open, expansionary, competitive and self-correcting, with an elaborate matrix of rules, principles and supervisory practices for regulating retail financial markets. Fairness is secured not so much by the setting of procedural or substantive standards against which to assess particular transactions, but through the use of the regulator's powers to constitute 'responsibilised' identities for the individuals who participate in market transactions,[4] identities that construct financial firms – and consumers – as self-regulating market actors.

According to this model, a responsibilised firm regards the fair treatment of consumers as fundamental to the marketing, making and execution of retail financial contracts. Moreover, as a self-regulating actor, entrusted with the governance of its own conduct, the responsibilised firm should have the capacity to demonstrate its performance of fairness not only in its front end dealings with retail consumers, but also in its conduct of those routine business operations – hiring, training, monitoring and rewarding – that support its market activities. Transactions between the responsibilised firm and the financial consumer (similarly responsibilised through capability enhancing financial education)[5] reflect and communicate each party's capacity for self-governance. Of equal importance to the regulatory project is the possibility that such transactions might generate corrective market discipline as the capable consumer rewards those firms that can signal their embrace of the regulator's fair dealing requirements and rejects those that cannot.

[3] O. Bar-Gill and E. Warren, 'Making Credit Safer' (2008) 157 *University of Pennsylvania Law Review* 1–101.

[4] G. Burchell, C. Gordon and P. Miller (eds.), *The Foucault Effect: Studies in Governmentality: with Two Lectures by and an Interview with Michel Foucault* (University of Chicago Press, 1991); J. Gray and J. Hamilton, *Implementing Financial Regulation: Theory and Practice* (Chichester: J. Wiley & Sons, 2006); N. Rose, *Powers of Freedom: Reframing Political Thought* (Cambridge University Press, 1999).

[5] T. Williams, 'Empowerment of Whom and for What? Financial Literacy Education and the New Regulation of Consumer Financial Services' (2007) 29 *Law & Policy* 226–56.

This chapter analyses a central component of the FSA's regulatory model, its Treating Customer's Fairly initiative (TCF), and explores the implications of this model for the protection of financial consumers. The next section of the chapter outlines the rationales for regulation that influence the Treating Customers Fairly initiative. After the discussion on rationales, the chapter proceeds to trace the development of TCF and describe its main responsibilising elements. The analysis then moves to consider implementation of TCF, by exploring some recent FSA enforcement decisions on the misselling of payment protection insurance, a topic that recently attracted the interest of many regulators and policymakers.

Rationale for fairness regulation

The FSA's approach to regulation of consumer financial products and markets rests on a familiar diagnosis of the relationship between the institutional structure of such markets and unfair treatment of consumers.[6] According to this diagnosis, the long-term nature and the credence and contingency characteristics of financial products create opportunities for profit-maximising firms to appropriate wealth from consumers, either by misselling the products or by stealthily redistributing the contract's explicit or implicit allocations of costs, risks and benefits after performance has begun.[7] Exacerbating the risk of opportunism is the limited capacity for self-defence of boundedly rational consumers when confronted with the complexity of many financial contracts and the information asymmetries that attend relationships between consumers and sellers of financial products. Nor, under such conditions, is competition likely to provide a solution since the inability of buyers to identify and avoid opportunistic sellers or dangerous products prevents the development of market constraints on opportunism or protections against it.[8]

Different but equally serious considerations arise in relation to consumers who do understand their vulnerability to opportunistic exploitation and those who do not. Some consumers who appreciate the risks may be deterred from participating in financial markets, denying

[6] I. Ramsay, *Rationales for Intervention in the Consumer Marketplace* (London: OFT, 1984); I. Ramsay, *Consumer Law and Policy: Text and Materials on Regulating Consumer Markets* (Oxford: Hart Publications, 2007).

[7] O. E. Williamson, *The Economic Institutions of Capitalism* (New York: The Free Press, 1987).

[8] Ibid.

themselves access to important services and products. Individual self-exclusion may thwart political projects to expand financial markets, and, more seriously for the consumers involved, self-exclusion from some products, including insurance and pension funds, may have long-term consequences for their personal economic security. Other consumers who are aware of the risk may yet decide to engage in financial transactions, but incur costs by trying to protect themselves against firms' strategies of 'self-interest seeking with guile',[9] expending resources on safeguards that they could have used for other purposes.

Consumers who do not understand their vulnerability to opportunism avoid the transaction costs of ineffective, or incompletely effective, self-protection. To the extent that opportunistic tendencies are endemic to the structure of consumer financial markets, however, unaware consumers risk incurring substantial error, regret and 'lemon' costs.[10] Financial firms and intermediaries may take advantage of consumer ignorance, bounded rationality and confusion in a variety of ways. They may, for example, tailor financial advice and recommendations to serve firms' interests in maximising commission payments, missell dangerous, defective, unsuitable or poor-quality financial products, impose tie-ins to companion products that consumers neither need nor want, lock-in buyers to long-term contracts thereby locking them out of better deals, erect spurious barriers to switching, ignore consumers complaints, deny them redress and so on.

A heightened risk of financial firms exploiting their informational advantages and other sources of relative power in consumer markets obviously affects the intra-contractual distribution between a firm and its consumer of the benefits, risks and costs of financial transactions. Perhaps of more significance to contemporary governments and regulators such as the FSA, however, are the perceived benefits of robust counter-opportunism measures for efficiency and competitiveness. An early FSA policy document on the TCF initiative, for example, explains that the requirement to treat customers fairly 'is key to the operation of an efficient retail market for financial services ... In a competitive marketplace, treating customers fairly (TCF) should be an important element (alongside service levels, pricing and customer satisfaction) in

[9] Ibid., 47–8.

[10] G. A. Akerloff 'The Market for "Lemons": Quality Uncertainty and the Market Mechanism' (1970) 84 *Quarterly Journal of Economics* 488.

determining the success of a firm in acquiring and maintaining market share.'[11] Opportunism control, in short, is just as important to aspirations to expand and develop financial markets as it is to the project of protecting vulnerable consumers.

Tools such as the FSA's rule-making, supervision and enforcement powers are constitutive elements of consumer financial markets and as such shape the extent to which particular markets are configured to facilitate or restrain opportunistic behaviour by firms. The FSA's responses to the risks of unfairness, however, appear to be driven less by a sense of the potential of such tools than by awareness of their limitations. For a central consequence of locating the reasons for unfair treatment in standard characteristics of consumer financial markets (the interaction of information asymmetry, product complexity and limited consumer capabilities with profit-maximising motivations of firms) is that regulation may be required to challenge established practices as well as those that substantially depart from the norm.

From a perspective that views the risk of unfair treatment as embedded in routine, everyday encounters of financial markets – rather than as a gross contravention of a standard that is generally observed – the enormity of the regulator's task becomes evident. Consumer financial markets are simply too large, complex, fragmented and diverse, and financial contracts too private, for a regulator equipped only with prescriptive rules and penalties for breach to have a significant impact on how firms relate to their customers. Rather than relying solely on penal action against manifest deviance, therefore, the FSA's fairness projects respond to opportunism by seeking to embed attentiveness to consumer welfare into the working rules of financial product design, development, and marketing, and financial contract formation, performance, complaint handling and redress.

The FSA's 'Treating Customers Fairly' initiative

1. The development of TCF

The Financial Services Authority (FSA) acquired statutory regulatory powers, including authorisation or licensing, rule-making, supervision and enforcement, on 30 November 2001, upon the coming into force of

[11] Financial Services Authority, *Treating Customers Fairly – Progress and Next Steps* (London: FSA, 2004).

the Financial Services and Markets Act 2000 (FSMA).[12] At that time, the FSA's jurisdiction covered pensions and investment products together with related intermediary and advisory services, and banks. Its regulatory authority was extended to first charge mortgages in October 2004 and to many non-investment insurance products on 14 January 2005. Since 2005, the FSA's jurisdiction has been extended to other consumer financial products, such as travel insurance, home reversion plans (a form of equity release) and Sale and Rent Back transactions.[13] In November 2009 the FSA took over conduct of business regulation for the deposit taking and payment services activities of retail banks, functions that were within its remit from 2001 but had been left with the Banking Code Standards Board.[14] Regulatory authority over unsecured credit and most aspects of non-first charge mortgages, however, remains with the Office of Fair Trading.[15]

Questions about how to institutionalise fair treatment of consumers in the business activities of financial firms have engaged the FSA from the beginning of its life as an integrated regulator, responsible for both conduct of business and prudent regulation of the financial sector. The FSA inherited the sector-specific regulatory standards of the second-tier self-regulatory organisations (SROs) that had been established under the 1986 regulatory scheme and a set of ten trans-sectoral principles on the conduct of financial firms that had been developed by the Securities and Investments Board (SIB), the financial industry's first-tier regulator and the FSA's immediate forerunner. Two of the SIB principles, 'integrity – A firm should observe high standards of integrity and fair dealing',[16] and a somewhat anaemic disclosure standard served as the point of departure for development of the Treating Customers Fairly (TCF) initiative.

Work on TCF started in early 2000 with the FSA's elaboration of the regulatory approach that it intended to adopt once the Financial Services and Markets Act came into effect and the Authority had received its

[12] The FSA began operating in October 1997 when the first tier regulator, the SIB, under the previous system, was renamed the Financial Services Authority and started to supply regulatory services to the other SROs (which retained their statutory powers until 2001).

[13] 'FSA to Protect Sale and Rent Back Customers', FSA/PN/071/2009, 3 June 2009, available at www.fsa.gov.uk/pages/Library/Communication/PR/2009/071.shtml.

[14] Financial Services Authority, *Regulating Retail Banking Conduct of Business: Feedback on CP08/19 and Final Rules* (London: FSA, 2009).

[15] Consumer Credit Act 1974, chapter 39 (as amended by Consumer Credit Act 2006, chapter 14).

[16] Cited in Financial Services Authority, *Fairness of Terms in Consumer Contracts: Statement of Good Practice* (London: FSA, 2005) para. 1.7.

statutory powers. *A New Regulator for a New Millennium*, the FSA's blueprint for its new 'risk-based' approach to regulation, synthesised the four FSMA objectives[17] – maintaining market confidence, promoting public awareness, protecting consumers, and reducing financial crime – into a general goal of 'maintain[ing] efficient, orderly and clean financial markets and help[ing] retail consumers achieve a fair deal'.[18] This report offers little by way of substantive content for the FSA's emerging construct of the 'fair deal'. As one might expect, however, *A New Regulator* is based on the dominant role of information inequality in rationales for regulating consumer financial transactions. It therefore identifies consumer-friendly disclosure obligations as an important regulatory response to problems of unfairness in consumer markets.

In terms of creating norms for the conduct of retail financial services business, the FSA took the position that regulation through 'high level principles' applicable to all financial firms, whatever the nature of their business, would better align its regulatory practice with the statutory considerations for good regulation.[19] Developing its regulatory toolkit around principles[20] also was regarded as more likely to advance consumers' interests in fair treatment than would reliance on detailed prescriptive rules for each sector and retail financial product. Firms, too, were thought to benefit from basing the new fairness requirements on principles, specifically through the construction of a less intrusive regulatory order than a rule-based system would require.[21]

[17] Financial Services and Markets Act 2001, s. 2(2)

[18] Financial Services Authority, *A New Regulator for the New Millennium* (London: FSA, 2000) para 21.

[19] Financial Services and Markets Act 2001, s. 2(3). These considerations are: 'efficiency and economy', 'proportionality', facilitating innovation, maintaining competition and the international competitiveness of the UK's financial industry, and recognition of the responsibilities of firms' managers for the conduct of business generally and regulatory compliance in particular.

[20] Recently refashioned as 'outcomes-based regulation', see e.g. H. Sants, 'Principles-Based Regulation – Lessons from the Sub-Prime Crisis', speech to Securities and Investments Institute Annual Conference, 15 May 2008, available at: www.fsa.gov.uk/pages/Library/Communication/Speeches/2008/0515_hs.shtml.

[21] Making these points, an early TCF policy document comments that 'we are reluctant to press on with ever more intrusive regulation, which could create defensive and costly markets which are smaller and less innovative. Instead we would prefer to see our rules supplemented by an intelligent, thoughtful and effective implementation by firms of the high-level principle that they must treat their customers fairly. We see a payback for firms in both market-based success and less intrusive, and therefore less costly, regulation': Financial Services Authority, *Treating Customers Fairly – Progress and Next Steps* (London: FSA, 2004).

Alongside the consolidation and repackaging of the conduct of business rules inherited from the rule books of its predecessor sector regulators, the FSA formulated eleven 'conduct of business' principles, which it regarded as providing firms with enough flexibility to innovate and thrive within a framework of sufficient constraint on unacceptable dealings with retail consumers. Several of the Principles bear upon the FSA's vision of 'achieving a fair deal for retail consumers'. TCF policy documents and enforcement proceedings, for example, may cite non-compliance with principles requiring firms to show integrity, and due skill, care and diligence, and to maintain 'responsible and effective business control systems including risk-management systems', as implicated in unfair treatment of customers.[22] Principles about fair management of conflicts of interest and protection of a client's assets also concern important aspects of consumer-firm relationships where a firm's judgement or actions may substantially affect a consumer's welfare or sense of being treated fairly.[23] Of most significance to the development of TCF, however, are: Principle 6, 'a firm must pay due regard to the interests of its customers and treat them fairly'; Principle 7, 'a firm must pay due regard to the information needs of its clients, and communicate information to them in a way which is clear, fair and not misleading'; and Principle 9, 'a firm must take reasonable care to ensure the suitability of its advice and discretionary decisions for any customer who is entitled to rely upon its judgment'.[24]

Mindful that the SIB's experience with principles appeared to have had little impact on the way that firms interacted with consumers, the FSA embarked on a process of fleshing out these basic tenets of fairness, a process that culminated in a formal regulatory requirement to Treat Customers Fairly.[25] It also has attempted to institutionalise the Treating Customers Fairly construct as a basic working rule of the business operations and consumer relations of financial firms. These processes of elaboration and institutionalisation have produced a substantial body of TCF publications, including discussion papers, consultation papers, qualitative research, policy documentation, speeches,

[22] Principles 1, 2 and 3, FSA Handbook PRIN, available at: http://fsahandbook.info/FSA//handbook/PRIN/2/1.pdf.

[23] Principles 8 and 10, ibid. [24] Ibid.

[25] Financial Services Authority, *FSA Update on the Treating Customers Fairly Initiative and the December Deadline* (London: FSA, 2008) 3.

thematic reviews of particular areas, examples of good and poor practice, speeches, 'Dear CEO' letters and enforcement decisions.[26] By 2004, the studies and consultations had coalesced into a package of norms, expectations and processes that the FSA was ready to demand of financial firms. Accordingly, the FSA's 2004/05 Business Plan declared that Treating Customers Fairly 'must be adopted and supported by the leadership of financial firms, and embedded throughout a firm's operations and within its culture'.[27] Since 2004, the FSA has published a lot more guidance about the requirements of TCF, added key customer outcomes to the TCF construct, stepped up enforcement action for TCF contraventions in particular markets, increased the level of fines for failure to meet TCF standards, and fully incorporated TCF into its core supervision of financial firms.[28]

2. *The requirements of TCF*

Treating Customers Fairly maps out a division of responsibilities between financial firms and the regulator for fair treatment of financial consumers, and directs firms generally as to the methods they should adopt to demonstrate that they have discharged their responsibilities. Firms are responsible for demonstrating fair treatment of customers and the FSA for ensuring that firms establish and maintain systems and controls that not only deliver fair treatment to customers but also allow regulators to observe firms' practices and thus assess how firms organise their dealings with consumers and how they perform their contracts. In terms of specifying the meaning(s) of fairness, the FSA provides extensive guidance to firms, but refuses to publish a formal 'definition', on the basis that a formal definition is likely to be overly

[26] See for example, Financial Services Authority, *Treating Customers Fairly – Building on Progress* (London: FSA, 2005); Financial Services Authority, *Treating Customers Fairly: The Consumers' View* (London: FSA, 2005); Financial Services Authority, *Treating Customers Fairly – What it Means for Small Firms* (London: FSA, 2005); Financial Services Authority, *Treating Customers Fairly after the Point of Sale* (London: FSA, 2001); Financial Services Authority, *Treating Customers Fairly – Progress and Next Steps* (London: FSA, 2004); Financial Services Authority, *Treating Customers Fairly – Towards Fair Outcomes for Consumers* (London: FSA, 2006); Financial Services Authority, *The Responsibilities of Providers and Distributors for the Fair Treatment of Customers* (London: FSA, 2006). A collection of key TCF publications is available at: www.fsa.gov.uk/Pages/Doing/Regulated/tcf/library/index.shtml.

[27] Financial Services Authority, *FSA Business Plan 2004/05* (London: FSA, 2004) 22.

[28] See sources cited in n. 26 above.

rigid, inappropriately prescriptive, and may be treated, at least by some firms, as representing a 'ceiling' on firms' obligations toward consumers or an invitation simply to add another factor to existing internal compliance processes.[29] Having positioned TCF as a comprehensive regulatory package for substantially changing the retail culture of firms, and how firms interact with consumers, the FSA regards the TCF standards as demanding far more of firms than the type of perfunctory cooperation and compliance that may occur in response to other regulatory reporting requirements.[30]

From the regulator's perspective – that firms must embrace and assume ownership of TCF – one of the FSA's more significant demands is that the managers of financial firms commit time and resources to figuring out what fairness means in relation to their products, their markets and the capacity, confidence and circumstances of their consumers.[31] Fairness may be a general – and to the FSA fundamental – ground rule of consumer financial markets, but its particular requirements are contextual; and as such will be significantly influenced by characteristics of a firm's consumers as well as their products. With respect to the 'key customer outcomes' added in 2006, for example, the FSA instructs firms as to what they must achieve, but insists that each firm must decide for itself, albeit with considerable guidance from the FSA, how it will secure each applicable outcome.[32]

It is thus the responsibility of the firm's management to decide what is meant by, for example, the most general key customer outcome of 'embedding fair customer treatment in the [firm's] corporate culture'; what specific changes are required to achieve this outcome in such areas of policy and practice as leadership, strategy, decision-making procedures, controls on staff discretion, recruitment, training and competence assessment practices, and reward system; how the firm will implement the changes; and how it will ensure that the changes have the desired

[29] *Treating Customers Fairly – Towards Fair Outcomes for Consumers*, n. 26 above.

[30] Ibid. See also Financial Services Authority, *Better Regulation Action Plan: What We Have Done and Why We Are Doing It* (London: FSA, 2005).

[31] *Treating Customers Fairly – Towards Fair Outcomes for Consumers*, n. 26 above; *The Responsibilities of Providers and Distributors for the Fair Treatment of Customers*, n. 26 above; Financial Services Authority, *Treating Customers Fairly: Measuring Outcomes* (London: FSA, 2007).

[32] *Treating Customers Fairly – Towards Fair Outcomes for Consumers*, n. 26 above; *Treating Customers Fairly: Measuring Outcomes*, n. 31 above.

effect. Similar analysis of consumer needs and interests and attentiveness to the specification of changes, systematic implementation and monitoring are expected of firms in relation to the more specific key outcomes as well. To these ends financial firms must consider what TCF demands of them with respect to product design, the targeting of marketing and selling practices; information disclosure 'before, during and after the point of sale'; the tailoring of advice to consumers' circumstances; consumer expectations about the performance of financial products and services; and the elimination of unreasonable impediments to customer switching, claiming and complaining.[33]

Planning, reviewing and monitoring the design, marketing, selling and supporting of financial products are, of course, standard business operations, at least in larger firms, but these operations normally are organised to support the firm's interests in maximising their profits, if necessary at the expense of consumers. Thus, the most striking aspect of the TCF initiative is not so much its conceptualisation of fairness as contextually related to characteristics of the product and the contractual parties – standards such as unconscionability or good faith, for example, reflect a similar approach[34] – nor that TCF standards draw on well-established consumer policy concerns about information disclosure and meeting consumer expectations. TCF's novelty, rather, is that the FSA explicitly demands firms to change aspects of their businesses that are traditionally conceived of as within management discretion in order to conform to the regulatory standard.[35]

Disregarding these demands may be risky. While the FSA may not tell financial firms specifically what fairness demands in relation to their business, the regulator does monitor the processes firms have created to achieve TCF goals. Moreover, the FSA's policy documentation and enforcement decisions provide ample evidence that the regulator considers the lack of robust implementation and monitoring to be indicative of failure to treat customers fairly, or at least of an

[33] Ibid.

[34] For extensive commentary on contractual concepts of fairness in the consumer setting, see C. Willett, *Fairness in Consumer Contracts: The Case of Unfair Terms* (Aldershot: Ashgate, 2007). For insightful analysis of different models of fairness in relation to financial transactions, see P. Cartwright, 'Conceptualising and Understanding Fairness: Lessons from and for Financial Services', Chapter 11 in this volume.

[35] Financial Services Authority, *Treating Customers Fairly – Guide to Management Information* (London: FSA, 2007); Financial Services Authority, *Treating Customers Fairly – Culture* (London: FSA, 2007).

unacceptable degree of risk of unfair treatment.[36] With its refusal to defer to managerial authority about how to measure a firm's performance in consumer markets, the FSA has prised open up the 'black box' of the firm's internal operations, exposing routine aspects of its retail business model to regulatory scrutiny.

TCF enforcement decisions: responding to unfairness in consumer financial markets

1. *Systemic risks and the FSA's presumption of unfairness:* Land of Leather *May 2008*

The FSA has incorporated into its supervisory work procedures for identifying the provisions that it expects to see in areas such as pay schemes, training and supervision, internal reporting and management priority setting. Unless firms have made suitable adaptations to these aspects of their operations, the FSA may regard the firm as presenting an unacceptable risk of dealing unfairly with its customers. This presumption of unfairness appears in some FSA reports on progress (or the lack thereof) towards its original target of TCF being fully 'embedded' in the culture of financial firms by the end of 2008 and sometimes in its enforcement actions.[37] In May 2008, for example, the FSA fined the

[36] In addition to the decisions discussed in this section see, for example, the final notice in *Egg Banking Plc*, 9 December 2008, available at: www.fsa.gov.uk/pubs/final/egg.pdf, where the facts that the regulator rather than the bank's management had identified the problems with the sales processes and that the problems had persisted despite several high profile FSA reports were treated as aggravating factors. The Final Notice in *GE Money Home Lending*, 22 September 2008, available at: www.fsa.gov.uk/pubs/final/gemhl.pdf, notes that management's failure to fix practices that the firm had long identified as harming consumers was an aggravating factor. Almost all of the policy documents on the implementation of TCF emphasise the responsibilities of managers to engage in proactive monitoring and supervision in order to safeguard consumer interests, see, for example: *Treating Customers Fairly: Measuring Outcomes*, n. 26 above; *Treating Customers Fairly – Guide to Management Information*, n. 35 above; *Treating Customers Fairly – Culture*, n. 35 above; Financial Services Authority, *Treating Customers Fairly Initiative: Progress Report* (London: FSA, 2007).

[37] The authority to impose penalties on authorised persons – firms and individuals – is found in s. 206 of the Financial Services and Markets Act 2000. As is true of most FSA procedures, a substantial body of regulatory rules and guidelines supplements the statutory provision; see, in particular, *Enforcement Guide* (EG) available at Handbook online, http://fsahandbook.info/FSA/html/handbook/EG and the *Decision Procedures and Penalties Manual* (DEPP) available at Handbook online, http://fsahandbook.info/FSA/html/handbook/DEPP.

furniture retailer Land of Leather £210,000, and its chief executive, Paul Briant £14,000, for selling payment protection insurance (PPI) while the firm lacked 'appropriate systems and controls ... to ensure that their customers are treated fairly'.[38]

This decision provides a good illustration of the FSA's emphasis on outcomes rather than policy documents and formal procedures. In this case the firm had taken professional advice about the organisational changes it needed to make to its systems for training staff, testing competence and monitoring sales before entering the PPI market on its own account. Managers had established a working compliance system that reported regularly as required. Senior management were said to have 'responded appropriately when specific issues were escalated to them for approval'.[39] More generally, however, the decision maker found that the firm's senior management had not treated such compliance information with sufficient seriousness and had been lax about implementation of the consultant's recommendations. Thus, the training programme that was required for sales staff after the firm received authorisation to sell PPI was not completed until six months after authorisation and the competence testing programme was still unfinished some thirteen months after authorisation.[40] The FSA decision maker also found that the systems for monitoring sales staff were wholly inadequate for the retail business model in which PPI was sold by more than 300 sales staff across a branch network of 90 stores.

The facts found by the FSA decision maker indicated that the vast majority (85 per cent) of the firm's buyers avoided any premium payment for PPI because they paid off the loan during a twelve-month payment-free period. For products such as PPI, however, even a small take-up rate by consumers may amount to a substantial sum. Thus the 8,000-plus customers who bought PPI from Land of Leather during the period under investigation were estimated to have paid £3.1 million in premiums with potential for an additional £2.8 million in interest payments. Interestingly, the firm's 'customer contact exercise', which was developed as a basis for consumer redress, did not identify 'widespread mis-selling' and only a few customers (less than 0.2 per cent) took up the

[38] *Final Notice: Land of Leather Limited*, 9 May 2008, para. 2.1, available at www.fsa.gov.uk/pubs/final/LandofLeather.pdf; see also *Final Notice: Paul Simon Briant*, 9 May 2008, available at: www.fsa.gov.uk/pubs/final/Paul_Briant.pdf.

[39] *Land of Leather*, n. 38 above, para. 2.3(4). [40] Ibid., para. 2.3.

firm's offer to cancel the PPI coverage.[41] The FSA decision maker accepted the results of the customer contact exercise in mitigation of the penalty, in effect concluding that there was a relatively small level of materialised consumer detriment. Nevertheless, the decision regarded the firm's inaction on implementation as disregarding consumers' interests in fair treatment and fined the firm on the basis that its indifference had exposed the entire population of its 57,950 customers to an unacceptable level of risk.

2. *The FSA's expectations of compliant outcomes:* GE Capital Bank *January 2007*

In January 2007, the FSA fined GE Capital Bank (GECB),[42] a large consumer credit financier, £610,000 for TCF failures in its systems and controls pertaining to PPI sales and consumer redress. The decision concerned just one part of the GECB's business: the PPI sold by retail store staff in support of high street department store cards. This business, which amounted to approximately 800,000 policies in 2005, relied on a highly dispersed retail distribution model that might involve up to half a million retail store workers per year. As in the *Land of Leather* case the focus of the FSA's enforcement decision was the risk to consumers from a sales model that it found to be seriously flawed. In this instance the firm had implemented systems for training its staff, monitoring sales practices and controlling sales, but the decision maker found these systems to be largely ineffective in terms of producing fair outcomes.

GECB had designed its sales procedures to comply with the FSA's requirements and it had consulted external experts as well as its own legal staff about these requirements. It delivered training on what it believed to be compliant procedures through a 'train the trainer model'; that is, GECB staff trained retail store managers, who then trained sales workers. GECB monitored retail sales through random mystery shopping and limited analysis of customer cancellation data, but did not systematically analyse its approximately 5,000 annual complaints. The FSA decision documented several inadequacies of GECB's monitoring systems, finding that its procedures were badly designed, poorly executed and

[41] Ibid., para. 2.8.

[42] *Final Notice: GE Capital Bank Limited*, 30 January 2007, available at: www.fsa.gov.uk/pubs/final/gecb.pdf.

insufficient 'to enable GECB to manage the regulatory risks presented by the nature and scale of its insurance business'.[43] It noted also, as further evidence of the failure of the sales model, that even GECB's seriously flawed monitoring measures had revealed a very high level of non-compliant sales (for example, a 57–75 per cent rate of failure to alert customers to the need to read a written policy summary) to which the firm had not responded. This was a clear contravention of the FSA's expectation that 'firms review their systems and controls and change them quickly if they are not operating as intended'.[44]

Another significant finding was the lack of a functional process to remedy non-compliant sales. GECB had not established appropriate procedures to initiate customer contact, and thus the firm had no reliable mechanism to recall missold products even when it identified defective sales. Nor had the firm established a system to trace the past sales of workers who were subsequently identified as making a non-compliant sale. It therefore lacked the capacity to locate previous customers of workers who may have made non-compliant sales. These findings exposed the GECB's provision for consumer redress as tantamount to 'a serious failure on the part of the firm to consider the interests of its insurance customers and a failure to treat them fairly'.[45]

The decision illustrates the FSA's expectations that management should not only aspire to TCF but also be able to demonstrate integration of the fair treatment of retail customers within sales procedures. It is not sufficient to establish policies and procedures to train staff on regulatory compliance, if the firm's training programmes and supervisory systems do not in fact produce TCF-compliant sales. While the FSA may not expect 'retail staff to have detailed knowledge of the FSA handbook', it does hold firms responsible for ensuring that their workers 'understand how to put the Principles into effect in their sales environment, so as to deliver a compliant outcome and the appropriate level of customer protection'.[46] Financial firm managers must develop adequate systems for monitoring, training and supervising staff; and they must ensure that the firm has the capacity to intervene rapidly to stop unfair sales practices and to adjust its training and reward systems where necessary. Managers are responsible for remedying non-compliant sales to individual consumers: and to this end it is for the firm's management to take the initiative to contact consumers and provide redress.

[43] Ibid., para. 4.19. [44] Ibid., para. 2.2. [45] Ibid., para. 4.28. [46] Ibid., para. 4.12.

3. *Misselling unsuitable products:* HFC Bank Ltd *16 January 2008*

In January 2008, the FSA imposed a fine of just over one million pounds on the finance company HFC Bank Ltd in respect of single premium PPI policies sold with unsecured loans,[47] a product that it has since banned.[48] As noted in the enforcement decision, HFC Bank specialises in lending to customers who have limited access to consumer finance, usually because of impaired or recent credit histories, that is to 'sub-prime borrowers who may be regarded as vulnerable because they lack viable alternatives'. PPI policies were added to 75 per cent of the loans sold during the period covered by the FSA enforcement action. In the sales sample reviewed by the FSA the average cost of the typical PPI policy was found to be £2,100, including £900 interest, which was estimated to increase by about 40 per cent the cost of the loan covered by the policy.

Unlike GECB and Land of Leather, HFC sold its policies on an advised basis. One important consequence of this sales model is that sellers actively interact with customers with a view to 'recommending' suitable products, a process that can all too readily descend into hard selling. A second important consequence is that the suitability of any advice or recommendation becomes an explicit element of the transaction, which opens up to regulatory observation the processes of giving advice or making a recommendation, and the training, monitoring and management of these processes. In addition to the sales scripts that may be available in non-advised cases as well, the regulator may have access to recordings and records of documents such as the customers' 'Statement of Demands and Needs' (the SODAN) that are required by the regulator's Conduct of Business rules.[49] These sources of data also are available to management, and as such create another site at which managers may be expected to show how they have met the requirements of Treating Customers Fairly.

[47] *Final Notice: HFC Bank Ltd*, 16 January 2008.

[48] In February 2009, the FSA sent a 'Dear CEO letter' to all firms that remained in the market to stop selling single premium PPI attached to unsecured loans by May 2009: Financial Services Authority, *FSA Wants All Firms to Stop Selling Single Premium PPI* (London: FSA, 2009). The Competition Commission's Report on competition in the PPI market had proposed a ban on such products but that proposal will not be fully implemented until December 2010: Competition Commission, *Market Investigation into Payment Protection Insurance* (London: TSO, 2009).

[49] FSA, *Insurance Conduct of Business Handbook* (ICOB), para. 4.4.1.

The decision reports numerous failings on the part of HFC front-line staff with respect to suitability assessments and sales practices, together with management systems that either implicitly encouraged unfair selling – through incentives such as bonuses, inadequate training and supervision and poor quality documentation – or did too little to stop it. Many of these problems stemmed from HFC's basic business model, which structured the sales process on the assumption that PPI was a suitable product for any eligible customer who did not insist that it was unnecessary. Working on this assumption, the firm did not train or supervise sales staff to gather detailed information about the specific needs, circumstances and requirements of individual customers. Staff would therefore assess expensive single premium policies as suitable for customers who: would not be able to claim during the loan period for reasons that were known or predictable at the start of the contract; had in place to the knowledge of the salesperson other coverage; were likely to refinance, therefore risked losing substantial sums because of the harsh contract terms on mid-term cancellation of the policies.[50] In addition to finding that HFC lacked appropriate procedures to govern the advising and sales process the FSA found that HFC's management systems were inadequate in almost all relevant respects, including staff training and supervision, reporting on compliance and complaints, and record-keeping.[51]

Conclusion

The FSA's 'Treating Customers Fairly' initiative offers an innovative model for achieving fairness in consumer financial markets. All three of the cases discussed in this chapter – as well as the other seventeen enforcement decisions on PPI consumer sales – suggest that unfairness in consumer financial markets may not be best understood as an exceptional transaction that departs radically from an unproblematic norm, a perspective that tends to influence judicial decisions. Absent regulatory oversight, monitoring, and strategic application of discipline, unfairness, instead, may be the norm. Thus, it may be salutary to note, but perhaps is scarcely surprising, that after three years of high profile regulatory action, a recent FSA enforcement decision found that Alliance & Leicester Plc had, throughout that time – notwithstanding multiple assurances of TCF

[50] *HFC Bank*, paras. 5.4(1)–(2). [51] Ibid., paras. 5.10–5.26.

compliance – substantially profited from PPI sales practices that the FSA has repeatedly condemned as unfair.[52]

Persistent stories of misselling and malpractice by providers and distributors of consumer financial products encourage the belief that unfair treatment of consumers may be endemic to the business models of many financial firms. Such stories also raise questions about the potential and the limits of regulatory action. One might conclude from reading the PPI decisions, for example, that even a regulator equipped with extensive rule-making powers to outlaw opportunistic behaviour and the necessary enforcement powers to sanction the offenders may have difficulty changing how financial firms treat their customers. It may be a mistake, however, to dismiss the TCF initiative too quickly as yet another example of an ineffectual regulator making demands that the regulated firms blithely ignore. More interesting to explore is the possibility that exposure of the internal systems and procedures of financial firms to regulatory scrutiny creates scope to think differently about how best to protect consumers' interests.

While the FSA may not have provided a neat definition of its complex fairness construct in terms of familiar ideas about 'oppression', 'extortion' or vulnerability attributable to 'weakness', its work on TCF sketches the contours of a new methodology for addressing unfairness in consumer markets. A starting assumption that unfairness is a normal rather than exceptional circumstance in consumer financial markets provides a basis for the regulator to require that firms spell out the demands of consumer fairness within the setting of their particular products and market activities and specify in detail how their businesses intend to change. Through this process of regulatory dialogue about how firms' practices should change, new conversations about consumers' expectations of fair dealing may emerge.

With respect to assessment of how firms perform against regulators and consumers expectations, the FSA's scepticism towards the formal policies of financial firms – their laws on the books – compels firms to

[52] Alliance & Leicester received a record £7 million penalty and also must fund a customer contact and redress exercise which has been reported to cost about £38 million: 'Payment Protection Complaints Triple', *FT.com* (London, 17 May 2009). Additional evidence of the intractable nature of the problem of unfairness in PPI sales are the substantial increases in complaints to the Financial Ombudsman Service. The numbers that increased substantially – five-fold – in 2007/08 and then tripled in 2008/09; and the FOS further reported that an exceptionally high proportion of the complaints are upheld: Financial Ombudsman Service, *FSA Annual Review 2008/09* (London: FOS, 2009).

demonstrate explicitly how their business models and sales practices work to deliver fair treatment of consumers. It is not sufficient for firms to create fair treatment policies if they do not then produce compliant results. Meta-regulatory aspects of the FSA's methodology may construct new sites and techniques of responsibility as managers become just as accountable for how their firms perform against fairness criteria as they are for the firm's performance against sales, revenue or costs targets.

The FSA is still a young regulatory agency, receiving its formal statutory powers less than ten years ago. Its jurisdiction was extended to key consumer financial products and markets, such as mortgages and insurance, even more recently. Furthermore, for much of the period since August 2007, the FSA has been pre-occupied with the global financial crisis. Thus it might be expected that its consumer fairness projects, including TCF, are works in progress and it remains to be seen whether the FSA's new model and methodologies for tackling unfairness in consumer financial markets can deliver on their promise. By prising open the black box of the firm's business model and exposing to regulatory – and public – scrutiny those critical internal processes that drive market activities, the FSA has suggested how ideas about the meanings of fairness for financial consumers might depart in the future from those of the past.

13

Conceptualising unconscionability in the context of risky financial transactions: how to converge public and private law approaches?

OLHA O. CHEREDNYCHENKO

1. Introduction

Financial services have become increasingly important in the EU. While such services are essential for the everyday life of EU citizens and for the EU economy at large, some of them entail very high risks which may particularly affect the vulnerable in financial transactions. Thus, for example, the provision of investment services by the bank may lead to huge financial losses beyond the client's ability to pay. By the same token, the provision of a business loan for one family member on the condition that another family member stand as a surety for the whole debt may result in financial ruin for the latter. The inequality of bargaining power and information asymmetry between the parties, coupled with huge risks involved in many financial transactions, give rise to the question of how and to what extent the vulnerable in such transactions must be protected.

Private laws of all European legal systems have developed concepts which aim to protect the weaker party against unconscionable bargains. Concepts such as good morals (*gute Sitten*) in German law, good faith (*redelijkheid en billijkheid*) and mistake (*dwaling*) in Dutch law or undue influence and unconscionability in English law may in certain circumstances relieve the weaker party from his or her onerous contractual obligations. There is a general agreement that the vulnerable should be protected against unconscionable transactions in private law. Major differences between the legal systems exist with regard to the concepts used for this purpose and particularly with regard to the *extent* to which the weaker party must be protected.

In the last two decades, however, the leading role of private law – in particular, contract law – in conceptualising unconscionability in the context of financial transactions has been put under pressure as a result of the growing influence of public law in this area. This influence has primarily manifested itself in two major developments, both of which have the potential to deeply affect private law. In the first place, in some legal systems, in German law in particular, there has been a noticeable change in the extent to which fundamental rights, i.e. human rights embodied in international human rights treaties and constitutional rights enshrined in national constitutions, have begun to have an impact on the relationships between private parties under contract law, i.e. a *horizontal effect in contract law*.[1] A famous judgment of the German Federal Constitutional Court (Bundesverfassungsgericht) in the *Bürgschaft* case,[2] which will be discussed in this chapter, has demonstrated that fundamental rights may have a crucial role to play in determining whether and to what extent a weaker party must be protected in contract law. Another major development is the growing importance of regulation in the field of financial services for the relationships between private parties under contract law. Of particular interest in the present context is the adoption of supervision legislation containing extensive rules of business conduct for financial service providers. The most important example available so far is the Markets in Financial Instruments Directive (MiFID)[3] which has the potential not only to supplement but also to supersede the contract law rules in the field of investment services.[4]

The aim of this chapter is to critically assess these developments and to discuss a possible interplay between public and private law in

[1] For a comprehensive study of the 'constitutionalisation' of private law, see O. O. Cherednychenko, *Fundamental Rights, Contract Law and the Protection of the Weaker Party: A Comparative Analysis of the Constitutionalisation of Contract Law, with Emphasis on Risky Financial Transactions* (Munich: Sellier, 2007), with further references to the extensive literature on this subject.

[2] Bundesverfassungsgericht (BVerfG) 19 October 1993, *BVerfGE* 89, 214 (*Bürgschaft*).

[3] Directive 2004/39/EC of the European Parliament and of the Council of 21 April 2004 on markets in financial instruments amending Council Directives 85/611/EEC and 93/6EEC and Directive 2000/12/EC of the European Parliament and of the Council and repealing Council Directive 93/22/EEC, OJEC 2004 L 145/1.

[4] On the relevance of the MiFID to contract law, see, inter alia, S. Grundmann, 'EC Financial Services: Developments 2002–2005' (2005) 1 *European Review of Contract Law* 482, 490; S. Grundmann and J. Hollering, 'EC Financial Services and Contract Law - Developments 2005–2007' (2008) 4 *European Review of Contract Law* 45, 68ff; Cherednychenko, *Fundamental Rights, Contract Law and the Protection of the Weaker Party*, chs. 7 and 8; P. O. Mülbert, 'The Eclipse of Contract Law in the Investment Firm-Client-Relationship: The Impact of the MiFID on the Law of Contract from a German Perspective', in G. Ferrarini and E. Wymeersch (eds.), *Investor Protection in Europe: Corporate Law Making, the MiFID and Beyond* (Oxford University Press, 2007) 299.

conceptualising unconscionability in the context of risky financial transactions. In view of the *comparative* nature of this analysis and the focus on *risky* financial transactions, I will use the terms 'unconscionability' and 'unconscionable' in a broad sense which goes beyond particular meanings attached to these concepts in common law countries.[5] For the purposes of this paper, an *unconscionable financial transaction* is a bargain which is (potentially) excessively disadvantageous for the weaker party whose freedom to form an independent judgement about the merits of the contract at the time the contract was made has been impaired because of what the stronger party has done or omitted to do. This definition of unconscionability includes the following three key elements. First, a relationship between the parties is characterised by an *imbalance in power*. Such an imbalance may result from the inequality of bargaining power between the parties and/or information asymmetry between them concerning the subject matter of the contract. Second, an unconscionable transaction in the meaning used in this chapter involves *excessive disadvantage* for the weaker party. In many financial transactions excessive disadvantage for the weaker party is to a greater or lesser extent the result of risk taking. Acting as a surety for a business loan of one's child or husband, for example, does not automatically result in financial ruin for the surety. The burden will be borne by the surety only if the business of the family member gets into financial difficulties. Similarly, an inexperienced retail investor who has invested all his savings in a particular investment product may not be prejudiced if the selected securities have performed well. The investor may suffer huge losses only if these securities drastically drop in value. These examples illustrate an important characteristic of many financial transactions – inherent risks involved therein for the weaker party which cannot be controlled by the stronger party.[6] The issue which the law of any legal system should therefore address is whether and to what extent the weaker party must be protected against entering into highly risky

[5] The equitable doctrine of unconscionability is grounded in the English common law tradition (*Earl of Chesterfield* v. *Janssen* [1750] 28 ER 82, 100). Although there are some cases in which the doctrine has been applied, they are relatively rare in England. In some other common law countries, however, the doctrine of unconscionability has taken on unique characteristics and played a much more prominent role in policing contracts. Notably in the United States (see, in particular, Uniform Commercial Code, s. 2–302 and E. A. Farnsworth, *Contracts* (New York: Aspen, 2004) para. 4.28); and in Australia (J. W. Carter and D. J. Harland, *Contract Law in Australia* (Chatswood, NSW: Butterworths, 2002) ch. 15).

[6] The risks are uncontrollable in the sense that the stronger party cannot normally guarantee that the risks will not materialise.

financial transactions. Should the investment firm, for example, be obliged to refuse to execute a certain transaction for the account of its client if such a transaction is extremely risky in view of the client's financial situation? Or should the client be able to enter into such a transaction subject to the condition that the investment firm, as a more professional party, has fully explained the transaction to the client, in particular by explaining the huge risks involved therein? These questions bring us to the third element of unconscionability in the sense used in this chapter – *the conduct of the stronger party* which *impairs the weaker party's freedom to form an independent judgement* about the merits of the transaction. Such conduct may not only consist of words or acts (such as making false statements about the subject matter of the contract or applying some form of pressure on the weaker party in order to obtain the contract), but also of an omission (such as a failure to inform or warn the weaker party about the risks involved in a transaction or a failure to prevent the conclusion of a potentially ruinous transaction even against the will of the weaker party).[7]

Proceeding from this understanding of unconscionable financial transactions, in the following sections I shall first consider the impact of fundamental rights on private law and their possible role in conceptualising unconscionability in Europe (section 2). Subsequently, I will turn to the conduct of business rules of financial service providers and discuss their relationship with and a possible impact on private law and the private law concepts of unconscionability (section 3). I will conclude with some observations on the issue of how to converge public and private law approaches to protecting the vulnerable against unconscionable financial transactions (section 4).

2. The private law concepts of unconscionability and fundamental rights

2.1 *Protecting the vulnerable in financial transactions by means of fundamental rights: the* Bürgschaft *case*

In most European legal systems, fundamental rights as an aspect of public law were for a long time considered to be defences for individuals

[7] The current definition of unconscionable financial transactions is particularly in this respect broader than the common law concepts of unconscionability in that it also covers situations which in common law countries fall under the doctrines of misrepresentation, undue influence or duress.

against excessive use of state power. In this function, they did not have any prominent impact on the relationships between private parties in private law. Recently, however, fundamental rights arguments have increasingly been used to protect weaker parties in contractual disputes.

The most striking example available so far of how the weaker party in financial transactions can be protected by means of fundamental rights is probably the judgment of the German Federal Constitutional Court (Bundesverfassungsgericht) in the *Bürgschaft* case.[8] In that case, a bank had offered a businessman a loan of DM100,000 (now approximately 50,000 Euros) subject to the condition that the businessman's daughter would sign the contract as a surety. Prior to the signing, a bank employee asked the daughter: 'Would you just sign this here, please? This won't make you enter into any important obligation; I need this for my files.' The daughter, who was 21, largely uneducated, with no property of her own and worked as an unskilled employee at a fish factory for a salary of DM1150 (575 Euros) per month, agreed to stand surety for the whole of her father's debt. Shortly afterwards, the father's business experienced financial difficulties and the bank claimed DM100,000 with interest, amounting to a total of DM160,000 (80,000 Euros), from the daughter under the original contract.

In the private law courts the daughter's defence met with alternating success. While the court of first instance (*Landgericht*), held that the contract was valid and ordered her to pay, the higher court, the Court of Appeal (*Oberlandesgericht*), maintained that the bank had violated its duty to inform the daughter (a case of *culpa in contrahendo*) and therefore the daughter was not bound by the suretyship signed by her. This decision was however overturned by the Federal Supreme Court in private law matters (*Bundesgerichtshof*). The latter examined whether the issue at stake was the collapse of the underlying basis for the suretyship (the doctrine of *Wegfall der Geschäftsgrundlage*) or acase of *culpa in contrahendo* as a consequence of the bank's breach of duty to inform. Neither of these grounds for releasing the daughter from her obligations under the contract was found to exist by the Supreme Court in the case at hand. The main argument of the Supreme Court was that any person of full age, even without business experience, knows that signing a suretyship entails a risk, and hence, as the daughter was over 18, the bank did not owe her a duty to inform.

However, this was not the end of the matter. The daughter appealed to the Constitutional Court and claimed that the Supreme Court, through its

[8] BVerfG 19 October 1993, *BVerfGE* 89, 214 (*Bürgschaft*).

decision, had, in particular, violated her constitutional right to private autonomy (Article 2(1) of the German Constitution (*Grundgesetz* (*GG*)) in conjunction with the principle of the social state (Article 20(1) and Article 28(1) *GG*). Her constitutional claim was successful. According to the Constitutional Court, in cases where a structural imbalance in the bargaining power has led to a contract which is exceptionally onerous for the weaker party, private law courts are obliged to intervene on the basis of the general clauses (§§ 138(1) and 242 of the Civil Code (*Bürgerliches Gesetzbuch* (*BGB*)) concerning, respectively, good morals and good faith). This obligation is based on the duty to protect the constitutional right to private autonomy in conjunction with the principle of the social state.

Thus, through the interpretation of constitutional rights, the German Constitutional Court, which is formally not the highest court in private law matters in Germany, was able to enter into the discussion on the issue of contractual justice in modern contract law. Constitutional rights were used by the Constitutional Court in order to resist the 'ice-cold wind of the late nineteenth-century private autonomy'[9] and to protect the weaker party. The significance of such a dictum by the Constitutional Court for German surety law cannot be underestimated, since it constituted the final word in the whole debate on the problem of contractual justice in the context of suretyships, which had to be followed by the ordinary courts of all instances, including the Federal Supreme Court in private law matters. Accordingly, as a result of the decision of the Constitutional Court in the case at hand, the 9th Senate of the Supreme Court had to change its approach to contractual justice in cases involving suretyship contracts and to start intervening in such contracts when they were concluded by family members of the main debtor. This was the only way to comply with the Constitutional Court's ruling and thus to act in conformity with the German Constitution.

2.2 *The complexity of conceptualising unconscionability by means of fundamental rights*

A striking feature of the approach of the German Constitutional Court in the *Bürgschaft* case[10] is the leading role of constitutional rights to protect

[9] H. Honsell, 'Anmerkung zum Urteil des BGH vom 19.11.1989 – IX ZR 124/88 (OLG Braunschweig)', *Juristenzeitung*, 44 (1989), 492, 495 (my translation).

[10] The decision of the German Constitutional Court in the *Bürgschaft* case is not the only case in which fundamental rights were used to set aside the private law solutions. See also

the weaker parties in the litigation of disputes arising under contract law. By holding the private law courts to be *obliged* to protect the constitutional rights of weaker parties, and for this purpose to intervene in contractual relationships by means of the general clauses in the German Civil Code, the Constitutional Court has significantly limited the role played by contract law, in particular by these general clauses, in determining whether a particular contract is unconscionable. Although fundamental rights were not formally *directly* applied to the relationship between private parties, and it was general contract law that remained applicable, in practice the Federal Constitutional Court determined the outcome of the case on the constitutional law level.[11]

Whether fundamental rights are, however, suitable for the direct regulation of the relationships between private parties in different phases of the life of a contract and, in particular, whether they are suitable for protecting the weaker party in financial transactions appears to be rather doubtful particularly in light of the following two difficulties.[12]

Firstly, the interests of the weaker party in a particular case can be protected not only by one fundamental right, but by several. In this case, competition between fundamental rights (*Grundrechtskonkurrenz*) arises, and the difficulty faced by the courts is to determine which of several fundamental rights that are potentially relevant in the circumstances of a particular case is ultimately applicable. Thus, for example, whereas the Federal Constitutional Court in the *Bürgschaft* case provided

BVerfG 7 February 1990, BVerfGE 81, 242 (*Handelsvertreter*); BVerfG 9 February 1994, BVerfGE 90, 27 (*Parabolantenne*); BVerfG 26 July 2005, (2005) 58 *Neue Juristische Wochenschrift* 2376. I have argued that this case law shows the tendency towards subordinating private law, in particular contract law, to fundamental rights law. On this in more detail, see, in particular, O. O. Cherednychenko, 'Subordinating Contract Law to Fundamental Rights: Towards a Major Breakthrough or towards Walking in Circles?', in S. Grundmann (ed.), *Constitutional Values and European Contract Law* (Alphen aan den Rijn: Kluwer, 2008) 35.

11 In this respect, the German Constitutional Court has, in my view, adopted the direct horizontal effect of constitutional rights in private law. On this in more detail, see Cherednychenko, *Fundamental Rights, Contract Law and the Protection of the Weaker Party*, s. 5.6. See also section 2.4 below.

12 In this chapter I will focus on practical aspects of the application of fundamental rights to private law relationships. Apart from more practical objections against the far-reaching effect of fundamental rights in private law disputes, an important theoretical objection against such an approach is the distinction between public and private law, which is currently maintained in the law in force in the continental legal systems, and generally the need to distinguish between public and private spheres. On this, see, Cherednychenko, *Fundamental Rights, Contract Law and the Protection of the Weaker Party*, in particular, ch. 1.

relief for the surety on the basis of her constitutional right to private autonomy, which follows from the constitutional right to the free development of one's personality, in conjunction with the principle of the social state, it would have been equally possible to argue that the case could have been decided on the basis of the surety's right to family life as guaranteed by Article 6(1) of the Federal Constitution. In such a case, the argument could have been put forward that a potentially ruinous suretyship entered into by a family member was problematic, from a constitutional point of view, not because such a contract was concluded as a result of the inequality of bargaining power between the parties, but because family solidarity had been exploited for economic purposes.[13]

If one follows the same line of reasoning a bit further, it could be concluded that the issue of whether or not the bank has informed the surety about the risks involved in a surety contract is no longer relevant because ruinous suretyships by family members must be prohibited *per se* because they severely interfere with the surety's constitutional right to family life.

It is submitted that the rules developed in German constitutional law for the purpose of resolving the problem of competition between two or more constitutional rights do not provide a satisfactory solution for such cases where there is competition between the constitutional right to private autonomy, taken in conjunction with the principle of the social state, and the constitutional right to family life.[14]

It follows that an examination of the validity of such contracts can be approached from two entirely different perspectives, both of which are equally possible under the Federal Constitution. On the one hand, it can be argued that a potentially ruinous surety contract, which may entail extremely onerous financial consequences for the family member of the principal debtor, is in principle illegal; even if the bank has informed the

[13] This argument was defended in German literature by Teubner in G. Teubner, 'Ein Fall von struktureller Korruption? Die Familienbürgschaft in der Kollision unverträglicher Handlungslogiken (BVerfGE 89, 214 ff.)' (2000) 83 *Kritische Vierteljahresschrift für Gesetzgebung und Rechtswissenschaft* 388, 389ff.

[14] In German constitutional theory one can distinguish three rules for resolving the problem of *Grundrechtskonkurrenz*: *Allgemeine Spezialität* (the more specific fundamental right prevails over the more general one), *Einzelfallspezialität* (the right which in a concrete case has a closer connection with the facts of the case will prevail) and, in case none of these two rules offer a solution, *Anwendungskonkurrenz* (in case two or more fundamental rights are equally relevant, the least susceptible to limitations will prevail). See, for example, H.-G. Pieper (ed.), *Grundrechte* (Münster: Alpmann und Schmidt, 1997) 72–3.

surety about the risks involved therein. Such a solution could be reached on the basis either of the constitutional right to family life or the principle of human dignity enshrined in Article 1(1) of the Federal Constitution. In such a case the whole issue of the inequality of bargaining power becomes completely irrelevant.

On the other hand, however, it can also be argued that a potentially ruinous surety contract by a family member of the principal debtor is valid as long as the bank has fulfilled its duties with regard to explaining all the risks involved to the surety so that he or she can then be presumed to have given not only free, but also informed consent to the contract. The surety's constitutional right to private autonomy, taken in conjunction with the constitutional principle of the social state, would then be most relevant.

Which of the two ways of dealing with potentially ruinous suretyships is ultimately chosen, in the absence of clear and workable criteria for dealing with competing fundamental rights in contractual disputes, depends solely on the subjective view of the judges. As a consequence, there is a danger of arbitrary choices between fundamental rights being made by judges guided primarily by their own views on the extent to which family sureties should be protected; the judges' choice can go either for or against the far-reaching protection of sureties against themselves.

Secondly, even when the problem of competition between two or more fundamental rights is resolved, the courts are confronted with another difficult issue. Whereas the main purpose of resorting to fundamental rights in contract law is to protect the interests of weaker parties to contracts, fundamental rights constitute a double-edged sword in the hands of both powerful creditors and weak debtors. This is so because in practice both the interests of the stronger and those of the weaker parties may be protected by them. Moreover, in certain cases one and the same fundamental right can be used to support both of the diametrically opposed claims of the two opposing parties. As a consequence, the courts must resolve the conflict which arises between the two fundamental rights. In the absence of a hierarchy between fundamental rights, essentially the only way of doing this is through balancing the two competing rights against each other. Thus, for example, in the *Bürgschaft* case, the conflict arose between the surety's constitutional right to private autonomy, taken in conjunction with the principle of the social state versus the bank's constitutional right to private autonomy. The balance had to be struck on the constitutional law level between the protection of the private autonomy of the weaker party and interference with the private autonomy of the stronger party.

That this task is not an easy one can already be seen from the broad drafting of the articles of the Federal Constitution delineating the constitutional rights involved and from the very fact that the same right protects the interests of both parties. Complexities relating to striking a balance between the conflicting interests of the two parties on the constitutional level, however, become most apparent in the outcome of the balancing reached by the Federal Constitutional Court which boils down to a directive for the private law courts. According to this directive, in cases where a 'structural inequality of bargaining power' has led to a contract which is 'exceptionally onerous' for the weaker party, the private law courts are obliged to intervene in contractual relationships between the parties in order to protect the weaker party.

While the directive clearly implies that the weaker parties must be protected by the private law courts, it does not make it clear how far this protection should extend in order to conform with the Federal Constitution. In particular, should potentially ruinous surety contracts by family members be held contrary to good morals as such or should they be considered valid provided that the surety has been informed about all the risks involved?

As in the case of competition between fundamental rights, here once again constitutional law does not provide an answer as to which of the two alternatives should be followed and why. In essence, therefore, resorting to fundamental rights in surety cases leads to the interpretation of well-established general clauses of a private law character on the basis of the newly created general clauses of a public law character, and the latter are even more difficult to grasp than the former.

The major problem, however, is that it is not at all obvious which outcomes should follow from the constitutional right to private autonomy, standing alone or in conjunction with the principal of the social state. What these rights require is respect for the private autonomy of both parties, but they do not give any clue as to how this should be done and leave this issue for private law to resolve. For this reason, one can argue that it would have been equally consistent with the Federal Constitutional Court's approach with regard to the effect of fundamental rights in private law to uphold the decision of the Federal Supreme Court in private law matters in the *Bürgschaft* case, reasoning that the surety's constitutional right to private autonomy had in fact been respected; every person who has reached the age of majority could not be unaware of the risks involved in acting as a surety.

This examination of the difficulties involved in deciding disputes between private parties on the basis of fundamental rights suggests that it is highly fallacious to believe that fundamental rights can help private lawyers to find a solution to the age-old problem of contract law – under what circumstances is a contract between the two private parties unconscionable? In essence, therefore, fundamental rights may be used both to promote the protection of the weaker party in contract law and to defend individual freedom and the binding force of contracts. In giving expression to both of these values, however, fundamental rights do not provide a concrete answer to the question of where individual freedom must stop and protection must begin. In particular, they do not help us out of our dilemma; where there is a risky contract, which may potentially result in extremely onerous financial consequences for one of the parties, should the contract be prohibited because it is contrary to good morals per se or, alternatively, should it be allowed subject to the condition that the stronger contractual party has taken the necessary steps to obtain the informed consent of the weaker party? Furthermore, if it is informed consent which is at stake, fundamental rights do not inform us about the circumstances under which the courts may hold that the stronger party has fulfilled his duty to explain the risks of the transaction to the weaker party.

Determining whether a particular transaction is unconscionable through the recourse to fundamental rights accordingly allows the real social and economic issues involved in restricting or extending the protection of the weaker party to be concealed under the guise of the interpretation of fundamental rights. In addition, such an approach involves the risk that, as fundamental rights do not contain the answers to the issues raised, they could become a political football between the proponents of paternalism and those of freedom.

2.3 Is there a need to shift the emphasis from private law to fundamental rights?

Against this background the question arises of whether, in order to protect the weaker party against unconscionable financial transactions, there is a real need to resort to fundamental rights. Will this lead to the enrichment of the legal discourse for the benefit of the vulnerable in financial transactions? It is notable in this context that neither in Dutch nor in English law have fundamental rights played any significant role in the family surety cases which were decided by the highest courts at approximately the same time as the German *Bürgschaft* case, although the facts of these cases were broadly similar.[15] Instead, relief for the family sureties was provided on the basis of well-established contract law concepts, such as mistake (*dwaling*) in Dutch law[16] and constructive notice in conjunction with undue influence in English law.

In fact, resorting to fundamental rights in these legal systems turned out to be unnecessary; a result comparable to that reached by the German Federal Constitutional Court on the basis of fundamental rights in the *Bürgschaft* case was achieved in both jurisdictions within private law. Although in both Dutch and English law the protection granted to sureties at present is limited to imposing on the creditor the duty to explain the risks of the transaction in detail to the surety and thus is of a solely procedural nature,[17] the contract law of both legal systems also contains concepts which could potentially be used in order to introduce (a certain degree of) substantive protection to sureties against themselves in those cases where there is a gross discrepancy between the amount of potential liability under the suretyship and the financial means of the prospective surety at the time of the contract's conclusion.

Whereas in Dutch law this could be done on the basis of mistake,[18] in English law the concept of constructive notice in conjunction with undue influence could potentially serve as a basis for moving from procedural protection of the weaker party in the direction of substantive protection. Moreover, the development by German private law courts of extensive substantive protection of family members against disproportionate obligations under surety contracts on the basis of good morals in the years

[15] See HR 1 June 1990, *NJ* 759 (*Van Lanschot Bankiers* v. *Bink*) and *Barclays Bank Plc* v. *O'Brien* [1994] 1 AC 180, for Dutch and English law, respectively. On these cases in more detail, see Cherednychenko, *Fundamental Rights, Contract Law and the Protection of the Weaker Party*, ss. 6.3 and 6.4. In contrast to Germany where there is a constitutional court, these legal systems do not have such a court. It is submitted, however, that the extent of the constitutionalisation of contract law in a particular legal system does not necessarily depend on the existence of a constitutional court. The reason for that is that in those legal systems where there is such a court, the latter may be reluctant to interfere with contract law, whereas in those legal systems where a constitutional court is absent, the far-reaching effect of fundamental rights in contact law may be granted by the private law courts.

[16] Section 6:228 of the Dutch Civil Code.

[17] For Dutch law, see HR 1 June 1990, *NJ* 759 (*Van Lanschot Bankiers* v. *Bink*). For English law, see *Royal Bank of Scotland* v. *Etridge (No. 2)* [2001] 4 All ER 449.

[18] Such an approach was advocated in the Dutch literature by Tjittes. See R. P. J. L. Tjittes, 'Ongeschreven zorgplichten van de schuldeiser jegens de aspirant-borg bij het aangaan van de overeenkomst van borgtocht' (2001) 132 *Weekblad voor pivaatrecht, notariaat en registratie* 347, 355ff.

following the Federal Constitutional Court's decision in the *Bürgschaft* case shows the enormous flexibility inherent in German contract law.[19] It also provides evidence that in this legal system, a change in the way sureties are treated was possible without any prompting by the Federal Constitutional Court.

The ability of modern contract law to address the problems faced by weaker parties is not surprising because the idea of protecting weaker parties has never been entirely repugnant to it. Contract law has always been concerned with imbalances of power which may arise, for example, between minors or poor and uneducated people in general, on the one hand, and other, potentially much more powerful market actors, on the other. It has tried to redress this imbalance through the use of general legal concepts such as good faith, good morals or public policy, defects of consent and even more specific legal rules to this effect.

What is at issue in modern contract law is therefore the extent of protection of weaker parties which is necessary in order to address the present challenges arising from changing social and economic conditions of everyday life. Examples of family surety litigation, taken from the private law case law of Germany, the Netherlands and England, show that contract law provides possibilities for addressing the problems faced by vulnerable sureties. Contract law has conducted debate on the extent of the protection that it should provide for weaker parties and it has developed this protection incrementally.

It follows that the *same* debate on the *extent* of protection of weaker parties against potentially highly risky financial transactions can be conducted both on the level of fundamental rights and on the level of contract law. On the level of fundamental rights, the question to be answered in the debate on the character of the protection of the weaker party, substantive or procedural, is which fundamental right – the right to human dignity, the right to family life or the right to private autonomy of the weaker party – ultimately prevails. In contrast, on the level of contract law the question to be answered in such a debate is whether, on

[19] See, for example, Bundesgerichtshof (BGH) (2001) 22 *ZIP Zeitschrift für Wirtschaftsrecht* 189; BGH (2001) 41 *Juristische Schulung* 606; BGH (2002) 55 *Neue Juristische Wochenschrift* 2228; BGH (2002) 55 *Neue Juristische Wochenschrift* 2230; BGH (2002) 55 *Neue Juristische Wochenschrift* 2634. Under this case law, for the presumption of immorality to arise it is sufficient that a close family member of the principal debtor has entered into a potentially ruinous obligation exceeding his financial potential, and it is immaterial whether or not his ability to make a free and responsible decision was impaired.

one hand, a particular risky transaction is, for example, contrary to good morals and therefore must be prohibited or prevented or whether, on the other hand, the conclusion of such a transaction should be allowed provided that the stronger party has taken reasonable steps to explain the risks inherent in the transaction to the weaker party so that the weaker party's consent can be presumed not to have been vitiated as a result of mistake, fraud or undue influence.

Similarly, whereas debate on the extent of procedural protection on the level of fundamental rights can take place along the lines of a balancing between the right to private autonomy on the one hand, and the right to private autonomy in conjunction with the principle of the social state or *Grundrecht auf einigermaßen faire Vertragsbeziehungen*[20] on the other, on the level of contract law such debate is conducted in terms of where the duty to inform ends and the duty to investigate begins.

What conceptualising unconscionability in the context of risky financial transactions on the level of fundamental rights accordingly entails is moving the debate on the same issue, i.e. where freedom ends and protection (against oneself) begins, to a higher level of abstraction. This adds further complication rather than offering a clear-cut solution. In other words, the problem of setting appropriate limits on the freedom of contract of stronger parties in order to secure the freedom of contract of weaker parties, as well as on the freedom of contract of weaker parties in order to protect the latter against themselves, is transformed into an issue of fundamental rights. Fundamental rights however do not add anything substantially new to possible ways of resolving this issue, and also do not provide any workable criteria for providing new answers. The case for moving the debate on the meaning of unconscionability in financial transactions to the level of fundamental rights is therefore very doubtful.

2.4 The role of fundamental rights in conceptualising unconscionability: a plea for the weak indirect horizontal effect

Do the arguments I have presented imply that fundamental rights have no role to play in protecting the vulnerable against unconscionable

[20] The recognition of this fundamental right has been advocated by Lurger for the purpose of preventing severe impairment of the interests of one of the parties. See B. Lurger, *Grundfragen des Vertragsrecht in der Europäischen Union* (Wien, New York: Springer, 2002) 242.

financial transactions? This is certainly not the case. Due to the growing relevance of fundamental rights to contract law, we face at present the important question of to *what extent* contract law will be affected by fundamental rights rather than *whether* these rights will have an impact on private law. This change in the perception of the relationship between fundamental rights and contract law should be welcomed. Both fundamental rights and contract law are extremely important for the legal order in general, and for each other in particular: fundamental rights as an important source of core values for the whole legal order; contract law as the source of concepts providing much sharper criteria developed by trial and error over a long period of time for determining whether a particular contract is unconscionable. The question which needs to be answered in the present context is therefore how to converge the two without undermining the importance of each in protecting the vulnerable in financial transactions.

The complexities involved in determining the meaning of unconscionability through fundamental rights speak against the adoption of such an analysis. What is necessary, in my view, is that fundamental rights and contract law *complement* each other in conceptualising unconscionability. This means that the values underlying these rights must be respected within contract law, but, at the same time, contract law must preserve its key role in accommodating these values within its own fabric. In the context of unconscionability in risky financial transactions, such a relationship between fundamental rights and private law implies that the value of private autonomy must be respected within contract law. National and international human rights instruments must be a guardian of the respect for private autonomy in private law. What the respect for private autonomy of the weaker party means in the particular circumstances of a dispute between private parties, however, should be left to contract law to determine.

To avoid the transformation of the private law issue on the meaning of unconscionability into a constitutional law issue and to ensure the complementarity between public and private law, it is necessary to limit the influence of fundamental rights on the relationships between private parties under contract law to their *weak indirect horizontal effect*.[21] In my understanding, such an effect means that the starting

[21] In the light of the analysis of the German, Dutch and English literature and case law, it is, in my view, useful to distinguish between the following three forms of the horizontal effect of fundamental rights in contract law: 'direct horizontal effect', 'strong indirect

point for the private law courts is to look for the solution in a particular case at the level of contract law and, in doing so, to consider any possible impact of fundamental rights. The private law court is considered to fulfil its duty if it has taken into account the impact of fundamental rights when applying contract law, and in reaching its decision the court enjoys a wide discretion which is guaranteed to it by the supervisory bodies, such as constitutional and international human rights courts.[22] In the case of weak indirect horizontal effect, contract law is therefore considered to be in conformity with fundamental rights once the values underlying fundamental rights are respected within it, and it is contract law which determines how this respect is to be ensured. There is accordingly no need for the private law courts to become involved in the controversial balancing of the competing interests of stronger and weaker parties on the level of fundamental rights.

In fact, if this approach had been used in the *Bürgschaft* case, the German Federal Constitutional Court would have upheld the decision of the German Federal Supreme Court in private law matters, since the latter noted that any person who has reached the age of majority knows that standing surety entails risks and so did take the fundamental right to private autonomy on the parts of both the bank and the surety into account. Essentially, by taking this approach the Federal Supreme Court can be regarded as having granted weak indirect horizontal effect to fundamental rights. It resolved the *Bürgschaft* case by taking into account that the right to be able to freely decide whether or not to enter into a certain transaction, as well as the possibility of enforcing said transaction, once it has been freely entered into by both parties, constitute expressions of the important value of private autonomy; a value which enjoys constitutional protection.

horizontal effect' and 'weak indirect horizontal effect'. On this differentiation, see Cherednychenko, 'Subordinating Contract Law to Fundamental Rights', 54ff and Cherednychenko, *Fundamental Rights, Contract Law and the Protection of the Weaker Party*, chs. 3 and 4, ss. 9.2.2 and 9.4, with further references.

22 Although until recently the tendency towards the constitutionalisation of private law has primarily manifested itself within domestic legal systems, private law, in particular contract law, may potentially also be considerably affected by fundamental rights as a result of the case law of the European Court of Human Rights and the European Court of Justice. On this, see O. O. Cherednychenko, 'Towards the Control of Private Acts by the European Court of Human Rights?' (2006) 13 *Maastricht Journal of European and Comparative Law* 195 and O. O. Cherednychenko, 'EU Fundamental Rights, EC Freedoms and Private Law' (2006) 14 *European Review of Private Law* 23, with further references.

The fact that the Federal Supreme Court nevertheless adopted a formal conception of private autonomy does not necessarily mean that it violated the surety's constitutional right to private autonomy in conjunction with the principle of the social state, as this right itself does not prescribe any particular outcome for the case and it should be balanced with the bank's constitutional right to private autonomy. The issue of the violation of a fundamental right, and thus a ground for interference by the German Federal Constitutional Court, would therefore have arisen only if private law courts had not considered the issue of free will at all. As fundamental rights do not contain the answer to this question, the Constitutional Court should not have chosen the path of *Einzelfallgerechtigkeit* (individual justice) and should have refrained from overturning the judgment of the Supreme Court. Although this outcome would certainly have been quite disappointing from the point of view of the need to protect family sureties, it must not be forgotten that, because of their highly abstract nature, fundamental rights in themselves do not necessarily entail an outcome which would favour the weaker party. The judgment of the Constitutional Court in *Bürgschaft* therefore provides a cautionary tale on the risks of reaching fair results at the expense of a well-considered and circumspect application of legal rules.[23]

3. Private law concepts of unconscionability and conduct of business rules

3.1 Protecting the vulnerable in financial transactions by means of conduct of business rules

Another major manifestation of the growing impact of public law in protecting weaker parties in financial transactions is the adoption of extensive conduct of business rules for financial service providers, in particular in

[23] These conclusions are not only true for the relationship between fundamental rights and contract law in the national legal systems of the EU Member States, but also for the relationship between fundamental rights and contract law at EU level. On this, see O. O. Cherednychenko, 'The Harmonisation of Contract Law in Europe by means of the Horizontal Effect of Fundamental Rights?' (2007) 1 *Erasmus Law Review* 37, www.erasmuslawreview.nl/past_issues/Volume01/harmonisation_of_contract_law. For a different view on the issue in question, see, for example, A. Colombi Ciacchi, 'The Constitutionalization of European Contract Law' (2006) 2 *European Review of Contract Law* 167; C. Mak, 'Harmonising Effects of Fundamental Rights in European Contract Law' (2007) 1 *Erasmus Law Review* 59, www.erasmuslawreview.nl/past_issues/Volume01/harmonisation_of_contract_law.

the field of investment services, as part of the specific legislation concerned with the supervision and regulation of the financial services industry. This development has been given a major impulse at the time of drafting the first Investment Services Directive (ISD).[24] Concerns of certain Member States that the Directive did not contain sufficient investor protection measures gave rise to the introduction of Article 11. This provision imposed a duty on the Member States to draw up rules of conduct which investment firms (and banks offering investment services) would be obliged to observe at all times in their relationship with (potential) clients. Whereas the ISD itself did not establish detailed conduct of business rules, it set out a list of principles aimed at ensuring the stability of the financial system and the protection of investors.[25]

Among the principles embodied in Article 11 the following three are of particular relevance in the present context. First, any provider of investment services must act honestly and fairly in the best interests of its clients (the loyalty principle). Second, the provider must adequately disclose relevant material information in its dealings with its clients (the informed consent principle). Third, it must seek from its clients information regarding their financial situation, investment experience and objectives as regards the services requested (the 'know your customer' principle).

In fact, by laying down these principles of conduct for investment service providers, the ISD included within its ambit the old contract law rules on the duties of care in relationships between an investment firm and its client and 'coined' these rules as standards whose compliance was to be checked by the supervisory authorities.[26] Moreover, it gave impulse to the same process in the national legal systems. The implementation of the ISD has led to the inclusion of an extensive catalogue of detailed conduct of business rules in the supervision laws. This has been done not only with a view to ensuring investor protection, but primarily to ensure the adequate functioning of the financial system.[27] The former has to a certain extent been a means to achieve the latter.

[24] Council Directive 93/22/EEC of 10 May 1993 on investment services in the securities field, OJEC L 141/27 (ISD I).

[25] See the Preamble to the ISD, para. 3.

[26] Compare Grundmann, 'EC Financial Services: Developments 2002–2005', 490.

[27] For German law, for example, see, inter alia, E. Schwark, *Kapitalmarktrechts-Kommentar* (München: Beck, 2004) 1282; for Dutch law, see C. M. Grundmann-van de Krol, *Koersen door het effectenrecht. Beschouwingen omtrent Nederlands effectenrecht* (The Hague: Boom Juridische Uitgevers, 2004) 497; for English law, see Financial Services and Markets Act (FSMA) 2000, ss. 2 (2)(a) and 3; ss. 2 (2)(b) and 4.

The conduct of business rules have largely originated within national private laws, in particular contract laws of the Member States, and, primarily as a result of the need to strengthen investors' confidence in the financial market, have been further elaborated and strengthened by public law enforcement mechanisms in the supervision legislation.[28] In German law, for example, the duty of investment service providers to disclose all relevant information in dealings with their (potential) clients, which was earlier derived from good faith (§ 242 of the Civil Code), has been accommodated in Section 31(2) no. 2 of the Securities Trading Act 1994 (*Wertpapierhandelsgesetz* (*WpHG*)). Similarly, the provider's duty to know one's customer included in Section 31(2) no. 1 of the WpHG corresponded with the principle developed in the case law according to which the content and scope of the duties to inform and to advise is determined by the investor's knowledge in the investment field and the risks involved therein as well as by the investor's investment objectives.[29]

While in German law the protection of non-professional investors by conduct of business rules was limited to procedural protection, other legal systems went further and introduced elements of substantive protection to prevent investors from taking excessively high risks relative to their financial resources. In Dutch law, for example, it was considered necessary to include in conduct of business rules the duty of investment service providers to check whether customers who trade in financial instruments which may give rise to obligations possess a sufficient balance on their bank accounts in order to meet such obligations (Article 28(3) of Further Regulations on Market Supervision of the Securities Trade (*Nadere Regeling gedragstoezicht effectenverkeer* (*NRge*) 2002)). This rule, known as the duty to supervise the compliance of orders with margin requirements, was earlier introduced by the private law courts in a series of cases which involved huge losses resulting from trading in derivatives.[30]

[28] On this in more detail, see Cherednychenko, *Fundamental Rights, Contract Law and the Protection of the Weaker Party*, chs. 7 and 8.

[29] BGH 6 July 1993, *BGHZ* 123, 126 (*Bond*), 128.

[30] See, for example, HR 13 November 1987, *NJ* 1988, 278 (*Rabobank* v. *Haanstra*); HR 24 January 1997, *NJ* 1997, 260 (*Dinkgreve* v. *Internationale Nederlanden Bank*); HR 23 May 1997, *NJ* 1998, 192 (*Rabobank* v. *Everaars*); HR 26 June 1998, *NJ* 1998, 660 (*Van de Klundert* v. *Rabobank*); HR 11 July 2003, *NJ* 2005, 103 (*Kouwenberg* v. *Rabobank*).

In one of these cases, *Kouwenberg* v. *Rabobank*,[31] in which the non-professional investor was left with an unsecured debt of approximately Dfl. 300,000 (145,000 Euros), the Dutch Supreme Court ruled that the bank, in principle, does not comply with its specific duty of care towards its clients if it yields to their explicit wishes to execute an order concerning a particular transaction despite a lack of sufficient securities. According to the Supreme Court, the bank's duty of care towards the client aims to protect the client against the danger of his own frivolity and lack of knowledge. If the bank fails to refuse to execute a transaction that does not comply with margin requirements, the warning of the risks involved in unsecured transactions in options is not always sufficient to exclude the bank's liability for the damage incurred by the client as a consequence of the margin being overdrawn. This is so, in the view of the Supreme Court, even if the client is stubborn and difficult to convince.

The duty to check the compliance of the customer's transactions with margin requirements was also included in conduct of business rules in the UK where it was laid down in the Handbook of Rules and Guidance issued by the Financial Services Authority (COB 7.10).

The tendency towards accommodating contract law duties of care towards clients within supervision rules has been further strengthened as a result of the adoption of the Markets in Financial Instruments Directive (MiFID) which has been described by some as Europe's 'new constitution' for investment services and secondary capital markets.[32] Whereas the ISD introduced only an 'embryonic degree of harmonisation'[33] of conduct of business rules in Europe, the MiFID aims to bring about their maximum harmonisation with a view to ensuring a high level of consumer protection, as well as integrity and the overall efficiency of the financial system.[34] The MiFID considerably clarifies three principles

[31] HR 11 July 2003, *NJ* 2005, 103. On this case in more detail, see Cherednychenko, *Fundamental Rights, Contract Law and the Protection of the Weaker Party*, s. 7.4.3, with further references.

[32] See, for example, K.J. Hopt, 'Grundsatz- und Praxisprobleme nach dem Wertpapierhandelsgesetz – insbesondere Insidergeschäfte und Ad-hoc-Publizität' (1995) 159 *Zeitschrift für gesamte Handelsrecht und Witrschaftsrecht*, 135; H-D. Assmann and U.H. Schneider, *Wertpapierhandelsgesetz* (Cologne: Otto Schmidt, 2006), Introduction n. 1.

[33] M. Tison, 'Conduct of Business Rules and their Implementation in the EU Member States', in G. Ferrarini *et al.* (eds.), *Capital Markets in the Age of the Euro: Cross-Border Transactions, Listed Companies and Regulation* (The Hague: Kluwer, 2002) 65, 69.

[34] See, inter alia, the Preamble to the MiFID, para. 44 and Article 4 of the Commission Directive 2006/73/EC implementing the MiFID which allows Member States to retain or impose requirements additional to those in this Directive only in exceptional cases.

referred to in Article 11 of the ISD. The meaning of these principles is further fleshed out by the Commission Directive implementing the ISD,[35] in particular as far as the rules of business conduct are concerned.[36]

A characteristic feature of the EC approach to investor protection is its procedural character. The MiFID aims to protect non-professional investors solely by procedural means such as extensive duties to inform, advise or warn the customer in combination with the duties to know one's customer and to assess the suitability of a particular investment service or financial instrument for the customer.[37] Special emphasis in this context is placed on ensuring that the investor understands the nature and risks of investment service and of the specific type of financial instrument to which the service relates. The MiFID does not impose on the providers of investment services duties aimed to prevent the conclusion of particularly risky investment transactions against the will of the client.

3.2 *The shift in focus from private law standards to conduct of business rules*

Conduct of business rules aim, in the first place to ensure the adequate functioning of the securities market and therefore lie within the competence of the supervisory authorities. As standards to be applied by investment service providers and to be checked by supervisors these rules are therefore of a public law nature. At the same time, there is a general agreement that as conduct of business rules also aim to protect investors, they can also have effect in private law.[38] Whereas general private law concepts had influenced the content of conduct of business rules, at present these rules have been exercising a profound impact on the content of the private law concepts.

[35] Commission Directive 2006/73/EC implementing Directive 2004/39/EC of the European Parliament and of the Council as regards organisational and operating conditions for investment firms and defined terms for the purposes of that Directive, OJEC L 241/26.

[36] The MiFID had to be transposed into national law before 1 November 2007. On the implementation of the MiFID in the Member States, see Grundmann and Hollering, 'EC Financial Services and Contract Law – Developments 2005–2007', p. 61, with further references.

[37] See Article 19 of the MiFID.

[38] On the nature of the conduct of business rules in German, Dutch and English law, see Cherednychenko, *Fundamental Rights, Contract Law and the Protection of the Weaker Party*, ss. 7.3.2, 7.4.2, 7.5.2.

In many legal systems, they have become the *main* source of specific duties of care on the part of investment service providers in private law, largely determining the *scope* of private law duties of care. In German law, for example, the conduct of business rules contained in the *WpHG* specify the meaning of more general private law concepts, such as precontractual liability (*culpa in contrahendo*) and a positive breach of contract (*positive Vertragsverletzung*) combined with the notion of a tacitly concluded (*stillschweigend abgeschlossen*) contract of advice (*Beratungsvertrag*).[39] In Dutch law, private law concepts, such as the general duty of care on the part of service providers (*zorgplicht van een goed opdrachtnemer*) laid down in Article 7:401 of the Civil Code, serve as an umbrella under which conduct of business rules enter into contract law.[40] Also in English law conduct of business rules have become highly influential in shaping common law standards of care, in particular the scope of the duty of care in the tort of negligence.[41] The violation of conduct of business rules does not *eo ipso* lead to liability in private law. Private law concepts still supply the basis for the service provider's liability for a breach of its duties of care towards the customer and hence determine whether there is a violation of a duty of care in private law and if so, what the consequences of such a violation are.

Although the conduct of business rules generally depend on private law as far as their enforcement in private law is concerned, it would not be an exaggeration to say that the adoption of conduct of business rules has led to the shift in focus from private law standards to supervision standards. After the enactment of conduct of business rules, the courts and commentators in the Members States largely focused on the conduct

[39] See, for example, BGH 11 November 2003, *Wertpapier-Mitteilungen* (2004) 24, 26; BGH 8 May 2001 (2001) 22 *ZIP Zeitschrift für Wirtschaftsrecht* 1580, 1581; BGH 5 October 1999, *BGHZ* 142, 345, 346.

[40] See, in particular, the case-law of the Dutch Securities Institute Complaints Board (*Klachtencommissie DSI (KCD)*) and the Appeal Commission of the Dutch Securities Institute (*Commissie van Beroep (KHCB)*), as well as their successor – the Financial Services Disputes Board (*Geschillencommissie financiële dienstverlening*) of the Financial Services Complaints Institute. E.g. KHCB 30 July 2002, JOR 2002/165; KCD 30 July 2003, no. 107; KCD 16 December 2005, 05–282.

[41] See, for example, *Lloyd Cheyham & Co. Ltd* v. *Eversheds* [1985] 2 Lloyd's Rep. P.N. 154; *Bankers Trust International Plc* v. *PT Dharmala Sakti Sejahtera* [1996] CLC 518; *Gorham & Others* v. *British Telecommunications Plc, Trustees of the BT Pension Scheme* v. *Standard Life Assurance Company* [2000] 1 WLR 2129; *Brandeis (Brokers) Ltd* v. *Black and others* [2001] 2 All ER (Comm) 980; *Loosemore* v. *Financial Concepts (a firm)* [2001] Lloyd's Rep P.N. 235; *Seymour* v. *Caroline Ockwell & Co* [2005] 39 PNLR 758.

of business rules. In Germany, for example, after the enactment of the *WpHG* the discussion concerning banks' duties to provide information as to securities transactions almost immediately concentrated on the new requirements contained in Section 31(2) of the *WpHG*, while the private law pre-contractual information duties declined in importance.[42] A similar development has also taken place in the Netherlands, where parties largely invoke conduct of business rules, in many cases, without even referring to the private law concepts providing the basis for liability in private law. The shift in focus from private law standards to conduct of business rules is even more evident in the UK where conduct of business rules not only specify the content of private law standards of care, but can also be *directly* invoked by private parties who have suffered loss as a result of their breach by the investment service provider.[43]

As a result, private law, in particular contract law, now increasingly 'follows' conduct of business rules.[44] Given that Article 19 of the MiFID contains much more detailed conduct of business rules than those contained in Article 11 of the ISD and that the MiFID aims at a much higher degree of uniformity than the former, the implementation of the MiFID will further intensify the shift in focus from private law standards to supervision law standards. This will lead to a 'partial eclipse of contract law' in the area of investor protection.[45]

3.3 The pros and cons of the leading role of conduct of business rules in conceptualising unconscionability

The shift in focus from private law concepts to conduct of business rules has significant implications for the protection of weaker parties from unconscionable financial transactions. The most important consequence

[42] On this in more detail, see Mülbert, 'The Eclipse of Contract Law in the Investment Firm-Client-Relationship', 302.

[43] This has become possible because the FSMA 2000 makes frequent use of the technique of expressly conferring a statutory right of action upon designated persons pursuant to section 150 of the FSMA where loss has been suffered as a result of a breach of duty under the Act or delegated legislation or other rules made under its aegis. The Financial Services Authority (FSA) has decided that a right of action would be available to a private person in respect of any rule within the Conduct of Business Source Book (FSA PS 45, para. 3.47). Invoking the tort of breach of an explicit statutory duty circumvents the need to establish that a duty of care should be recognised at common law.

[44] Compare Grundmann and Hollering, 'EC Financial Services and Contract Law – Developments 2005–2007', 62.

[45] Mülbert, 'The Eclipse of Contract Law in the Investment Firm-Client-Relationship', 320.

of this development is that in certain areas, such as the area of investment services, supervision standards will largely determine the scope of private law duties of care and thus the scope of the protection of non-professional investors against highly risky financial transactions in private law. However, what does this mean in more concrete terms for the protection of the vulnerable in financial transactions in particular, and for the development of law in this area in general?

There are two major advantages to the enactment of conduct of business rules. In the first place, in contrast to broadly formulated and rather vague general private law rules, supervision laws supply a more detailed standard of care which is applicable to a particular activity. In this way, they provide more legal certainty, which is beneficial for both the providers of financial services and non-professional investors. As Gower put it, speaking of the proposed conduct of business rules in the UK: '[T]hey seem to me to be a practical working-out of the gentlemanly ethics, on which the City has traditionally prided itself (even if all its members have not invariably lived up to them) that you should "do as you would be done by" and not do anything that you would not want found out.'[46] In fact, the absence of clear rules in private law which would provide investment institutions with certainty as to their duties towards (potential) clients, which they needed in order to function efficiently, was one of the main reasons behind the choice in favour of regulation and the adoption of conduct of business rules.

The second advantage of including conduct of business rules in supervision laws is their public enforcement. Quite apart from the private law action which an individual investor may pursue, the investor benefits from the protection of collective interests of all investors by the supervisory authorities through the control over the compliance by investment service providers with conduct of business rules.[47]

At the same time, the leading role of conduct of business rules in determining the contents of the legal relationship between the client and the investment firm, combined with the maximum harmonisation of

[46] L. C. B. Gower, Review of Investor Protection – Part II, Cmnd 9125, 1985.

[47] For a recent study of public and private enforcement of securities laws, see H. E. Jackson and M. J. Roe, 'Public and Private Enforcement of Securities Laws: Resource-Based Evidence' (2009), http://papers.ssrn.com/sol3/papers.cfm?abstract_id=1000086, with further references.

such rules in Europe, also has serious defects. A major concern in this respect is that contract law will be prevented from shaping the relationship between investment service providers and their (potential) clients in accordance with its own principles and values and that it will be turned into a tool to achieve public goals such as the smooth functioning of the financial system and market integration. This result is particularly disturbing considering that the effectiveness of regulation in the area of investment services still needs to be proved.[48] While the EU's regulatory strategy for the retail investment market, as expressed in the conduct of business regime, aims to produce well-informed and active investors who are able to make autonomous investment choices, the exclusive character of regulation as the retail markets strategy also carries significant risks given, inter alia, the untried nature of the regulatory standards and unpredictable changes in market behaviour. Private law and private litigation have an important role to play as the last resort to those seeking protection, should the regulation fail. In fact, 'every private law case may be seen as a failure of regulation'.[49] It is important therefore that private law does not become wholly instrumental to the achievement of public goals and retains the potential to discover problems encountered by the vulnerable in financial transactions and to generate and develop concepts for protecting the vulnerable against unconscionable transactions.[50]

Another deficiency of the regulatory measures affecting financial service contracts, including the regulatory regime under the MiFID, is their particular focus on the duties of financial service providers. The role of the client is normally not dealt with in EC legislation. For many complex financial services, such as investment services, however, a continuous cooperation and mutually coordinated exchange of information between the parties is required for the purpose of achieving the

[48] On this see N. Moloney, 'Effective Policy Design for the Retail Investment Services Market: Challenges and Choices Post FSAP', in G. Ferrarini and E. Wymeersch (eds.), *Investor Protection in Europe: Corporate Law Making, the MiFID and Beyond* (Oxford University Press, 2007) 381.

[49] T. Wilhelmsson, 'The Paradox of the Risk Society and the Fragmentation of Consumer Law', in I. Ramsay *et al.* (eds.), *Risk and Choice in Consumer Society* (Athènes: Ant. N. Sakkpulas; Bruxelles: Bruylant, 2007) 1, 11.

[50] On the role of private law in the investment firm–client relationship after the introduction of the (EC) Conduct of Business Rules, see O. O. Cherednychenko, 'European Securities Regulation, Private Law and the Investment Firm–Client Relationship' (2009) 17 *European Review of Private Law* 925.

objective which the parties have in mind for their contract.[51] This fact has been acknowledged in national private laws where the client's behaviour is also taken into account when considering whether the client's consent to the contract has been vitiated by mistake or misrepresentation or whether the client has negligently contributed to his or her loss. The leading role of the conduct of business rules of European origin in determining the relationship between providers of financial services and their (potential) clients gives rise to the difficult issue concerning the consequences of the violation of conduct of business rules in private law.

Last but not least, regulating the protection of weaker parties in some areas by means of conduct of business rules while leaving such protection in other areas to private law may lead to peculiar differences in the extent to which weaker parties are protected in different financial transactions. Thus, for example, in German law family sureties enjoy substantive protection against excessively onerous obligations, while non-professional investors are denied such protection altogether; in contrast to the treatment of family sureties, where a potentially ruinous obligation exceeding the surety's ability to pay gives rise to the presumption of immorality,[52] no such consequences are attached to the fact that the investor has entered into a highly risky investment transaction which was highly disproportional to his financial resources.[53] In Dutch law, apparently the concern for the effectiveness of the financial system has produced even more odd results. While family sureties enjoy only procedural protection by means of the information duties incumbent on the bank,[54] non-professional investors trading in derivatives enjoy a combination of substantive and procedural protection aimed at protecting such investors against themselves.[55] The question which arises in this respect, however, is whether non-professional investors are more vulnerable in risky financial transactions than family sureties.

[51] On this in more detail, see O. O. Cherednychenko and C. E. C. Jansen, 'Principles of European Law on Financial Service Contracts?' (2008) 16 *European Review of Private Law* 443, in particular, s. 3.

[52] See the case law cited in n. 19 above.

[53] See, for example, BGH 8 May 2001, *BGHZ* 147, 343, 350; BGH 11 November 2003, *Wertpapier-Mitteilungen* (2004) 24, 27.

[54] See HR 1 June 1990, *NJ* 759 (*Van Lanschot Bankiers* v. *Bink*).

[55] See the case law cited in n. 30 above and, in particular, *Kouwenberg* v. *Rabobank* discussed in section 3.1 above.

3.4 *The need for a coherent body of contract law rules for financial service contracts*

Against this background, it may be reasonable to consider the possibilities for converging conduct of business rules as laid down in supervision legislation and contract law. Given that the conduct of business regime has been largely harmonised in Europe, one may consider integrating the regulatory standards for the conduct of business into European private law.

The first step in this direction can be the inclusion of a comprehensive body of rules for financial service contracts into the 'Common Frame of Reference' (CFR). It remains to be seen what purpose the Commission has in mind with the CFR, but it is generally expected that it will provide fundamental principles, definitions and model rules in the field of European private law; these could be of help in the improvement of the existing *acquis communautaire*, serve as a guide for legislators and even form a basis for an optional instrument.[56] Recently, an academic draft CFR (DCFR) has been published.[57] It contains, inter alia, slightly modified versions of the Principles of European Contract Law (PECL)[58] and the Principles of European Law on Service Contracts (PEL SC).[59] Whereas the PECL provide general contract law rules applicable to all contracts, the PEL SC contain specific rules for service contracts. Financial services, however, are explicitly excluded from the scope of application of the PEL SC.

It is submitted that an additional module on Principles of European Law on Financial Service Contracts (PEL FSC) can be embedded in the PEL SC and hence in the DCFR.[60] The PEL FSC may accommodate the conduct of business rules within themselves, further elaborating,

[56] See Communication from the Commission to the European Parliament and the Council, *A More Coherent European Contract Law: An Action Plan* (COM, 2003) 68; Report from the Commission, *Second Progress Report on the Common Frame of Reference*, 25 July 2007 (COM, 2007) 447, p. 11.

[57] Study Group on a European Civil Code and the Research Group on EC Private Law (Acquis Group), *Principles, Definitions and Model Rules of European Private Law: Draft Common Frame of Reference* (DCFR), outline edition (München: Sellier, European Law Publishers, 2009).

[58] O. Lando and H. Beale (eds.), *Principles of European Contract Law* (The Hague: Kluwer, 2000).

[59] M. Barendrecht *et al.*, *Principles of European Law: Service Contracts (PEL SC)* (Munich: Sellier, 2007).

[60] For the analysis of this possibility, see Cherednychenko and Jansen, 'Principles of European Law on Financial Service Contracts?', 443.

correcting or supplementing them, if necessary. In addition, the PEL FSC may also establish the duties of (potential) clients which are generally not dealt with in the supervision legislation. Laying down such duties in the PEL FSC will make it much more transparent in which cases the financial service provider or the client may be (co-)responsible for an unsatisfactory outcome of a financial service process. While drafting mutual duties of financial service providers and their (potential) clients, special attention should be paid to ensuring coherence between these duties and the general contract law rules as laid down in the PECL. In this way, the PEL SC may play an important role in providing a coherent body of private law rules governing service contracts in general, and financial service contracts in particular, taking into account the experience of regulation on the one hand, and that of private law on the other. This would allow the convergence of the two to protect weaker parties in financial transactions.

4. Concluding remarks

The growing impact of public law on the private law relationships between private parties in the context of risky financial transactions puts the role of private law in protecting the vulnerable against unconscionable bargains under pressure. What is at issue today is how the public law and private law approaches to the protection of the weaker party can be converged.

In this chapter I have tried to show that the shift in emphasis from private law to public law may not necessarily be beneficial for the weaker party. Conceptualising unconscionability on the level of fundamental rights may lead us to walk in circles whilst trying to resolve the old problem of contractual justice, moving again and again from one level of abstraction to another. Whilst doing this the substantive arguments remain essentially the same. In contrast, casting the standards of financial service providers' conduct in their dealings with (potential) clients in terms of regulatory requirements did bring something new under the sun for weaker parties. The old contract law rules were not merely copied from private law and pasted into the supervision law; their content was further elaborated. Shifting our focus from private law to regulation, however, also carries significant risks given, inter alia, the untried nature of the regulatory standards and unpredictable changes in market behaviour. Denying private law the possibility to incrementally develop the concepts to protect the vulnerable in financial transactions may adversely affect the vulnerable themselves. Moreover, incorporating the standards of contractual behaviour into the supervision laws puts the coherence between the legal rules governing financial transactions at risk.

It is important therefore that private law retains a considerable degree of autonomy in relation to public law and preserves its leading role in determining the relationships between private parties under private law. Private law should be able to conceptualise unconscionability and to assess liability in financial transactions without being bound to the applicable standards as defined in public law.

This does not mean that in doing so private law should be completely independent from public law. Public and private law should certainly interplay in conceptualising unconscionability in the context of risky financial transactions. The values underlying fundamental rights must be respected within private law, and this can be accomplished through the weak indirect horizontal effect of fundamental rights in disputes between private parties. Being derivatives of private law, the regulatory standards of the conduct of business, in their turn, may return home and be accommodated within a coherent body of European private law governing the provision of service contracts in general, and financial service contracts in particular.

It is only when there is a dialogue between public and private law that major breakthroughs in conceptualising unconscionability may be achieved, and it is these breakthroughs, in providing new and better solutions, which will truly benefit the vulnerable in financial transactions.

14

Conceptualising unconscionability in the post-Soviet era: the Lithuanian case of legal transplants

ANDRIUS SMALIUKAS

Unconscionability, embracing both procedural and substantive unconscionability,[1] is a multi-dimensional legal concept.[2] It evolved at common law, where traditional doctrines such as fraud, duress and mistake did not cover every situation in which a contract might be oppressive. Thus, the concept of unconscionability was developed to achieve justice in cases of unconscionable dealing, inequality in bargaining power and special disadvantage.[3] However, application of this doctrine differs substantially even in the common law jurisdictions.[4] Moreover, in the civil law jurisdictions, while a comprehensive concept of unconscionability may not exist, there are a number of legal doctrines and instruments that

[1] A. A. Leff, *Unconscionability and the Code – The Emperor's New Clause* (1967) 115 *University of Pennsylvania Law Review* 485, 487.

[2] 'Unconscionability is not a mono-dimensional concept under judge-made law. It has at least three different levels of meaning. At the widest level, it enshrines the basic principle underlying much or all of the law of equity. At another level down, it also operates as the unifying rationale for a discrete set of equitable actions, such as duress, estoppels, relief against forfeiture, imposition of constructive trust, and the doctrine of penalties. At a third level, it is most often associated with a distinct ground of equitable relief based on unconscionable dealing, inequality in bargaining power, and special disadvantage.' See B. Horrigan, *Unconscionability Breaks New Ground – Avoiding and Litigating Unfair Client Conduct After the ACCC Test Cases and Financial Services Reforms* (2002) 7 *Deakin Law Review* 73, 76.

[3] See P. B. Marrow, *Contractual Unconscionability: Identifying and Understanding its Potential Elements* (2000) 72 *Journal of the New York State Bar Association* 18.

[4] As leading precedents should be mentioned *Williams* v. *Walker-Thomas Furniture Co.*, 350 F.2d 445 (D.C. Cir. 1965) in US; *Lloyd's Bank* v. *Bundy* [1975] QB 326 in UK; *Harry* v. *Kreutziger* (1978) 9 BCLR 166 in Canada; *Commercial Bank of Australia Ltd* v. *Amadio* (1983) 151 CLR 447. See – Janine Pascoe, *Guarantees, Financial Services Regulation and the role of the ASIC*, 2006, CLTA Conference papers http://0-users.austlii.edu.au.prospero.murdoch.edu.au/clta/docs/pdf/2006-conf-papers/pascoe.pdf.

ensure fairness in contract law and, inter alia, in financial transactions; they all define unconscionability *largo sensu*.

The harmonised regulation of unconscionability in financial transactions would provide both parties with greater legal certainty since the validity of the contract or its terms would not depend on the peculiarities of the applicable national law.[5] The regulation of unconscionability is closely linked to the free movement of capital and consumer protection and, therefore, it is especially important in the EU.[6]

In this chapter, taking Lithuania as an example, I will investigate some issues relating to the harmonisation of the legal rules that deal with unconscionability *largo sensu* in financial transactions and attempt to evaluate the pros and cons of such harmonisation. I will demonstrate that Lithuania has transplanted the major rules on unconscionability from the UNIDROIT Principles of International Commercial Contracts (1994) and the Principles of European Contract Law. I will not consider specific provisions of financial law that may be related to the concept of unconscionability, such as insider dealing or market manipulation. Similarly, the issues of unconscionability as specifically tackled by the laws on consumer protection will not be discussed.

Unconscionability in the context of Lithuanian reform of private law

Due to the post-Soviet heritage and the need to create a system of private law from scratch, Lithuania has a harmonisation-friendly legal culture. For example, despite the fact that Lithuanian private law is mostly based on the Romano-Germanic legal tradition, Lithuania follows the common law doctrine of judicial precedent and has adopted, for example, the general trust. Such an approach has some shortcomings: the transplanted rules are often not fully and easily compatible with the 'old' rules and the

[5] Opponents of legal harmonisation should not discourage the harmonisation process in financial services as this field has nothing to do with the 'national cultural background' argument. See L. A. Mistelis, *Regulatory Aspects: Globalization, Harmonisation, Legal Transplants and Law Reform – Some Fundamental Observations* (2000) 34 *The International Lawyer* 1065; M. van Hoecke, *The Harmonisation of Private Law in Europe: Some Misunderstandings* in M. van Hoecke and F. Ost (eds.), *Harmonisation of European Private Law* (Oxford: Hart, 2000) 2–5.

[6] Whilst Directive 2008/48/EC of the European Parliament and of the Council of 23 April 2008 on credit agreements for consumers and repealing Council Directive 87/102/EEC ((2008) OJ L133/66) promotes an internal market in cross-border consumer credit, other fields of financial law still require harmonisation.

legal system as a whole. Nevertheless, there are cases where legal transplants turn out to be a huge success; and one of these cases is the transplantation into the Lithuanian legal system of the rules that deal with unconscionability in contract law.

The Lithuanian legal system was not familiar with the concept of unconscionability before the reform of its private law, which was started after the restoration of independence in 1990.[7] However, the draftsmen of the new Civil Code of the Republic of Lithuania,[8] which came into force as of 1 July 2001, fully realised the necessity to deal with contractual unfairness. The draftsmen of the Civil Code did not attempt to introduce a comprehensive concept of unconscionability. Instead, the new Civil Code contains a number of separate provisions dealing with unfairness in pre-contractual dealings and substantive unfairness as well as grounds for invalidation of contracts, such as provisions related to dealings in good faith and gross disparity. Most importantly, these legal provisions were not created from scratch or intercepted from other jurisdictions, but were transplanted from two major sources – the UNIDROIT Principles of International Commercial Contracts 1994 (hereinafter referred to as 'UNIDROIT Principles') and the Principles of European Contract Law proposed by the Commission on European Contract Law (hereinafter referred to as 'PECL').[9] The major architect of Lithuanian private law reform, Professor Valentinas Mikelenas, is a strong supporter of the voluntary harmonisation of private law and therefore believed Lithuania would benefit from incorporating the non-binding provisions from the UNIDROIT Principles and PECL into its national law.[10]

[7] For a more detailed introduction to Lithuania's new contract law, see D. Mikeleniene and V. Mikelenas, 'Contracts: Lithuania', in *International Encyclopedia of Laws: Contracts* (The Hague: Kluwer Law International 2004).

[8] The Civil Code of the Republic of Lithuania (with alterations and supplements), Valstybės žinios (2000) No. 74–2262.

[9] For more about borrowing and transplantation, see A. Watson, *Aspects of Reception of Law* (1996) 44 *American Journal of Comparative Law* 335; A. Watson, *Legal Transplants: An Approach to Comparative Law* (Athens and London: University of Georgia Press, 1993); U. Mattei, 'Efficiency in Legal Transplants: An Essay in Comparative Law and Economics' (1995) 14 *International Review of Law and Economics* 3.

[10] 'It was decided to incorporate into the Civil Code as many provisions of the UNIDROIT Principles of International Commercial Contracts as possible, taking into account the social and economic realities in Lithuania. As a result, most of the provisions of the UNIDROIT Principles were incorporated into the draft Civil Code.' See V. Mikelėnas, 'Unification and Harmonisation of Law at the Turn of the Millennium: The Lithuanian Experience' (2000) *No. 2 Uniform Law Review*.

In this chapter I describe the incorporation of the concepts of good faith and gross disparity into the Lithuanian legal system and analyse the rules on standard contract terms. I also discuss other relevant provisions of the Lithuanian Civil Code and evaluate the efficiency of the new Lithuanian rules in protecting the aggrieved party to financial transactions, with particular focus on non-professional parties.

The principle of good faith

Financial contracts must be negotiated, concluded and performed in good faith. Article 1.5 of the Lithuanian Civil Code (CC) contains a general rule that in exercising their rights and duties parties shall act according to the principles of justice, reasonableness and good faith; a provision which was transplanted from Article 1.7 of the UNIDROIT Principles ('Each party must act in accordance with good faith and fair dealing in international trade')[11] and Article 1.201 (ex Article 1.106) of the PECL[12] ('Each party must act in accordance with good faith and fair dealing').

Article 1.5 CC enshrines the principle of good faith within the new framework of Lithuanian private law. It demonstrates the fundamental importance of the good faith principle, stipulating that in exercising their rights and duties all persons shall act according to the principles of justice, reasonableness and good faith. Moreover, when the law does not prevent persons from determining their mutual rights and duties in mutual agreement, they shall act according to the principles of justice, reasonableness and good faith. Further, the courts are also obliged to apply the principle of good faith; Article 1.5 paragraph 3 states that if laws or an agreement between the parties provide for certain issues to be decided by a court according to its discretion, the court shall act in accordance with the principles of justice, reasonableness and good faith. Finally, the court has a general obligation in interpreting and applying laws to be guided by the principles of justice, reasonableness and good faith.

Article 1.5 is further extended by Articles 6.4, 6.38, 6.158 and 6.200. Article 6.4 sets a general rule of the law of obligations, that a creditor and a debtor must act in good faith and reasonably both at the time the obligation is entered into and throughout its performance. Further, in the framework of contract law, a similar rule stems from Article 6.158 CC, which, in

[11] See UNIDROIT Principles of International Commercial Contracts, at www.unidroit.org/english/principles/contracts/main.htm.

[12] Principles of European Contract Law' (Parts I and II revised 1998, Part III 2002), at www.jus.uio.no/lm/eu.contract.principles.parts.1.to.3.2002/4.109.html.

line with Article 1.7 of the UNIDROIT Principles, requires each party to act in accordance with good faith and fair dealing. In general, that means the obligation of good faith is imposed on every party in every contract and this rule is mandatory and cannot be excluded or limited by contract. Article 6.38 CC, paragraph 1 provides that all obligations must be performed in good faith, properly and without delay, pursuant to the requirements indicated both in general statute or in the terms of the contract, and in case the relevant requirements are absent, obligations must be performed in accordance with the criteria of reasonableness. This provision extends the rule in Article 6.200 CC, paragraph 1 to cover the performance of all obligations, including non-contractual obligations.

Thus, the principle of good faith, as it is applied in Lithuania, implies that the parties should act freely and disclose all necessary information, retain a due balance of the parties' interests as well as perform their obligations and exercise their rights in accordance with the provisions of the contract, the law and the general principles of justice and reasonableness. This principle is also applied to pre-contractual negotiations (Article 6.163 CC).[13] In performing a contract, each party is bound to contribute to and to cooperate with the other party. The parties are bound to use the most economical means in the performance of the contract. A reasonableness standard is used in assessing whether a party has performed contractual duties using his/her best efforts.[14]

The good faith principle in the Lithuanian Civil Code often operates *supplendi causa* (so as to supplement the law): it specifies the way in which the contractual performance has to be rendered and gives rise to a host of ancillary duties that may arise under the contract, such as duty of information, cooperation and disclosure. This provision also serves to limit the abusive exercise of contractual rights, such as proceeding ruthlessly against and without due consideration of the other party's interests.

To act in good faith and deal fairly, the parties must act honestly toward each other when performing or enforcing a contract. The parties shall not

[13] See the Civil Case Division of the Supreme Court of Republic of Lithuania, decision of 19 January 2005 *UAB Vingio kino teatras* v. *UAB Eika* (case No. 3K-3-38/2005, category No. 42.5).

[14] See V. Mikelėnas, *Lietuvos Respublikos Civilinio kodekso komentaras: šešta knyga. Prievolių teisė (I)* (Commentary of the Civil Code of the Republic of Lithuania. Sixth book. The Law on Obligations (I), in Lithuanian) (Justitia: Vilnius, 2003) 197–8 and 252–3; Civil Case Division of the Supreme Court of Republic of Lithuania, decision of 10 October 2001, *Ž. Budros individuali įmonė Sėkmės sistemos* v. *AB Lietuvos telekomas* (case No. 3K-3-927/2001, category No. 31.4); Civil Case Division of the Supreme Court of Republic of Lithuania, decision of 14 April 2004, *UAB Libra Vitalis* v. *UAB Homo Faber* (case No. 3K-3-274/2004, category No. 37.6).

do anything that will have the effect of destroying or injuring the right of the other party to derive the benefits due under the contract. The good faith obligation in the performance of contracts means that both parties must adhere to general standards of behaviour and, in case of commercial contracts, commercial standards of fair dealing, but contractual acceptance of unreasonable commercial risk by one party does not presuppose a breach of good faith and contractual equilibrium.[15] For example, if the party has an option and chooses a performance that is not the most efficient for the other party, such performance might prove incompatible with the principle of good faith. Similarly, if one party has a discretion to set the terms of performance and sets the terms so that the other party is unable to perform his/her obligations, such actions might be incompatible with the notion of good faith. Most importantly, leading Lithuanian scholars – inspired by the UNIDROIT Principles in Article 5.3 – treat the duty to cooperate with the other party as part of the good faith principle.[16] This means that the party that receives performance shall provide all relevant information as well as other necessary assistance to the performing party. On the other hand, the performing party shall inform the other party without undue delay about any hardship that might prejudice the performance.[17] The duty of cooperation must of course be confined within certain limits, so as not to upset the allocation of duties in the performance of the contract.[18]

It is noteworthy that despite the fact the principle of good faith in the Lithuanian Civil Code has been primarily drafted to take the relevant provisions of the UNIDROIT Principles into account, provisions on the general duty of good faith has much in common with the German

[15] See Civil Case Division of the Supreme Court of Republic of Lithuania, decision of 19 September 2005, *bankrutuojanti UAB Bivainis* v. *A.Bartkevičiaus firma Arum* (case No. 3K-3–406/2005, category No. 35.5).

[16] See V. Mikelėnas, *Lietuvos Respublikos Civilinio kodekso komentaras: šešta knyga. Prievolių teisė (I)* (Commentary of the Civil Code of the Republic of Lithuania. Sixth book. The Law on Obligations (I), in Lithuanian) (Vilnius: Justitia, 2003) 70–1, 198; Civil Case Division of the Supreme Court of Republic of Lithuania, decision of 29 October 2003, *Nadoc Nr.1 A/S* v. *Valstybinio socialinio draudimo fondo valdyba* (case No. 3K-3–1036/2003, category No. 18.1).

[17] See Civil Case Division of the Supreme Court of Republic of Lithuania, decision of 18 June 2001, *G. Šeršiovaitė* v. *E. Medonio individuali įmonė Beilė* (case No. 3K-3–704/2001, category No. 45.5); Civil Case Division of the Supreme Court of Republic of Lithuania, decision of 29 May 2002, *UAB Remolita ir Ko* v. *UAB Autopartis* (case No. 3K-3–795/2002, category 47.3).

[18] See Civil Case Division of the Supreme Court of Republic of Lithuania, decision of 15 September 2003, *UAB Sauliuta* v. *AB Lytagra* (case No. 3K-3–813/2003, category No. 31.4).

principle of *Treu und Glauben*, developed by the courts and academic authorities under the auspices of Article 242 of the German Civil Code of 1900 (BGB).[19] The position of German academic and judicial authorities could often be successfully used to fill the current lacunae in the interpretation of the good faith obligation pursuant to the Lithuanian Civil Code.

Finally, it must be stressed that acts in bad faith include cases where one party receives an excessive advantage against the other. Lithuanian academic and judicial authorities agree that good faith implies that the obligations of the parties shall be proportionate, i.e. good faith ensures the contractual equilibrium.[20] At a theoretical level this test of equilibrium could be very welcome, but in commercial practice it is difficult to establish specific requirements that would satisfy this equilibrium, because case law has yet to develop and sometimes produces contradictory decisions and reasoning. For example, the equilibrium test was applied in the case *UAB Birių krovinių terminalas* v. *AB Klaipėdos Smeltė et al.* where it was recognised that a party could not withdraw a promise to refuse priority rights in favour of a subtenant even if the subtenant infringed the payment obligations under the subletting agreement. It is hard to say how this conclusion builds an equilibrium. The main argument for this decision was that the owner of the building, here the subtenant, should be allowed to use the land necessary for the use of buildings. In my opinion, the equilibrium test was instrumentalised in this case. In another case, *G. Brencius* v. *UAB Ūkio investicinė grupė*, the Lithuanian Court of Appeal decided that it would be against the contractual equilibrium to request the full payment for shares which had wholly lost their value. But the Lithuanian Supreme Court reversed the decision stating that only performance of the contract could be adapted to the requirements of reasonableness and justice and not liability after breach of payment obligations, given, in particular, that the buyer had accepted the risk of share value fluctuation.

The test of equilibrium is closely related with the principles of reasonableness and justice. In establishing the contours of equilibrium it should

[19] See R. Zimmermann and S. Whittaker, 'Good faith in European contract law: surveying the legal landscape', in R. Zimmermann and S. Whittaker (eds.), *Good Faith in European Contract Law* (Cambridge University Press, 2000) 18–22.

[20] See, for example, Civil Case Division of the Supreme Court of Republic of Lithuania, decision of 7 December 2004, *UAB Birių krovinių terminalas* v. *AB Klaipėdos Smeltė et al.* (case No. 3K-7–541/2004, category No. 45.7); Civil Case Division of the Supreme Court of Republic of Lithuania, decision of 19 May 2003 *G. Brencius* v. *UAB Ūkio investicinė grupė* (case No. 3K-3–612/2003, category No. 16.3.2.1).

be noted that in the *obiter dicta* in *V. Juozaitis* v. *E. Jacėno įmonė* it was held that termination per se of the contract – even for a relatively minor payment breach – does not contravene the requirements of reasonableness and justice as long as it is contractually agreed upon.[21] Therefore, not every unfair advantage might create the right for the disadvantaged party to invoke a legal remedy. Apart from the general principle of good faith, the aggrieved party in a financial transaction may invoke the special provisions of Article 6.228 CC, which deal with gross disparity.

The concept of gross disparity

Article 6.228 CC deals with the concept of 'gross disparity' and transplanted Article 3.10 of the UNIDROIT Principles[22] into Lithuanian law. The draftsmen of the Civil Code also took Article 4.109 (ex Article 6.109) of PECL, which deals with so-called 'Excessive benefit or unfair advantage'[23] into consideration.

[21] See, for example, Civil Case Division of the Supreme Court of Republic of Lithuania, decision of 12 October 2005 *V. Juozaitis* v. *E. Jacėno įmonė* (case No. 3K-3–473/2005, category No. 42.11.1). In this case it was concluded that the due payment was prevented by the claimant himself by objecting to the indicated purpose of the payment and refusing to accept it.

[22] Article 3.10, UNIDROIT Principles: 'A party may avoid the contract or an individual term of it if, at the time of the conclusion of the contract, the contract or term unjustifiably gave the other party an excessive advantage. Regard is to be had, among other factors, to (a) the fact that the other party has taken unfair advantage of the first party's dependence, economic distress or urgent needs, or of its improvidence, ignorance, inexperience or lack of bargaining skill, and (b) the nature and purpose of the contract. (2) Upon the request of the party entitled to avoidance, a court may adapt the contract or term in order to make it accord with reasonable commercial standards of fair dealing. (3) A court may also adapt the contract or term upon the request of the party receiving notice of avoidance, provided that that party informs the other party of its request promptly after receiving such notice and before the other party has reasonably acted in reliance on it. The provisions of Article 3.13(2) apply accordingly.' See www.unidroit.org/english/principles/contracts/main.htm.

[23] Article 4.109 (ex art. 6.109) of PECL: 'A party may avoid a contract if, (a) at the time of the conclusion of the contract: it was dependent on or had a relationship of trust with the other party, was in economic distress or had urgent needs, was improvident, ignorant, inexperienced or lacking in bargaining skill, and (b) the other party knew or ought to have known of this and, given the circumstances and purpose of the contract, took advantage of the first party's situation in a way which was grossly unfair or took an excessive benefit. (2) Upon the request of the party entitled to avoidance, a court may if it is appropriate adapt the contract in order to bring it into accordance with what might have been agreed had the requirements of good faith and fair dealing been followed. (3) A court may similarly adapt the contract upon the request of a party receiving notice of avoidance for excessive benefit or unfair advantage, provided that this party informs the party who gave the notice promptly after receiving it and before that party has acted in reliance on it.' See www.jus.uio.no/lm/eu.contract.principles.parts.1.to.3.2002/4.109.html.

This rule provides that in cases where, at the time of the conclusion of the contract, the contract or a contract term unjustifiably gives the other party an excessive advantage, the disadvantaged party may avoid the contract or its terms. Moreover, upon the request of the party entitled to avoid the contract or separate terms, a court may revise the contract or its terms and adapt them to make the contract or its separate terms meet the requirements of fairness and reasonable standards of fair dealing (Article 6.228 CC). In order to apply the remedies of Article 6.228 in favour of an aggrieved party, the court shall take into consideration the circumstances in which the contract was concluded, in particular the economic weakness, lack of information or experience, improvidence, ignorance and lack of bargaining skills of the parties. Moreover, a court may similarly adapt the contract upon the request of a party receiving notice of avoidance for gross disparity, provided that this party informs the party who gave notice promptly after receiving it and before that party has acted in reliance on it.

For example, in the case *UAB Sauluva* v. *B.R.* the Supreme Court of Lithuania decided not to apply the provisions of a lease agreement stipulating the obligation for the landlord (a natural person) to pay the penalty equal to LTL 30,000 for the early termination of a contract. The key argument for the gross disparity was the great discrepancy between the contractual penalty and the rent payment, which was many times lower.[24] In *R. K. L.* v. *J. G* the Lithuanian Court of Appeal dealt with a credit agreement whereby the borrower was obliged to pay a daily default interest equal to 1 per cent if the borrower failed to settle the debt at maturity. The court followed Article 6.228 and reduced the rate of default interest to 5 per cent per annum.[25]

I believe that Article 6.228 CC could extend effective protection to non-professional parties to financial transactions. This rule of the Civil Code has already been applied by the courts to avoid unfair contract terms, most often in cases dealing with the reduction (or setting aside) of the contractual penalties or default interest rate provided for by the contract.

Standard term contracts

In case the standard terms are used to conclude a financial transaction (adhesion contracts) the party of the contract may additionally rely upon Articles 6.185 and 6.186 CC. The use of standard terms is very

[24] Civil Case Division of the Supreme Court of Republic of Lithuania, decision of 24 April 2006, *UAB Sauluva* v. *B.R.* (case No. 3K-3–296/2006).

[25] Lithuanian Court of Appeal, decision of 20 May 2008, *R. K. L.* v. *J. G* (case No. 2A–339/2008).

common in Lithuanian banking practice, where credit institutions prepare provisions for general and repeated use in advance.

Article 6.185 CC provides that standard terms prepared by one of the parties shall bind the other party only if the latter was provided with an adequate opportunity of acquainting him/herself with these terms. The 'adequate opportunity' is established case by case, and the court shall take into consideration all the relevant circumstances that existed at the time the contract was concluded. Lithuanian legal doctrine supports the position that in case one of the parties is a non-professional, standard terms may not be invoked against such a party on the mere ground that a reference to them was made in a contractual document, even if that party signed the document. Such a position is based on Article 2.104 (ex Article 5.103 A) of PECL ('Terms not individually negotiated').[26] For example, in *UAB Pozicija* v. *AB Lietuvos draudimas*[27] the Lithuanian Supreme Court decided that the provision in an insurance policy that the insured party had knowledge of a specific standard term (No. 021) – even though the insured party had signed the insurance policy – did not per se mean the proper disclosure of the content of standard terms.

Furthermore, Article 6.186 CC provides that no term contained in standard terms, which is of such a character that the other party could not reasonably have expected it (i.e. 'surprising term'), is effective unless it has been expressly accepted by that party. This rule was transplanted into the Lithuanian Civil Code from Article 2.1.20 ('Surprising terms') of the UNIDROIT Principles.[28] In determining whether a term is 'surprising' regard shall be had to its content, language and presentation.

Finally, Article 6.186 CC entitles the party agreeing standard contract terms to claim for the termination or modification of that contract where the standard terms, despite not conflicting with mandatory provisions,

[26] Article 2.104 (ex Art. 5.103 A), PECL: '(1) Contract terms which have not been individually negotiated may be invoked against a party who did not know of them only if the party invoking them took reasonable steps to bring them to the other party's attention before or when the contract was concluded. (2) Terms are not brought appropriately to a party's attention by a mere reference to them in a contract document, even if that party signs the document.' See www.jus.uio.no/lm/eu.contract.principles.parts.1.to.3.2002/2.104.html.

[27] Civil Case Division of the Supreme Court of Republic of Lithuania, decision of 3 May 2000, *UAB Pozicija* v. *AB Lietuvos draudimas* (case No. 3K-3–486/2000).

[28] Article 2.1.20, UNIDROIT Principles: 'No term contained in standard terms which is of such a character that the other party could not reasonably have expected it, is effective unless it has been expressly accepted by that party. In determining whether a term is of such a character regard shall be had to its content, language and presentation.' See www.unidroit.org/english/principles/contracts/main.htm.

exclude the party's rights commonly granted in such contracts, or exclude or limit the civil liability of the party who prepared the standard conditions, or establish other provisions which are incompatible with the principle of equality of parties, cause imbalance in the parties' interests, or are contrary to the principles of reasonableness, good faith and justice. This provision has been drafted along the lines of Article 4.110 (ex Article 6.110) of PECL, which deals with unfair terms that have not been individually negotiated.[29]

Therefore, with the reference to Articles 6.185 and 6.186 CC, the aggrieved party may escape the performance of the contract by requesting the court to modify the agreement or not to apply particular clauses or the contract *in corpore*. Moreover, in conjunction with the defences provided in Articles 6.185 and 6.186 CC, the aggrieved party may rely on Article 6.193(4), which stipulates the *contra proferentem* rule. For example, in *UAB Algava* v. *AB Lietuvos draudimas*,[30] the Lithuanian Supreme Court concluded that the interpretation of the agreement provided by the respondent (the insurer) could not be accepted because the respondent was the person who suggested and drafted the rules in question and the interpretation provided by the insurer conflicted with the insured person's interests. Articles 6.185 and 6.186 CC, when applicable, could also provide effective protection to non-professional parties to financial transactions.

Legal basis for invalidation of financial contracts

A financial transaction may be declared null and void pursuant to the general rules of the Civil Code on the invalidity of contracts and other transactions. All of these rules can be grouped into four categories: i.e. they can be classified on the basis of why the enforcement of the contracts would be unconscionable. Hence, the contract can be declared null and void because of the:

[29] Article 4.110, PECL: 'A party may avoid a term which has not been individually negotiated if, contrary to the requirements of good faith and fair dealing, it causes a significant imbalance in the parties' rights and obligations arising under the contract to the detriment of that party, taking into account the nature of the performance to be rendered under the contract, all the other terms of the contract and the circumstances at the time the contract was concluded.' See www.jus.uio.no/lm/eu.contract.principles.parts.1.to.3.2002/4.110.html.

[30] Lithuanian Court of Appeal, decision of 26 July 2004, *UAB Algava* v. *AB Lietuvos draudimas* (case No. 2A 250/2004).

1. fault/illegal actions of the counterparty;
2. fault/illegal actions of the third person;
3. fact that the transaction per se contravenes the requirement of good faith;
4. defects as to intention of one of the parties.

The first category includes the situations regulated by Article 1.91 CC. Article 1.91 CC has been drafted along the lines of Article 3.8 ('Fraud') and 3.9 ('Threat') of the UNIDROIT Principles and Article 4.107 (ex Article 6.107) ('Fraud') and Article 4.108 (ex Article 6.108) ('Threat') of PECL, which deals with the concepts of fraud and threat. Following this rule, a transaction that has been concluded due to fraud, duress, economic pressure or real threat can be declared null and void. Article 1.91 CC can be applied where the illegal acts in question are performed by a party to the agreement. This rule also covers transactions where one party assumes unfair obligations due to harsh and exceptional circumstances and the counterparty takes advantage of the said circumstances.

The instances of the second category are regulated by Articles 1.82, 1.91 and 1.92 CC. Hence, contracts can be found null and void (i) where the transaction is *ultra vires* (Article 1.82 in case of legal persons, and Article 1.92 in case of a natural person), or (ii) where the agreement was formed by a malicious agreement of the agent of one party with the counterparty.

The third category is addressed by Articles 1.81, 1.86 and 1.87 CC. The contract itself shall be null and void without the need for any declaration, where the transaction: (i) conflicts with public order or norms of good morals (Article 1.81 CC), (ii) has been made for the sake of appearance without any intention to create legal effects (Article 1.86 CC), or (iii) is made exclusively with the purpose of suppressing the real intentions of the parties. There is no need to find fault on the part of any person; the transaction is contrary to good faith in its very essence and is therefore null and void.

The fourth category involves transactions which are null and void because the particular transaction is made by (i) incapable natural persons (Article 1.84 CC), (ii) natural persons whose legal capacity is limited (Article 1.85 CC), (iii) minors without the consent of their parents or guardians (Article 1.88 CC), (iv) capable natural persons who are unable to comprehend the meaning of their acts or to control them (Article 1.89 CC), or (v) because the transaction in question results from consent given because of mistake, where the mistake is an erroneous assumption of essential facts that existed when the contract was concluded (Article 1.90 CC[31]). Article 1.90 CC transplants into Lithuanian law Article 3.4 ('Mistake is an erroneous assumption relating to facts or to law existing when the contract was concluded.') and Article 3.5 ('Relevant mistake') of the UNIDROIT principles. Similarly, the draftsmen of the Civil Code took Article 4.103 (ex Article 6.103) of the PECL ('Mistake as to facts or law') into account.

All of the cases discussed above are connected by the same feature – i.e. that their enforcement would undoubtedly be unconscionable. Therefore, they can be found null and void without being declared to contravene statutory requirements. Such transactions are incompatible with the criterion of rationality or reasonableness. Furthermore, the transactions contravening statutory requirements can be declared null and void on the grounds of Articles 1.80 and 1.94 CC.

I believe that Articles 1.90 and, especially, 1.91 of the Civil Code are the most helpful provisions and furnish the legal grounds for declaring financial contracts (or their provisions) void. In practice, the scope of their application covers most cases of unfair contracts as they are understood in Lithuanian legal doctrine and case law. First of all, the non-professional party may consider invoking the 'real threat' provision

[31] Article 3.5, UNIDROIT Principles: 'A party may only avoid the contract for mistake if, when the contract was concluded, the mistake was of such importance that a reasonable person in the same situation as the party in error would only have concluded the contract on materially different terms or would not have concluded it at all if the true state of affairs had been known, and (a) the other party made the same mistake, or caused the mistake, or knew or ought to have known of the mistake and it was contrary to reasonable commercial standards of fair dealing to leave the mistaken party in error; or (b) the other party had not at the time of avoidance reasonably acted in reliance on the contract. (2) However, a party may not avoid the contract if (a) it was grossly negligent in committing the mistake; or (b) the mistake relates to a matter in regard to which the risk of mistake was assumed or, having regard to the circumstances, should be borne by the mistaken party.' See www.unidroit.org/english/principles/contracts/main.htm.

Article 4.103 (ex Art. 6.103) of the PECL reads as follows: 'A party may avoid a contract for mistake of fact or law existing when the contract was concluded if: (a) (i) the mistake was caused by information given by the other party; or (ii) the other party knew or ought to have known of the mistake and it was contrary to good faith and fair dealing to leave the mistaken party in error; or (iii) the other party made the same mistake, and (b) the other party knew or ought to have known that the mistaken party, had it known the truth, would not have entered the contract or would have done so only on fundamentally different terms. (2) However a party may not avoid the contract if: (a) in the circumstances its mistake was inexcusable, or (b) the risk of the mistake was assumed, or in the circumstances should be borne, by it.' See www.jus.uio.no/lm/eu.contract.principles.parts.1.to.3.2002/4.109.html.

where the economically stronger party puts the weaker party under pressure to conclude a transaction subject to exceptionally disadvantageous conditions. In addition, the non-professional party to a contract may rely on exceptionally harsh circumstances that in fact forced him/her to enter into the contract. However, only under some exceptional circumstances (old age or illness), will contracts of persons unaware of the associated financial risks be declared void pursuant to Article 1.90 CC (mistake).[32] Such legal provisions could also hardly be invoked in cases where contracting parties, although perfectly aware of the risk, nevertheless had no choice but to sign the agreement because, for example, a refusal would have impaired family harmony or close relationships. Moreover, the mere fact that obligations under the terms of the contract are manifestly disproportionate to the party's financial means would not be sufficient to avoid the contract and declare it void.

Conclusions

The Lithuanian example of voluntary harmonisation illustrates that it is indeed possible to achieve at least the partial harmonisation of national financial laws by transplanting the results of non-binding harmonisation efforts produced by leading international scholarship. However, such harmonisation in the field of unconscionability still remains fragmented because the concept of unconscionability is diverse per se and, moreover, even after transplantation, national case law has to elaborate the interpretation and application of the rules in a context peculiar to that jurisdiction, a context which may differ substantially from other jurisdictions with identical rules.

[32] See Decision of the Lithuanian Court of Appeal 3 May 2004, *UAB A.L.* v. *UAB Šiaulių dujotiekio statyba* (case No. 2A-176/2004).

15

Bank loan contracts in Polish law: the legal position of the borrower

STANISLAWA KALUS AND MAGDALENA HABDAS*

Introduction

The purpose of this chapter is to examine the legal position of the borrower under a loan agreement entered into with a bank. As Polish financial and capital markets develop, a growing amount of banking products have become available. This is particularly evident with respect to bank loans, which have become increasingly affordable.

Despite the fact that many banks are present on the market, the competition to secure a client base does not always guarantee that contracts equally protect the interests of the client and the bank. Apart from including abusive clauses and burdening the borrower with onerous duties, banks assume that the borrower is aware of the legal effects of creating security for the loan. However, in practice, the borrower does not comprehend the effect this has on his legal position. Moreover, this position entails legal effects not only for the borrower during his lifetime, but also for his heirs upon his death.

Poland's accession to the European Union must be viewed as having had a positive influence on the development of banking practice and consumer protection in the field of bank loans. Directives such as the Consumer Credit Directive, Door-Step Selling Directive, e-Commerce Directive, Distance Marketing Directive, and the Unfair Terms Directive are aimed at increasing the safety and transparency of transactions, with particular attention paid to the protection of consumers. Although these directives have brought about much needed change in Polish law, it must be pointed out that European law in this field is often contradictory and over-regulation causes difficulties in transposing it into domestic regulations.[1]

* Faculty of Law and Administration, University of Silesia, Katowice, Poland.

[1] R. W. Kaszubski, 'Wpływ prawa europejskiego na funkcjonowanie polskiego systemu bankowego' (2005) 6 *Prawo bankowe* 49–50.

The bank-client relationship began to evolve before Poland became a member of the European Union. As early as 2001 the Union of Polish Banks passed a resolution in which the role of the banks as institutions of public trust and the need for an open dialogue with clients was emphasised.[2] Institutions such as the Bank Arbiter or the Office of Competition and Consumer Protection increased awareness of the legal issues connected with financial services. Their practice also shows that, as Polish law concerning bank loans and the protection of borrowers develops, there are still a number of issues that must be addressed in order to protect borrowers, who are invariably the weaker parties in bank loan contracts.

This chapter focuses on the main legal characteristics of the bank loan contract in Polish law, the methods of securing a bank loan, the most common abusive clauses in loan contracts and the influence of these issues on the borrower's legal position. It is argued that knowledge of the risks involved in these arrangements should influence market practice and lead to a better protection of the borrower's interests.

The bank loan (credit) contract

According to Polish law banks make cash available to physical and legal persons either by means of a loan contract or a bank loan (bank credit) contract. The bank loan contract, regulated in Article 69 of the Banking Law Act 1997 (BLA),[3] is derived from the loan contract which is defined in Article 720 of the Polish Civil Code (PCC).[4] In a loan contract the lender assumes the obligation to transfer to the borrower the ownership of a specified sum of money or a specified amount of things designated only as to their kind; and the borrower assumes the obligation to return the same sum of money or the same amount of things of the same kind and quality.

In a bank loan contract the bank assumes the obligation to make a specified amount of money available to the borrower for a time specified in the contract and for a specified purpose; and the borrower assumes the obligation to use the money according to contractual provisions, return the used amount of money with interest in designated instalments and to

[2] K. Marczynska, 'Stosunki między bankiem, a klientem na tle skarg klientów do Arbitra Bankowego' (2005) 6 *Prawo Bankowe* 53.

[3] Act of 29 August 1997, Dz.U. 2002, no. 72, item 665 with subsequent amendments.

[4] Act of 23 April 1964, Dz.U.64, No.16, item 93 with subsequent amendments.

pay a commission charge on the loan.[5] The *essentialia negotii* of the bank loan contract consists of the following elements: the agreement of the parties to the contract; the amount and the currency of the bank loan; the purpose for which the bank loan has been granted; the conditions and times of instalments; the commission due on the bank loan in question; the means of securing the bank loan; the means and times of making the money available to the borrower and the scope of the bank's rights to monitor the use and payment of money advanced in a bank loan.[6] The contract may be characterised as consensual and causal, in which both parties have mutual obligations and consideration is given. Also, the lender in a bank loan contract must be an entity, which according to Polish law fulfils the criteria of a bank (Article 2 and 5 BLA).[7] The borrower, on the other hand, may be either a business entity (sole trader, entrepreneur, company), a professional or a consumer.

Polish law adheres to the principle of freedom of contract expressed in Article 353^1 PCC, according to which the parties may shape their legal relationship as they deem proper, providing that the contents or the purpose of the contract are not contrary to the nature of the relationship and do not violate statutory law and principles of community life. Banking practice, however, cannot function without standard contracts, which make the contracting process faster and cheaper, but may also allow the bank to take advantage of its stronger position and deprive the client of the possibility to individually negotiate contract conditions. Control mechanisms have to operate in order to prevent the inclusion of abusive clauses (unfair contract terms) in standard contracts. It is not difficult to imagine the impact of finding an abusive clause in a standard contract which has been entered into by clients of any particular bank nationwide.[8]

Conducting negotiations with the client is not rare, but negotiated issues (frequently the interest rate, the bank's commission and times of repayments) usually include only a fraction of the matters important to

[5] See T. Narozny, *Czynnosci kredytowe banku. Zagadnienia prawne* (Warsaw: Zarządzanie i Finanse, 2000) 15; A. Szpunar, 'O umowie pozyczki' (1992) 12 *Państwo i Prawo* 30.

[6] A. Strzelecki, *Zarys prawa bankowego* (Wloclawek: Wyższa Szkoła Humanistyczno-Ekonomiczna, 2005) 100–4.

[7] W. Popiolek, 'Pozyczka', in K. Pietrzykowski (ed.), *Kodeks cywilny. Tom II. Komentarz* (Warsaw: C. H. Beck 2004) 357.

[8] J. Pisulinski, 'Niedozwolone klauzule umowne w obrocie bankowym na wybranych przykładach' (2005) 6 *Prawo bankowe* 15; A. Swistak, 'Luki we wzorcach umownych i ich interpretacja' (2004) 7/8 *Prawo bankowe* 85.

the client, who may not even be aware of the possible wider scope of negotiations. It is also important to note that presently the range of various bank loans offered on the market is very wide and the client may have difficulties in comparing and choosing a loan that best protects his interests.

The bank, on the other hand, will not, as a rule, grant a bank loan to a party who is not creditworthy or who is unable to pay the debt along with interest and bank costs (Article 70 s. 1 BLA). Such a situation is permissible under Article 70 s. 3 BLA on the condition that the loan is adequately secured and the borrower presents a repayment plan which, in the bank's opinion, will allow the borrower to become creditworthy within a specified period of time.

The means of securing a bank loan

There are different types of protective measures taken by banks to decrease the risk of not recovering the capital sum and the interest. They may be classified into three groups: economic, psychological and legal securities.[9] The first group includes the borrower's financial standing, his equity capital and his fixed and current assets. The second group involves analysing the borrower's previous cooperation with the bank. If the borrower has shown himself to be creditworthy and reliable then the risk of granting him a bank loan is decreased. Finally, the third group includes legal securities. These may be divided into *personal securities*, which include a surety, bill cover, bank guarantee, blocking access to money in bank accounts, guarantee deposit and *real securities* which include the pledge, registered pledge (floating charge), and mortgage and mortgage of goods by security bill of sale.[10] An analysis of banking practice shows that banks do not employ only one type of security, but resort to a combination of different instruments. For example, in order to secure one claim, a mortgage and a registered pledge are set up, the latter typically on the debtor's car.

Personal securities, particularly in the form of a surety, are most widely used to secure bank loans granted to physical persons where the credit rating is assessed on the basis of earnings. In order for a suretyship to fulfil its protective function, the person (physical or legal) acting as surety must have at least the same or a better credit rating than the

[9] T. Narozny, *Prawo bankowe* (Poznan: Wydawnictwo Wyzszej Szkoły Bankowej, 1998) 48.
[10] See further A. Strzelecki, n. 6 above, 109–10.

borrower. It is important to note that according to a Supreme Court judgment a surety is void if it concerns an undefined set of the debtor's liabilities or all of the debtor's liabilities in relation to the creditor (general surety).[11] A surety is not employed in bank loans granted for the purpose of purchasing real estate, as they are commonly secured by a mortgage.

Another instrument frequently employed is the bill of exchange, particularly the bill of security. A blank bill is issued when the amount of the debt cannot be specified because it depends on payments being made by the borrower. Once the borrower defaults, the bank will fill in the amount of a bill in accordance with a separate agreement (bill declaration), in which the conditions and the amount are stipulated. Unfortunately in practice such a declaration is seldom prepared and this causes disputes between the banks and issuers of bills. The blank bill is often connected with a bill guarantee (aval), which encompasses either the whole debt or a part of that debt identified in the bill. The bill guarantor and the bill issuer are jointly liable, but their liability expires together with expiry of the debt.[12]

Popular means of securing bank loans also include bank guarantees, which banks readily accept as security but are not equally enthusiastic about issuing.[13] One should also mention the cession of borrower's claims/receivables, which may be a global cession (including all of the borrower's claims/receivables) or a limited cession, when a specified claim/receivable is being transferred to the bank.

The most popular real securities employed by banks include the registered pledge (or floating charge) and the mortgage. Banks seldom use the regular pledge, as they are not interested in being in possession of a movable, particularly since the creditor does not automatically become its owner upon the debtor's default, but must go through foreclosure proceedings (*postepowanie egzekucyjne*).

As far as the mortgage of goods by security bill of sale is concerned Polish law does not have any equitable securities, only legal ones. The effect of this is that in the case of a mortgage of goods by security bill of sale, ownership of real property is transferred to the creditor (a contract by which both an obligation and a conveyance is made), but the creditor

[11] Judgment of 29 May 2005 (V CK 827/04).

[12] See further A. Strzelecki, n. 6 above, 109–10.

[13] G. Tracz, *Umowa gwarancji ze szczególnym uwzględnieniem gwarancji bankowej* (Kraków: Zakamycze 1998) 113–15.

is obliged to transfer the ownership of that property back to the debtor when he pays his debt (only an obligation is created – Article 157 § 1 PCC). In order for ownership to be transferred back to the debtor, he and the creditor must create a new contract in which they agree to unconditionally and immediately transfer the aforementioned ownership (Article 157 § 2 PCC).[14] If the creditor refuses to enter into such a contract, despite the fact that the debt has been repaid, the debtor may apply for a court judgment, which essentially substitutes the creditor's declaration of intent (Article 64 PCC and Article 1047 § 1 Polish Civil Procedure Code (PCPC)).[15] This judgment may then be presented to the notary who prepares the contract for the transfer of ownership back to the debtor in the form of a notarial deed.

This option of securing a bank loan is not, however, commonly employed. Numerous Polish banks are of the opinion that their main activity involves financial operations and that they do not have staff specialised in real property management. However, some banks do employ mortgage of goods by security bill of sale, because a mortgage does not always lead to the satisfaction of the bank's claim. This is due to the fact that money raised in foreclosure sales must be divided to cover costs and creditors in a given order of priority, as prescribed in Article 1025 PCPC (see below).

Real securities allow the bank to recover the money due under the bank loan contract, regardless of who becomes the owner of the encumbered movables (pledge, floating charge) or immovables (mortgage). The law does not, however, provide the creditor with the possibility of out of court recovery of money due, such as foreclosure and repossession of the encumbered item. Apart from the floating charge, where there are different ways of recovering the money by the bank, including foreclosure, in the case of pledges and mortgages the bank must initiate foreclosure proceedings in order to recover its money. According to the PCPC the entitled parties acquire a right to satisfy their claims from the amount for which the immovable or movable is sold by the bailiff in foreclosure proceedings (Article 1000 §1 PCPC). This is done according to the order prescribed in Article 1025 PCPC. Out of the ten categories listed, mortgages and registered pledges are in fifth position following foreclosure costs, alimony payments, unpaid

[14] G. Tracz and F. Zoll, *Przewłaszczenie na zabezpieczenie* (Kraków: Zakamycze 1998) 36–40.
[15] Act of 17 November 1964, Dz.U.64, no. 43, item 269 with subsequent amendments.

employee salaries up to three months and receivables secured by a sea vessel's mortgage.

Consequently, the bank's position in foreclosure proceedings is quite strong. Moreover, the bank's access to these proceedings is also simplified. The general rule is that in order to start foreclosure proceedings, one must present an implementation title, i.e. a foreclosure title with a power of sale *(klauzula wykonalnosci)*. According to Article 777 PCPC the following constitute foreclosure titles:

1. A court (or a court clerk's) judgment in force or subject to immediate enforcement, a consent judgment, which means that the creditor must first obtain a judgment in which the amount (claim) secured by the mortgage is acknowledged;
2. a judgment of a settlement court or a settlement reached in such a court, as well as a settlement reached in front of a mediator;
3. other judgments, settlements and decisions which are subject to court foreclosure on the basis of statutory provisions;
4. a notarial deed in which the debtor voluntarily agrees to foreclosure proceedings and which stipulates the obligation to pay a given sum of money at a given date; and
5. a notarial deed in which the debtor voluntarily agrees to foreclosure proceedings and which stipulates the obligation to pay a sum of money up to an indicated amount, or up to an amount which can be calculated in accordance with a valorisation clause. Furthermore, the deed specifies the conditions in which the creditor may instigate foreclosure proceedings.

However, unlike other creditors, banks do not need to go to court to obtain a judgment which acknowledges the existence of the debt. According to Article 96 BLA the bank's accounts and other documents are proof that a specified debt exists, and therefore are the basis for issuing a banking foreclosure title. This title may be issued if the debtor voluntarily agrees to foreclosure (Article 97 s. 1 BLA), which in practice is one of the clauses commonly included by banks in bank loan contracts.

Banking foreclosure titles have been the subject of controversy, because they are the only titles issued exclusively by the creditor without the courts' supervision. It is the bank which states the amount of the debt, based on banking documents, which in Polish law have the status of official documents (Article 95 s. 1 BLA) and the debtor has no influence over the contents of that statement. The debtor's consent to issue a banking foreclosure title cannot be viewed as his conscious decision, since it is one of many clauses included in the bank loan contract.[16]

In a judgment of 26 January 2005[17] the Constitutional Tribunal stated that banking foreclosure titles do not violate the Polish Constitution[18] because the debtor may bring an action against foreclosure (Article 840 PCPC) or a declaratory action, to ascertain the existence and the amount of his debt (Article 189 PCPC) and so the constitutional right of access to the court is not violated. Moreover, if the banking foreclosure title were to be replaced with the other most common foreclosure title, namely a notarial deed, in which the debtor voluntarily agrees to foreclosure proceedings and which stipulates the obligation to pay a given sum of money at a given date, the process of entering into a bank loan contract would be more onerous and costly. In practice such a situation would lead to increased costs for the borrower. Therefore, it is important that clients are made aware of the bank's power of sale and that the bank fulfils its information duties towards the borrower.[19] These duties may be derived from general provisions of the PCC concerning contracts, but also from more specific provisions on granting bank loans,[20] for example from Article 69 BLA or Article 4 of the Consumer Credit Act 2001 (CCA).[21]

Mortgages as instruments of securing a bank loan

Among the securities mentioned above, only mortgages and the mortgage of goods by security bill of sale may be created with respect to immovables (real estate). The economic effectiveness of these securities depends on the adequacy of a given immovable as loan collateral. The immovable should achieve the required amount upon its sale in foreclosure proceedings in the case of default on the loan.

Unquestionably for certain types of real estate there is a high demand: principally residential property, but less so for recreational or industrial property. However, other factors, not only the type, influence the value of

[16] J. Szczesny, 'Konstytucyjnosc bankowych tytulow egzekucyjnych. Glosa do wyroku TK z 26.I.2005r. (P 10/04)' (2005) 11 *Prawo bankowe* 38.

[17] P 10/04. [18] English version: www.sejm.gov.pl/prawo/konst/angielski/kon1.htm.

[19] For more on the bank's information duties in the context of consumer credit, see E. Rutkowska, 'Ochrona kredytobiorcy – konsumenta uslug bankowych' (2005) 6 *Prawo bankowe* 89–94.

[20] J. Szczesny, 'Konstytucyjnosc bankowych tytulow egzekucyjnych. Glosa do wyroku TK z 26.I.2005r. (P 10/04)' (2005) 11 *Prawo bankowe* 40–1.

[21] Act of 20 July 2001, Dz.U.01, no. 100, item 1081 with subsequent amendments.

the immovable in foreclosure. These include its location, permitted use (zoning) and the general market situation. It is important to bear in mind that a mortgage only ensures that the creditor will be able to recover his money from a foreclosure of the encumbered immovable, regardless of its owner and with priority to other personal creditors (Article 65 Land Register and Mortgages Act 1982 – LRM[22]) but, as discussed above, an out of court recovery of money due is not permissible.

In the course of a foreclosure conducted by the bailiff, the real property is described and valued. The only individuals entitled to value real estate are real estate valuers (Article 174 and 177 of the Management of Real Property Act – MRP[23]) who possess special qualifications to value real estate and who also give expert opinions in court (Article 948 PCPC). According to Article 150 MRP, if a market value for the real property in foreclosure can be determined, because similar properties have been traded on the market, then its sale should be based on its market value. If there is no comparable evidence, then according to Article 150 s. 4 MRP, the valuer should calculate the replacement value, which will serve as the basis of the auction sale.

The borrower is often not aware of the fact that during the foreclosure the bailiff seizes (attaches) not only the immovable and its fixtures (constituent parts) but also movables (Article 929 §1 PCPC and Article 84 LRM), which have the legal status of appurtenances, that is movable things functionally (not physically) connected to the principal thing (Article 51 PCC). Therefore, if the attached immovable is used as a fish pond, the boats used for fishing, even though they are not fixtures of land, will be attached as appurtenances of the immovable. This rule is particularly important in the attachment of farms or immovables where business activity is conducted. Consequently, in foreclosure proceedings, it is not only the debtor's land that is being sold, but often valuable movables as well.

The borrower also needs to realise that the price obtained in foreclosure proceedings will usually be much lower than the immovable's market value. The foreclosure is a forced one and there is no proper time for marketing and negotiations. Additionally the starting sale price at the first auction may be lowered to three-quarters of the determined value (Article 965 PCPC), and to two-thirds of the value at the second auction (Article 983 PCPC). As has already been stated, the money

[22] Act of 6 July 1982, t.j. Dz.U.01, no. 124, item 1361 with subsequent amendments.

[23] Act of 21 August 1997, t.j. Dz.U.04, no. 261, item 2603 with subsequent amendments.

received from the sale will not be used to satisfy the bank's claim in its entirety if there are entities whose claims have a higher priority (i.e. the bailiff with respect to his costs of carrying out the foreclosure). Therefore, the borrower should realise that, despite having lost one of his most valuable assets, he may still be personally liable to the creditor for outstanding debts with all his remaining assets. In such cases, in order to make him optimise his legal position, the borrower should avoid foreclosure proceedings and whenever possible chose mediation/arbitration procedures.

A mortgage comes into legal existence only after it has been entered on the land register. The waiting period for registration is liable to be quite long and in the interim the bank remains uncertain as to whether the court will consider registration to be admissible. Since Poland does not have a notice system, the register court examines if there is a valid legal basis to make the requested registration. The court will not allow registration if such a basis does not exist or is flawed and consequently the mortgage will not be established. Although a mortgage does not exist until it has been registered, once it is registered its effects are retroactive and begin at the time the registration was filed with the court (Article 29 LRM). Because of these delays to effective registration the bank, for a substantial period of time, will be unsure whether a mortgage will in fact be created. Therefore, banks usually require the debtor to insure the bank loan with an insurance company, which makes the bank loan even more expensive.

The borrower should be careful when considering the creation of a joint mortgage encumbering more than one immovable. The immovables do not need to be owned by the debtor or even by one person. Joint mortgages come into existence *ex lege*, when a previously encumbered immovable is divided into two or more separate ones (Article 76 s. 1 LRM) but they may also be created by contracting parties who agree that a given debt will be secured by one mortgage which will be created over two or more immovables (contractual joint mortgage, Article 76 s. 3 LRM). The essence of a joint mortgage is that the secured creditor may choose from which immovable he shall satisfy his claim. He may choose to satisfy his claim from one of the immovables encumbered, a few of them, or all of them and specify the amount he wishes to recover from the foreclosure sale of a given immovable (Article 76 s. 2 LRM). It is obvious that joint mortgages are an attractive means of securing the interests of creditors, particularly when the encumbered properties differ in function/use. This not only diversifies the creditor's risk, but also allows him, depending on the state of the market at any given time, to choose which property, out of the ones encumbered by the joint mortgage, to sell in order to achieve the highest price. The debtor, however, should be aware of the fact that a joint mortgage often leads to the creditor's overprotection, especially when the amount of the debt is low when compared to the value of the mortgaged immovables. In such cases the mortgage is onerous and unnecessarily weakens the debtor's legal position in relation to third parties.[24] The creditor secured by a joint mortgage has an advantage over the debtor for two reasons. First, the creditor's mortgage will have a higher priority than subsequent mortgages created over any of the debtor's immovables (already encumbered by the joint mortgage). Secondly, the debtor does not know from which immovables the creditor will choose to satisfy his claim. In extreme situations, the creation of a joint mortgage may be viewed as an abuse of rights by the creditor and may be raised as an objection by the debtor against the creditor in court proceedings.[25]

In this context it is also necessary to mention the Mortgage Bonds and Mortgage Banks Act 1997 (MBMB).[26] Special provisions on ascertaining the mortgage lending value of immovables often lead to a lower value estimate and to the creation of joint mortgages, thus negatively influencing the borrower's legal and financial situation. According to Article 2 s. 1 MBMB, the mortgage lending value of immovables is the value which, in the bank's opinion, reflects the risk associated with a given immovable as the object of security created to protect bank loans granted by the mortgage bank. The calculation of the mortgage-lending value must be done in a prudent and careful manner with consideration given only to those aspects of the property and its income, which under the assumption of rational use are sustainable and obtainable by any user (Article 22 s. 1 MBMB).

In Directive 2006/48/EC relating to credit institutions, the mortgage-lending value is defined as:

> the value of the property as determined by a prudent assessment of the future marketability of the property taking into account long-term sustainable aspects of the property, the normal and local market conditions, the current use and alternative appropriate uses of the property. Speculative elements shall not be taken into account in the assessment of the mortgage lending value. The mortgage value shall be documented in a transparent and clear manner.

[24] A. Malarewicz, 'Hipoteka laczna jako zabezpieczenie kredytu hipotecznego' (2006) 2 *Prawo bankowe* 71–2.

[25] S. Rudnicki, *Komentarz do ustawy o ksiegach wieczystych i hipotece oraz do przepisow o postepowaniu w sprawach wieczystoksiegowych* (Warsaw: Lexis Nexis 2002) 228.

[26] Act of 29 August 1997, t.j. Dz.U.03, no. 99, item 919 with subsequent amendments.

The Directive also requires property to be valued by an independent valuer at or less than the market value. Valuation at or less than the mortgage-lending value is allowed in Member States where rigorous criteria for the assessment of the mortgage-lending value have been set out in statutory or regulatory provisions; however, such a valuation must still be prepared by an independent valuer.[27]

Polish legislation allows for this value to be determined by the mortgage bank on the basis of an expert opinion prepared either by the bank (Article 22 s. 2.1; this probably means an in-house valuer), or other persons agreed to by the borrower including professional real estate valuers licensed according to the provisions of the MRP. Detailed principles for calculating the mortgage lending value are set out in bank regulations that must be approved by the Polish Financial Supervision Authority. These provisions of the Polish MBMB seem to violate the requirements set out in the Directive 2006/48/EC, as the former allow for the determination of the mortgage-lending value by in-house valuers, who cannot be viewed as independent. Additionally, it is doubtful whether bank regulations may be treated as 'regulatory provisions' within the terms of the Directive.

It is also essential to point out that a mortgage-lending value is not a basis of valuation, so it is not a type of value (i.e. market value, investment value, special value), but it is a long-term risk assessment technique.[28] The borrower wishing to take out a bank loan with a mortgage bank (which to a borrower does not differ from other banks) is unaware of the fact that the immovable that will serve as collateral for the loan is not valued in accordance with internationally accepted valuation principles, but is appraised with the use of a risk assessment technique developed by the mortgage bank and based on long-term, sustainable aspects of the property. These aspects are also difficult to identify, as even the property's location, which obviously remains the same, will have a different impact on the value depending on changes in development plans, the use of neighbouring properties, the occupiers of properties in the vicinity, etc. The determined mortgage value is often lower than the market value of a given property. Therefore, the property may not provide adequate security. Consequently, the borrower will need to create an additional security in favour of the bank.

[27] Official Journal L 177, 30.06.2006, 150.

[28] International Valuation Standards Committee, *International Valuation Standards*, 8th edn (London: IVSC, 2007) 141.

The legal position of the borrower's heirs

By entering into a bank loan contract, the borrower not only alters his own legal position, but also influences the legal position of his heirs. Bank loans are often the most important debts of the estate inherited after the death of the testator.

In Polish succession law the estate of the deceased, consisting of rights and duties, devolves at the time of his death to one or more persons. The estate does not, however, include rights and duties strictly connected with the deceased as well as those rights, which at the time of his death devolve to designated persons, regardless of whether they are his heirs (Article 922 PCC). The acquisition of the estate by heirs occurs *ex lege*, at the time of the testator's death, without any additional actions by the heirs and regardless of whether the persons that are heirs are even aware of the fact that they have just inherited an estate. The heirs inherit the estate instantly on the testator's death, but the acquisition is temporary as each heir, from the day on which he learns about his title to inherit, has six months to reject the estate. Furthermore, the acceptance of the estate may be made without limitation of liability for debts (simple acceptance) or with limitation of liability for debts up to the value of the estate's assets.

As far as a bank loan contract is concerned, for the borrower it is a source of both rights (e.g. to receive a specified amount of money for a specified purpose from the bank) and duties/obligations (e.g. to repay the capital sum with interest in a given time along with other bank fees). The main issue which needs to be addressed is whether those rights and duties do form a part of the deceased person's estate or whether their connection with the deceased is so strong that they do not devolve to heirs.

It is difficult to deny that the bank loan contract has a strong link to the borrower, as the bank analyses his credit rating and on that basis decides whether to grant the bank loan, its amount, conditions of repayment and means of security. Therefore if the money that was to be made available to the borrower under a bank loan contract has not yet been transferred to his or another account, the heirs do not have the right to demand the transfer. The bank cannot be held to be obliged to make money available to persons whose credit capacity has in no way been ascertained. The borrower's claim under the bank loan contract is therefore strictly connected with the borrower and does not constitute a part of the inherited estate.[29]

[29] D. Rogon and T. Spyra, 'Wplyw spadkobrania na bankowe stosunki umowne' (2007) 9 *Prawo bankowe* 77.

If money has already been made available to the borrower in accordance with a bank loan agreement, the duty to repay the capital sum with interest has a clear financial connotation and is distinct from duties that may be connected exclusively with the borrower himself. The heirs inherit the duty to repay sums which were already due at the time of the borrower's death along with any penalties for delays in making payments as well as the duty to pay sums which become due after the borrower's death.

There are no provisions in the BLA or CCA which allow for the bank to rescind the bank loan contract upon the borrower's death and it seems that if such a clause were to be included in the contract itself, resort to it by the bank could be treated as an abuse of a right (*naduzycie prawa podmiotowego*) (Article 5 PCC) and could be objected to by the heirs in court. It is not clear whether the same can be said about a contractual clause stipulating that a bank loan contract expires and becomes due in its entirety upon the death of the borrower. Such a clause has *mortis causa* effects and has major implications for the borrower's heirs. It may be argued that such a clause is admissible and would allow the bank to utilise the securities it has established to guarantee the repayment of the loan. However, the bank would not be able to make any claims against the heirs before a court judgment – stipulating the acquisition of the estate by specified heirs – is issued and comes into force. Until that moment, there is no certainty as to who the heirs are and who has accepted or rejected the estate.[30]

Nevertheless, banks have repeatedly attempted to recover money from the presumed heirs, who, in turn, have brought disputes to courts or the Bank Arbiter. The heirs also frequently point out that if the bank requires them to pay back the entire loan in a short period of time their legal position becomes much worse than that of the original borrower. In such cases the banks usually take into account the heirs' arguments and a satisfactory settlement is reached.[31]

In the absence of such a clause in the bank loan contract, the bank may approach the heirs identified in the court judgment, informing them about the duty to pay the loan instalments. If the heirs do not begin performing their obligations, the bank may rescind the contract (Article 75 BLA) on the grounds that the conditions of the bank loan are not

[30] Ibid., at 85.

[31] K. Marczynska, 'Stosunki między bankiem, a klientem na tle skarg klientów do Arbitra Bankowego' (2005) 6 *Prawo Bankowe* 57.

fulfilled.[32] It is also important to emphasise that the bank and the heirs may reach a settlement as to their respective obligations arising out of the bank loan contract.[33]

Unfair contract terms (abusive clauses)

Unfair contract terms relate to the broad issue of consumer protection, which is recognised in the Polish Constitution. According to Article 76 of the Constitution, public authorities shall protect consumers, customers, hirers or lessees against activities threatening their health, privacy and safety, as well as against dishonest market practices. The scope of such protection is to be specified by statute.

The most fundamental piece of legislation in this area is in the PCC, where Article 385^1 §1 stipulates that provisions of contracts with consumers which are not individually agreed are non-binding if they formulate consumer rights and obligations against good practice and amount to gross violations of consumer interests (abusive clauses). This does not apply to fundamental conditions including price or remuneration, if they have been identified in a clear manner. If a consumer had no actual influence on the contents of a provision, it is to be treated as not individually agreed (Article 385^1 §3 PCC). The Polish Supreme Court pointed out that an unjustified disproportion in the rights and duties of the consumer may amount to a gross violation of consumer interests; that a formulation of consumer rights and obligations contrary to good practice may be seen where a clause disturbs the contractual balance of the legal relationship.[34]

In banking practice the use of standard contract terms is widespread and the vast majority of bank loan contract clauses are not individually agreed with the consumer. There are, however, elements of the bank loan contract which, according to Article 69 BLA, should be included in the contract itself and not in standard contract terms, but banking practice shows that this principle is often ignored.[35] The Polish Supreme Court and the Court of Competition and Consumer Protection have already emphasised the requirement to agree individually, clearly, exhaustively

32 B. Smykla, *Prawo bankowe. Komentarz* (Warsaw: C. H. Beck 2005), at 252.

33 For more on settlements see A. Portalska and O. Kornatowicz, *Odzyskiwanie należności pieniężnych* (Warsaw: C. H. Beck, 2003) 75.

34 Judgment of 13 July 2005 (I CK 832/04).

35 A. Swistak, 'Luki we wzorcach umownych i ich interpretacja' (2004) 7/8 *Prawo bankowe* 91.

and directly the obligatory elements of the consumer credit contract and have pointed out that regulating these elements in standard contract terms, bank regulations or other general contract conditions is unacceptable.[36]

Standard contract terms may undergo an 'incidental' or an 'abstract' control procedure, the latter carried out by the District Court in Warsaw, the Court of Competition and Consumer Protection (CCCP). Incidental control relates to a particular dispute between a consumer and another contracting party which concerns a clause contained in standard contract terms. It is carried out by a court competent to try specific types of case in accordance with the general provisions of PCPC. The court judgment is effective only between the parties involved in the dispute. With relation to bank loan contracts incidental control often takes place when a consumer questions the validity of the bank's rescission of the contract and claims that a clause allowing the bank to rescind in standard contract terms is not binding.[37]

Abstract control occurs when a standard contract term is questioned but not in relation to a contract entered into by particular parties. A judgment recognising a specific clause as abusive is entered in the Register of Abusive Clauses kept by the President of the Office of Competition and Consumer Protection and becomes effective against third parties (Article 479^{43} PCPC). The function of abstract control is to eliminate abusive clauses from contract practice and thus protect the consumer interest, but the precise consequences of such judgments are disputable, particularly with respect to the 'extended effectiveness' (*rozszerzona skutecznosc*) of such judgments.[38] It should be emphasised, that a clause which has been entered into the register as abusive may not be abusive as regards a different set of standard contract terms. A clause is frequently abusive not by virtue exclusively of its content, but also by virtue of its function and relation to other standard contract terms which together bring about gross violation of the consumer interest. Consequently, the fact that a given clause is entered into the Register of Abusive Clauses does not mean that such a clause cannot be used in any standard contract term, but merely that its

[36] Judgment of 20 June 2006 (III SK 7/06), OSNP 2007/13–14/207; judgment of 7 March 2005 (XVII Ama 6/04), Dz.Urz.UOKiK 2005/2/26.

[37] J. Pisulinski, 'Niedozwolone klauzule umowne w obrocie bankowym na wybranych przykładach' (2005) 6 *Prawo bankowe* 19.

[38] M. Skory, *Abusive Clauses– Application of the Provisions of Directive 93/13 in Poland and in Selected Countries of the European Union (Germany, Great Britain, France, the Czech Republic, Slovakia and Hungary)* (Warsaw: Office for Competition and Consumer Protection 2007) 3, 12–13.

application in other standard contract terms should be carefully considered.[39] The most common abusive clauses entered into the register concerning bank loan agreements include:

1. The borrower's obligation to open a bank account with the bank granting a bank loan as a condition of making the loan available;
2. the bank's right to rescind the bank loan contract for reasons which are described in standard contract terms in an unclear manner; and
3. where the repayment of the bank loan will consist of the bank deducting the respective amounts from the borrower's current bank account, even when the debtor gave no such instructions to the bank.

Conclusions

Concluding a bank loan contract greatly influences the borrower's legal position and although the duty to repay the bank loan is obvious to most borrowers, other more subtle but serious effects often remain underestimated. The contract may be characterised as consensual and causal, in which both parties have mutual obligations and consideration is given. Also, the lender in a bank loan contract must be an entity which, according to Polish law, fulfils the criteria of a bank (Articles 2 and 5 BLA).

The first issue that the borrower should be aware of is that the bank loan must be secured by the borrower. As has been pointed out, banks employ a combination of economic, psychological and legal securities, but the borrower should carefully consider which securities best reflect his own interests.

Real securities allow the bank to recover the money due under the bank loan contract, regardless of who becomes the owner of the encumbered movables (pledge, floating charge) or immovables (mortgage). The law does not, however, provide the creditor with the possibility of out of court recovery of money due. In the case of mortgages the bank must initiate foreclosure proceedings to recover its money. The bank's access to these proceedings is simplified because, unlike other creditors, banks do not need to go to court to obtain a judgment which acknowledges the existence of the debt. According to Article 96 BLA, the bank's accounts and other documents are proof that a specific debt exists and therefore constitute the basis of issuing a foreclosure title. Banking foreclosure

[39] J. Pisulinski, 'Niedozwolone klauzule umowne w obrocie bankowym na wybranych przykładach' (2005) 6 *Prawo bankowe* 6 (2005) 20–2; see also Skory, *Abusive Clauses*, n. 38 above, 13–14.

titles are the only titles which can be issued by the creditor without judicial supervision. It is the bank which states the amount of the debt, based on banking documents that in Polish law have the status of official documents (Article 95 s. 1 BLA) and the debtor has no influence over the contents of that statement. The debtor's consent to issue a foreclosure title cannot be viewed as his conscious decision, since it is one of many clauses included in the bank loan contract.

The borrower also needs to realise that the price obtained in foreclosure will usually be much lower than the immovable's market value. The foreclosure sale is a forced one and there is no time for marketing and negotiations. Additionally, the starting sale price at the first auction may be lowered to three-quarters of the determined value (Article 965 PCPC), and to two-thirds of the value at the second auction (Article 983 PCPC). During the foreclosure the bailiff seizes (attaches) not only the immovable and its fixtures (constituent parts) but also movables (Article 929 §1 PCPC and Article 84 LRM), which have the legal status of appurtenances (Article 51 PCC). Consequently, in foreclosure proceedings it is not only the debtor's land that is being sold, but often valuable movables as well.

Creating joint mortgages often leads to overprotection of the creditor, especially when the amount of the debt is low when compared to the value of the mortgaged immovables. In such cases the mortgage is onerous and unnecessarily weakens the debtor's legal position in relation to third parties. In extreme situations, the creation of a joint mortgage may be viewed as an abuse of rights by the creditor and may be raised as an objection by the debtor against the creditor in court proceedings.

By entering into a bank loan contract, the borrower not only shapes his own legal position, but also influences the legal situation of his heirs. If the money that is to be made available to the borrower under a bank loan contract has not yet been transferred to his or another identified account, the heirs do not have the right to demand this transfer from the bank. The borrower's claim and the bank's obligation to make money available in accordance with the bank loan contract is strictly limited to these two parties, does not pass to the borrower's heirs and does not constitute a part of the inherited estate. The converse is true with respect to the duty to repay the money made available to the borrower before his death. The heirs inherit the duty to repay sums which were already due at the time of the borrower's death along with any penalty fees for delays in making payments, as well as the duty to pay sums which become due after the borrower's death. However, the bank cannot make any claims against the heirs before a court judgment is issued and comes into force stipulating the acquisition of the estate by specified heirs. Until that moment, there is no certainty as to who the heirs are and who has accepted or rejected the estate.

Finally, the borrower should be aware of the bank's requirement to agree individually, clearly, exhaustively and directly the obligatory elements of the consumer credit contract. These elements may not be regulated in standard contract terms, bank regulations or other general contract conditions. Additionally, 'abstract' control of standard contract terms brings about the entry of a specific unfair contract term in the Register of Abusive Clauses kept by the President of the Office of Competition and Consumer Protection. However, it should be emphasised that a clause which has been entered in the register as abusive, may not be abusive within a different set of standard contract terms. Nevertheless, the fact that a given clause is entered into the Register of Abusive Clauses should cause the borrower to carefully consider before signing a bank loan contract that has a similar clause.

16

Financial contracts and 'junk title' purchases: a matter of (in)correct information

CRISTINA AMATO

Introduction

Financial contracts[1] are mainly characterised by inherent risks undertaken by both parties. Investors in particular should never expect that contracts for the purchase of bonds or other financial titles would be subject to the rule (if any) of 'adequacy of consideration'.[2] Although issues like 'contractual unconscionability' are rarely discussed in relation to these types of contract, the economic balance of a financial contract might become a relevant issue for a court when the 'consideration' exchanged is striking in its unfairness. This was demonstrated in a case of 'bad loans' tendered by a Southern Italian bank:[3] the transaction concerned loans subject to the purchase of 'atypic' titles – those which are expressly created and issued by the bank and unknown to the financial market – as well as the purchase of shares in mutual funds. The consideration for the loan charged to investors consisted of a 6.8 per cent interest rate. The overall economic aim of the financial transaction consisted of inducing investors to borrow money from the bank in order

[1] In this chapter 'financial contracts' include any agreement having as its object financial products as defined by the Italian fundamental financial provisions, L. 24 February 1998, n. 58 (*Testo Unico Finanziario*, hereinafter: TUF): 'a financial product is a financial instruments or any other form of investment product having financial nature, except cash at bank not represented by a financial instrument' (TUF Art. 1, lett. u). This definition also includes 'financial instruments issued by insurance companies, except for life assurance policies [. . .]' (TUF lett.w-*bis*).

[2] It Is generally acknowledged in the Western legal tradition that there is no principle of 'adequacy of consideration', but rather that the contracting parties are free to assess their own deal. See, for example, H. Collins, *The Law of Contract*, 3rd edn (London: Butterworths, 1997) 58; C. Scognamiglio, 'Problemi della causa e del tipo', in V. Roppo, *Trattato del contratto* (Milano: Giuffré, 2006), vol. II, G. Vettori (ed.), 'Il regolamento', 83–191.

[3] Trib. Brindisi, 21.06.2005, *I contratti* (2006), 884, comment of V. Velluzzi, '"4 you": C'è "spazio" per il contratto immeritevole di tutela?'

to purchase 'atypic' titles (named: '4 you') issued by the lending bank itself; the loan would have a high interest rate (6.8 per cent per year), exceeding the titles' output. Once the titles proved to be false in their face value, investors sued for damages and the judge struck down the loan agreement on the basis of its 'total failure of consideration'. According to the first instance court, the unconscionability of the 'bargain', consisting of an excessive inbalance to investors as well as of a striking conflict of interest, completely defeated the existence of a *causa* (economic meaning of the transaction). The court therefore held that the transaction deserved no protection within the legal system and it was declared void.

The scenario described above can, however, be regarded as an 'easy case' of unconscionability; however, the issues discussed in this paper are concerned not with such easy cases but with a 'grey stream' of legal problems, related to negligent misstatements and consequential legal remedies deriving from incomplete, mistaken or late information. As Cherednychenko points out elsewhere in this volume,[4] important triggers for 'unconscionability' in financial contracts include: the information asymmetry inherent in financial transactions; the excessive disadvantages that may affect the weakest party in a financial contract, that is the retailer investor; and the misconduct of the stronger party, that is, the financial providers involved in financial transactions.

It is generally acknowledged that there is an inherent information gap between investors and issuing companies. However, protecting investors from negligent misstatements which may lead to economic detriment is not a problem that can be viewed as a one-sided legal issue. In this special area of financial relationships, duties to disclose are certainly owed by most of the subjects involved: issuing companies and their directors; the company board of directors; brokers; gatekeepers: rating companies; auditors; and supervisory financial authorities. By the same token, a negligent/incorrect/late financial statement shall have different economical effects depending on whom the information fell: title underwriters (who agree to underwrite the issue of titles launched by the lead manager and managers of the company) or retailer investors (responsible for selling financial products onto the secondary market). Assuming that title underwriters in the primary market deal 'at arm's length' – at least as regards the information asymmetry – the main concern in this chapter is

[4] See ch. 13 in this volume, O. Cherednychenko, 'Conceptualising Unconscionability in the Context of Risky Financial Transactions: How to Converge Public and Private Law Approaches?'

to highlight the position – in terms of legal liability – of issuers, retailers and other financial service providers involved in financial business vis-à-vis investors.

For this purpose, the chapter firstly separates the different roles played by different subjects in financial products placement. Secondly, it discusses the legal issues springing from the purchase of titles by retail investors, should the financial products prove not to have the face value advertised in the information statements.

The roles of subjects in financial products placement

The Italian legal system has recently elaborated statutory as well as case law rules in order to regulate the investment market, which are mainly derived from European Directives on investments services.[5] Since the 1990s, Italy has had specific legislation to govern the organisation, duties and liabilities of banks and other subjects operating in the financial market. The main statutory rules regulating financial products are: Law n. 385/1993 (*Testo Unico Bancario* (TUB)); Law n. 58/1998 (*Testo Unico Finanziario*, (TUF)), as amended by Law n. 262/2005 and D.lgs. n. 303/2006, concerning specifically the protection of investors' savings. The range of applications of these rules is wide and complex. This chapter will focus on exploring special aspects of this regulatory frame concerning duties of disclosure in the interest of investors, and the possible legal remedies given to protected purchasers.

Case law in the past decade has developed such a framework, relating mainly to bond issue and purchases of titles in the secondary market.[6] For one thing, investors entering into financial contracts should be conscious of the risks they are undertaking: the procedural correctness of the issuing process of titles, as well as the truthfulness and completeness of the information circulating on the market, are of the utmost

[5] See in particular: Directive 2004/39/EC of the European Parliament and of the Council of 21 April 2004 on markets in financial instruments, amending Council Directives 85/611/EEC and 93/6/EEC; Directive 2000/12/EC of the European Parliament and of the Council (repealing Council Directive 93/22/EEC), implemented by: d.lgs. 17 September 2007, n. 164; Directive 2004/109/EC of the European Parliament and of the Council of 15 December 2004 on the harmonisation of transparency requirements in relation to information about issuers whose securities are admitted to trading on a regulated market (amending Directive 2001/34/EC), implemented by: d.lgs. 6 November 2007, n. 195; Directive 2004/25/EC of the European Parliament and of the Council of 21 April 2004 on takeover bids, implemented by: d.lgs. 19 November 2007, n. 229.

[6] See further, nn. 23, 27, 34–36, 39.

importance for the balance of the purchase contract. In the end, what investors can complain of is not that the inherent risk has come true; but that it was not consciously undertaken. The information process is therefore the central issue in the topic at stake, and the subjects involved in this process enter into play at different levels.

On the first level, the company directors shall take the decision of issuing titles to be placed on the secondary market (Art. 2410 Civil Code (CC)). Under Italian law, the relevant provisions dealing with the directors' role as well as their liability can be found in the Civil Code: see Articles 2380–2396 CC; moreover, most of the TUF discipline involves the directors' and board of directors' activity in issuing companies and financial brokers' companies (Part IV TUF). A company's directors or the board of directors are charged with *general* duties to take reasonable care prescribed by the law and by the company by-laws (Art. 2392 CC). In particular, the strategic role of directors in any decision to be taken on behalf of the company they lead is relevant vis-à-vis: the company itself; the company shareholders or third parties; the company's creditors. In each case the law provides three different types of action in respect of directors' liability: (i) to the company (breach of the duty of care: Arts. 2392–3 CC); (ii) to the company's shareholders or to third parties (breach of the duty not to provoke the shareholders' or a third party's economic loss: Art. 2395 CC – see further below); and (iii) to the creditors (breach of the duty to preserve the company's asset integrity: Art. 2394 CC).

On the second level, it is important to consider the process by which titles are placed on the 'grey market' and onto the secondary market. At this level, many groups of professionals are involved. In particular, the procedures for a bond issue involve three different groups acting in a three-stage process:

1. the managers, who are responsible for managing the issue and who commonly delegate the preparation of the relevant documents to a lead manager. Their task consists of launching the issue and undertaking the quantity, pricing, credit opinion and rating of the issuing company, with the knowledge and evaluation of other subjects joining the launch;
2. the underwriting group, comprising a larger group of financial institutions who agree to underwrite the issue of the title. It is to the underwriting group that the managers and other underwriters transfer the titles within the primary market; thus the underwriting group bear the full risk associated with the financial deal;
3. brokers/retailers who are responsible for selling financial products to private clients, thus reaching the so-called secondary market. The

'selling group' often comprises several hundred professional dealers in securities who place the bonds with outside investors.

It is important to remember that managers and underwriters are usually also members of the selling group. It is at this third stage that the risk of the operation is spread by the retailers to the secondary market; this third stage is also somewhat remote from the analysis and evaluation of titles which is carefully carried out by the lead managers at the time of the launching (stage 1).

In particular, while a wide set of information is provided at the first stage by lead managers when they are offering circular bonds, this information is not carried across to the later stages of the transaction. When bonds are subsequently transferred from retailers to private investors, only a modest abstract of the offering circular is tendered to investors with no control over the abstract, thus depriving the offering circular of all the technical characteristics of the titles that are explained in depth in the offering circular when the product is launched on the 'grey market'. In the Italian system, the statutory provisions dealing with information duties are: Article 21 TUF, as enlarged by Law n. 262/2005; Articles 28, 29 of the regulatory provisions n. 11522 of the Italian regulatory authority (CONSOB), and these are discussed in more detail below.[7] While these provisions refer to the 'brokers' involved in such transactions, defined as banks and other purchasers/retailers of titles in the secondary market, lead managers, underwriters and rating analysts involved in stages 1 and 2 of the transaction are not mentioned.

With regard to rating agencies, their specific purpose is to give an overall assessment of the financial reliability of the issuing company, expressed into alphanumeric characters comprehensible to retail investors. The authoritative judgement of a rating company derives from the professional profile of the rating analysts and the standardised procedures they adopt to achieve a final rating of the issuing company. In the case of a 'solicited rating',[8] the analysts establish a strong fiduciary

[7] See further, n. 30 and associated text.

[8] The 'unsolicited rating' occurs when the rating has not been requested by a company, and the rating company undertakes autonomously the evaluation of titles in order to promote the rating company's own professional profile on financial markets. In this case there is no contractual and fiduciary relationship between the rating company and the issuing company, and the rating is assessed on the basis of general information available on the market for the financial operators at large. Since this is a less accurate and reliable evaluation than that offered in cases of 'solicited rating', it is appropriate that the rating company liability should be less strict.

relationship with their clients, with whom they maintain a close link during the rating process as well as at any subsequent point in the transaction when the original judgment is reviewed; therefore they acquire a deep knowledge of the financial situation of their client, through a significant amount of confidential information. Though this information cannot be disclosed to the public at large, it contributes to the formulation of an overall assessment of the rated company as well as of the titles issued, not restricted to the annual or consolidated financial statements, but involving discretionary evaluations deriving from the deep and confidential insights into the company's activities (for example, information concerning the company's involvement in obtaining a new copyright concerning a revolutionary product; a prospective take-over; or simply information relating to management quality).[9] It cannot be denied, therefore, that all this information, though not disclosed to investors, determines the price of the rated titles through the rating issued, and that these ratings in turn influence the behaviour of several subjects operating in the financial market, including the clients themselves, their creditors and investors.[10]

In cases of public placement of financial titles, Article 97 paragraph 3 of the TUF prescribes that the annual and consolidated financial statements of a company involved in public placement of financial titles shall be submitted to the auditors' revision. Should the auditing company deliver a financial statements report expressing a negative judgment, the public placement cannot take place. As discussed below, no civil liability of the auditing company is expressly prescribed by the Italian TUF: besides criminal penalties,[11] a negligent review of the financial statements has prima facie a very weak impact on investors.[12] Though, having regard to the contractual relationship existing between the issuing company and the auditing company, any negligent performance by the latter would have much greater negative effect on investors than on the issuing company itself.

According to Law n. 58/98 (TUF) the regulatory authority in financial markets (CONSOB) has a pivotal role in controlling the performances of all the parties involved in the issuing process, from the company and any of the subjects representing it to brokers and financial providers.

[9] This procedure has been approved and standardised by the Basilea Agreements, 2004, adopting the 'Core Principles for the Effective Banking Supervision'.

[10] M. Marianello, 'La responsabilità dell'agenzia di rating nei confronti dei terzi risparmiatori', *Resp. civ.*, 7 (2008), 635.

[11] See Articles 175–179 TUF.

[12] See Article 164 TUF., discussed below.

Legal issues after (mis)information is provided

The discussion in the previous section outlined the different role played by each of the financial services providers in the financial services market. From this discussion, it should be clear how their roles may have different effects on the investment services market when it comes to disclosing to investors the relevant data needed in order to fill the information gap and avoid placing retailer investors at an excessive disadvantage, whereby they are unconscionably led to enter into high risk financial contracts. Having considered the subjects taking part in this financial process, this section proceeds to discuss the liability issues attendant on these transactions.

The first group of financial service providers which can be considered includes the directors and the auditors of the issuing company. When considering their duties to provide correct information when launching a product onto the financial market, special consideration must be given to situations involving contracts for the sale/purchase of shares in listed companies. According to Article 114, Law n. 58/1998, a listed company issuing financial products, as well as its holding company, has a duty to inform the public at large about any relevant fact concerning the activities of the company (or its holdings) that might be price sensitive.[13] A number of important issues are raised by this statutory provision. The first issue concerns whether (and when) a company is expected to announce to the public at large that a contract for the sale or purchase of shares (or any other deal) has been carried on between listed companies. As a matter of fact, the law does not list the relevant facts that can be regarded as price sensitive for an issuing company. So, therefore, an important task which must be carried out by the directors is to evaluate whether (and when) a contract for the sale/purchase of shares, as well as the preliminary agreements linked to the sale/purchase,[14]

[13] Art. 114: *Comunicazioni al pubblico* 1. Fermi gli obblighi di pubblicità previsti da specifiche disposizioni di legge, gli emittenti quotati e i soggetti che li controllano informano il pubblico dei fatti che accadono nella loro sfera di attività e in quella delle società controllate, *non di pubblico dominio e idonei, se resi pubblici, a influenzare sensibilmente il prezzo degli strumenti finanziari* (emphasis added).

[14] It is generally acknowledged in Italian scholarship that during preliminary agreement and before a contract has been signed there is no duty to inform under Art. 114 TUF. On the contrary, those who have a role in negotiations between prospective parties to a contract are under a duty of confidentiality in respect of any information acquired in that role. If, despite such duty of confidentiality, information concerning the negotiations has been disclosed to the market, the parties involved have a duty not to publish false information; for example, they would be estopped from denying that negotiations were taking place. See L. Picone, 'Trattative, *due diligence* ed obblighi informativi delle società quotate', *Banca, borsa, titoli di credito*, II (2004), 237–55.

might significantly influence the price of the financial titles issued by the involved (listed) companies. Directors have to contextualise the relevant facts which might possibly be able to influence the financial products' price, taking into account: (a) the quantitative aspect of the activity – for example, the consistency of the assets of the selling/purchasing company; (b) the proprietary assets of the companies involved in the perspective or actual deal – for example, a new holding acquisition, instead of a simple raising of the actual minority share in the company; (c) the strategy of the deal at stake – for example, a holding in a small business might turn into a new entry of a competitor into the market.[15]

A second issue concerns whether (and when) the directors have a duty to disclose to one or more prospective purchasers, confidential information concerning the selling company. Reference is made to the due diligence process (once again according to Art. 114 TUF), especially as regards the sale or purchase of company shares, when the due diligence requirement represents a fundamental pre-condition to the formulation of free and informed consent to the contract. And, in fact, during the negotiations the directors have a duty to disclose to the prospective purchaser any confidential information that shall be part of the prospective contract. At the same time, passing confidential information to people who are not members of the selling company may violate the 'right of privacy' of the target company, and the related duty of care on directors or board of directors prescribed by Article 2392 CC. In other words, during the due diligence process there is a need to balance two different and conflicting interests: the target company's interest to protect its own private business, on one side; and the purchaser's right to acquire all the relevant information in order to achieve a correct and informed consent as to the contract's contents, on the other. Once again, it is the directors' delicate as well as discretionary task to balance these conflicting interests of the target company and the buyer. As a general rule, a duty to disclose rests on the issuing company's directors whenever the information represents a fundamental element of the contract.[16]

[15] See A. Frignani, 'I primi orientamenti della Consob concernenti la diffusione di informazioni "price sensitive" a terzi', *Società*, 9 (1999) 1114.

[16] Once again, during the due diligence process it is the board of directors' difficult task to take into account all the relevant elements: (a) the quality of the information to be disclosed (there may be information that, although undisclosed, cannot be defined as 'confidential'); (b) the purchaser's commitment to enter into a contract; (c) the confidentiality duties undertaken by the parties; (d) the undertakings already assumed by the parties and the actual possibilities to reach a final agreement (for example, whether a letter of intent has been signed or not); (e) the overall importance of the deal (for example, whether a significant amount of shares are to be sold/purchased). See

It is striking that in relation to both of these issues the law does not specify the consequences that result from a breach of the statutory provisions: in other words, it is not at all clear whether damages would be owed to investors should the directors negligently exercise their discretionary duty to inform as set out in Article 114 TUF.

Italian statutory law, the civil code in particular, does, however, provide some general answers. According to Article 2395 CC the board of directors, as well as the individual directors, are liable in the event of the managers' negligent (or fraudulent) behaviour vis-à-vis: (a) the company shareholders; (b) *any third party who has suffered: loss or damage* deriving from the negligent (or fraudulent) behaviour. While liability to shareholders springs from a breach of the contract that exists between the company's management and the company's shareholders, the third party liability is more difficult to understand, as no contractual relationship exists between investors and managing directors. The same problem is raised by Article 164 TUF, according to which auditors are held legally liable vis-à-vis shareholders and *any third party who has suffered loss or damage* deriving from the auditors' negligent performance.[17] Since the law is silent as to the nature of the action that can be brought against directors and auditors, it can alternatively be argued that the action might lie either in tort or in contract. Yet, both arguments are difficult to support in the Italian system: first, as a general rule, to establish tortious liability, plaintiffs have to prove that the financial loss represents 'unfair damage' by the terms and conditions of Article 2043 CC. In particular, a plaintiff must prove that she has been deprived by a defendant of a 'right' or 'interest' which is recognised in law. The second possibility, of contractual liability, is also inappropriate, as contractual liability is limited by the doctrine of 'privity of contract', as stated in Article 1372 CC.[18] Although both arguments have recently been advanced, both in case law and in legal

A. Agostoni, 'L'informazione societaria nei gruppi quotati dopo l'emanazione del d.lgs. 58 del 1998', *Società* (1999) 279; Picone, n. 14 above, 255–61.

[17] Art. 164: '*Responsabilità*. 1. Alla società di revisione si applicano le disposizioni dell'articolo 2407, primo comma, del codice civile. 2. I responsabili della revisione e i dipendenti che hanno effettuato l'attività di revisione contabile sono responsabili, in solido con la società di revisione, per i danni conseguenti da propri inadempimenti o da fatti illeciti nei confronti della società che ha conferito l'incarico e *nei confronti dei terzi danneggiati*' (emphasis added).

[18] Art. 1372 CC states: '1. Il contratto ha forza di legge fra le parti [. . .]. 2. Il contratto non produce effetto rispetto ai terzi che nei casi previsti dalla legge'.

scholarship,[19] the debate on the correct basis of liability remains open. What is clear is that losses suffered as a result of the reasonable reliance on mistaken, incomplete or late information that induced investors to purchase titles is protected in principle, although the basis of the defendant's liability is still fluctuating between contract and tort.[20]

Some further comments can also be made with particular regard to auditing companies, whose specific professional task is to certify the accountability and the financial statements of a company, including expressing a final judgement on both. Once again, there are of course 'easy cases' concerning the auditing company's liability in cases of fraud as well as vis-à-vis the certified company, which are of less interest for the purposes of the discussion in this chapter. In these instances, in fact, there is no difficulty in attributing liability to the auditors, whether as a result of the invalidity of the contract for fraudulent misrepresentation;[21] or imposing criminal penalties in the first instance,[22] or civil penalties for

[19] Art. 2395, para. 2 CC gives a limitation period of five years to bring an action against directors: as the limitation period for the general action in contract is ten years, while the limitation period for the general action in tort is five years, the nature of the special action in Art. 2395, para. 2, should consequently be tortious. But this literal argument does not fully address the issues, leaving questions as to whether the Italian legislator was really aware of the tortious nature of the liability when setting this limitation period; or whether the five-year limitation period should be regarded as a special provision for directors' liability, but not related to any general rule.

[20] From a comparative point of view, the abovementioned Italian statutory provisions are reminiscent of the 'intended beneficiary doctrine' as stated in § 552 of the *American Restatement 2nd on Torts*:

(1) One who, in the course of his business, profession or employment, or in any other transaction in which he has a pecuniary interest, supplies false information for the guidance of others in their business transactions, is subject to liability for pecuniary loss caused to them by their justifiable reliance upon the information, if he fails to exercise reasonable care or competence in obtaining or communicating the information.

(2) Except as stated in Subsection (3), the liability stated in Subsection (1) is limited to loss suffered:

   (a) by the person or one of a limited group of persons for whose benefit and guidance he intends to supply the information or knows that the recipient intends to supply it; and

   (b) through reliance upon it in a transaction that he intends the information to influence or knows that the recipient so intends or in a substantially similar transaction.

(3) The liability of one who is under a public duty to give the information extends to loss suffered by any of the class of persons for whose benefit the duty is created, in any of the transactions in which it is intended to protect them.

[21] *Annullamento per dolo*: see Art. 1439 CC. [22] See Part v of TUF.

breach of contract in the second case. The more interesting question for the purposes of this analysis concerns the auditors' liability vis-à-vis investors, that is, liability to third-party beneficiaries who are not in a contractual relationship with the auditing company. At present, in order to protect investors' reliance on information given to them, Italian jurisprudence[23] and scholars[24] seem to favour – unlike the *Caparo*[25] 'bright non-liability rule' – a triggering of liability in tort in compliance with Article 2043 CC. Nevertheless, as in the case of directors' liability, the legal questions raised fall once again in the so-called 'no-man's land' between tort and contract.

A second group of financial service providers is represented by the rating companies. As the discussion in the previous section has illustrated, the rating companies are responsible for carrying out the difficult task of analytically and critically collecting all the relevant information referring to the credit risk of the issuing company. This is particularly significant in cases of 'solicited rating', when the alphanumeric results made public to the world at large by the rating analysts represent the sum of a critical, though partly discretionary, evaluation of confidential data not available on the market. The role played by the rating analysts can thus be compared to the role of 'financial brokers', whose main concern is to make offers and manage the demand for financial products on the secondary market and whose main duties are set out in Part II of TUF (see in particular: Art. 21, discussed further below).

Since this 'information brokering' is the role of the rating company, it should be regarded as reasonable for other brokers on the retail market, as well as investors, to rely on the information so provided, once the rating has met the secondary market. Yet, although the TUF charges

[23] Cass. 18.07.2002 n. 10403, *Società*, 10 (2002), 1513, comment of R. Salafia, 'Responsabilità extracontrattuale delle società di revisione per danno a terzi'; App. Milano, 07.07.2000, *Banca, borsa, titoli di credito*, II (2003), 319; Trib. Milano, 21.10.1999, *Giur.it.*, 1 (2000), 554; Trib. Milano 18.06.1992, *Giur. it.*, I, 2 (1993), 1, comment of Montalenti 'Responsabilità extracontrattuale della società di revisione per negligente certificazione'.

[24] R. Cozzi, *Tutela dei mercati finanziari e responsabilità delle società di revisione*, (Naples: Jovene, 2002); B. Addante, 'Responsabilità nell'esercizio della revisione contabile', *Danno e resp.*, 2 (2003), 353; P. Casadei, *La responsabilità delle società di revisione*, (Milan: Giuffré, 2000).

[25] *Caparo Industries Plc* v. *Dickman and Others* [1991] 1 WLR 210 HL (per Lord Oliver). On the issue of the auditing company's liability vis-à-vis third party beneficiaries, see recently in the Italian literature: G. M. Buta, 'La responsabilità civile dei revisori nei confronti dei terzi nella *common law*', *Banca, borsa, titoli di credito*, I (2004) 342–90.

information brokers with duties to perform with the utmost care, the only reference to rating analysts made by the TUF (as modified by law n. 262/2005) is to expressly exempt them from any duty to correctly inform or to avoid conflicts of interests.[26] Indeed, dissatisfaction with this statutory position was such that Italian courts[27] (and scholars[28]) have rejected the 'exemption rule', including creating a graduated duty of care, and consequently graduated liabilities, for rating analysts in the different contexts of solicited and unsolicited ratings. In the case of information given by rating analysts to other financial providers in the secondary market there is a contractual relationship between the parties: so, therefore, late, mistaken or incomplete information concerning the credit risk of the issuing company can certainly be submitted to the general discipline of breach of contract. On the other hand, in the case of information which is made available to third party beneficiaries, such as investors, the absence of a direct contractual relationship raises a question concerning the nature of the rating analysts' liability. The debate around the nature and discipline of the 'social contact'[29] can be extended to the issue at stake: it is commonly believed that the reasonable reliance

[26] Art. 14 law n. 262/2005: '(2) il comma 8 dell'art. 114 T.U.F. è sostituito dal seguente':

> 8. I soggetti che producono o diffondono ricerche o valutazioni, *con l'esclusione delle società di rating* [emphasis added], riguardanti gli strumenti finanziari indicati all'articolo 180, comma 1, lettera a), o gli emittenti di tali strumenti, nonché i soggetti che producono o diffondono altre informazioni che raccomandano o propongono strategie di investimento destinate ai canali di divulgazione o al pubblico, devono presentare l'informazione in modo corretto e comunicare l'esistenza di ogni loro interesse o conflitto di interessi riguardo agli strumenti finanziari cui l'informazione si riferisce.

[27] Trib. Pinerolo, 14.10.2005; Trib. Cagliari, 02.01.2006; Trib. Cosenza, 01.03.2006; Trib. Milano, 24.04.2006; Trib. Catania, 05.05.2006; Trib. Parma, 24.05.2007; Trib. Firenze, 06.07.2007: www.ilcaso.it

[28] V. Carbone, 'La responsabilità degli intermediari', *Danno e resp.* (2002) 109; A. Monti, 'Le asimmetrie informative e le attività di rating: una proposta per l'Italia', *Bancaria* (1995) 16; G. Facci, 'Il rating e la circolazione del prodotto finanziario: profili di responsabilità', *Resp. civ.* (2007) 679; C. Mazzoni, 'Osservazioni in tema di responsabilità civile degli analisti finanziari', *Analisi giur.econ.* (2002), 232.

[29] On the so-called 'social contact' liability see C. Castronovo, *La nuova responsabilità civile* (Giuffré, 2006). According to this author and to some sharing his view, there can be situations where, besides the fundamental obligation arising from a contract, there are further obligations arising from 'social contact' in favour of third parties. Besides the case of directors' liability to third parties' investors (Art. 2395 CC quoted hereabove), the most important instances concern the liability of a doctor in a hospital to the patient; or the liability of a teacher in a school to a student: in cases concerning personal injuries, a contract exists between the patient and the hospital, as well as between the student and

of investors on financial information stated by risk management professionals should be protected according to a special discipline, which occupies a 'no-man's land' between contract and tort.

A third group of financial service providers are the brokers who are responsible for placing titles on the secondary market. Several statutory provisions in the TUF (as modified by Law n. 262/2005) regulate the brokers' duties to act correctly vis-à-vis investors. In particular, for the purposes of this chapter it is interesting to consider Article 21 TUF[30] and Articles 28 and 29 of CONSOB regulatory provisions n. 11522 1 July 1998. These rules set out four main duties that are attributed to investment brokers: (1) the duty to use the utmost diligence, and to act honestly and fairly in the (private) interest of investors as well as in the (public) interest of the financial markets; (2) the duty to disclose to investors any relevant information; (3) the duty to obtain from their client-investors any relevant information in order to define their correct risk profile, especially having regard to the inherent risks of the advertised titles in relation to the clients' assets (the 'know your client rule'; 'suitability rule'); (4) the duty to advertise the financial products fairly, clearly and in a non-misleading manner.

Yet, although these statutory provisions seem clear and effective as to the brokers' duties, no reference was made by the law to the nature and to the extent of liability. Indeed, dealing with the well-known scandals of Cirio,[31]

the school. The doctor's or teacher's liability for causing personal injury to a patient or student should therefore spring from the 'social contact' between them, that is a relationship connected to the primary contract though not having contractual nature. See: Cass. 22.01.1999, n. 589, *Resp. civ. prev.*, 3 (1999), 661, comment of M. Forziati, 'La responsabilità contrattuale del medico dipendente: il "contatto sociale" conquista la cassazione'; Cass. S.U., 27.06.2002, n.–9346, *Resp. civ. prev.*, 4–5 (2002), 1022, comment of G. Facci, 'Minore autolesionista, responsabilità del precettore e contatto sociale'. This theory derives from the German doctrine of 'duties of protection' towards third party beneficiaries owed by the parties to a contract: see Larenz, *Lehrbuch des Schuldrechts* (Munich, 1976).

30 Art. 21 (implementing EC Dir. 2003/71):

1. Nella prestazione dei servizi e delle attività di investimento e accessori i soggetti abilitati devono:

(a) comportarsi con diligenza, correttezza e trasparenza, per servire al meglio linteresse dei clienti e per lintegrità dei mercati;
(b) acquisire, le informazioni necessarie dai clienti e operare in modo che essi siano sempre adeguatamente informati;
(c) utilizzare comunicazioni pubblicitarie e promozionali corrette, chiare e non fuorvianti;
(d) disporre di risorse e procedure, anche di controllo interno, idonee ad assicurare.

31 The background to the Cirio bonds case took place in 2002, when the incorporated company, Cirio Finance Luxemburg Ltd, related to an Italian group belonging to

Parmalat,[32] and Argentine[33] bonds, the Italian courts have adopted very different positions on the issues at stake. A first group of decisions opted to find financial contracts for the purchase of 'junk titles' to be invalid, arguing that since the statutory provisions are mandatory in their nature, their breach leads to the radical invalidity (*nullità*) of the agreement;[34] however, others have preferred to employ the doctrine of

Mr Cragnotti and producing food commodities, declared the impossibility of refunding investors bonds previously issued by the company for a total amount of €150 million. As a matter of fact, during the previous years the Cirio group's indebtness towards the banks had increased in different areas of food production. Such indebtness had induced the group to raise up to € 1.25 billion through bonds between 2000 and 2002, for the purpose of: (a) obtaining fresh money through a financial product (bonds) to be directly placed on the European market; and (b) restyling the group's indebtness by postponing the debts' expiry date. It was therefore clear that the main role was played by the Italian banks, which were responsible for placing Cirio's bonds to investors. Instead of selling to qualified investors, the Italian banks sold Cirio's bonds to more than 35,000 private investors, thus transferring the insolvency risk of Cirio's group onto the public at large. From 2003, several actions were filed by private investors or investors' associations against the banks involved in the placement of Cirio bonds. Among the most famous cases, see: Trib. Genova, 15.03.2005, *Danno e resp.*, 5 (2005), 609.

[32] A similar situation arose in the Parmalat cases (another Italian group involved in the food commodities market). Parmalat indebtness exploded in 2000: Italian and international banks were involved in the financial collapse, placing Parmalat bonds to private investors despite being aware of the serious indebtness the Parmalat group was incurring. Once again, the risk of the Parmalat insolvency was distributed onto private investors, while the banks dismissed all titles having no value. See: Trib. Venezia, 17.10.2005, *Giur. comm.*, II (2007), 1252, comment of C. A. Russo, 'Il caso Parmalat: tra conflitto d'interesse del lead manager e tutela risarcitoria'.

[33] In the Argentine cases, the issuer of bonds was the Argentine state. Several Italian banks had advertised these bonds as extremely safe and profitable, thus inducing private investors to the purchase. For case law, see n. 34. See also: V. Roppo, 'La tutela del risparmiatore fra nullità e risoluzione (a proposito di Cirio bond & tango bond)', *Danno e resp.*, 5 (2005), 614.

[34] See with reference to Argentine bonds: Trib. Mantova, 18.03.2004, *Banca, borsa, titoli di credito*, II (2004) 440 comment of D. Maffeis, 'Conflitto di interessi nella prestazione di servizi di investimento: la prima sentenza sulla vendita a risparmiatori di obbligazioni argentine'; see also: *Giur. comm.*, II (2004) 690, comment of Scimeni, 'La prima sentenza italiana sulla vendita di tango bonds'; Trib. Venezia, 22.11.2004, *I Contratti* (2005) 5, commento of D. Maffeis, 'Il dovere di consulenza al cliente nei servizi di investimento e l'estensione del modello al credito ai consumatori (bond argentini, nullità per conflitto di interessi)'; Trib. Firenze, 30.05.2004, *Resp.civ. prev.* (2005) 136, 'reverse convertible' titles; Trib. Milano, 06.062005 and Trib. Ferrara, 25 febbraio 2005, both in *I Contratti*, 2006, 12; Trib. Firenze, 19.04.2005, *Corr. giur.* (2005) 1279; Trib. Avezzano, 23.06.2005 and Trib. Palermo, 26.03.2005, both in *Foro it.*, *I* (2005) 2536.

A second argument leading to the radical invalidity of the financial contract is based on the breach of form requirements: Trib. Genova, 15.03.2005, *Danno e resp.*, 5 (2005), 609.

breach of contract,[35] or have chosen to use the pre-contractual liability doctrine (according to Arts. 1337, 1338 CC)[36] in order to assess the investment broker's liability.[37] After the Cirio, Parmalat and Argentine bonds' cases, this issue has been recently faced by the legislator (L. n. 262/2005, Art. 11, para. 2) who has introduced a new provision in the TUF, that is, Article 100-*bis* dealing with so-called 'indirect public offers'. According to this new provision a public offer originally meant for qualified (that is, professional) investors, and thus not circulating together with an information memorandum, is considered as *void* if it subsequently reaches private investors. This defect of the indirect public offer can be raised by private investors only, dealing outside the scope of his/her professional activity, vis-à-vis any financial brokers (banks in particular) responsible for violating the law by

[35] Trib. Genova, 02.08.2005, *Danno e resp.*, 5 (2005), 618; Trib. Roma, 25.05.2005, *Corr. giur.*, 11 (2005) 1282; Trib. Milano, 25.07.2005, *Nuova giurisprudenza civile commentata*, I (2006) 593, comment of Dellacasa, 'Negoziazione di titoli obbligazionari e insolvenza dell'emittente: quale tutela per il risparmiatore non adeguatamente informato?'

[36] Cass. 29.09.2005, n. 19024, in *Danno e resp.*, 2006, 25, comment of V. Roppo, G. Afferni, 'Dai contratti finanziari al contratto in genere: punti fermi della Cassazione sulla nullità virtuale e responsabilità precontrattuale', *Danno e resp.*, 1 (2006), 30 ss.; Trib. Taranto, 27 ottobre 2004, *Diritto e Giustizia*, n. 46 (2004), 102.

[37] Pre-contractual liability represents an original and innovative peculiarity of the Italian Civil Code. Art. 1337 CC prescribes a general duty to bargain in good faith on the prospective parties of a contract that shall never be entered into ('Le parti, nello svolgimento delle trattative o nella formazione del contratto, devono comportarsi secondo buona fede'). Art. 1338 CC applies such general duty to bargain in good faith to cases where a contract has been stipulated, but has shown itself to be ineffective for some reason: in this case the party who knew, or should have known, of the reason that rendered the contract ineffective is held liabile to the innocent party who resonably relied on the validity of the contract ('La parte che, conoscendo o dovendo conoscere l'esistenza di una causa di invalidità del contratto, non ne ha dato notizia all'altra parte è tenuta a risarcire il danno da questa risentito per aver confidato, senza sua colpa, nella validità del contratto'). The breach of such duty to act in good faith gives the innocent party a right to reliance damages. The contents of the duty are very broadly defined by the courts under three main headings: (1) fair dealing; (2) duty to disclose relevant information to the other party; (3) a duty of confidentiality. As to the nature and discipline of the general duty to bargain in good faith, case law and literature do not agree, but the majority of the opinions consider this liability as tortious. See: G. Grisi, *L'obbligo precontrattuale di informazione* (Jovene, 1990); R. Sacco and G. De Nova, *Il contratto*, vol. 2, in *Trattato di diritto civile* diretto da R. Sacco, (Turin, 2004) 223 ff.; V. Roppo, 'L'informazione precontrattuale: spunti di diritto italiano, e prospettive di diritto europeo', *Riv. dir. priv.* (2004), 747; P. Gallo, 'Resp, precontrattuale: il quantum', *Riv. dir. civ.*, I (2004), 487 (with complete references to Italian case law on pre-contractual liability). See also: Cass. S.U. 10.07.2003, n. 19896; and Cass. 11.9.2003, n. 13390, *Resp. civ. prev.*, 4 (2004), 400.

placing on the secondary market titles originally offered to qualified investors.

And yet, it should also be underlined that a recent decision delivered by the full board of the Corte di Cassazione[38] has resolved the legal issue under debate applying different principles and rules. According to the highest Italian Court, information duties belong to the so-called 'rules of fair dealing'. Consequently, the proper remedies to be applied to the breach of those rules cannot stand on the validity/invalidity of the contract; rather they must stand on the content of the agreement as related to the defendant's behaviour. This leads to the conclusion that the broker's liability depends, as to its nature and discipline, on the content of the information as well as on the very moment it was delivered. In sum, the financial broker's liability can be either pre-contractual, if it concerns a conduct and a set of information delivered *before* signing the purchase of specific titles; or it may be contractual, if it concerns the financial provider's conduct *in the course of the performance* of the purchase contract, resulting in a breach of contract. In both cases damages shall be awarded to the client-investor: reliance damages, in the former instance; expectation damages in the latter.

Finally, it is important to take account of the financial regulatory authority's liability. The CONSOB has deep and effective supervisory powers over the broker's activities (Part II TUF) as well as on the issuing companies (Part IV TUF). Yet, once again, no specific rule has been prescribed as regards the authority's liability vis-à-vis investors. However, in a famous decision, the Supreme Court (Corte di Cassazione)[39] held CONSOB liable for failing to exercise a deep control over the bonds issuing process, where the face value of the bonds dropped dramatically soon after sale on the secondary market. In this case, investors were oriented to the purchase of the 'junk titles' by mistaken and incomplete reports, which had been signed by directors and auditors. According to the Italian judges the supervisory authority was not only under a duty to supervise the procedural correctness of the bonds issue; it should also have checked the substantial reliability of the information before it was circulated on the market. As a result, the financial losses suffered by the purchasers were qualified as 'unfair' for the purposes of the terms and conditions set out in Article 2043 CC. The rationale underlying

[38] Cass, Sez. Un., 19.12.2007, n. 26724, *Danno e resp.*, 4 (2008), 525, comments of V. Roppo: 'La nullità virtuale del contratto dopo la sentenza Rordorf'; and Bonaccorsi, 'Le sezioni unite e la responsabilità degli intermediari finanziari'.

[39] Cass., I sez. civ., 03.03.2001, n. 3132, *Foro it.*, I (2001), 1139, comment of A. Palmieri, 'Responsabilità per omessa o insufficiente vigilanza: si affievolisce l'immunità della pubblica amministrazione'. See also Trib. Roma, 26.07.2004, *Foro it.*, I (2005), 560.

this approach demonstrates, once again the court's recognition of the need to protect the reasonable and detrimental reliance of third parties acting on such information, although there remain some concerns regarding the random search for a 'deep pocket' to protect investors' detrimental reliance.

Conclusions

There are three key points to emphasise at the end of this overall review. First, that protection of purchasers in unconscionable financial transactions should focus on the nature and consequences deriving from reliance liability triggered by negligent misstatements on economical information that induce investors to enter into the sale/purchase of 'junk titles'. Absent special statutory provisions on the liability issue, the relevant criteria (particularly as regards the award of damages) can be derived from the general theory of obligations (liability in tort; duties to protect the intended beneficiary; or social contact theory). Reliance liability should arise when the intended beneficiary of a professional service is negligently induced to act to his or her detriment by reasonably relying on the high professional standard of qualified professionals. However, as the discussion above has demonstrated, a more practical problem in this context concerns the assessment of damages.

Second, the complex process underlying the issue and placement of financial titles involves different professional profiles, whose liability should be recognised at different levels. Lead managers, gatekeepers, rating analysts, auditors, regulatory authorities and retailer brokers all play a role in inducing investors to make unconscionable financial titles purchases, in reliance on their professional skills. While the interrelationships between the roles of these actors might suggest that joint and several liability between the parties would be appropriate, this would not in fact help in this context, as it is important to reflect the different roles in a graduated scale of liability for each player in the provision of these financial products. Consequently, a proportionate liability perspective should instead be adopted, which operates by isolating the duties attendant on each role and, further, by controlling for the remoteness of negligent conduct by each party vis-à-vis the investors' economic loss.[40]

[40] A model of 'modified proportional liability' has recently been adopted in the United States. According to Art. 21(g)(4)(A)(ii) of the Exchange Security Act, 1934, as amended by the Private Securities Litigation Reform Act (PSLRA) 1995, in case of liability for damages to investors based on recklessness, or negligence or strict liability of the auditing company, it can be charged only with liability deriving from its own conduct, and no more.

Third, it is noted that civil liability remedies do not provide the only possible answer to the protection of investors against unconscionable financial contracts: in addition, one can consider how alternative remedies subsequent to the occurrence of damages (for example, stricter criminal penalties), preventive measures (rules of conduct) or collateral sanctions (reputational risks) may be able to support and protect investors more effectively than civil liability rules. There is evidence to suggest that Italian law has recently begun to move towards the American model of the class action suit, as an efficient instrument of access to justice, in contrast to the expensive and exhausting individual legal actions which are available to investors under Article 140-*bis* of the Italian Consumer Code, as reflected in Article 32-*bis* of TUF. Though Article 140-*bis* has not yet come into force,[41] there is great interest in this provision within Italian scholarship,[42] as it introduces a collective action in favour of consumers and (through Art. 32-*bis* TUF) for investors as well.[43]

[41] The entry into force of this provision has been postponed to 1 July 2009: see Art. 2, para. 446, L. 24 December 2007, n. 244.

[42] R. Lener 'L'introduzione della *class action* nell'ordinamento italiano del mercato finanziario', *Giur. comm.*, II (2005), 270; F. Camilletti, 'L'azione collettiva risarcitoria: profili processuali', *I Contratti*, 5 (2008), 639; G. D'Alfonso, 'La tutela risarcitoria delle pretese seriali tra "azioni di classe" ed "azioni collettive". Il nuovo Art. 140-*bis* del Codice del consumo (Seconda parte)', *Studium iuris* (2008), 665; L. Frata '"Class actions" e "azioni collettive risarcitorie": un primo confronto', *Danno e resp.*, 3 (2008), 439; C. Consolo, 'E' legge una disposizione sull'azione collettiva risarcitoria: si è scelta la via svedese dello "opt-in" anziché quella danese dello "opt-out" e il fitro ("L'inutil precauzione")', *Corr. giur.* , 1 (2008), 5; G. Costantino, 'La tutela collettiva risarcitoria: note a prima lettura dell'art. 140 bis cod. consumo', *Foro it.*, V (2008), c. 17; M. Bove, 'Azione collettiva: una soluzione all'italiana lontana dalle esperienze straniere più mature', *Guida al dir.*, 4 (2008), 11.

[43] The main features of the 'Italian' class actions are that: (1) class actions are admitted in three situations only, that is: (i) If standard contracts are involved; (ii) If there is the professional's tortious liability; (iii) If there is a violation of competition laws; (2) there must be a plurality of plaintiffs (*numerosity requirement*: see Rule 23 of the American Rules of Civil Procedure); (3) class actions can be filed by representative associations only, never by individual consumers/investors; (4) consumers/investors are free to enter into a class action once they belong to the 'class' and once they have knowledge of it (*opt in* system, as opposed to the *opt out* choice of Rule 23 of the American Rules of Civil Procedure); (5) the first instance Court shall provide the 'certification' of the class action, in accordance with the requirements listed in the law; and (6) the final decision of the first instance court may recognise the existence of consumers'/investors' rights, without assessing damages. The assessment of damages shall be made by the defendant, in accordance with the criteria and minimum amount set by the first instance court.

17

Kickback payments under MiFID: substantive or procedural standard of unconscionability?

AXEL HALFMEIER AND PETER ROTT

1. Outline

In this chapter, we discuss problems related to kickback payments in financial transactions. After a short introduction into the nature of kickback payments, we identify these problems and briefly address solutions that have been discussed under German law (section 2). We then turn to EC legislation, in particular Directive 2004/39/EC on Markets in Financial Instruments[1] (the MiFID Directive) and subsequent instruments that are meant to elaborate this Directive and demonstrate the way in which the Directive addresses kickback payments as 'inducements' (section 3). While the new rules have been the subject of heated debate between the banks and consumer groups, the German implementation of EC legislation is, at first glance, scandalously bank-friendly (section 4). In contrast, we propose to use findings from research on behavioural finance to interpret the law correctly and to propose a stricter reading of the EC rules on inducement and implementing legislation (section 5). We also discuss whether more stringent national rules on kickback payments are still allowed following the adoption of the MiFID Directive (section 6). Finally, we return to the general issue of deciding between procedural and substantive mechanisms to protect customers of investment services against unconscionable transactions (section 7).

2. Kickback payments in financial transactions and related problems

Kickback payments

First of all, what are kickback payments? Here we are looking at investors who use a bank or any other investment firm (for simplicity's sake, we

[1] O.J. 2004 L 145/1.

will refer to banks) to get advice with regard to investment decisions – such as the purchase of stocks, shares in investment funds or other investment instruments. Today, it is general practice that the issuer of such financial instruments pays a commission to the bank if the bank manages to sell this issuer's products. This would be a kickback payment – in the broad sense of the word, although some writers use it more technically[2] – since part of the money paid by the customer in exchange for the investment instrument is 'kicked back' to the bank.

At first glance, kickback payments are beneficial to everybody. The issuer of financial instruments uses them to increase its sales, the bank makes extra money from them, and the customer gets free advice from the bank since the bank does not charge the customer with fees for advice but instead hopes to get revenue from the kickback payments.

There are however some serious problems regarding this practice, namely conflicts of interest and hidden fees, which are described below. And although there are some technicalities of banking law here, the big issue behind the regulation of kickback payments is relevant to many other areas of financial services (and other services): can the free and informed choice of services be guaranteed through information about the relevant circumstances? Such an approach would involve a 'procedural' standard of unconscionability. Alternatively, should certain dealings be prohibited as such, regardless of the level of information: should we adopt a 'substantive' standard of unconscionability?

Conflicts of interest

The first problem with kickback payments is a structural conflict of interest for the bank.[3] On the one hand, it should, or rather is contractually obliged to, give good advice to its customer regarding the choice of the most appropriate investment instruments and the best investment strategy for that customer. On the other hand, the bank aims to make profits and may therefore be tempted to recommend those investments

[2] P. O. Mülbert, 'Auswirkungen der MiFID-Rechtsakte für Vertriebsvergütungen im Effektengeschäft der Kreditinstitute', *Zeitschrift für das gesamte Handelsrecht*, 172 (2008), 170, at 174.

[3] In economic terms this is a principal/agent problem, see S. Grundmann and W. Kerber, 'Information Intermediaries and Party Autonomy – The Example of Securities and Insurance Markets', in S. Grundmann, W. Kerber and S. Weatherill (eds.), *Party Autonomy and the Role of Information in the Internal Market* (Berlin: de Gruyter, 2001), 264, at 277.

to the customer that result in a maximum commission or kickback to the bank but are not in the customer's best interest. This is easily possible since the customer is dependent on the bank's advice due to the complexity of financial products, which is prominently recognised in recital (3) of the MiFID Directive.[4] Possible reactions by the legislator or the courts to such a conflict of interest are, essentially, an outright prohibition of kickback payments or similar disincentives, or disclosure requirements.

(a) Prohibition of kickback payments

An almost complete prohibition of kickback payments exists in the law on advertising medical products. Article 94(1) of Directive 2001/83/EC states that where medicinal products are being promoted to persons qualified to prescribe or supply them, no gifts, pecuniary advantages or benefits in kind may be supplied, offered or promised unless they are inexpensive and relevant to the practice of medicine or pharmacy. Doctors and other persons who are qualified to prescribe or supply medicinal products shall not solicit or accept any inducement, according to Article 94(3). The obvious reason for this prohibition is to avoid any risk of inappropriate medical treatment caused by financial inducements. In contrast, no explicit prohibition of kickback payments exists under European or German law on financial instruments.

(b) A customer's claim to have kickback payments reimbursed?

A similarly radical solution would consist in a rule according to which commissions or kickback payments must be reimbursed. In fact, there is an ongoing discussion in German academic literature on whether or not such a rule can be derived from the general rules of the German Civil Code regarding the law of mandate.[5] Under the law of mandate, the mandatee is required to hand over everything he or she receives out of

[4] See, e.g., C. Brömmelmeyer, 'Der Königsweg der Information? Informations- und Beratungspflichten auf Märkten für Finanzinstrumente nach der Richtlinie 2004/39/EG', in T. Siegel *et al.* (eds.), *Unternehmungen, Versicherungen und Rechnungswesen: Festschrift zur Vollendung des 65. Lebensjahres von Dieter Rückle* (Berlin: Duncker & Humblot, 2006), 13, at 17 f.

[5] See, e.g., I. Koller, '§31', in H.-D. Assmann and U.H. Schneider (eds.), *Wertpapierhandelsgesetz*, 4th edn (Cologne: O. Schmidt, 2006), margin nos. 18, 83 and 135 (in favour of transfer to customer); against W. Hadding, 'Sind Vertriebsvergütungen von Emittenten an Kreditinstitute geschäftsbesorgungsrechtlich herauszugeben?', *Zeitschrift für Wirtschaftsrecht*, 29 (2008), 529, at 538; Mülbert, n. 2 above, at 206 (both against transfer to customer).

the performance of the mandate:[6] a rule that was meant, from the outset, to ensure that conflicts of interests are avoided since the mandatee has nothing to gain from performing the mandate. The mandator's right to the reimbursement of commissions can, however, be waived in the contract.[7] Thus, this right would be of particular importance in older cases where kickback payments were not disclosed. In contrast, investment firms could get around the problem in the future, provided that they disclose receipt of kickback payments.

(c) Disclosure

The most modest approach is disclosure. The German Federal Court, for example, recently held that banks or other intermediaries in financial services have to disclose the amount of kickbacks they receive before the client makes his or her investment decision. If they fail to do so, they are liable for damages in the sense that the customer may reverse his investment decision at the bank's risk.[8]

Hidden costs

The second problem associated with kickback payments is that unless disclosed to the customer, they represent hidden costs of the respective investment instrument and may thus mislead the customer in the evaluation of the value of that instrument.[9] Hidden costs have, in particular, been discussed in the context of investment in overpriced real property, or real property funds, since excessive and undisclosed kickback payments were ubiquitous in this area. Again, there is some German case law on this issue, although German courts have been reluctant to hold that contracts are void due to such hidden costs.

The courts' starting point is that the law does not protect people from paying more than the price that is equivalent to the objective value of a good or service. Bad bargains are enforceable unless they constitute immoral bargains under §138 of the German Civil Code (BGB). Under normal

[6] §667 of the Civil Code reads: 'The mandatee is obliged to surrender to the mandator everything received to carry out the mandate and what he has obtained from the contract for services.'

[7] See C. Kumpan and A. Hellgardt, 'Haftung der Wertpapierdienstleistungsunternehmen nach Umsetzung der EU-Richtlinie über Märkte für Finanzinstrumente (MiFID)', *Der Betrieb*, 59 (2006), 1714, at 1718.

[8] BGH, 19 December 2006, *Neue Juristische Wochenschrift*, 60 (2007), 1876.

[9] See also U. Kulke, 'Anmerkung', *Zeitschrift für Immobilienrecht*, 9 (2005), 726, at 727.

circumstances, bargains are immoral, in German case law, where the purchase price exceeds objective value by 100 per cent. Hidden kickback payments may be taken into account in this calculation but even a kickback payment of 50 per cent may only lead to a purchase price that exceeds objective value by 80 per cent and which is therefore not immoral.[10]

Otherwise, hidden costs may have to be disclosed where the customer is particularly vulnerable, and this has been accepted by the Federal Court in cases where intermediaries used prospectuses describing the investment in detail but failed to disclose the kickback payments. In these cases, the Federal Court argued that a customer who has no other means of assessing the quality of the investment relies on the information being comprehensive. The non-disclosure of kickback payments – where their scale is unusual or exceeds the level disclosed in the prospectus – was held to be a breach of pre-contractual obligations and led to a claim for damages. The normal cost of the distribution of an investment product was estimated by the Supreme Court at 15 per cent of the purchase price.[11]

The investor as a consumer – or: what is not the problem

We should also separate the problem of kickback payments from other consumer law problems which may occur in financial transactions. Although one may call an investor a consumer – as the German Federal Court has done[12] and as the MiFID Directive implies by mentioning consumer organisations' rights of appeal[13] – the MiFID rules are not designed to protect consumers against a surprising approach by traders, or against pressure applied at the doorstep as seen in the junk property

[10] See BGH, 14 March 2003, *Neue Juristische Wochenschrift*, 56 (2003), 1811. For an analysis of earlier case law: H. G. Graf Lambsdorff, 'Die Pflicht der Kreditinstitute zur Angabe von verdeckten Innenprovisionen', *Zeitschrift für Immobilienrecht*, 7 (2003), 705 ff.

[11] BGH, 12 February 2004, *Entscheidungen des Bundesgerichtshofs in Zivilsachen (BGHZ)*, 158 (2004), 110, confirmed by BGH, 28 July 2005, *Zeitschrift für Immobilienrecht*, 9 (2005), 722. The figure of 15 per cent was criticised in academic writing as being overly high, although it appears to be common practice in the investment in property business (see also OLG Munich, 7 February 2008, *Wertpapier-Mitteilungen*, 62 (2008), 581 ff., and K.-G. Loritz, 'Innenprovisionen bei Kapitalanlagen, insbesondere beim Immobilienvertrieb', *Wertpapier-Mitteilungen*, 54 (2000), 1831 ff.). The problem with the notion 'common practice' is of course that it is still unknown to the customer since we are talking of hidden costs. See Kulke, n. 9 above, at 727.

[12] BGH, 23 October 2001, *Neue Juristische Wochenschrift*, 55 (2002), 368, at 369.

[13] See Art. 52 of Directive 2004/39/EC.

(*Schrottimmobilien*) cases, amongst others, those of *Heininger*,[14] *Schulte*[15] and *Crailsheimer Volksbank*.[16] MiFID is also unrelated to the abuse of a personal relationship that has found much attention in the field of family guarantees. Instead, we are looking at a bank's customer who freely decides to invest and to approach a bank for that reason.[17]

Accordingly, the notion of the consumer as a person who is especially vulnerable does not really apply in the MiFID context of inducements. The MiFID rules, including those on inducements, apply regardless of the role or identity of the bank's customer. They do not differentiate, for example, between natural and legal persons as customers, or 'clients' in the language of MiFID. Although MiFID otherwise contains specific rules regarding different types of transactions and transacting parties,[18] the rules on conflicts of interest are not limited to 'consumer' transactions. We are therefore not talking about 'consumer law' in the sense that it requires a specific consumer definition.

The MiFID inducement regime

We do not, at this point, want to go into the fine detail of the German approaches to kickback payments but rather to look at the regime of the MiFID Directive that has now been implemented in Germany and most other Member States. MiFID itself does not use the term 'inducement', but speaks generally of 'conflicts of interests' which shall be identified, avoided if possible and disclosed where necessary by the investment firms (Article 18 MiFID). In addition, an investment firm must always act 'honestly, fairly and professionally in accordance with the best interests of its clients' (Article 19 (1) MiFID). What the term 'acting honestly, fairly and professionally in accordance with the best interests of its

14 ECJ, 13 December 2001, Case C-481/99, *Georg Heininger and Helga Heininger* v. *Bayerische Hypo- und Vereinsbank AG* [2001] ECR I–9945.

15 ECJ, 25 October 2005, Case C-350/03 *Elisabeth Schulte, Wolfgang Schulte* v. *Deutsche Bausparkasse Badenia AG* [2005] ECR I-9215.

16 ECJ, 25 October 2005, Case C-229/04 *Crailsheimer Volksbank eG* v. *Klaus Conrads, Frank Schulzke und Petra Schulzke-Lösche, Joachim Nitschke* [2005] ECR I-9273.

17 Although banks do employ pressure selling methods, trying to persuade customers to invest.

18 See recitals (31) and (41), and also Art. 24 of Directive 2004/39/EC. For an account see, e.g., C. Duve and M. Keller, 'MiFID: Die neue Welt des Wertpapiergeschäfts', *Betriebs-Berater*, 61 (2006), 2425, at 2427 ff.; R. Kasten, 'Das neue Kundenbild des § 31a WpHG – Umsetzungsprobleme nach MiFID & FRUG', *Zeitschrift für Bank- und Kapitalmarktrecht*, 7 (2007), 261 ff.

clients' means is elaborated in the MiFID Implementing Directive 2006/73/EC.[19] This Directive is also called the 'Level 2' Directive since, in the 'Lamfalussy process',[20] the MiFID is supposed to provide general principles – the 'level 1' – which are then broken down to more specific rules by the European Commission in such 'level 2' directives. There is also a third level, which comprises the informal recommendations issued by the 'Committee of European Securities Regulators' (CESR).[21] These are not legally binding but of high practical relevance.[22]

The level 2 regulation of inducements is enshrined in Article 26 of the Implementing Directive 2006/73/EC:

> Member States shall ensure that investment firms are not regarded as acting honestly, fairly and professionally in accordance with the best interests of a client if, in relation to the provision of an investment or ancillary service to the client, they pay or are paid any fee or commission, or provide or are provided with any non-monetary benefit, other than the following:
>
> (a) a fee, commission or non-monetary benefit paid or provided to or by the client or a person on behalf of the client;
>
> (b) a fee, commission or non-monetary benefit paid or provided to or by a third party or a person acting on behalf of a third party, where the following conditions are satisfied:
>
> (i) the existence, nature and amount of the fee, commission or benefit, or, where the amount cannot be ascertained, the method of calculating that amount, must be clearly disclosed to the client, in a manner that is comprehensive, accurate and understandable, prior to the provision of the relevant investment or ancillary service;
>
> (ii) the payment of the fee or commission, or the provision of the non-monetary benefit must be designed to enhance the quality of the relevant service to the client and not impair compliance with the firm's duty to act in the best interests of the client;
>
> (c) proper fees which enable or are necessary for the provision of investment services, such as custody costs, settlement and exchange fees, regulatory levies or legal fees, and which, by their nature, cannot

19 OJ 2006 L 241/26.

20 See the Final Report of the Committee of Wise Men on the Regulation of European Securities Markets of 15 February 2001, available at ec.europa.eu/internal_market/securities/docs/lamfalussy/wisemen/final-report-wise-men_en.pdf. See also Duve and Keller, n. 18 above, at 2425 f.

21 The CESR was established by a Commission Decision of June 2001. See also EC Doc. IP/01/792.

22 See also Duve and Keller, n. 18 above, at 2426.

> give rise to conflicts with the firm's duties to act honestly, fairly and professionally in accordance with the best interests of its clients.
>
> Member States shall permit an investment firm, for the purposes of point (b)(i), to disclose the essential terms of the arrangements relating to the fee, commission or non-monetary benefit in summary form, provided that it undertakes to disclose further details at the request of the client and provided that it honours that undertaking.

Accordingly, inducements are defined as payments or non-monetary benefits given to the bank or paid by the bank in relation to investment services provided to the client. In practice, such non-monetary benefits include access to the issuer's research or databases which can in turn be used by the bank for its own purposes.

It is important to note that Article 26 generally regards inducements as being not in the client's best interest. Therefore, they are in principle prohibited under Article 19(1) MiFID. From this prohibition there are only three exceptions in point (a) to (c) of Article 26 of the Implementing Directive. These have been interpreted by the CESR in a recommendation on inducements of May 2007.[23]

Transaction fees and costs

The most obvious of these exceptions is Article 26(c) which allows for the payment of 'proper fees' that are necessary for the provision of the investment service offered by the bank. Therefore, if the bank pays or gets paid for certain transaction costs associated with the service provided by the bank this is not a prohibited inducement. However, the commissions or kickbacks we are talking about clearly do not fall under this category since they do not aim to reimburse specific costs but are instead designed to reward the sale of certain instruments.

Fees paid by or on behalf of the client

The second exception is Article 26(a), and it is a little less obvious. It states that fees paid to the bank 'by or on behalf of the client' are not considered to be prohibited inducements. Where the client consciously and directly pays something to the bank for the service he contracted for, there are no hidden costs and no conflicts of interest. This is, however,

[23] CESR, 'Inducements under MiFID', CESR Recommendations May 2007, CESR/07-228b, available at www.cesr.eu/index.php?docid=4608.

less clear in cases where somebody else pays something to the bank 'on behalf of the client'. In Germany, some investment firms have tried to use this phrase to legitimise kickback payments by inserting language into the respective contract forms according to which commissions paid to the bank are paid 'on behalf of the client', arguing that kickback payments ultimately come out of the client's pocket.[24] This strategy is obviously unacceptable since it would defeat the purpose of Article 26 if all inducements were allowed simply by a small change in the issuer's contractual terms. The term 'on behalf of the client' therefore cannot be interpreted as meaning the issuer but applies only to other persons who may be involved in the dealings, such as the client's attorney or other representative.[25]

Inducements allowed under circumscribed circumstances

Apart from such creative readings of Article 26(a), the most problematic provision is Article 26(b) which allows commissions given to the bank by 'third parties' under specific circumstances. Here, we are in the typical kickback situation and therefore the interpretation of this rule is decisive for the future of kickback payments in the European banking and finance landscape.

The two conditions for legal kickback payments may be called 'disclosure' and 'quality improvement without impairment'. The disclosure requirement is enshrined in Article 26(b)(i) of Directive 2006/73/EC. It requires clear disclosure to the client of the 'existence, nature and amount of the fee, commission or benefit' including its methods of calculation where applicable. This information must be given prior to the provision of the relevant investment service so that the customer has a chance to include this information in his or her decision regarding the choice of investment instruments.

(a) Disclosure

The disclosure obligation adds another set of documents to each financial transaction and it is doubtful whether clients will in fact read the respective documents and adjust their decisions accordingly. In addition, Article 26 allows for a disclosure of the 'essential terms' of the

[24] See discussion in F. Schumacher, 'Rückvergütungszahlungen von Investmentgesellschaften an Kreditinstitute', *Zeitschrift für Bank- und Kapitalmarktrecht*, 7 (2007), 447–9.

[25] Ibid., at 449, and see also CESR, n. 21 above, n. 8 at p. 6.

inducements 'in summary form' provided that further details are disclosed at the client's request. Again, it is unclear what 'summary form' means and whether clients will really make use of the possibility of asking for further information. The CESR recommendations state that a 'generic disclosure which explains merely that the firm will or may receive' inducements was not sufficient. Instead – according to the CESR – the investor must be able to relate the disclosure to the particular service in question.[26]

(b) Quality improvement without impairment

In view of these factual problems with disclosure, it is noteworthy that Directive 2006/73/EC contains a second condition for the legality of inducements, which is of a substantive nature. Article 26(b)(ii) Directive 2006/73/EC requires that the payment of the commission 'must be designed to enhance the quality of the relevant service to the client and not impair compliance with the firm's duty to act in the best interests of the client'. This requirement again consists of two sub-conditions: the 'design to enhance quality of the relevant service', and the requirement that the firm's compliance with its duties towards the client is not negatively affected.

What kind of inducements would be able to enhance the quality of the service provided? Clearly, such quality improvement could be the result of non-monetary benefits. If – as mentioned above – an issuer lets the bank use its research facilities, research results or databases, this can enhance the quality of the investment advice given by the bank. And would it impair compliance with the firm's duty to act in the interest of its client? Probably not if the non-monetary benefit is given unconditionally, that is, regardless of whether or not the bank recommends or sells the issuer's instruments. If it is attached to such conditions, then this second condition of non-impairment becomes less clear and must be discussed in detail later. But what is the situation with monetary inducements – the kickback payments? Can they be 'designed to enhance the quality of the service'? Certainly not in a direct way, since the ability of a bank employee to make or recommend good investment decisions is independent of what money the bank gets later on. So there is already a big difference between monetary benefits and non-monetary benefits, the latter being able to directly improve the bank's consulting quality.

[26] CESR, n. 23 above, box 6 at p. 11.

In contrast, the banks argue that since they must spend money on staff and offices, their service quality will improve if they earn money to pay staff and facilities, and improve even more if they receive more kickback payments so that they can hire more or better staff and improve their facilities.[27] In essence, what is claimed is that payments are in an indirect way designed, or even necessary, to provide a certain service, especially if the customer is not willing to pay directly for that service through fees. This argument is not a very good interpretation of Article 26(b)(ii) since that norm speaks of payments that are 'designed to enhance quality' – which usually means that their main purpose is to improve quality which probably is not the case with kickback payments. On the other hand, the European legislator has obviously not intended to prohibit kickback payments completely. Since the EC has not done so, one has to admit that even monetary payments may be 'designed to enhance the quality of the relevant service' in the terms of Article 26.

This interpretation is supported by recital (39) of Directive 2006/73/EC which is often cited in this context as if it were the law[28] and not only a source of interpretation.[29] Recital (39) explicitly addresses the receipt of commissions by an investment firm 'in connection with investment advice or general recommendations' and states that such payments should be considered as 'designed to enhance the quality of the service' as long as the advice or recommendations 'are not biased as a result of the . . . commission'. Technically, what is the effect of this rule – if it is one – on Article 26(b)(ii) of the same Directive? The recital says that one condition (quality-enhancement) shall be considered to be met if the other condition is met (unbiased service in the client's best interest). This means that under the circumstances envisaged by recital (39), the requirement of a quality-enhancing effect becomes irrelevant, and only the unbiased-service requirement remains as the test of the lawfulness of the inducement. Obviously, such interpretation of Article 26(b)(ii) and recital (39) offends against the golden rule of interpretation that one must assume that the legislator does not include terms in the law that are entirely meaningless. Thus, the two requirements of quality enhancement and unimpaired decision-making must be kept separate.

[27] M. Rozok, 'Tod der Vertriebsprovisionen oder Alles wie gehabt?', *Zeitschrift für Bank- und Kapitalmarktrecht*, 7 (2007), 217, 221.

[28] See, for example, CESR, n. 23 above, at no. 20 ff.

[29] Which triggers once more the question of the logic and the legal nature of recitals in EC legislation.

(c) When do kickback payments impair compliance with the bank's duties towards its client?

The remaining question is therefore whether and under what conditions inducements do 'not impair compliance with the firm's duty to act in the best interest of the client'. Unfortunately, neither the directive nor the CESR recommendations give much guidance on this. The CESR recommendations only give a list of factors to be considered in answering this question.[30] These factors include the specific type of the service provided to the client (including special agreements), whether there will be incentives for the bank not to act in the client's interest and the relationship between the bank and the entity providing the inducement.

None of these factors is helpful in a simple everyday situation where a customer shows up in his bank and wishes advice on how to invest his inheritance of 100,000 Euros and where the bank receives inducements from all kinds of investment entities. A German commentator remarked that the quality of the CESR recommendations was ridiculously low and that an inbuilt defect of the Lamfalussy procedure was that it 'listens only to the frogs when the location of the frog pond is discussed'.[31]

The German implementation of Directive 2006/73/EC

Under the MiFiD regime, even the Implementing Directive 2006/73/EC has to be implemented by the Member States. Germany did so in its Securities Trade Act (*Wertpapierhandelsgesetz*; WpHG) which was amended in December 2007 to incorporate the rules discussed above. The act now contains a new §31d WpHG which mainly copies the language of Article 26 of Directive 2006/73/EC. In addition, it also copies from recital (39) and thus lifts this recital to the status of a legal norm. However, in §31d paragraph 4 WpHG, a specific procedural twist is added by establishing a 'presumption' that inducements are designed to enhance the quality of the service if that service is performed in an unbiased manner even if payments are collected.

In German law, a presumption means that the court has to use the presumed facts unless the other side can rebut the presumption by demonstrating that the facts were different. But how should any client,

[30] CESR, n. 23 above, box 4 at p. 9.

[31] H.-D. Assmann, 'Interessenkonflikte aufgrund von Zuwendungen', *Zeitschrift für Bankrecht und Bankwirtschaft*, 20 (2008), 21, 32.

or even the supervising authority, prove that a kickback payment is *not* designed to enhance the quality of the service? If one accepts the argument of the banking industry – that any earnings enable banks to provide a better service – then there is hardly any way to rebut this presumption.

German law also requires that the party relying on a presumption has to prove the presumption's factual requirements. In the case of §31d paragraph 4 WpHG, the precondition is that services are being provided in an unbiased manner notwithstanding the kickbacks. Accordingly, it is for the bank to prove that its employees acted without bias.[32] How can this be done? One answer would be that the bank has to show objective facts which allow the conclusion of unbiased action regardless of any commission. This could be the case if the recommendation was indeed in the client's best interest. Since it is hard to say which investment recommendations are and which are not in the client's best interest, such a reading would create a large grey area where unbiased action would have to be assumed. Only recommendations that are clearly not in the client's interest – such as 'churning' – would lead to the finding that there was biased action and that the inducements were therefore illegal.[33]

Such a reading would allow kickback payments to continue as usual – with the exception of severe and obvious violations of the duties towards the clients. Indeed, this is what German banks' lawyers assume: they argue that as the banks have to act in their clients' best interest anyway, the requirements of the presumption in §31d paragraph 4 WpHG are met and that therefore inducements can be accepted as before.[34] The banks' business model of 'seemingly-for-free' investment advice, financed by kickback payments, remains intact according to this argument; with the slight modification that the kickback payments now have to be disclosed to the customer. A different business model, where clients would have to pay directly for advice or other services, is dismissed as being unrealistic because of customers' perceived unwillingness to pay direct fees.[35] Even critical academics see no alternative but to accept that in the area covered by §31d paragraph 4 WpHG – especially general investment advice – there

[32] For the relevance of the burden of proof see also Grundmann and Kerber, n. 3 above, at 299.

[33] Assmann, n. 31 above, at 27.

[34] Rozok, n. 27 above, at 221 and 225.

[35] Rozok, n. 27 above, at 221.

will be almost no limit to the legality of inducements under existing EC and German law.[36]

In our opinion this cannot be the end of the story. European law started out in Articles 18 and 19 MiFiD with a very firm stance regarding conflicts of interest in the finance industry and with the goal of eliminating or alleviating them as far as possible. In fact, the avoidance of conflicts of interest was one of the core aims defined in the proposal for the Directive.[37] An unbiased look at Article 26 Directive 2006/73/EC shows that inducements are regarded as unwelcome exceptions, not as the rule. This approach would conform to Article 19(1) MiFiD which states that the aim of these rules is to 'ensure that an investment firm act honestly, fairly and professionally in accordance with the best interests of its client'. It is therefore necessary to read the Implementing Directive in accordance with this high standard. This is supported by Article 64(2) and (2a) MiFID which state that the implementing measures cannot change the essential provisions of MiFID itself.

The question therefore is: are inducements allowed in situations of general investment advice as long as they are properly disclosed? Or do kickback payments create a conflict of interest that structurally impairs the bank's ability to act in its client's best interest? If the latter is the case, then the receipt of kickback payments cannot be accepted as a matter of daily routine, but has to be limited to special circumstances.

A procedural or substantive approach to the inducement problem?

By asking this question we return to the general issue of procedural or substantive standards of protection against unconscionability. The solution proposed in German law focuses on the procedural aspect: as long as the bank's client is provided with sufficient information, inducements are considered legal.

[36] Assmann, n. 31 above, at 23 ('this absurdity of freeing the investment services with the highest potential of conflict from the prohibition of inducements') (authors' translation); for other critical comments on the legality of inducements, see Kumpan and Hellgardt, n. 7 above, at 1719; G. Spindler and R. A. Kasten, 'Der neue Rechtsrahmen für den Finanzdienstleistungssektor – die MiFID und ihre Umsetzung', *Wertpapier-Mitteilungen*, 60 (2006), 1797, at 1803.

[37] See the proposal for a directive on investment services and regulated markets, COM (2002) 625, at 18f.

(a) Information only of limited use for the client

This idea seems to be based on a model of the well-informed consumer who is able to see the bank's conflict of interest and can calculate the risk this represents for his investment decision. However, research in 'behavioural finance' shows that investment decisions are not necessarily made according to the classical model of the rational man that was long assumed in economic theory.

Today, there has been a paradigm shift in economics which involves injecting psychological and empirical findings on decision-making situations into the models of economic theory. Some of the main points are the lack of stability in people's preferences, the so-called over-confidence-bias and the relevance of fairness instead of pure cost-benefit-analysis.[38]

If we relate these findings to our inducement problem, it becomes clear that the mere disclosure of existing kickback schemes does not help the client in making a better decision. Instead, his or her investment decision will be largely influenced by the behaviour of the bank's employee giving the investment advice.

Psychologists tell us that people do not make decisions on the basis of stable preferences but that, instead, decisions are 'framed' by the way that they are presented to the decision-maker.[39] This means, for example, that the amount of financial risk that somebody is willing to accept may depend on which products are offered to him: an investment with high risk can be 'framed' as a medium risk choice if it is presented together with even riskier alternatives. People prefer 'middle' solutions, but the 'middle' is defined by the extremes it is contrasted with.[40]

Furthermore, since people typically overestimate their decision-making abilities, the disclosure of inducements will probably not change

[38] For an overview of behavioural economics see the Nobel prize lecture of D. Kahneman, 'Maps of Bounded Rationality: Psychology for Behavioral Economics', *American Economic Review*, 93 (2003), 1449; for a summary treatise: J. Dowling and Y. Chin-Fang, *Modern Developments in Behavioral Economics* (Singapore: World Scientific Pub., 2007); with a specific view to law, see C. Sunstein (ed.), *Behavioral Law and Economics* (Cambridge University Press, 2000). For a different critique of the traditional law and economics approach, see R. P. Malloy, *Law and Market Economy* (Cambridge University Press, 2000) who understands market interaction as a creative use of signs and a production of social meaning.

[39] A. Tversky and D. Kahneman, 'The Framing of Decisions and the Psychology of Choice', *Science*, 211 (1981), 453–58.

[40] From a legal point of view, see M. Kelman, Y. Rottenstreich and A. Tversky, 'Context-Dependence in Legal Decision Making', *Journal of Legal Studies*, 25 (1996), 287.

much in their investment decision. If one firmly but falsely believes that one knows better than others what is best and what the future will bring,[41] the disclosure of countervailing conflicts of interests will not make much difference.

On the contrary, information on inducements may even be dysfunctional for the decision-making process given that people use fairness aspects in addition to or even instead of a strict utility calculation.[42] In a pure cost-benefit analysis, it would be of no relevance at all whether the issuer of a financial instrument gives the bank a commission or not. If, for example, an investment fund is sold with a 5 per cent commission fee, then the 5 per cent are 'sunk costs' which have to be calculated in evaluating the asset's performance regardless of who profits from them. If the buyer only looked at costs and benefits, it would be completely irrelevant whether some of this money is transferred to the bank, or kept by the issuer or given to charity. In reality, however, people assess not only their own benefits with regard to economic decisions, but also the perceived 'fairness' of a deal. From a fairness perspective, it may look strange if the bank makes large profits from a specific investment, even if that investment may be very good from a pure utility perspective.

It therefore makes sense that some authors have even opposed the disclosure of commissions, arguing that the amount of commission is entirely unrelated to the quality of the investment and that therefore its disclosure may be an irritant to the client who may wish to save money on the commission, thereby making a bad investment decision.[43]

Even from a common sense point of view, one can question what it means to the client if the bank discloses that it receives a higher commission from one of the possible issuers and a lower commission from another? Certainly, where the commission is exorbitant, the investor would suspect that first, the product cannot be very good and second, that a significant part of the invested money is not spent on the product

[41] See, e.g. S. Taylor, *Positive Illusions* (Basic Books, New York 1989) *passim*, finding that only people with permanent depression are able to realistically assess risks in their lives (at 39), whereas all others are over-confident (including university professors 94 per cent of whom believe that they are better professors than their colleagues).

[42] The most prominent example is the 'ultimatum game', see C. Jolls, C. Sunstein and R. Thaler, 'A Behavioral Approach to Law and Economics', in Sunstein (ed.), n. 38 above, at 13, 21 ff.

[43] See A. Matusche-Beckmann, 'Berufsrecht und zivilrechtliche Beratungs- und Informationspflichten für Versicherungsvermittler', *Neue Zeitschrift für Versicherungsrecht*, 5 (2002), 385, at 390. See also P. O. Mülbert, 'Anlegerschutz bei Zertifikaten', *Wertpapier-Mitteilungen*, 61 (2007), 1149, at 1160.

itself.[44] In contrast, the difference between a commission of 6 per cent and a commission of 7 per cent is less telling. It may only enable the investor to live out his or her fairness bias and choose the investment that causes the lowest extra cost, which is the investment where the bank receives the lowest commission – but this may also be the worst investment in terms of profitability. In essence, the client still depends on the bank's advice regarding the choice of the best investment even if he or she knows about the respective commissions. In economic terms the principal/agent problem remains.

(b) Conflict of interest management at the bank

Since inducements give rise to a potential conflict of interest at the bank, it is crucial to analyse how this conflict can be managed and how the bank can make sure that its employees still act in the client's best interest as required by the MiFID rules.

First, the disclosure requirement on inducements may aggravate the conflict of interest problem: in the past, the employee advising the client did not necessarily know the exact details of the kickback payments between the bank and the issuers of the financial instruments, since this was handled mainly by the bank's back office.[45] If, in contrast, this employee now gives those details to the client, the employee will have that information and possibly even discuss the information with the client.

In a situation where there is a choice between different possible investment tools, it would therefore be only natural for the bank employee to recommend the strategy that generates the highest revenue for the bank. If the bank encouraged such behaviour, for example through revenue-related bonuses that would not be in the client's best interest and would violate the MiFID rules.[46]

Therefore, the banks are trying to put in place schemes to mitigate this problem by instructing their employees to disregard the information on inducements and only focus on the client's best interest. While such instructions are helpful and indeed necessary under the MiFID regime, they are certainly not sufficient. If a bank employee knows about the

[44] This point has been made by German courts when they justified their opinion that (only) commissions that are unusually high must be disclosed. See BGH, n. 8 above.

[45] Rozok, n. 27 above, at 224.

[46] See also C. Kumpan and P. C. Leyens, 'Conflicts of Interest of Financial Intermediaries', *European Company and Financial Law Review*, 5 (2008), 72, at 99, on performance-related remuneration schemes.

revenues gathered by the bank as a result of his or her actions, it is unrealistic to expect him or her to suppress this information while giving investment advice. It is only rational for any employee to try to maximise earnings for his or her employer, since this is why he or she is employed by the bank. Especially with a view to wage negotiations or even possible lay-offs, it is always helpful to be a 'profitable' employee.[47]

Thus, a simple instruction to the bank's employees cannot possibly be sufficient to alleviate the inducement problem. One possible way would be to separate the front office employees from the inducement-collecting back office so that only the latter have knowledge of the existence and amount of kickback payments. Such a 'Chinese wall' would require that information on inducements which is to be given under the MiFID regime must be given by a separate division of the bank, for example in a letter sent from the back office to the client which is not given to the front office employee. However, even with such precautions, there is still room for some conflicts of interest since it would be obvious to any bank employee – even without detailed information – that some investment products are likely to bring more revenue for the bank than others, for example that the bank's own products are more profitable for the bank than state treasury bonds.

A lot more could be said about managing conflicts of interest but even this short discussion shows that simply informing the client about inducements is not good enough and may even be counterproductive. In order to fulfil the MiFID requirement of acting in the client's best interest, a bank has to devise a specific strategy which probably must include the 'Chinese walls' described above, general instructions to the front office, a policy on how to deal with the problem in the human resources department and further strategies to minimise remaining problems.

Consequences for the law on inducements

For the EC and German law on inducements one cannot simply assume that banks always act in the client's best interest. Beyond the procedural aspect of giving the customer adequate information, there must be a substantive standard for the bank's management of the conflicts of interest arising from kickback payments; compliance with this standard must be proved by the bank as described above.

[47] In Germany, it is well known that due to fierce competition in the banking sector, bank employees are nowadays under enormous pressure to sell financial products.

For German law, this means that the presumption laid down in §31d paragraph 4 WpHG may only become effective if the bank can prove that it has established a system in which unbiased investment advice is possible in the context of inducements.

If the bank is unable to prove such a system, inducements are unlawful since the requirements established by Article 26 of Directive 2006/73/EC, as implemented in §31d paragraph 1 WpHG, are not met. Such an interpretation is consistent with the main idea of Article 26 that inducements are generally prohibited and can only be allowed in exceptional circumstances. Whoever wants to show that these exceptions apply in a specific case has to prove the factual requirements of the exception.

In practice this may lead to the conclusion that the existing practices of kickback payments are illegal. Would this be a problem? The banks would say so since their model of free-of-charge investment advice would have to come to an end, in the absence of kickback payments to finance this model. There are, however, alternative models to serve the clients' investment interests: one model would be the charging of hourly fees for investment advice,[48] or fees that are directly related to the purchase of a financial instrument, just as this is common practice (in Germany) if property is purchased through a broker. Both models would be compatible with the MiFID regime and would eliminate the conflict of interest inherent in the kickback model.

Such a solution would require a change of behaviour on both sides: the banks would have to devise new models as to how to provide investment advice and the customers would have to accept that investment advice is a valuable service which cannot be provided for free.

Room for more radical solutions?

As mentioned at the outset, there is an ongoing debate among German academics as to whether kickback payments have to be reimbursed to the client under the law on mandates, which would of course make them unattractive for investment firms. Before considering the law on mandates, the primary question is whether such a national regime is at all possible after the implementation period for the MiFID Directive has elapsed. In other words, does the MiFID Directive fully harmonise the contract law of kickback payments in the field of the investment services?

[48] See also Grundmann and Kerber, n. 3 above, at 277, who however also point out that in such a system there might be an incentive to prolong the consulting process.

This question is difficult to answer since the Directive neither contains a minimum harmonisation clause, as many other Directives especially in consumer law do, nor does it provide for a maximum harmonisation clause, such as Article 22(1) of the new Consumer Credit Directive 2008/48/EC.[49] According to the explanation of its first proposal, the Commission aimed to establish a 'bed-rock of harmonised investor protection obligations in order to facilitate cross-border activities of investment firms needed to support mutual recognition of authorisation and operational requirements'.[50] Recital (22) of the MiFID Directive now states that Member States are in principle required to mutually recognise another Member State's competent authority's decision to authorise an investment firm. However, recital (22) also mentions 'stricter standards' that are in force in another Member State, which arguably implies that not all Member States have to apply the same standards. Thus, one could conclude that Member States are allowed to maintain investor protection standards that go beyond the requirements of the Directive. However, due to the principle of mutual recognition, they cannot be enforced by national authorities against foreign investment firms, for example by a prohibition to operate in the Member State that has adopted a higher standard of protection.

Moreover, the extent to which Directive 2004/39/EC is of relevance to the contractual relationship between the investor and the investment firm is entirely unclear. The Directive itself only talks of harmonisation aiming at mutual recognition of authorisations by the competent authorities. The question has two dimensions: one is the question as to whether a breach, for example of the duty to act 'honestly, fairly and professionally in accordance with the best interests of its clients', triggers the private law liability of the investment firm.[51] The German Federal Court has

[49] O.J. 2008 L 133/66. [50] See only COM(2002) 625 final, at 23.

[51] In favour of such an effect on contract: N. Reich, 'Informations-, Aufklärungs- und Warnpflichten beim Anlagengeschäft unter besonderer Berücksichtigung des "execution-only-business" (EOB)', *Wertpapier-Mitteilungen*, 51 (1997), 1601, at 1603 f.; P. Balzer, 'Der Vorschlag der EG-Kommission für eine neue Wertpapierdienstleistungsrichtlinie', *Zeitschrift für Bankrecht und Bankwirtschaft*, 15 (2003), 177, at 186; R. Veil, 'Der Schutz des verständigen Anlegers durch Publizität und Haftung im europäischen und nationalen Kapitalmarktrecht', *Zeitschrift für Bankrecht und Bankwirtschaft*, 18 (2006), 162, at 171; idem, 'Anlageberatung im Zeitalter der MiFID', *Wertpapier-Mitteilungen*, 61 (2007), 1821 ff.; T. Weichert and T. Wenninger, 'Die Neuregelung der Erkundigungs- und Aufklärungspflichten von Wertpapierdienstleistungsunternehmen gem. Art. 19 RiL 2004/39/EG (MiFID) und Finanzmarkt-Richtlinie-Umsetzungsgesetz', *Wertpapier-Mitteilungen*, 61 (2007), 627, at 635; Mülbert, n. 43 above, at 1157. For more details: Kumpan and Hellgardt, n. 7 above.

recognised that §31 WpHG (implementing the investor protection regime of the MiFID Directive) may be relevant for the content and the extent of pre-contractual information obligations and the duty to advise the investor 'insofar they aim to protect the investor'.[52] In contrast, the court has, under the predecessor Directive 93/22/EEC, denied tortious liability for non-compliance with the rules on the internal organisation of investment firms that were meant to avoid conflicts of interest.[53] This latter case law does, however, not necessarily apply to inducements since the duty to disclose kickback payments (where allowed) directly concerns the investor/investment firm relationship and aims to protect the investor. Contractual liability for damage for failing to disclose is indeed essential since the duty to disclose would otherwise not be effectively enforceable.[54]

The second dimension is whether the principle of mutual recognition for the purposes of authorisation also impacts on the Member States' civil laws. Indeed, it does not seem to make much sense to harmonise rules on, for example, inducements for matters of supervision whilst leaving it to the Member States to prohibit the identical practices under contract or tort law. As recital (2) of Directive 2004/39/EC prominently confirms, the Directive aims to facilitate cross-border investment services, as does the Lamfalussy process in the field of financial services. Thus, where Directives 2004/39/EC and 2006/73/EC contain specific rules on a particular issue, they would imply maximum harmonisation of related private law as well.[55] An outright national prohibition of kickback payments therefore appears to be barred by EC legislation.[56]

[52] See BGH, 19 December 2006, *Wertpapier-Mitteilungen*, 61 (2007), 487, at 489. See also P. Balzer, 'Anlegerschutz bei Verstößen gegen die Verhaltenspflichten nach §§31 ff Wertpapierhandelsgesetz (WpHG)', *Zeitschrift für Bankrecht und Bankwirtschaft*, 9 (1997), 260, at 262 ff.

[53] See BGH, 8 May 2001, *Betriebs-Berater*, 56 (2001), 1865, at 1867. Whether this will change after the implementation of Directive 2004/39/EC has been discussed controversially. In favour of civil liability G. Spindler and R. Kasten, 'Organisationsverpflichtungen nach der MiFID und ihre Umsetzung', *Die Aktiengesellschaft*, 51 (2006), 785, at 791.

[54] Ibid., at 791, and see generally for financial intermediaries, P. Rott, 'Europäisierung des Rechts der Finanzintermediäre', *Europäisches Wirtschafts- und Steuerrecht*, 19 (2008), 21, at 28 ff.

[55] See also Mülbert, n. 43 above, at 1157.

[56] See also Mülbert, n. 43 above, at 1160, who however maintains that an obligation to pass kickback payments on to the customer would still be possible; which seems somewhat contradictory.

In contrast, Member States have undoubtedly retained the competence to regulate those issues that are not addressed by the Directive. In particular, this applies to the above-mentioned issue of hidden costs that amount to a usurious price of the investment product. The new Consumer Credit Directive, which explicitly prohibits stricter consumer protection measures in areas containing harmonised provisions[57] shows that even the most detailed information obligations do not exclude the Member States' competence to define usury limits beyond which a contract is null and void.[58]

Furthermore, EC legislation does not address the legal consequences of unlawful or undisclosed kickback payments but only adopts, in Article 51(1) of Directive 2004/39/EC, the formula that Member States have to ensure that appropriate administrative measures can be taken or administrative sanctions be imposed against the persons responsible where the provisions adopted in the implementation of this Directive have not been complied with, and that these measures are effective, proportionate and dissuasive. Thus, it is left to the Member States to determine the legal consequences in private law, and there are no clear-cut solutions available, one reason being that kickback payments are, as mentioned above, largely unrelated to the value of an investment product. Can the customer, for example, rescind the contract? Or can the customer claim damages, and what is the damage? In principle, the customer would have to prove that he or she would not have concluded the contract, if he or she had known of the kickback payments, in the first place; although courts may alleviate the burden of proof in cases of fraudulent non-disclosure. Moreover, is there any real damage if the investment was still worth the price? Does the damage correspond with the amount of the kickback payment? And what if the investment dropped in value for other reasons?[59]

What different standards of protection would mean for the contractual relationship between an investment firm in a lower-standard Member State and a client in a higher-standard Member State is yet another story

[57] See Art. 22(1) of Directive 2008/48/EC.

[58] See the explanation on Art. 30(1) of the first proposal for the new Consumer Credit Directive, COM(2002) 443 final, at 27, and P. Rott, 'Die neue Verbraucherkredit-Richtlinie 2008/48/EG und ihre Auswirkungen auf das deutsche Recht', *Wertpapier-Mitteilungen*, 62 (2008), 1104, at 1106.

[59] Detailed analysis of German law: S. Geibel, 'Schadensersatz wegen verdeckter Innenprovisionen und ähnlicher Zuwendungen', *Zeitschrift für Bankrecht und Bankwirtschaft*, 15 (2003), 349 ff.

that has to be decided under the rules of private international law. Clearly, in a contract between an investment firm and a non-consumer client, unrestricted choice of law is possible, and a reasonable investment firm would incorporate a clause in the contract that points at its own (lower-standard) Member State's law. In contrast, where a consumer contract is concerned, under Article 5 of the old Rome Convention and also under Article 6 of the new Regulation 593/2008 on the law applicable to contractual obligations (Rome I),[60] the more protective consumer laws of the Member State of the consumer's habitual residence may apply on top of the law that otherwise governs the contract, so that ultimately the investment firm would have to take into account the higher standard of protection of the Member State in which the consumer has his or her habitual residence. This latter regime also ensures that all investment firms that operate in the same Member States have to operate under the same rules.

Conclusions

Returning from the specific discussion of the lawfulness or unlawfulness of kickback payments to the general theme of this chapter, we would like to emphasise that there are situations where purely procedural protection against unconscionable conduct through disclosure is likely not to work. This is not only the case where a vulnerable contracting party is unable to understand the information provided, or where one contracting party is in a particularly emotional state of mind, which is the reason for protective mechanisms against family suretyships that the German Constitutional Court has derived from the constitutional right to freedom of contract.[61]

Thus, even where investment decisions of more or less reasonable investors are at stake, disclosure alone – here, on kickback payments – may be insufficient since the disclosed information does not help the investor to make a reasonable decision. The truly disturbing factor is not the

[60] OJ 2008 L 177/6.

[61] See Constitutional Court, 19 October 1993, *Neue Juristische Wochenschrift*, 47 (1994), 36, confirmed by Constitutional Court, 5 August 1994, *Neue Juristische Wochenschrift*, 47 (1994), 2749, and by Constitutional Court, 6 December 2005, *Wertpapier-Mitteilungen*, 60 (2006), 23. See also P. Rott, 'German Law on Family Suretyships: An Overrated System', in A. Colombi Ciacchi (ed.), *Protection of Non-Professional Sureties in Europe: Formal and Substantive Disparity* (Baden-Baden: Nomos, 2007), 51 ff.

informational asymmetry between advisor and investor but the incentive for the adviser to give inappropriate advice. Such disturbance can only be effectively avoided by abolishing the incentive, that is, ideally by disallowing inducements, which is not a procedural but a substantive way of protecting the investor. At least outside the scope of application of the MiFID Directive, this approach should be taken.

18

Unfairness under the Consumer Protection from Unfair Trading Regulations 2008

CHRIS WILLETT

1 Introduction

The Unfair Commercial Practices Directive (UCPD) was adopted in 2005[1] and requires Member States to empower bodies to take preventive action against unfair business-to-consumer practices.[2] This has been implemented in the UK by the Consumer Protection from Unfair Trading Regulations (CPUTR) 2008,[3] which define such practices as forms of 'Community infringement' under the Enterprise Act (EA), thereby providing enforcement authorities with the powers to seek enforcement orders against such practices.[4] This now coexists with the pre-existing powers to seek enforcement orders against other practices

[1] 2005/29/EC; and see generally U. Bernitz and S. Weatherill (eds.), *The Regulation of Unfair Commercial Practices under EC Directive 2005/29: New Rules and New Techniques* (Oxford: Hart Publishing, 2007); H. Collins (ed.), *The Forthcoming EC Directive on Unfair Commercial Practices: Contract, Consumer and Competition Law Implications* (Hague and London: Kluwer International, 2004); R. Schulze and H. Schulte-Nolke, *Analysis of National Fairness Laws Aimed at Protecting Consumers in Relation to Commercial Practices*, available at www.europa.eu.int/comm./consumers/cons%20/int/%20/safeshop/fair%20/bus%20/pract/green%20/pap%20/comm./studies/unfair%20/practices20en.pdf; G. Howells, H.-W. Micklitz, T. Wilhelmsson, *European Fair Trading Law: The Unfair Commercial Practices Directive* (Aldershot: Ashgate, 2006); C. Willett, *Fairness in Consumer Contracts* (Aldershot: Ashgate, 2007) chapter 9.

[2] See UCPD, Articles 3 and 11. [3] CPUTR 2008, SI 1277.

[4] Enterprise Act 2002, s. 212 and Schedule 13 (as amended by CPUTR, reg. 26). Acting unfairly within the meaning of the Directive has also been criminalised (CPUTR, regs. 3–12), subject to the traditional defences based on the default of another, due diligence and innocent publication of an advertisement (CPUTR, regs. 16–18); while the pre-existing criminal measures (under the Trade Descriptions Act 1968 and Part III of the Consumer Protection Act 1987) on false statements as to goods, services and prices have been repealed (CPUTR, Schedule 4, Part 1). For the full background to consultation on, and implementation of, the Directive see www.berr.gov.uk/consultations/page39674.html.

that represent 'Community infringements' and those that represent 'domestic infringements'.[5]

This chapter considers the concept of unfairness in the CPUTR, in particular what it adds to regulatory ideas of unfairness in the financial services sector.

The regime clearly catches financial service transactions, covering commercial transactions in relation to 'any goods or service including immovable property, rights and obligations'.[6] Indeed, financial services transactions are given special treatment, in that they are excluded from the 'internal market clause',[7] which, when applicable, will prevent Member States from exceeding the level of protection provided for in the Directive. It is expressly provided by Article 3 (9) that in relation to 'financial services':[8]

> Member States may impose requirements which are more restrictive or prescriptive than this Directive in the field which it approximates.[9]

2. Coverage, regulatory context and the general notion of unfairness

The UCPD unfairness concept is of particular importance because of the sheer range of activities it regulates within any given transaction. It catches 'any act, omission, course of conduct, representation or commercial communication ... by a trader, directly connected with the promotion, sale or supply of a product to consumers'.[10] Such a practice may be 'before, during or after' a transaction.[11]

What we have then is a 'cradle to grave' approach, applicable to promotion, negotiation, conclusion, performance and enforcement of the contract. It covers practices such as advertising, promotion, persuasion and negotiation at the pre-contractual stage; post-contractual

[5] Enterprise Act 2002, ss. 211–212. 'Domestic infringements' cover actions amounting to breaches of traditional domestic norms, including breaches of contract and duty and of criminal law standards; while 'Community infringements' cover actions in breach of EU consumer protection directives.

[6] UCPD, Article 2 . [7] UCPD, Article 4.

[8] As defined in Directive 2002/65/EC on Distance Marketing of Financial Services, i.e. (as per Art. 2(b)), 'any service of a banking, credit, insurance, personal pension, investment or payment nature.'

[9] UCPD, Article 3 (9) allows Member States the same leeway in relation to immovable property; meaning that, even if mortgages were not found to be covered by the financial services definition, they would be covered in any event.

[10] UCPD, Article 2 (d). [11] UCPD, Article 3 (1).

alterations or variations; performance, delivery etc. by the trader; performance, payment etc. by the consumer; complaint handling; after-sales service; and enforcement by either party.

This new regime sits alongside other regimes which can also be described, to varying degrees, as taking a 'cradle to grave' approach; but which are focused specifically on the financial services sector. First of all, there is the general clause in the Consumer Credit Act 1974 (CCA) which focuses on 'unfair credit relationships'. Such a relationship can be caused by (a) the way the lender has exercised or enforced his rights or (b) anything done or not done by the lender before or after the agreement.[12] Then there are the Treating Consumers Fairly (TCF) principles, developed and administered by the Financial Service Authority (FSA);[13] and the Banking Code.[14] These two regimes are 'cradle to grave' in the sense that their commitments to treat customers fairly are applicable across the course of the relationship.[15]

In addition to these 'cradle to grave' approaches there are, of course, a range of specific 'fairness-oriented' requirements and constraints. So, for example, there are requirements to disclose certain specific elements of information at certain pre- and post-contractual points;[16] consumers have cancellation rights in certain circumstances;[17] the contract terms must not be unfair;[18] and there are specific information-based and other protections in the context of enforcement action against consumers.[19]

[12] CCA 1974, s. 140 (1) (b) and (c).

[13] FSA, *Treating Customers Fairly – Towards Fair Outcomes for Consumers*, July 2006; see also J. Black, M. Hopper and C. Band, 'Making a Success of Principles-based Regulation' (2007) 1 *Law and Financial Markets Review* 191.

[14] For detailed information see www.bba.org.uk/bba/jsp/polopoly.jsp?d=140.

[15] Both refer to issues that arise both pre- and post-contractually. See, for example, FSA, n. 13 above, TCF Outcome Three, p. 3, on providing clear and appropriate information 'before, during and after the point of sale', and the Banking Code, n. 14 above, section 2, 'Fairness Commitment', on advertising and promotional literature that is clear and not misleading and, also, on dealing 'quickly and sympathetically with things that go wrong'. Of course, neither these, nor the CCA regime, necessarily focus on all of the same issues as those relevant to the new CPUTR regime and some possible divergences will be alluded to below.

[16] See CCA, s. 44 on the form and content of advertisements and CCA, ss. 77–79 on information as to the amounts paid and payable under credit agreements.

[17] See, for example, CCA, ss. 67–73; and the Financial Services (Distance Marketing) Regulations 2004, reg. 9.

[18] Unfair Terms in Consumer Contracts Regulations 1999, SI 2083.

[19] See CCA, s. 76 on pre-enforcement information; and also the equitable rules on forfeiture, on which see the chapter by Sarah Nield, ch. 10 in this volume.

Under the new regime unfairness is conceptualised first of all by a kind of 'master clause', which defines as 'unfair' practices that are 'contrary to the requirements of professional diligence' and likely to 'materially distort the economic behaviour' of consumers.[20] However, it then goes on to provide that, in particular, practices are unfair where they are either misleading or where they are aggressive.[21] Here, I will deal with the misleading and then the aggressive concepts, before turning to the various consumer 'benchmarks' applicable to the unfairness concept.

3. Misleading actions and omissions

(i) Introduction – misleading actions

A practice is misleading where it is either a 'misleading action' (positive provision of misleading information)[22] or a 'misleading omission' (failure to provide material information).[23] The misleading action concept broadly reflects that in the (now repealed) Control of Misleading Advertisement Regulations (CMAR) (the issue being whether the practice 'deceives or is likely to deceive'[24]). It is broader than the CMAR concept in applying right across the relationship and not being restricted (as was CMAR) to statements *promoting* the goods or services.[25] However, as already indicated, the CCA general clause, the TCF regime and the Banking Code also apply right across the relationship. The TCF regime refers to giving 'clear' information 'before, during and after the point of sale';[26] and the Banking Code refers to not being 'misleading' at the pre-contractual stage and to keeping consumers informed as to changes in interest rates, charges and terms.[27] As to the CCA, we have seen that there can be an unfair relationship based on anything done or not done before or after the agreement, which surely covers misleading behaviour. How the new misleading action concept compares to the CCA, TCF and Banking Code regimes is a matter requiring much more detailed analysis than there is space for here.

[20] UCPD, Article 5(1)/(2).
[21] UCPD, Article 5(4) (a) and (b); and there is an Annex of practices that are, in all circumstances, regarded as unfair (Art. 5 (5) and Annex 1).
[22] UCPD, Article 6. [23] UCPD, Article 7.
[24] See CMAR, reg. 2 (2) and UCPD, Article 6 (1).
[25] CMAR, reg. 2 (1). [26] FSA, n. 13 above, TCF, Outcome 3, p. 3.
[27] Banking Code, n. 14 above, Section 2.

However, one question is whether the TCF regime actually goes further than the new misleading action concept in that the TCF regime also focuses on the 'suitability' of advice[28] and the financial products meeting the 'expectations' generated.[29] There might be scope for debate as to whether there has always been a 'misleading' statement as such where advice is unsuitable or expectations are generated but not met by product performance.

Another potential restriction on the protective effects of the new misleading action concept is that the practice must not only be likely to deceive, it must also be likely to cause the average consumer[30] to take a 'transactional decision' that he would not take otherwise.[31] It may well be that this is a fairly easy hurdle to clear, the idea being that any action that would be likely to deceive in a material way will generally be taken to have such an effect on transactional decision making. However, we cannot be sure of this and, in any case, the greater the number of conceptual hurdles that have to be crossed, the more difficult it is in practice for regulators to persuade businesses that a practice satisfies the criteria.

(ii) *Misleading omissions*

There is a misleading omission where the trader omits:

> material information that the average consumer needs, according to the context, to take an informed transactional decision and [this] causes or is likely to cause the average consumer to take a transactional decision that he would not have taken otherwise.[32]

Where invitations to purchase are concerned, particular types of information are deemed (expressly) to be 'material', and therefore needed for an informed decision.[33] There are, of course, similar requirements to

[28] FSA, n. 13 above, TCF, Outcome Four, p. 3.

[29] Ibid., Outcome Five, p. 3.

[30] Or average member of the relevant benchmark group of consumers, on which see further below.

[31] UCPD, Article 6(1). This 'average consumer' is not part of the notion of a misleading practice under the TCF principles; and neither is it used in relation to unfairness under the CCA test.

[32] UCPD, Article 7(1). Even if information is provided there is still a misleading omission if it is hidden, unclear, unintelligible, ambiguous or untimely (Art. 7(2)).

[33] Information as to the main characteristics of the goods/services; the price and other charges; the identity and address of the trader; any cancellation right; and arrangements for payment, delivery, performance and complaint handling if they depart from the requirements of professional diligence (UCPD, Art. 7(4) (e)).

disclose particular types of information in the pre-existing regimes applicable to various types of financial services contracts.[34] Here, however, the focus is on the general 'consumer needs' test (set out above) that determines what must be disclosed in cases other than where the specific requirements on invitations to purchase apply.

The omissions rule rejects the idea that consumers must exercise total self-reliance in discovering whatever they think might be important; they are to be helped to make more informed decisions.[35] Such an approach is clearly premised on a recognition that businesses often have limited incentives to highlight issues;[36] and that, for a variety of reasons, consumers have limited capacity to work out what they need to know and to search for it.[37]

By comparison with trading sectors in general (and leaving aside requirements to disclose specific pieces of information), requiring disclosure based on the informational 'needs' of the consumer does represent a more protective approach than has generally existed in pre-existing law. Sometimes, a failure to provide information *can* amount to a misrepresentation[38] or fall foul of (now repealed) rules on false trade descriptions and misleading advertising.[39] However, the starting point for these rules is/was not consumer 'need' as such; but, rather, the positive provision of incorrect information. What tends to be required under these rules is some statement or representation that in some way does not tell the whole truth and therefore triggers an obligation of disclosure.[40] This model retains a significant freedom-oriented ethic; the trader being liable only when there has been some form of voluntary 'assumption of responsibility' and the consumer (beyond such situations) having the (self-reliant) responsibility to assess what information may be required and seek it out. By contrast, as we have seen, under the new concept the question is whether the consumer 'needs' the

34 See, e.g. the Financial Services (Distance Marketing) Regulations 2004, regs. 7 (1), 8 (1) and Schedule 1.

35 See Willett, n. 1 above, 2.4.2.2 and 2.4.3.4.

36 See OFT, *Consumer Detriment under Conditions of Imperfect Information*, OFT Research Paper 11, prepared by London Economics, August 1997; and (in particular relation to banking) P. Cartwright, *Banks, Consumers and Regulation* (Oxford: Hart Publishing, 2004), chapter 3.

37 Willett, n. 1 above, 2.4.2.2.

38 See, for example, *Dimmock* v. *Hallett* (1866) 2 Ch App 21 and *Spice Girls Ltd* v. *Aprilia World Service BV* [2002] EWCA Civ 15.

39 *Cottee* v. *Douglas Seaton* [1972] 1 WLR 1408.

40 See *Spice Girls Ltd* v. *Aprilia*, n. 38 above, and *R* v. *Ford Motor Co* [1974] 1 WLR 1221.

information to take an informed decision; whether the trader has in any way assumed responsibility for the information would appear to be irrelevant.

In fact, the approach under the TCF initiative seems to fall somewhere in between the approaches just described. The idea under the TCF regime is that consumers should be 'kept appropriately informed before, during and after the point of sale';[41] so, there is no need for some form of 'half truth' or the like, in order to trigger a disclosure requirement. At the same time, what is 'appropriate' might be something to be decided not only from the perspective of consumer needs, but also taking into account the interests of the trader; whereas the 'needs' formula is squarely focused on the consumer interest.[42]

Of course, the type of information required under the TCF and banking regimes may often provide a good indication as to what is 'needed' under the new regime. So, for instance, the TCF regime refers to (pre-contractual) information to aid understanding of the product;[43] ongoing information as to product performance;[44] and information as to changes to terms and conditions.[45] It seems likely that such information would be regarded as 'needed' under the new regime. More generally, there is a theme here of disclosure where key benefits and risks are concerned; and this approach is often to be found in other European systems with more of a disclosure tradition[46] (this being relevant to the extent that the ECJ chooses to draw upon such traditions in developing an autonomous Community approach to omissions).

The next question is whether the 'needs' test moves beyond the notion of risks associated with the product or service as such, and focuses on risks associated with the *trader*, e.g. risks (to consumers making significant deposits) of impending trader insolvency, or risks posed by a history of poor customer care (in particular where this involves consistent breaches of consumer protection laws). There is certainly no requirement to disclose such information under the TCF and Banking Code

41 FSA, n. 13 above, TCF Outcome Three, p. 3.

42 The Banking Code (see, n. 14 above) does not contain a *general* disclosure rule applicable to all stages of the transaction; although there are commitments to give information on specific issues, such as the nature of various products (section 3.1), interest rates, charges and changes to terms and conditions (see sections 4–6).

43 FSA, n. 13 above, TCF, p. 12. 44 Ibid.

45 On the latter see also the Banking Code, n. 14 above, section 6.

46 See, for example, the Danish Marketing Practices Act, s. 2 (1) and the Finnish Consumer Protection Act, Chapter 2, s. 1.

initiatives. However, it might be argued that such information is sometimes needed (at least in extreme cases) in order to allow for informed decisions as to whether to deal with the trader in question.

Another issue arises in relation to consumer rights.[47] One of the most vital forms of information for consumers (particularly at the post-contractual stage when there is a dispute) is information as to the rights that are available to the consumer and how to enforce them. Such rights are not matters that are likely to have been noticed and 'logged' by the 'average consumer' at the formation stage (not being core matters as to subject matter or price). In fact, the issue as to disclosure of rights arose a few years ago when the House of Lords considered whether a term was made unfair (at least in part) by the failure of a Bank (at the stage of seeking a judgment in relation to consumer debts) to draw the attention of consumers to court review processes (which would only take place if the consumer asked for them expressly) which would (potentially) have protected consumers from the effects of the term (a term allowing the bank to recover contractual interest on top of the amount awarded in the judgement).[48] The House of Lords (in denying that any such disclosure obligation existed) said that this was not a common practice, it was not required by independent rules of law and what was needed was that the law be reformed so that the consumer be informed of these matters independently.[49]

However, surely considerations such as these cannot have a place under a test based on consumer 'need', which must surely focus squarely on the importance of the information to the consumer and his ability to access it if it is not provided. This being the case, it is certainly arguable that consumers may need the sort of information under analysis in the above case in order to make an 'informed transactional decision', i.e. a decision as to whether to ask for a review that might significantly reduce their liabilities.

For all that has been said above about how the misleading omissions rule may be more protective than pre-existing approaches, there is a key limitation on the potential effectiveness of the omissions rule. This is because of the severe limitations on consumer information processing powers that are highlighted by behavioural science research.[50]

[47] Neither the TCF principles (n. 13 above) nor the Banking Code (n. 14 above) focus on disclosure of consumer rights.

[48] *First National Bank* v. *DGFT* [2001] 3 WLR 1297.

[49] Ibid., see Lord Bingham at 1310.

[50] See I. Ramsay, *Consumer Law and Policy* (Oxford: Hart, 2007) 71–85; and G. Howells, 'The Potential and Limits of Consumer Empowerment by Information' (2005) 32 (3) *Journal of Law and Society* 349.

Essentially, the point is that consumers will often simply not focus on and digest the information that is provided. First of all, there may be a large quantity of information to be processed prior to the decision in question;[51] meaning that consumers focus only on the core aspects of the transaction. Further, consumers may suffer from over-optimism and an inclination to discount future risks.[52] This may be partly because of factors such as the very positive general marketing messages, the deeply embedded nature of consumption culture, prior psychological commitment to purchases[53] and the particular way in which certain risks and benefits are 'framed'.[54] Of course, these problems are most intense at the pre-contractual stage; so it may be that there is more chance of consumers taking notice of information (e.g. as to rights) that is provided at the enforcement stage.

4. Aggressive practices

(i) Introduction

A practice is aggressive if:

> in its factual context, taking account of all its features and circumstances, by harassment, coercion, including the use of physical force, or undue influence, it significantly impairs or is likely to impair the average consumer's freedom of choice or conduct with regard to the product and thereby causes him or is likely to cause him to take a transactional decision that he would not have taken otherwise.[55]

As a concept that can be enforced by preventive means, several introductory comparisons can be made with pre-existing approaches. First of all, it appears to be a broader principle – providing the potential to cover a broader range of practices – than anything in the TCF initiative or the Banking Code. Although these might be said to address certain enforcement practices that could be viewed as aggressive,[56] neither contains a

[51] On quantity, in particular, see Better Regulation Executive and the National Consumer Council, *Warning: Too Much Information Can Harm* (Interim Report, 2007).

[52] So called 'hyperbolic discounting', on which see S. Frederick, G. Lowenstein and T. O'Donoghue, 'Time Discounting and Time Preference: A Critical Review' (2002) 40 *Journal of Economic Literature* 351.

[53] See Willett, n. 1 above, at 2.4.2.2. [54] See Ramsay, n. 50 above, at 73–4.

[55] Art 8. For comparison with common law duress and equitable undue influence see below at section 6 (Concluding comments).

[56] See the discussion of barriers to consumer enforcement and aggressive trader enforcement below at section 4 (iii).

general principle against aggressive practices. Second, the CCA general clause is very open-textured[57] and so is capable of covering a very broad range of practices (possibly more than the aggressive practices concept in that it is not restricted to specific forms of aggression and there is no requirement that there be an impact on transactional decision making). However, the aggressive practices clause may provide a useful complement to this; in providing a more focused approach to aggressive practices, that highlights particular elements of aggression, i.e. coercion, harassment and undue influence. Third, the aggressive practices concept catches practices that were not caught by the pre-existing powers under the EA. These EA powers allow the seeking of an enforcement order against a so-called 'domestic infringement'. In very broad terms, this covers a range of behaviour that breaches private law, criminal and statutory standards.[58] As far as 'coercion' and 'undue influence' are concerned, we would think of a comparison with private law concepts such as duress and undue influence; and ask whether behaviour of this nature counts as a domestic infringement. In fact, neither undue influence nor duress counts as a domestic infringement. What counts as such infringement is defined specifically in the Enterprise Act 2002 (Part 8 Domestic Infringements) Order 2003.[59] Insofar as private law standards provide a benchmark here, all that is covered is behaviour that amounts to either a breach of contract or breach of a duty of care in tort.[60]

By contrast with coercion and undue influence, preventive control of *harassment* is not new for the UK, in two respects. First of all, there is the Protection from Harassment Act (PHA) 1997, which makes harassment a criminal offence.[61] This, in turn, means that it is a domestic infringement; which means that there is a power to seek an enforcement order to prevent it.[62] However, it must be borne in mind that the harassment concept in the PHA (although potentially covering trader behaviour towards consumers) is essentially aimed at the problem of 'stalking' and it does not appear that much attention has been given to the concept of harassment by local authority or OFT enforcers in the consumer protection context. Perhaps of more practical significance are the rules on harassment of debtors under the Administration of Justice Act (AJA) 1970, section 40. These render various forms of harassment subject to criminal sanctions.[63] This, in turn, means that they are domestic

[57] See above at section 2. [58] S. 211 [59] SI 1593.

[60] Art. 2(2) and Part 3 to the Schedule. [61] Ss. 1 and 2.

[62] EA, s. 211(2)(a). [63] Consumer 'distress, alarm or humiliation' being key (s. 40(1)(a)).

infringements and there is therefore power under the EA to seek an enforcement order to prevent them. These rules are more relevant to the current discussion than the general harassment rules under the PHA. This is because they are specifically focused on consumer debtors.

(ii) Aggression, choice and informed decision making

In deciding whether a practice uses coercion, harassment or undue influence, account is to be taken of:

(a) its timing, location, nature or persistence;
(b) the use of threatening or abusive language or behaviour;
(c) the exploitation by the trader of any specific misfortune or circumstance of such gravity as to impair the consumer's judgement, of which the trader is aware, to influence the consumer's decision with regard to the product;
(d) any onerous or disproportionate non-contractual barriers imposed by the trader where a consumer wishes to exercise rights under the contract, including rights to terminate a contract or to switch to another product or another trader; and
(e) any threat to take any action that cannot legally be taken.[64]

It is also very important to focus on the precise ways in which it is imagined that any given aggressive practice affects consumer choice. After all, practices are only aggressive if there is a restriction on freedom of choice that is likely to lead to a transactional decision that would not otherwise be taken.

One notion of choice constraint seems to be that of *uninformed* decision making. This certainly seems to be *the* issue where undue influence is concerned. It is true that the above definition refers more generally to whether undue influence (or coercion or harassment) restricts the 'freedom of choice' of the consumer. However, where undue influence is concerned, the restriction of choice that leads to an actual or likely transactional decision cannot be just any restriction of choice. It must, specifically, be a restriction of choice that results from an information problem. We know this because the undue influence (that must lead to the restriction of choice) is (separately) defined in terms of:

[64] UCPD, Article 9.

> exploiting a position of power in relation to the consumer so as to apply pressure, even without using or threatening physical force, in a way which significantly limits the consumer's ability to make an *informed* decision.[65]

The model, in other words (as with *misleading* practices) is one in which there is impairment of the ability of consumers to reflect fully (or at all) on decisions, although here the cause of the impairment is not a *misleading* omission as such; but, rather, trader exploitation of a position of power through pressure.

We then turn to the more general 'freedom of choice' concept applicable in cases of coercion and harassment. Whatever this may mean *beyond* informed decision making,[66] it is arguable that 'freedom of choice' requires informed decision making as a basic minimum. This conclusion is premised on the view that a choice is not free (at least in the sense arguably intended in a consumer protection measure) if there are not at least the conditions for the consumer to understand what is on the table.

To sum up, the trader may be viewed[67] as exploiting a position of power through pressure that is likely to prevent consumers from reflecting properly on the decision in question. In such a case, there will be undue influence as there is no 'informed decision'. However, even where there is not the necessary power relationship and/or pressure for undue influence, trader actions that prevent consumers from reflecting on the decision may, depending on application of the listed factors, be sufficient to amount to coercion or harassment; on the basis that if there is no informed decision, there is no 'freedom of choice'.

In terms of particular applications, one can imagine various possibilities. There might be high pressure sales of financial products where the effect is that consumers are unlikely to reflect adequately on the benefits and risks of the transaction. The problem will often derive from the fact that the salesperson creates the need for a quick decision (e.g. because the consumer is made to feel that otherwise he will not escape the attentions of the salesperson or the salesperson will not leave his house, or because there are promised benefits only available to those making an early commitment).[68] Another possible problem is that an insurance salesperson exploits concerns or emotions relating to risks that consumers or their families face, with the result that consumers do not properly reflect on the benefits and costs of the insurance.[69]

[65] UCPD, Article 2 (j). [66] See section 4 (iii) below.
[67] In light of the Article 9 guidelines set out above [68] See guideline (a) above.
[69] See guideline (c) above.

Post-contractually, there might also be the possibility for exploitation of emotions or concerns. Here, the consumer may be struggling with existing commitments and the trader might exploit the consumer's concern over this to persuade him (without proper reflection on the risks) to take on further commitments that expose the consumer to the same or perhaps greater risks.[70]

Another possibility (where the consumer is in default) is that the trader threatens to take action that cannot legally be taken,[71] e.g. to take criminal proceedings.[72] Here the informed decision-making problem lies in the fact that the consumer may pay what is demanded without appreciating that there is no actual risk of the action threatened, as it cannot legally be taken. (Note here that a threat to take criminal proceedings is a criminal offence under s. 40(1)(1) of the AJA 1970.)

So, in all of the above cases there is the notion of the trader creating a situation in which the consumer may not make an informed decision (whether in the sense that he does not reflect adequately on the risks or in the sense that he does not understand the limits of the legal powers that can be applied against him). Of course, it has long been recognised that where credit and other financial services contracts are made at home or by distance selling, then (even in the absence of any proven pressure, harassment or coercion) there is a risk that consumers may not have fully reflected on the decision; and, for this reason, there are rights to cancel the contract for a certain period after its conclusion.[73] (These particular types of contract apart, there is no such general cancellation right). However, the question now is how to react to cases where pressure, harassment or coercion *is* proven.[74]

[70] See OFT/BERR Guidance on the CPUTR, 2008 (available at http://www.oft.gov.uk/shared_oft/business_leaflets/cpregs/oft1008.pdf), at 8.4.

[71] See guideline (e) above.

[72] See Law Commission, *A Private Right of Redress for Unfair Commercial Practices*, November 2008, at para. 2.77, where this is cited as a form of aggressive practice.

[73] See the Consumer Credit Act 1974, ss. 67–73; Cancellation of Contracts made in a Consumer's Home, Work etc. Regulations 2008, SI 1816, reg. 7; and the Financial Services (Distance Marketing) Regulations 2004, SI 2095, reg. 9.

[74] This may occur in contracts where there is no cancellation right. Equally, it might occur in cases where the result is not a contract at all (but nevertheless involves a 'transactional decision' and is therefore covered by the CPUTR), e.g. the above situation in which the consumer is simply being pressured to pay a debt that is owed. Further, as will be suggested below, a cancellation right (whether a short statutory one or a longer one applied in cases of aggression) will not necessarily ensure informed decision making (especially where there has been aggression).

What model of informed decision-making is at work here and what part might a cancellation right play? One possibility is a model based on transparency. So, at the very least, the nature of the transactional decision and the risks associated with it must be made very transparent. In some cases, there would also need to be a cancellation period to give an extended opportunity for the consumer to reflect on the risks.[75] In short, on this model, traders would always be able to engage in harassment, coercion or pressure, so long as there was a sufficient degree of transparency and, sometimes, the chance to cancel (this transparency/period for reflection being viewed as guaranteeing informed decision-making, the presence of which indicates that there is not an aggressive practice).

There is no space to investigate this matter fully here. However, it seems likely that the model is more protective than this; particularly if we interpret the concept of informed decision making in the light of the consumer protection and confidence goals of the UCPD.[76] So, it seems likely that harassment, coercion or pressure can be viewed as having the potential for such a significant impact on the consumer that standardised transparency (and even time for reflection) will not necessarily be enough to create the conditions for an informed decision. The case for such an approach is strengthened if we bear in mind (i) the information processing difficulties likely to be faced by consumers when dealing with standardised literature from traders[77] and the fact that these difficulties are likely to be exacerbated by the harassment, coercion or pressure, and (ii) the empirical research as to the limited impact of cancellation periods.[78]

Another matter needing further consideration is the extent to which the notion of informed decision-making is viewed not only in light of the harassment, coercion or pressure, but also in light of the substantive risks involved in the decision. On such an approach, the more the substantive risk increases, the greater reflection is called for; and, *on this basis*, transparency/time for reflection may not be viewed as enough to guarantee the requisite level of informed decision making. In other words, even though transparency/time for reflection might be sufficient if the focus were solely on the degree of harassment, coercion or pressure,

[75] In contracts where there is already a statutory cancellation period, the added problem of the harassment, pressure or coercion would surely mean that the least that would be required would be an extension of this period (in order to recognise the added consumer difficulty in making an informed decision that has been caused by the aggressive practice in question).

[76] UCPD, Articles 1 and 4. [77] I.e. those that were discussed above at section 3.

[78] See the discussion by Ramsay, supra, n. 50, at 345–6.

those factors may not be enough due to the substantive risks involved. There is no space to consider this issue in full. However, once again, if we interpret the concept of informed decision making in the light of the consumer protection and confidence goals of the UCPD, there seems a reasonable prospect that the substantive risks to the consumer would be considered relevant to the way in which we view informed decision making in the context of the aggressive practices concept.

(iii) Aggression, choice and substance

Thus far, we have been discussing those cases in which the actions of the trader have restricted the consumer's scope to reflect properly on the risks, burdens etc. involved in the decision in question (or possibly the consumer is threatened with an action that – unbeknownst to him – cannot be taken) and considering whether transparency/time for reflection is sometimes (or even often) not enough to cure the problem, i.e. to 'reinstate' informed consent. However, there seems to be a quite separate category of cases in which the fundamental problem is not that consumers are not well enough informed about risks or not well enough informed about the legality of what is being threatened. The problem, rather, is that that the trader creates a situation in which there are substantively unreasonable consequences for the consumer if he takes a certain decision; so that he may decide, as a result, to take another decision. The point is that the substantively unreasonable consequence does not become substantively reasonable just because it is clear, so that the basic issue is not a lack of informed consent; and, therefore, transparency does not provide a solution.

Certainly, it seems that there is potential for such cases to be recognised under the aggressive practices concept. As we have seen, in the case of harassment and coercion, the question is whether there is a restriction on 'freedom of choice or conduct'. While, as suggested above, this may *include* cases in which freedom of choice is restricted in the sense that there is not an informed decision; it arguably also covers cases in which choice is restricted in that taking a certain decision involves a substantively unreasonable consequence.

There may be support for this analysis in that one of the guidelines, as we have already seen, is whether there is a threat to take action that cannot lawfully be taken.[79] Sometimes (as in the example given above)

[79] UCPD, Article 9, guideline (e).

this is an informed decision-making problem in that the consumer does not realise that the action cannot be taken. However, it could be that, for example, a trader threatens to break a contract with the consumer if the consumer does not agree to some change. Breaking a contract can be viewed as 'unlawful'; but is the threat to do so necessarily one that causes an informed decision-making problem? The consumer may well know that the trader is not entitled to break the contract. The problem, rather, is that if the trader breaks the contract then, in practice, the consumer will suffer a loss of some type and may only recoup this loss if he goes to the trouble of taking court action. In short, there is an unreasonable consequence for the consumer; so, rather than facing this prospect, the consumer may decide to agree to the change.

There seems also to be support for a 'substantively unreasonable consequences' model in the guidance that refers to:

> any onerous or disproportionate non-contractual barrier imposed by the trader where a consumer wishes to exercise rights under the contract . . .[80]

Here, again, the issue does not seem to be whether the consumer is informed or not. Indeed, he is likely to be perfectly well aware as to what barriers he faces; and he may also be perfectly well aware as to what he stands to lose if he does not enforce his rights. The problem, rather, is that he may decide to give up on enforcing his rights due to the trouble, costs etc. involved in taking whatever unreasonable steps are required in order to enforce these rights. The further significance of this example is that it is a case where there is not necessarily anything independently unlawful about what the trader is doing. In the case of the threat to break the contract (above), there is a threat to do something which, in itself, can be viewed as being unlawful; while, here, the erection of the barrier to enforcement is not, independently, unlawful (it is not a tort and neither is it a threat of any type, much less to break a contract).

If this is indicative of a more general approach, it could have implications for the approach to enforcement by the *trader*. It could mean that there is an aggressive practice where, although the consumer may owe the money in question (so that there is nothing unlawful in seeking to recover it), the means of enforcement are considered to involve unreasonable substantive consequences for the consumer (and the threat, or

[80] UCPD, Article 9, guideline (d); and see the similar TCF principle to the effect that consumers should not face 'unreasonable post-sale barriers' when they wish to 'submit a claim or make a complaint' (Outcome 6).

actuality, of these consequences can be said to be such as to impair, significantly, the freedom of choice of the consumer, making it likely that he will decide to make immediate payment). This may provide an explanation for examples that the Office of Fair Trading views as aggressive. These include pressurising the consumer to perform, pay up etc.[81] by contacting him at unreasonable times and/or places (e.g. late at night, at work etc.)[82] and requiring consumers to discuss debts by making contact on premium rate telephone lines.[83] Again, the consumer may be perfectly well informed as to what is required; so that the problem is not that he is uninformed in this sense. Equally, the trader may be legally owed the money, so that the problem is not that the trader is taking action in respect of a 'debt' that the consumer does not really owe (the consumer being uninformed in that he believes it *is* legally due). Further, the type of enforcement action being threatened may be normal civil proceedings; so that the problem is not that the trader is threatening a type of action that he cannot take (the consumer being uninformed in the sense that he does not realise this). The problem is simply that the consumer may decide to pay up rather than face the substantively unreasonable impact of home/work contact or needing to pay for premium rate calls.

What is being suggested, then, is that any form of enforcement by the trader could be regarded as aggressive where what is being done/proposed/threatened etc., if the consumer does not pay the debt, is unreasonable (even though it is not necessarily independently unlawful[84]). Such a principle could be of particular assistance, given the greater than normal numbers of consumers that may find themselves in default in the (extraordinary) current economic circumstances. It could, conceivably, mean that there is an aggressive practice where the trader threatens immediate court action, giving little or no leeway or scope for an alternative solution or compromise, unless there is immediate payment. Such a threat might be considered unreasonable, especially where consumers have already paid significant parts of the debt, where they are suffering from a drop in income etc. This might lead consumers to make the payment, when a compromise (whether reducing the amount or giving

[81] I.e. to take a 'transactional decision' to do so.

[82] OFT/BERR, n. 70 above, at para. 8.11.

[83] Ibid., para. 8.11, n. 29 and OFT Debt Collection Guidance, July 2003 (updated December 2006), at 2.2 (h).

[84] As long as this unreasonableness is likely significantly to restrict freedom of choice and cause the consumer to decide to cave in to the demands.

more time to pay) might have been more reasonable. Of course, where cases actually go to court there are powers[85] allowing the court to review matters and potentially protect consumers (whether from full payment, immediate payment, forfeiture of property etc.). The problem is that consumers will not benefit from these protections if they cave in at an earlier stage;[86] so it is potentially significant if there is a control over trader actions that might cause this to happen. The AJA s. 40 catches 'distress, alarm or humiliation', e.g. contact at unreasonable times rather than simple refusal to compromise. The Banking Code says that 'with your co-operation we will develop a plan with you for dealing with your financial difficulties',[87] which may well address the issue. Treating uncompromising enforcement as unfair would also be in keeping with the recently agreed Civil Justice Council Protocol applicable to mortgage arrears. This recommends that there should be discussion, for instance, as to whether the causes of arrears are temporary or long-term and whether payment could be made within a reasonable time.[88]

5. Consumer benchmarks

One of the key features of the CPUTR regime is the way in which practices are assessed by reference to various consumer 'benchmarks'. Generally, the benchmark is the 'average consumer' (presumably meaning the average member of the general body of consumers). So the question is whether such an average consumer would be likely to be deceived by a practice (misleading actions); would need information to make an informed decision (misleading omissions); or would have his

85 E.g. rules against forfeiture, and rules under CCA, ss. 127–140, as amended by relevant provisions of CCA 2006.

86 Of course, one reason that consumers may pay up immediately is that they may not realise that the courts have such powers that could protect them. However, it does not seem correct to therefore say that the problem is simply one of uninformed decision-making. The powers in question may or may not be exercised in favour of the consumer and the court action generally involves stresses and risks (including a judgment being issued and the attendant problems of obtaining future credit, for example). So, taking court action (where no leeway or solution is explored) may be viewed, in some cases, as substantively unreasonable (whatever the consumer does or does not know about his rights in court).

87 See n. 14 above, at 14.2.

88 Civil Justice Council, October, 2008, available at www.civiljusticecouncil.gov.uk/files/cjc-new-pre-action-protocol-mort-poss-cases.pdf; particular options that are recommended for discussion are extending the term, changing the type or deferring payment of interest due under, the mortgage and capitalising the arrears.

freedom of choice significantly impaired (aggressive practices).[89] However, this benchmark can be altered (i) to the average member of a 'clearly identifiable group' that is 'particularly vulnerable to the practice or the underlying product because of their mental or physical infirmity, age or credulity in a way which the trader could reasonably be expected to foresee'[90] or (ii) to the average member of a particular group at which a practice is directed.[91] The pre-existing regulatory regimes do not contain any such clearly articulated benchmarking approach.[92] So, it is of particular importance to consider some of its implications.

It seems clear that the issue will often be the *procedural* ability of the average member of the relevant benchmark group, i.e. the ability to protect one's interest in the context of the decision-making process. So, for instance, in order to decide whether consumers need information to make an informed decision,[93] we must consider how capable they are of working out for themselves what they need to know and of searching out this information. To decide when informed decision making is compromised by pressure, coercion or harassment, we must assess consumer ability to withstand such tactics and fully assess the risks. The general average consumer benchmark certainly allows for consideration of such questions. What guidance there is focuses on the notion of a consumer that is 'reasonably well informed and reasonably circumspect';[94] and there is a rich vein of ECJ case law applying this concept.[95] It must be said, of course, that the main focus of this case law has been on assessing whether consumers would be *misled* by positively provided information. So, while the case law may be of help in developing the misleading action concept, it may be of less use in assessing the procedural questions relevant to the other concepts, i.e. how capable consumers are of working out for themselves what they need to know and of searching it out and how capable they are of withstanding pressure, coercion or harassment

[89] And in all cases the question is also whether the transactional decision-making of this same average consumer would be affected.

[90] UCPD, Article 5 (3). [91] UCPD, Article 5 (2) (b).

[92] Although there is some reference in the TCF initiative to considering the impact of practices on different target groups of consumers (2.15).

[93] The issue where misleading omissions are concerned.

[94] Preamble to the UCPD, recital 18.

[95] See, for example, Case C-210/96, *Gut Springheide GmbH* v. *Oberkreisdirektor des Kreises Steinfurt* (1998) ECR I-4657 (para. 37); *Verein gegen Unwesen in Handel und Gewerbe* v. *Mars GmbH*, C-470/93 [1995] ECR 1-1923; *Estee Lauder* v. *Lancaster* C-220/98; and see S. Weatherill, 'Who Is the "Average Consumer"', in Bernitz and Weatherill, n. 1 above for a review of the cases.

and remaining capable of calmly assessing the risks. However, the basic point is that the general average consumer concept seems flexible enough to accommodate consideration of these procedural questions.

The alternative consumer benchmarks also seem to allow for consideration of procedural abilities. This line of enquiry is certainly *demanded* in the case of members of groups that are vulnerable based on 'mental or physical infirmity, age or credulity' (see category (i) of the alternative consumer benchmarks above). It is obvious that factors such as infirmity, age and credulity may affect the ability to protect one's interest in the context of the decision-making process. So, there might be actions or omissions that would not be misleading (or practices that would not be aggressive) when assessed against the 'average member of the general body of consumers' benchmark. However, as we have seen above, if the practice affects a clearly identifiable group of consumers that the trader can reasonably foresee would have the procedural limitations mentioned (infirmity, age, credulity), the practice is to be assessed by reference to the (more limited) procedural abilities of the average member of such a group. In other words, a higher standard of fairness is set in order to recognise the procedural vulnerabilities and needs of the more vulnerable groups. So, for example, for those affected by infirmity, age or credulity, more information may be required to avoid the finding of a misleading omission; and trader selling or enforcement tactics are more inclined to be viewed as likely to affect informed decision making (and, therefore, as aggressive).

In order to work out when this should happen, it will be vital to work out when the market contains a 'clearly identifiable group' that traders can 'reasonably be expected to foresee' will have these limitations. Clearly many practices affecting children, the elderly and the infirm will be covered. However, in the financial services context, a key question will be whether consumers with poor financial literacy could be viewed in this light on the basis that they suffer from 'credulity'. This could be very significant in providing the basis for the application of higher standards of fairness (better information, more explanations, a lower acceptable threshold of pressure in selling etc.) for such consumers.

In the other benchmark scenario (i.e. category (ii) above, where certain groups are actually *targeted*) there is, in fact, no reference to particular characteristics/weaknesses. However, it must surely be intended that we take into account the procedural ability of the average member of such a group (to emphasise, again, this meaning the ability to protect one's interest in the context of the decision-making process). Here, again, where the target group is especially vulnerable in this regard, the result could be higher levels of protection (better information, more explanations, a lower acceptable threshold of pressure in selling etc.). However, in the case of category (ii) the result could also be a *lower* level of protection, where the average member of the particular targeted group is viewed as having *greater* procedural abilities than the average member of the general body of consumers.

A key question in the case of category (ii) will be when a practice is 'directed at' a particular group, although in some cases the nature of the product and the marketing may make it fairly obvious that groups such as children or the elderly are the target. Again, however, there is the question of those with poor financial literacy – when can a practice be viewed as 'directed at' such a group, thereby triggering application of a higher standard of procedural fairness?

Of course, sometimes the issue goes beyond the *procedural* abilities of consumers. *Substance* may also be relevant. So, for example, we saw above that the substantive risks of the transaction as a whole are possibly relevant to the question of informed decision making under the aggressive practices concept;[96] and that the question (again under the aggressive practices concept) as to whether there is a restriction on freedom of choice may depend on whether taking a certain decision involves a substantively unreasonable consequence.[97]

This would logically suggest that when we consider the practice from the point of view of the average member of a given benchmark consumer group, we consider (in addition to procedural abilities) the *impact* on the average member of this group of the substantive risks or consequences in question. This might, in turn, mean that account is taken of the financial resources of the average member of the benchmark group. However, this sort of approach may, in fact, only be able to be taken where the general body of consumers or particularly targeted groups are concerned. In these cases there is no clear indication that we should consider only *procedural* abilities. But, the same cannot be said in the case of the other benchmark group which, as we have seen, is one in which there is particular vulnerability to the practice based on reasonably foreseeable 'mental or physical infirmity, age or credulity', i.e. apparently *not* on the basis of reasonably foreseeable weaknesses (e.g. poverty, unemployment etc.) that could cause substantive risks or consequences to have a more serious impact.

[96] See above at section 4 (ii). [97] See above at section 4 (iii).

It seems, then, that substantive risks and consequences (when relevant) should be assessed by reference to the financial resources of the average member of either (i) the general body of consumers or (ii) a group at whom the practice was directed. In relation to this second category, as in the case of procedural abilities, the average member of such a group may have more or less in the way of financial resources than the average member of the general body of consumers; and, depending upon this, the result could be that a lower or a higher standard of fairness is applied than would otherwise be the case. A very important question in this context is as to when, exactly, groups who are particularly financially vulnerable will be regarded as having been targeted by a practice (and, thereby, benefit from a higher level of protection). The nature and marketing of some loans may make it clear that they are directed at low income consumers.[98] However, there may be a more difficult question at the enforcement stage. Many of the consumers who are in arrears of some kind have particularly limited financial resources (this often being the cause of the arrears building up). One could say that, as long as the same enforcement practices are used for members of all income groups who happen to be in arrears, such a practice cannot be said to be 'directed at' those badly off consumers who just happen to be the ones that are normally affected. On the other hand, it could be said that a practice is indeed 'directed at' those that are, in reality, normally affected by it. On this latter approach, it is the particularly weak financial position of these consumers that informs how we determine whether the substantive consequences of certain decisions have such an unreasonable impact that freedom of choice is significantly impaired. In short, an enforcement practice may well be aggressive unless it displays a fairly high level of sensitivity to the very weak financial position of most of those that are on the receiving end of it.

6. Concluding comments

This chapter has highlighted various key aspects of the new concept of unfairness emanating from the UCPD. It has been suggested that this

[98] So, arguably, in deciding whether there has been aggressive selling, account needs to be taken of the fact that the substantive risks involved in such a transaction are greater for low income consumers than for the general body of consumers (meaning that the degree of scope for reflection required for informed decision making is greater and, consequently, that there is less tolerance of trader action that might compromise this scope for reflection).

concept may make some important contributions to the framework of protection in the financial services sector, e.g. in relation to non-disclosure, pressure selling, being obstructive in the face of consumer complaints and being uncompromising in dealing with defaulting consumers.

Also, the chapter has sought to illustrate how the standards of fairness required on these various issues can increase, based on the particular procedural and substantive vulnerabilities of particular categories of consumers. Inter alia, this could mean that the standard of fairness expected of traders is particularly high when dealing with consumers who are in arrears.

A question for the future in relation to the unfairness concept is whether a practice can be unfair even where it is not misleading or aggressive as such, but on the basis that it simply involves an abuse of superior bargaining power. The issue here is whether this might be said to put it in breach of the 'master clause' on 'professional diligence'.[99]

A further question is as to the impact of the concept on private law. Although the Directive is said to be 'without prejudice to contract law and, in particular, to the rules on the validity, formation or effect of a contract',[100] it is hard to imagine that the concept of unfairness will not, ultimately, have some impact on the private law of contract. First of all, it seems inevitable that it will have an impact on contracting *practice*, as traders shape the way that they interact with consumers by reference to this regulatory backdrop. Second, it would be remarkable if courts were not pressed by at least some lawyers to develop common law concepts such as misrepresentation, duress and undue influence in ways that reflect the unfairness concept from the UCPD; and it would be surprising if this did not meet with at least a degree of sympathy. Third, the government has already considered the introduction of private law remedies for breach of the unfairness standard in the Directive; and the issue has now been given an initial review by the Law Commission;[101] It is therefore vital to better understand the concept in order to inform the debate surrounding any possible reception into private law (whether this is an incremental, common law reception or a statutory reception).

There is no space here to develop the issue. However various points seem to arise:

(i) The omissions concept is almost certainly broader than the existing notion of misrepresentation, which takes disclosure requirements as

[99] See above at section 2. [100] UCPD, Article 3 (3). [101] See n. 72 above.

exceptional;[102] (ii) the sort of practices identified above as potentially aggressive seem to be outside what would generally be taken to count as equitable relational-based undue influence;[103] (iii) threats to do something unlawful would already be caught by economic duress, but it is more difficult to say just to what extent economic duress currently covers lawful threats to do unreasonable things;[104] (iv) the rescission remedy might need to be developed to allow for the setting aside of a 'transactional decision' short of a contract; (v) interconnected issues as to fault and damages need to be resolved. Should there be the same damages for negligent and fraudulent practices that are misleading?[105] Should there be damages/an indemnity for innocently misleading practices? Should there be damages for omissions and, if so, what role should fault play?[106] Should there be damages for aggressive practices; and, if so, what, if any, notion of fault should this be based on?

[102] See section 3 (ii) above and see Law Commission, n. 72 above, at 2.43–2.64.

[103] Normally a relationship of trust is needed (see generally *RBOS* v. *Etridge* (No. 2) [2001] 4 All ER 449 and this will not usually exist in routine financial services cases (see also Law Commission, n. 72 above, at 2.73) .

[104] I.e. the sort of things that may well be covered by the new concept, see above at section 4 (iii). There is certainly some recognition that duress can cover threats of lawful action where what is being demanded is unreasonable or unconscionable (see *R* v. *Attorney General for England and Wales* [2003] UKPC 22). See the Law Commission view (n. 72 above, at 2.75) that threats may be illegitimate (and therefore caught by duress) on the simple basis that they breach the CPUTR.

[105] This already being an issue of controversy: J. Poole and J. Devenney, 'Reforming Damages for Misrepresentation: The Case for Coherent Aims and Principles' (2007) *Journal of Business Law* 269–305, which there is now an opportunity to resolve in the context of any reform of private law remedies.

[106] See Law Commission, n. 72 above, at 2.63.

Conclusions

19

Conceptualising unconscionability in Europe: in the kaleidoscope of private and public law

MEL KENNY, JAMES DEVENNEY AND LORNA FOX O'MAHONY

1. Introduction

The aim of this project has been to explore particular conceptions of, and responses to, unconscionability and similar notions, with specific reference to financial transactions across Europe. Such an endeavour is difficult for at least five reasons.

First, the process can be obscured by the nuances of emphasis[1] and language[2] both within jurisdictions and at a pan-European level.[3] Secondly, as the chapter by Waddams[4] suggests, particular jurisdictions may choose, to varying degrees, to respond (sometimes indirectly) to unconscionability issues through a variety of devices rather than through an independent doctrine of unconscionability. Thirdly, as we have suggested elsewhere,[5] conceptions of, and responses to, unconscionability may be shaped by,

1 See, for example, R. Bigwood, 'Undue Influence: "Impaired Consent" or "Wicked Exploitation"' (1996) 16 *Oxford Journal of Legal Studies* 503 and J. Devenney and A. Chandler, 'Unconscionability and the Taxonomy of Undue Influence' (2007) *Journal of Business Law* 541.

2 See, for example, J. Elvin, 'The Purpose of the Doctrine of Undue Influence', in P. Giliker (ed.), *Re-examining Contract and Unjust Enrichment: Anglo-Canadian Perspectives* (Leiden: Martinus Nijhoff Publishers, 2007) and the review thereof by J. Devenney, (2008) *Legal Studies* 477 at 479.

3 M. Kenny, '*Standing Surety in Europe: Common Core or Tower of Babel*, (2007) 70 *Modern Law Review* 175 in particular at 180 ff.

4 Waddams, Chapter 2.

5 J. Devenney, L. Fox O'Mahony and M. Kenny, 'Standing Surety in England and Wales: The Sphinx of Procedural Protection' (2008) *Lloyds Maritime and Commercial Law Quarterly* 527 and J. Devenney, M. Kenny and L. Fox O'Mahony, '[The Protection of Non-Professional Sureties in England and Wales]', in A. Colombi Ciacchi and S. Weatherill (eds.), *Regulating Unfair Banking Practices in Europe: The Case of Personal Suretyships* (forthcoming, OUP). See also M. Kenny and J. Devenney, 'The Fallacy of the Common Core: Polycontextualism in Surety Protection – a Hard Case in Harmonisation Discourse', in M. Andenæs and

for example, the social security and insolvency regimes within a particular jurisdiction.[6] Fourthly, as Capper demonstrates, conceptions of unconscionability may be dependent on context[7] and, as Swain and Fairweather[8] clearly demonstrate, may vary over time. Indeed a week after the conference upon which this collection of essays is based, Lehman Brothers collapsed and the landscape of financial transactions and many of the assumptions underlying traditional approaches to the protection of the vulnerable in financial transactions was radically challenged; our perception of risk, attitudes towards regulation and understandings of risk may never be the same again. As Capper[9] demonstrates, even within particular jurisdictions conceptions of unconscionability can be contested.[10] Indeed Waddams thought-provokingly suggests that unconscionability 'has had multiple dimensions, and that it has not been confined to a single conceptual category'.[11] This idea is elaborated in Wightman's approach to the neglected dimension of unconscionability and the specific issue of transactional risk, where the characteristics of particular kinds of transaction, in interaction with the conduct of the parties, create unusual risk for one party.[12] Transactional risk is, as Rott and Halfmeier analyse, endemic in financial services' contracts.[13]

In this chapter we will seek to pull together some of the key issues and themes which emerge from this collection of essays and the conference upon which it is based. We will also comment on the challenges for programmes of harmonisation in this area.[14]

C. Andersen (eds.), *The Theory and Practice of Harmonisation* (forthcoming, Edward Elgar Publishing).

6 See also R. Parry, 'The Position of Family Sureties within the Framework of Protection for Consumer Debtors in European Member States' (2005) 13 *European Review of Private Law* 357.

7 See also J. Devenney and A. Chandler, 'Unconscionability and the Taxonomy of Undue Influence' (2007) *Journal of Business Law* 541.

8 Swain and Fairweather, Chapter 8.

9 Capper, Chapter 9.

10 Compare, for example, P. Birks and Y. Chin, 'On the Nature of Undue Influence', in J. Beatson and D. Friedmann (eds.), *Good Faith and Fault in Contract Law* (Oxford: Clarendon, 1995) with Devenney and Chandler, 'Unconscionability and the Taxonomy of Undue Influence', n. 1 above.

11 Waddams, Chapter 2. 12 Wightman, Chapter 6.

13 Rott and Halfmeier, Chapter 17.

14 See also J. Devenney and M. Kenny, 'Unfair Terms, Surety Transactions and European Harmonisation: A Crucible of Europeanised Private Law?' (2009) *Conveyancer and Property Lawyer* 295.

2. Challenging private law elaborations of unconscionability

Public vs. private, common law vs. civil law?

A central issue which arises from this project relates to the respective roles of private and public law in responding to issues of unconscionability. Common lawyers would automatically tend to understand unconscionability as a private law problem, as an exception to the primacy of notions of freedom of contract. Traditionally at least, the central place of freedom of contract led to the assumption that exceptions should be avoided, or at the very least restricted to the bare minimum. Civil lawyers might more naturally tend to view equivalent concepts to unconscionability such as good morals (*gute Sitten*) in German law, good faith (*redelijkheid en billijkheid*) and mistake (*dwaling*) in Dutch law,[15] contractual unfairness as elaborated through doctrine, consumer protection and pre-contractual fraud (*la réticence dolosive)* in France,[16] as, in certain circumstances, relieving vulnerable parties from the full play of their contractual obligations.

Yet why should freedom of contract continue to play such an important and constricting role in the elaboration of unconscionability? Surely, as Colombi Ciacchi challenges, a case can be made to fundamentally revamp private law, to make the law relevant for the twenty-first century by ensuring a tangible freedom from unconscionable transactions rather than a one-dimensional notion of freedom of contract. Indeed, in more recent times the traditional private law approaches to fleshing out the content of unconscionability have been increasingly challenged; and all European jurisdictions have had to find ways to respond to this challenge. The challenge, as this volume demonstrates, has arisen on at least three fronts: by public law/constitutional principles (fundamental rights); attempts at European regulation (see in this connection, in particular, Rott and Halfmeier on the MiFID); and the challenge presented to traditional private law approaches by broader exercises in private law codification (for example, the Common Frame of Reference project).[17] At this stage we can briefly describe the three respective challenges to the private law elaboration of unconscionability:

(a) Constitutional challenge: this is strikingly seen in the German Constitutional Court's decision in the *Bürgschaft* case, in which it

[15] Cherednychenko, Chapter 13. [16] Saintier, Chapter 4.
[17] See generally Kenny and Devenney, 'The Fallacy of the Common Core', n. 5 above.

was held that courts were obliged to give effect to extensive substantive protection of family members against disproportionate obligations in suretyship agreements on the basis of good morals. The case shows the enormous flexibility inherent in German contract law to import or transplant constitutional principles: but also begs the question of whether this truly represents the triumph of, or the constitutionalisation of, German private law.[18]

(b) European regulation: for example, the tendency towards accommodating contract law duties of care towards customers within regulatory supervision rules, especially in financial transactions, has been further strengthened as a result of the adoption of the Markets in Financial Instruments Directive (MiFID), described by some as Europe's 'new constitution' for investment services and secondary capital markets.[19] A characteristic feature of the EC approach to investor protection is its procedural nature and consequent reliance on the information paradigm. Despite the objections to the model adopted in overstating the capacity of consumers to process the information given, expanded upon in Rott and Halfmeier's contribution, the MiFID aims to protect non-professional investors solely by procedural means: extensive duties to inform, advise or warn the customer in combination with the duties to know one's customer and to assess the suitability of a particular investment service or financial instrument for the customer.[20] As with the suretyship constellation, in the context of financial transactions consumers may simply not respond to such steps, no matter how extensive the information given.

(c) Codification: given the fragmentation of law which uneven patterns of national private law and consumer protection across different European jurisdictions have produced, a fragmentation further exacerbated by the piecemeal, sectoral adoption of vertical instruments of European regulation, can a case be made for the wholesale codification of European private law?

[18] Rott and Halfmeier, Chapter 17 elaborating the German approach: Bundesgerichtshof (BGH) *ZIP Zeitschrift für Wirtschaftsrecht*, 22 (2001), 189; BGH *Juristische Schulung*, 41 (2001), 606; BGH *Neue Juristische Wochenschrift*, 55 (2002), 2228; BGH *Neue Juristische Wochenschrift*, 55 (2002), 2230; BGH *Neue Juristische Wochenschrift*, 55 (2002), 2634.

[19] See, K. J. Hopt, 'Grundsatz- und Praxisprobleme nach dem Wertpapierhandelsgesetz – insbesondere Insidergeschäfte und Ad-hoc-Publizität', *Zeitschrift für gesamte Handelsrecht und Witrschaftsrecht*, 159 (1995), 135, 135; H-D. Assmann/U. H. Schneider, *Wertpapierhandelsgesetz* (Cologne: Otto Schmidt, 2006).

[20] See Article 19 of the MiFID.

Furthermore, and even more subtly, if courts – whether common law or civil law – make judgments about particular norms such as unconscionability or equivalent concepts,[21] can a pan-European concept of unconscionability emerge indirectly through judicial harmonisation rather than through the more invasive codification exercise announced in the CFR initiative? Can the emergent concept be influenced by a mixture of private and public law concepts as elaborated in domestic case law? Smaliukas in his analysis suggests that European private law regimes may indeed be more resilient in their capacity to import or transplant legal doctrine than we may think;[22] a point which Willett also alludes to in his chapter.[23] As Cherednychenko notes, to an extent the challenges which have arisen have at least been accommodated within the private law: the *Bürgschaft* case can be seen not simply as a case of constitutionalisation but also, if more subtly, as a prime example of a more piecemeal *judicial harmonisation* of private law. What is important with such judicial harmonisation is, ultimately, that the results produced are similar and here, though the facts of the Dutch and English suretyship cases were broadly similar, unlike in Germany, in neither jurisdiction did fundamental rights play any significant role.[24]

Constitutionalisation

The intervention of fundamental rights to protect the vulnerable family member in the German *Bürgschaft* case[25] represents at one level, as previously alluded to, a constitutionalisation of unconscionability; a valuable assertion, as Colombi Ciacchi observes, of freedom from unconscionable transactions. It comes as a qualification of the traditional model which looked to the fundamental importance of freedom of contract. Under the 'constitutionalised' approach, in cases where a structural imbalance in bargaining power has led to a contract which is exceptionally onerous for the vulnerable party, private law courts are obliged to intervene on the basis of general clauses of good morals and good faith.[26] Through the

[21] See also Devenney and Kenny, 'Unfair Terms, Surety Transactions and European Harmonisation', n. 14 above.

[22] Smaliukas, Chapter 14. [23] Willett, Chapter 18.

[24] See HR 1 June 1990, *NJ* 759 (*Van Lanschot Bankiers* v. *Bink*) and *Barclays Bank plc* v. *O'Brien* [1994] 1 AC 180, for Dutch and English law, respectively. On these cases in more detail, see O. Cherednychenko, *Fundamental Rights, Contract Law and the Protection of the Weaker Party* (Munich: Sellier, 2007).

[25] BVerfG 19 October 1993, *BVerfGE* 89, 214 (*Bürgschaft*).

[26] §§ 138(1) and 242 of the German Civil Code.

interpretation of fundamental rights, the Constitutional Court in Germany thus entered into the kaleidoscope of public and private law; into the elaboration of contractual justice in modern contract law. By holding the private law courts to be *obliged* to protect the constitutional rights of weaker parties, the judiciary can thus be seen to be limiting the role played by contract law in determining when a contract is unconscionable.

Cherednychenko criticises this approach: the interests of the vulnerable party can be protected by several fundamental rights; a competition between the applicable fundamental rights or *Grundrechtskonkurrenz* is possible, begging in turn the question as to when the courts should determine which fundamental right/s is/are applicable. Whereas the German Constitutional Court in the *Bürgschaft* case provided relief on the basis of the right to private autonomy in conjunction with the social state, it would have been equally possible, as Cherednychenko suggests, to argue the case on the basis of the surety's right to family life within the framework provided by Article 6(1) of the German Constitution. Moreover, even when the *Grundrechtskonkurrenz* can be resolved, in certain cases one and the same right can be used to support both of the claims of the parties involved in the case. Consequently, the courts are charged with resolving the conflict between the two fundamental rights. In the absence of a clear hierarchy of fundamental rights, the only way of doing this is by mediating or balancing the competing rights against each other. Here, in the *Bürgschaft* case, the 'conflict of fundamental rights' arose between the surety's right to private autonomy versus the bank's right to private autonomy. A balance had to be struck on the constitutional level between the protection of the private autonomy of the vulnerable and interference with the private autonomy of the stronger party to the contract.

The major problem with this approach is that, as it is not clear which outcomes should follow from the individual fundamental right, the issue – unsatisfactorily – is simply left to private law courts to resolve. In this regard, as Cherednychenko goes on to argue, it would have been equally consistent with the Constitutional Court's approach to the effect of fundamental rights to uphold the original decision of the Supreme Court in the *Bürgschaft* case: after all, it could be argued that the surety's constitutional right to private autonomy had been respected; every person would have to have been aware of the risks involved.

But are we really dealing with the constitutionalisation of private law? Surely, as Cherednychenko argues, is this not simply a case in which judicial innovation has transplanted constitutional rights into private law analysis? Moreover, a comparable or at least equivalent result to the *Bürgschaft* case was achieved, in the context of surety agreements, in both England and Wales and the Netherlands on the basis of different concepts within a traditional private law approach. Although in both Dutch and English law the protection granted to sureties is limited to procedural protection,[27] the contract law of both legal systems also contains concepts which can be resorted to in order to introduce substantive protection in those cases where there is a gross discrepancy between the amount of liability potentially faced by the surety and the financial means of the prospective surety at the time of the conclusion of the surety agreement. [28]

Between the positions adopted by Cherednychenko and Colombi Ciacchi, Teubner points to a subtle transformation of the notion of freedom of contract itself. Freedom of contract in a layered context of private law instruments, doctrines and protective levels, becomes a much broader concept: 'While ... freedom of contract was limited to the protection of free choice in the market against fraud, deception, and ... political interference, the new freedom of contract ... extend(s) to a protection of contract against the free market itself.'[29] In this model the need to limit autonomy, to respect a complex array of social expectations and third party interests is accentuated, Teubner concluding that constitutional law will play a mediating role in this hybridised, discursive contract law:[30] '[C]ontract as interdiscursivity raises ... the issue of constitutional rights ... these rights can no longer be seen as protecting only the individual actor against the repressive power of the state, but ... need to be reconstructed as "discourse rights" ... The ... correlate of contract as translation would be an extension of constitutional rights into the context of private governance regimes.'[31] Yet the implications of such

[27] For Dutch law, see HR 1 June 1990, *NJ* 759 (*Van Lanschot Bankiers* v. *Bink*). For English law, see *Royal Bank of Scotland* v. *Etridge (No. 2)* [2001] 4 ALL ER 449.

[28] J. Devenney, L. Fox-O'Mahony and M. Kenny, 'Standing Surety in England and Wales', n. 5 above.

[29] G. Teubner, 'Das Recht hybrider Netzwerke', *Zeitschrift für das gesamte Handelsrecht and Wirtschaftsrecht*, 165 (2001), 550. English version: G. Teubner, 'In the Blindspot: The Hybridisation of Contracting', available at www.jura.uni-frankfurt.de/ifawz1/teubner/dokumente/VERTRAG_eng_TheoreticalInquiries.pdf., at 14.

[30] S. Weatherill, 'The Commission's Options for Developing EC Consumer Protection and Contract Law: Assessing the Constitutional Basis' (2002) 13 *European Business Law Review* 497, O. Gerstenberg, 'Private Law and the New European Constitutional Settlement' (2004) 10 *European Law Journal* 766, H. Schepel, 'The Enforcement of EC Law in Contractual Relations: Case Studies in How Not to "Constitutionalise" Private Law' (2004) 12 *European Review of Private Law* 661.

[31] Teubner, 'In the Blindspot', n. 29 above, at 18.

constitutionalisation or quasi-constitutionalisation on the constitutional democracy are, as Hirschl observes, massive and potentially pernicious; launching a process in which lawyers intervene to insulate traditional hierarchical patterns:

> By keeping popular decision-making mechanisms at the forefront of the formal democratic political processes while simultaneously shifting the power to formulate and promulgate certain policies from majoritarian policy-making arenas to semiautonomous professional policy-making bodies, those who have disproportionate access to and have a decisive influence upon such bodies minimize the potential threat to their hegemony ... the current global trend toward judicial empowerment through constitutionalisation is part of a broader process whereby self-interested political and economic elites ... *attempt to insulate policy-making from the vagaries of democratic politics ... [I]t can best be understood as an attempt to defend established interests from the potential threats posed by the voices of cultural divergence, growing economic inequality, regionalism, and other centrifugal forces that have been given a public platform through the proliferation of representative democracy.*[32]

Constitutionalisation and harmonisation vs. regulation and codification

Given the legitimacy caveats regarding constitutionalisation, which can perhaps be seen as a type of judicial harmonisation or innovation, can a case be made for a more formal, regulatory harmonisation through European secondary law or, even more radically, a comprehensive codification of European private law? Given the differences between Member States' financial services' laws, the Commission had, until September 2008, taken the view that improving access to credit, enhancing consumer protection through responsible lending, and thus 'promoting' consumer debt and encouraging, in particular, the active consumer could generate significant economic growth. The aim of promoting the depth, liquidity and dynamism in financial markets so as to allow for more efficient resource allocation and enhanced competition[33] was

[32] R. Hirschl, *Towards Juristocracy* (Harvard University Press, 2004) at 217 (emphasis added).

[33] Green Paper on Financial Services Policy (2005–2010) (COM(2005) 177 final) at: http://ec.europa.eu/internal_market/finances/docs/actionplan/index/green_en.pdf. Financial Services White Paper 2005–2010: http://ec.europa.eu/internal_market/finances/docs/white_paper/white_paper_en.pdf. identifying EC objectives of an integrated, open, inclusive, competitive and efficient financial market; removal of the remaining barriers to financial services; high levels of financial stability; consumer protection; deepened relations with other global financial market places and globally enhanced European influence.

also an aspect of the Lisbon strategy.[34] To these ends, in 2002, the Commission proposed the adoption of a new, maximum harmonisation Directive on consumer credit.[35] The Commission's interest in the integration of the financial services' market can be illuminated: extrapolating from UK levels of secured and unsecured debt, there appeared – at least up to the advent of the Credit Crunch – to be a potential for a European debt market in excess of 13 trillion Euros.[36]

Increasingly, therefore, the question to emerge was not whether but how a single financial services' market could be achieved: through selective measures of sectoral harmonisation or more adventurous measures of 'internal market', maximum harmonisation. In this volume Rott and Halfmeier examine the virtues of the sectoral approach to harmonisation. Moreover, even if the question as to the depth of harmonisation or the feasibility of codification can be resolved, what type of financial services' regulation would recommend itself: the traditional Anglo-American model of unregulated financial services' provision[37] or a more European model involving a higher level of consumer protection? Alternatively, is the integration of the financial services' market best left after all to less invasive, non-legislative, judicial harmonisation,[38] to a competition of legal orders[39] or to the market and spontaneous

[34] Presidency Conclusions, Lisbon European Council, 23–24 March 2000 (Lisbon Strategy): http://ue.eu.int/ueDocs/cms_Data/docs/pressData/en/ec/00100-r1.en0.htm. 'to become the most competitive and dynamic knowledge-based economy in the world, capable of sustainable economic growth with more and better jobs and greater social cohesion'.

[35] Proposal for a Directive of the European Parliament and of the Council on the harmonisation of the laws, regulations and administrative provisions of the Member States concerning credit for consumers, Brussels 11.9.2002, (COM(2002) 443 final) Explanatory Memorandum, Section 1.2. at 3: http://europa.eu.int/eur-lex/lex/LexUriServ/site/en/com/2002/com2002_0443en01.pdf. Section 3, Explanatory Memorandum emphasising the information paradigm, at 8: 'The directive also covers surety agreements. The harmonisation being sought for these agreements will centre mainly on the information to be provided to consumers concluding such agreements, even if they guarantee credit that is granted for employment-related purposes'.

[36] In February 2006, the UK secured lending at GBP 981.8 bn and consumer credit at GBP 192.6 bn making a total indebtedness of GBP 1.174 trillion. For policy initiatives: www.creditaction.org.uk/debtstats.htm and www.debt-on-our-doorstep.com.

[37] C. McCreevy, DG Internal Market, Speech at Centre for European Reform, 'Financial Markets Integration', London, 9 March 2006: http://ec.europa.eu/commission_barroso/mccreevy/docs/speeches/2006-03-09/centreeureform_en.pdf.

[38] A. Colombi Ciacchi, 'Non-Legislative Harmonisation of Private Law under the European Constitution: The Case of Unfair Suretyships' (2005) 13 *European Review of Private Law* 285.

[39] J. H. M. van Erp, 'European Private Law: Post-modern Dilemmas and Choices' (1999) 3 *Electronic Journal of Comparative Law*, www.ejcl.org/31/art31-1.html.

harmonisation,[40] or is it best achieved through a mediation of claims through a constitutionalisation of private law?[41] Clearly, the scale of intervention identified as necessary – whether substantive control or the need for procedural rules and behavioural change to bank practice – will inform the choice and location of measures to be adopted.

3. Key themes demarcating unconscionability

Across the range of topics and contributions covered in this collection, it is possible to identify a number of key themes that emerge across the 'unconscionability scholarship' in the context of financial transactions. These key themes are vulnerability, risk and responsibility.

Vulnerability

Our perception of vulnerability and the adequacy of private law, regulatory and codification responses aimed at protecting the vulnerable has altered dramatically in the last months. Again, different legal orders have focused on different categories as particularly vulnerable,[42] for example, whether consumer, family member or non-professional; and some of the fragmentation of European approaches to unconscionability can be attributed to these different and sometimes inconsistent demarcations of vulnerability across legal orders.[43]

The understanding of unconscionability may also hinge on one's approach to freedom of contract, in particular on whether a freedom to conclude contracts should be understood in a formal or a substantive sense. This conflict goes to the heart of modern European contract discourse between private autonomy and social justice, as alluded to above – between the assertion of freedom of contract and the assertion of the importance of fairness and solidarity in contract law; it shapes the extent of the class of vulnerable contracting parties. Increasingly, as Colombi Ciacchi observes, a new substantive understanding of freedom of contract is emerging, requiring the judge to consider the contractual

[40] A. I. Ogus, 'Competition between National Legal Systems: A Contribution of Economic Analysis to Comparative Law' (1999) 48 *International and Comparative Law Quarterly* 405.

[41] O. Gerstenberg, 'Private Law and the New European Constitutional Settlement' (2004) 10 *European Law Journal* 766.

[42] See generally, Devenney and Kenny, 'Unfair Terms, Surety Transactions and European Harmonisation', n. 14 above.

[43] Kenny and Devenney, 'The Fallacy of the Common Core' n. 5 above.

parity in the given case. Colombi Ciacchi points to a range of cases in Germany, Slovenia, Greece and the Netherlands in which judges have been asked to address the imbalance between the parties and to ensure substantive freedom of contract. [44]

Thus, the question Cherednychenko sets as to whether and to what extent the weaker party must be protected against entering into highly risky financial transactions: should the financial institution be obliged to refuse to execute transactions where the transaction is extremely risky in view of the customer's financial situation? Clearly this may lead to an unstable definition of vulnerability: the customer's solvency may be irrelevant in determining his/her protection where the risk involved in the investment is significant. Alternatively, should the customer be able to assume such risks subject to the condition that the investment firm, as a more professional party, has fully explained the transaction, in particular by explaining the risks involved?[45]

Here Rott and Halfmeier's critique is instructive: both the MiFID Directive (2004/39/EC) and the German implementation of the Implementing Directive 2006/73/EC[46] adopt, in their view, far too bank-friendly an approach to non-professional investment advice, adopting an information-based solution towards kickback payments rather than a substantive approach. Interestingly, a substantive 'prohibition' as used with medicines (Directive 2001/83/EC) was not adopted for financial services on the basis that there is no special vulnerability with financial advice, the investor being neither consumer nor vulnerable towards another contracting party. However, Rott and Halfmeier analyse the appropriate approach to protection by incorporating behavioural finance research and disrupt the picture of the 'well-informed consumer' assumed by both the European and domestic legislator to be at the heart of the transaction, concluding that 'the disclosed information does not help the investor to make a reasonable decision' and that only substantive protection is appropriate where conflicts of interest are responsible for incentives to give inappropriate advice. The psychology of the context may thus rephrase the traditional view of the invulnerability of the non-professional investor.

Family members, meanwhile, would seem more naturally a vulnerable group than non-professional investors; as the suretyship cases confirm, no amount of information will be liable to influence the family member

[44] Colombi Ciacchi, Chapter 1. [45] Cherednychenko, Chapter 13.
[46] Rott and Halfmeier, Chapter 17.

in a meaningful way.[47] This explains the intervention of fundamental rights in the German *Bürgschaft* case[48] in which an appeal that the Supreme Court had violated the surety's constitutional right to private autonomy (Article 2(1) of the German Constitution) in conjunction with the principle of the social state (Article 20(1) and Article 28(1)) succeeded. According to the Constitutional Court, in cases where a structural imbalance in bargaining power has led to a contract which is exceptionally onerous for the weaker party, the private law courts are obliged to intervene on the basis of the general clauses (§§ 138(1) and 242 of the Civil Code) on good morals and good faith. Thus, through the interpretation of constitutional rights, the German Constitutional Court entered into the discussion of contractual justice in modern contract law. Constitutional rights were used to challenge the logic of private autonomy. By holding the private law courts to be *obliged* to protect the constitutional rights of weaker parties, the Constitutional Court significantly limited the role played by contract law in determining whether a particular contract is unconscionable. What is at issue in modern contract law is therefore the extent of protection of weaker parties which is necessary in order to address the present challenges arising from changing social and economic conditions of everyday life.

Last but not least, regulating the protection of weaker parties in some areas by means of the conduct of business rules such as European secondary law, exemplified in the MiFID Directive, while leaving such protection in other areas to private law – in particular where the private law concept has been shaped by fundamental rights – may lead to peculiar differences in the extent to which weaker parties are protected in different financial transactions. Thus, for example, as Rott and Halfmeier observe, in German law family sureties enjoy substantive protection against excessively onerous obligations while non-professional investors are denied such protection altogether; in contrast to the treatment of family sureties, where a potentially ruinous obligation exceeding the surety's ability to pay gives rise to the presumption of immorality, no such consequences are attached to the fact that the investor has entered into a highly risky investment transaction which

[47] Kenny, 'Standing Surety in Europe' n. 3 above, in particular at 176 citing J. Gernhüber, 'Ruinöse Bürgschaften als Folge familiärer Verbundenheit' (1995) *Juristenzeitung* 1086, at 1093: 'Warnings and advice . . . are only useful where the addressee is prepared to accept them' (authors' translation).

[48] BVerfG 19 October 1993, *BVerfGE* 89, 214 (*Bürgschaft*).

was highly disproportional to his financial resources.[49] In Dutch law, as Cherednychenko elaborates, the concern for the effectiveness of the financial system has produced even odder results. While family sureties enjoy only procedural protection by means of the information duties incumbent on the bank,[50] non-professional investors trading in derivatives enjoy a combination of substantive and procedural protection aimed at protecting such investors against themselves.[51] The question which arises in this respect, however, is whether non-professional investors are more vulnerable in risky financial transactions than family sureties.

Risk

It is generally accepted that financial transactions carry risks.[52] Until recently, these risks have been valorised within neoliberal policy, with exposure to risk accepted as part of the modern identity of consumers as 'enterprising entrepreneurs' – as 'the bearer of risk who makes "choices" as to which risks he/she will manage, to what degree, and by what provision, and who must live with the consequences of the mistakes they make'.[53] With 'risk' identified as the leitmotif,[54] and neoliberal policies emphasising the individualisation of citizens,[55] individuals are presented as: 'prudent, rational, desiring to be responsible for themselves'.[56] Within this framework, protection for vulnerable parties has tended to operate at the

[49] See, for example, BGH 8 May 2001, *BGHZ* 147, 343, 350; BGH 11 November 2003, *Wertpapier-Mitteilungen* (2004), 24, 27.

[50] See HR 1 June 1990, *NJ* 759 (*Van Lanschot Bankiers* v. *Bink*).

[51] Cherednychenko, Chapter 13.

[52] P. Bernstein, *Against The Gods: The Remarkable Story of Risk* (J. Wiley & Sons, 1996), which provides a historical account of risk in financial transactions; K. Byrne, 'How Do Consumers Evaluate Risk in Financial Products?' (2005) 10 *Journal of Financial Services Marketing* 21–36; H. Van Greuning and S. Brajovic Bratanovic, *Analyzing and Managing Banking Risk* (World Bank Publications, 3rd edn, 2009).

[53] M. Cooper, 'The Inequality of Security: Winners and Losers in the Risk Society' (2008) 61 *Human Relations* 1229 at 1233.

[54] A. Giddens, *Modernity and Self-Identity: Self and Society in the Late Modern Age* (Cambridge: Polity Press, 1991); U. Beck, *Risk Society: Towards a New Modernity* (New Delhi: Sage, 1992). See also A. Giddens, 'Risk and Responsibility' (1999) 62 *Modern Law Review* 1.

[55] N. Rose, 'The Death of the Social? Refiguring the Territory of Government' (1996) 25 *Economy and Society* 327; P. O'Malley, 'Risk and Responsibility', in A. Barry, T. Osborne and N. S. Rose (eds.), *Foucault and Political Reason: Liberalism, Neo-liberalism and the Rationalities of Government* (London: UCL Press, 1996); P. Leonard, *Postmodern Welfare* (London: Sage, 1997).

[56] Cooper, n. 53 above, at 1234.

margins, with what Williams describes as a (judicial) tendency to regard 'unfairness in consumer financial markets . . . as an exceptional transaction that departs radically from an unproblematic norm'.[57]

Yet, within this model, two major contemporary challenges can be identified. On the one hand, the emergence of scholarship critiquing Giddens' and Beck's portrait of the 'reflexive individual'[58] has important implications for the 'value of choice' theory delineated by Voyiakis in his analysis.[59] This account of contract law puts the contracting consumer in context, taking account of the structures that frame people's choices in respect of financial transactions, and proposing a more complex, 'pluralist' response.

Meanwhile, the global financial crisis has demonstrated the way in which the risks in the financial system can potentially impact on *all* consumers, and called into question the 'overly optimistic view of self-regulating markets',[60] informing much law-and-economics scholarship. Indeed, even before the 'credit crunch', the relationship between risk, responsibility and regulation had emerged as an important theme in UK policy,[61] with the growing reach of the FSA providing an example of the shift towards growth in the use of regulatory approaches as a response to the risks associated with financial transactions. Yet the way in which *risk* is conceptualised has also been transformed by the global financial meltdown,[62] with the suggestion that permissive regulatory conditions played a role in creating the conditions for the crisis, leading to increased calls for fundamental reviews of the way in which financial transactions are regulated.[63]

This theme is explored in several contributions. Nield's analysis of the new notion of unconscionability that has emerged through a range of statutory provisions and regulatory responses to the risks posed to those who borrow against the security of domestic property, raises questions

57 Williams, Chapter 12.

58 Cooper, n. 53 above; A. Aldridge, 'Habitus and Cultural Capital in the Field of Personal Finance' (1998) 46 *Sociological Review* 1; V. Gillies, 'Raising the Meritocracy: Parenting and the Individualization of Social Class' (2005) 39 *Sociology* 835.

59 Voyiakis, Chapter 5.

60 R. P. Malloy, 'Mortgage Market Reform and the Fallacy of Self-Correcting Markets' (2009) 30 *Pace Law Review* 79.

61 Better Regulation Commission, *Risk, Responsibility and Regulation: Whose Risk is it Anyway?* (London: Cabinet Office, 2006).

62 E. Heilpern, C. Haslam and T. Andersson, 'When it Comes to the Crunch: What are the Drivers of the US Banking Crisis?' (2009) 33(2) *Accounting Forum* 99–113; V. Acharya and M. Richardson (eds.), *Restoring Financial Stability* (J. Wiley & Sons, 2009).

63 M. Wolf, 'Why the Credit Squeeze is a Turning Point for the World' *Financial Times* 11 December 2007.

about the way in which risk is conceptualised:[64] for example, should transactions which put one's home at risk be regarded as 'higher order risks', on the basis that the harms that may result from a 'bad' outcome are particularly adverse? Across the range of papers, particular sets of risk and different responses to those risks across the nodes of scholarship and the various jurisdictions represented can be identified. For example, Williams demonstrates how the risk of adverse consequences for consumers, even where this risk is not actualised, has been sufficient to justify fines against providers of financial products under the remit of the FSA.[65] From another perspective, Williams' chapter also highlights the emergence of a new methodology for addressing unfairness in consumer markets, which recognises that fairness is contextually related to the characteristics of the product and the parties.[66] This approach is rooted in recognition of the variable measure of risk posed by particular products, to particular parties. Further, it makes a crucial connection in identifying the relationship between the exposure of consumers to risk – whether actualised in a 'bad' outcome or not – and adverse consequences for financial service providers.[67]

It is also valuable to note the debates concerning provision of adequate and qualitative information in the tests seeking to identify unconscionability in financial transactions. Here, Cartwright emphasises the centrality of information as part of a complex, multi-faceted conceptualisation of 'unfairness' within the context of financial regulation, a theme which resonates strongly with conceptualisations of the risk society as characterised by the expansion of choice and the proliferation of information, often in respect of an inherently uncertain future.[68]

However, it is also important to bear in mind that the party with whom the potentially vulnerable consumer is transacting is in a stronger position by virtue of being 'the expert' party. This issue is discussed in Viñals' analysis, where she notes that consumers can be regarded as a weaker party per se by virtue of their non-expert status, particularly in the context of mass or standard form contracts.[69] Viñals notes that 'a mass contract offered to a fungible contractor is drawn up by a class of experts that depend on their technological background of knowledge', thus

[64] Nield, Chapter 10. [65] Williams, Chapter 12.
[66] Ibid. [67] Ibid.
[68] J. Ford, R. Burrows and S. Nettleton, *Home Ownership in a Risk Society: A Social Analysis of Mortgage Arrears and Possessions* (Bristol: Policy Press, 2001) 6.
[69] Viñals, Chapter 3.

placing all consumers in a relatively vulnerable position as the weaker party to the transaction. Yet, it is important to bear in mind the need to balance the tensions between this type of vulnerability, and the need to facilitate efficient business practices through standard form contracts. Cartwright also identifies the problem of 'information asymmetry' between the consumer and the service provider as one of the catalysts of regulation,[70] with reference to the difficulties in putting into practice the objective 'average consumer test' standard and in light of the FSA's recognition that 'there is a lot more to do before information from firms to consumers could generally be regarded to be fair and clear'.[71]

Meanwhile Zhou's contribution looks to the rationale for the operation of the doctrine of unconscionability as being grounded both in the asymmetry of information between the parties and the need to correct the allocative inefficiency caused by the parties' bounded rationality. From an economic perspective, the choice of appropriate remedy among the remedial options, as Zhou observes, depends upon the emphasis placed by the lawmaker. If the lawmaker focuses on deterrence, damages are the preferable option; if the major concern is the disincentive to trade, then judicial modification is the most suitable choice. If, however, the lawmaker seeks to achieve some level of compromise, both invalidation of contract and rescission are plausible alternatives.[72]

Furthermore, what is striking to Rott and Halfmeier is less the informational asymmetry than the prevalence of conflicts of interest affecting financial institutions' ability to act in their clients' best interests and incentives embedded in current practice for advisers to give inappropriate advice. The proceduralisation of risk in this context is simply unequal to the task; instead, Rott and Halfmeier argue that to deal with the risks inherent in investment contexts more substantive protection has to be organised: to disallow inducements for investment advice, introduce fees for such services and pattern regulation so as to divorce front-office investment advice from back-office inducement-collecting.[73] A similar problem, as Kalus and Habdas observe, seems to arise in practice with bank loans in Poland; with banks employing a combination of economic, psychological and legal securities to secure their lending, such that the borrower needs to carefully consider which securities best reflect his/her interests.[74]

[70] Cartwright, Chapter 11.
[71] FSA, *Treating Customers Fairly: Measuring Outcomes* (London: FSA, 2007) 5.
[72] Zhou, Chapter 7. [73] Rott and Halfmeier, Chapter 17.
[74] Kalus and Habdas, Chapter 15.

Moreover, viewing the evolution of legal responses to unconscionability, Swain and Fairweather provided an account of the genesis of 'unconscionable conduct' as behaviour that 'shocks the conscience of the court'.[75] In reviewing the evolution of unconscionability against the current global financial crisis, it is interesting to reflect on how our conceptualisation of the 'normal' levels of risk in financial transactions will provide important context for the development of unconscionability. Finally, given the levels of risk and vulnerability identified in this volume, and the capacity of unconscionable behaviour to shock the conscience of the court one might begin to ask, as does Amato in her contribution, whether the civil law is ultimately equal to the task of addressing such behaviour. As Amato concludes:

> civil liability remedies do not provide the only possible answer to the protection of investors against unconscionable financial contracts: in addition, one can consider how alternative remedies subsequent to the occurrence of damages (for example, stricter criminal penalties), preventive measures (rules of conduct) or collateral sanctions (reputational risks) may be able to support and protect investors more effectively than civil liability rules.[76]

Responsibility

Another core theme to be drawn from these chapters relates to responsibility: Who is responsible when the risks to which vulnerable consumers are exposed are actualised, leading to harm? Who is responsible for miscalculation of risk or bad outcomes? The relationship between risk and responsibility is an important theme; Giddens has stated that '[r]isk is ... always connected to responsibility';[77] however, the neoliberal perspective that tends to dominate in the UK typically emphasises the *self*-responsibility of the individual consumer, rather than regarding the provider of financial services, or the state or legal system, as bearing responsibility for the harms that may result when risks lead to bad outcomes. Nevertheless, as the chapters which trace the growing regulatory role of the FSA and the OFT in the UK, including the growth in mandatory codes of conduct, demonstrate, the model of absolute individual consumer responsibility has come under increasing pressure. Nield contrasts the theory of a 'decentered regulatory approach' underpinned by a mantra of 'responsible lending and responsible borrowing',

[75] Swain and Fairweather, Chapter 8. [76] Amato, Chapter 16.
[77] Giddens, 'Risk and Responsibility', n. 54 above, 7.

with evidence that, in practice, this model has clearly failed in both respects.[78]

A central question is the appropriate allocation of responsibility between the individual consumer or debtor who undertakes financial obligations within what Williams identifies as the 'responsibilised' identity of a self-regulating market actor,[79] and the provider of financial services, constructed as a 'responsibilised firm', also regarded as a 'self-regulating actor, entrusted with the governance of its own conduct'.[80] Yet, Williams demonstrates a significant development in the FSA's approach to such 'responsibilised firms', whereby they are required to demonstrate the performance of fairness, not only in their 'front end dealings', but in their routine business operations. Furthermore, it is increasingly recognised that responsible behaviour on the part of financial institutions requires a contextualised approach, which recognises the importance of distinguishing advice and products, on the basis of their suitability for particular types of consumer. This issue has emerged within the meaning of the FSA's definition of unfairness – as 'taking advantage of the customer' – and represents an important dimension in the regulatory standard of responsibility which the FSA wishes to apply to financial services providers,[81] although, again, it is recognised that considerable work remains to be done before the goals of the FSA in being able to implement and enforce the standards of fairness and responsibility which it has conceptualised are achieved.

The difficulties in giving effect to standards of responsibility in the context of financial markets were recognised by Giddens in his seminal paper on 'Risk and Responsibility'.[82] Giddens set out three models of 'responsibility', a term which he described as 'an interestingly ambiguous or multi-layered term', which connotes (1) being the author of an event; (2) acting in an ethical/accountable manner; and (3) obligation or liability.[83] The evolving approach to regulation of financial services discussed in several papers provides an interesting point of reflection on the shift from 'good practice' approaches to 'responsible lending, responsible borrowing', towards a more enforceable set of obligations and liabilities to which firms are held to account, including by the levying of fines where actions are deemed contrary to the standards of responsibility required in dealing with consumers. Giddens noted, however, that in a

[78] Nield, Chapter 10. [79] Williams, Chapter 12.
[80] Ibid. [81] Cartwright, Chapter 11.
[82] Giddens, 'Risk and Responsibility', n. 54 above. [83] Ibid, 8.

context where risk is viewed as 'an energising principle . . . responsibility can neither easily be attributed nor assumed'.[84] Giddens went on to suggest that this gives rise to the phenomenon which Beck described as 'organised irresponsibility', where 'there are a diversity of humanly created risks for which people and organisations are certainly "responsible" in a sense that they are its authors but where no one is held specifically accountable'.[85] The difficulty, he argues, is how to allocate responsibility for such risks: 'Who is to determine how harmful products are, what side effects are produced by them, and what level of risk is acceptable?'[86] Giddens predicted that:

> Coping with situations of organised irresponsibility is likely to become more and more important in the fields of law, insurance and politics, but this won't be easy to do precisely because of the rather imponderable character of most circumstances of manufactured risk.[87]

It is clear that the degree of regulatory responsibility to which firms involved in financial transactions with potentially vulnerable consumers are expected to comply is increasingly under scrutiny and that, while the mantra of 'responsible borrowing' continues to impose expectations on consumers as self-regulating market actors, which may present particular challenges for vulnerable or marginalised consumers, the expansion of regulation in recent years is expanding the standard of responsible conduct required of firms, both in its breadth and in the extent to which the FSA is willing to enforce standards of fairness and 'conscionable' behaviour. Nevertheless, in the context of financial transactions, the question of responsibility is a complex, multifaceted issue, which poses contextual challenges which the regulatory regimes continue to grapple with.

4. Conclusions

A number of propositions emerge from this project. Perhaps the most important are the caveats which we have introduced to the understanding of European private law as a law possessing a clearly identifiable common core, as a body of law amenable to a broad exercise in codification. Looking at the law in action, we find substantial divergence rather than convergence, and a picture of polycontextualism, legal fragmentation and tension. Amid the general mood of euphoria connected to the

[84] Ibid. [85] Ibid. [86] Ibid. [87] Ibid.

Commission's codification exercise, it is important to stress the fact that Europe's private law can best be described in terms of a lack of commonality rather than by reference to an imagined, simplistic commonality.

As we have seen, the growing impact of public law on private law relationships in the context of risky financial transactions subjects the role of private law in protecting the vulnerable against unconscionable bargains to heightened scrutiny. The central issue to emerge is how the kaleidoscope of public and private law approaches to the protection of the vulnerable can be converged without sacrificing the full autonomy of private law to standards developed by public law. Here Cherednychenko argues that it is only when there is a dialogue between public law and private law that an advance in conceptualising unconscionability may be achieved, and it is only with such a re-conceptualisation, providing new and better solutions, that we will be able to protect the vulnerable in financial transactions.

Polycontextualism in Unconscionability

This survey has made clear that unconscionability involves a plurality of parties and competing interests. The doctrine has a polycontextual function, and the balancing or mediation of the interests involved can take place at a number of levels and fields of law, for example in: contract law (traditional defences: fraud, duress, mistake, misrepresentation); procedural protection (duties to inform of financial risks); consumer law (formal requirements and duties to inform); family law (protection of family interests); insolvency law (regulation of rights of recourse, symmetry of fresh start protection); constitutional law (proportionality considerations); property law. The polycontextual function of unconscionability and the location of protective mechanisms within this matrix of levels and fields of law affects both the level of protection and the prevalence of different types of agreements. As we have observed, this may lead to inconsistencies: for example, between the level of protection offered the family surety on a fundamental rights basis and the relatively low level of protection offered non-professional investors via European secondary law under the implementation of the MiFID framework directive. In contrast, other legal regimes establish quite different levels of protection for different categories of vulnerable contracting parties. In the Netherlands, for example, the non-professional investor enjoys substantive protection whilst the family surety must rely on a quite different standard of procedural protection.

The uncommon core

Whilst, at a basic level of abstraction common elements of unconscionability can be recognised in all legal systems, the coherence of this picture of commonality becomes fragmented the higher the level of abstraction. Member States' legal orders have their own demarcations and differentiations, locating protection in different legal institutions and fields of law. Even at a conceptual level the differences are striking: in the suretyship context, for example, either involving three parties in a two-transaction agreement[88] or a trilateral agreement.[89] This leads to further demarcational problems as between legal orders: thus whilst the creditor may be seen in some legal orders as the professional (Germany), in others he may also be a non-professional (Belgium and France). A major distinction emerges in the balances struck between market-liberal formalism and interventionist, substantive approaches. The market-liberal approach, underscores the central importance of freedom of contract and allows the individual the freedom to enter 'unwise' obligations. Meanwhile, the substantive approach focuses on the bargaining power of the parties and the social implications of disproportionate guarantees.[90] Whilst substantive analysis discloses the limits to the information model, at its outer limit it appeals to the horizontal effect of fundamental rights.

Spectral analysis

A major reason for the uncommon core of European private laws lies in the fragmentation of the contexts in which they operate; unconscionability being correctly seen as an element or part of a wider spectrum, of a *layering* of divergent protective mechanisms. Against this background, standards of protection are fleshed out in the framework of national standards of consumer/debtor protection. This means that we need to

[88] Two-transaction: underlying and unilateral contract. See generally, M. Siems, 'No Risk, No Fun? Should Spouses be Advised before Committing to Guarantees? A Comparative Analysis' [2002] *European Review of Private Law* 509 at 517; O. Cherednychenko, 'The Constitionalisation of Contract Law: Something New under the Sun?' (2004) 8 *Electronic Journal of Comparative Law*, www.ejcl.org/81/art81-3.html.

[89] Art. 7:850(1) Dutch Civil Code, provides: 'Suretyship is a contract whereby one party, the surety, obliges himself towards the other party, the main creditor, to perform an obligation to which a third person, the main debtor, is or will be bound towards the main creditor.'

[90] U. Reifner, 'Konsumentenkreditrichtlinie im Europaparlament – Zurück zu den Siebzigern?' (2004) *Verbraucher and Recht* 85. Current critique contained in a modified proposal for a directive on credit agreements for consumers: www.responsible-credit.net/media.php?id=1812.

consider a number of legal institutions in comparing the level of protection of the vulnerable. In turn, this variety hinders the integration of a European credit market. Moreover, social and behavioural factors can play a decisive role in determining the real extent of liability. The level of social welfare may influence the likelihood of default, whilst banking practice will also influence the treatment of the vulnerable. As alluded to above, legislators and judiciary have to find the balance between competing interests in the law of polycontextual unconscionability: between contractual security and the interests of guarantors; between family and bank interests; between the parties' rights in bankruptcy; and between family members' rights. In the following a cross-section of national protection systems are charted.

Towards a unitary network

It can be countered that some commonality is present in the law on unconscionability, but at a different level; that a type of uniformity emerges from the tension at the heart of the uncommon core. If we can understand unconscionability as the law of an interface or layering of overlapping legal systems, then, whilst some elements may require uniform treatment, we can otherwise rely on a conflicts' approach, competition and spontaneous harmonisation. In describing uniformity through tension we have to change our perception of law. The central idea here is that law depends on contradiction; that a multiplicity of systems can also work as a unitary network, producing, as Teubner notes, a hybridised, ambivalent unity: '[O]nly the combination of both sides of the difference . . . brings out the special nature of the hybrid: neither mediation nor synthesis, but extremely ambivalent unity.'[91]

A tripartite approach?

Given its polycontextual function and uncommon core, an incremental tripartite approach involving a combination of measures of (1) legislative regulation, (2) non-legislative harmonisation admitting selective constitutionalisation, and (3) non-legislative harmonisation (judicial convergence) recommends itself for the required elaboration of the doctrine of unconscionability in Europe. Despite calls for full-blown private law codification it is, in these authors' assessment, unlikely that ultimately

[91] Teubner, 'Das Recht hybrider Netzwerke', n. 29 above.

anything more than selective, vertical measures of legislative harmonisation (EU secondary law) will be adopted in those narrow areas of functional similarity where uniform law produces clear efficiency gains. Whilst such areas, given the heterogeneity identified in this chapter, will be rare, EU legislation could be important, for example, in ensuring access to credit, establishing criteria for responsible lending or criteria relating to community reinvestment initiatives along US lines.[92] More common will be measures of non-legislative harmonisation through judicial convergence, a common law turn, and an effective, sensitive and legitimate way of harmonising private law.[93] Finally, in these authors' view the elaboration of unconscionability, inspired by the German example, should admit selective constitutionalisation where the fundamental rights of the vulnerable party require more substantive and not merely procedural protection. Substantively, all that matters is that the courts achieve the same results regardless of which norms, doctrines or procedures they apply in order to come to this end. Such a pragmatic approach, avoiding the superficial attraction of codification, could, in Teubner's terms, more effectively illuminate the 'blindspots' in the elaboration of European unconscionability.

Finally, the virtue of such a tripartite strategy lies in its simultaneous appeal to advocates of the uniform law and the unitary network, as well as incidentally appealing to the financial services industry and the European executive, and in its acknowledgment of the interplay of private and public in the kaleidoscopic concept of unconscionability in Europe.

[92] Cf. US Community Reinvestment Coalition: www.ncrc.org.
[93] A. Colombi Ciacchi, 'Non-Legislative Harmonisation of Private Law', n. 38 above.

INDEX